D1091083

Liberals and Social Democrats

LIBERALS AND SOCIAL DEMOCRATS

Peter Clarke

These are matters that we must leave, I suppose, to those learned men who are described as 'future historians', though it is with distrust that I leave them.

H. W. Nevinson

Cambridge University Press

CAMBRIDGE

LONDON - NEW YORK - MELBOURNE

Published by the Syndics of the Cambridge University Press
The Pitt Building, Trumpington Street, Cambridge CB2 1RP
Bentley House, 200 Euston Road, London NW1 2DB
32 East 57th Street, New York, NY 10022, USA
296 Beaconsfield Parade, Middle Park, Melbourne 3206, Australia

First published 1978

Printed in Great Britain by
Western Printing Services Ltd, Bristol

Library of Congress Cataloguing in Publication Data

Clarke, Peter, 1942–

Liberals and social democrats.

Includes bibliographical references and index.

1. Political science – Great Britain – History.
2. Liberalism – Great Britain – History.
3. Socialism in Great Britain – History. I. Title.

JA84.G7C57 320.5′0941 78–6970

ISBN 0 521 22171 4

For DILLON
who gave the 2 Hobs house room

Contents

Preface

My chief feeling on finishing this book is one of gratitude. I have been helped by many librarians, scholars and students. The staff of the manuscripts department at the Bodleian Library made my frequent visits to Oxford both productive and pleasurable; and for permission to quote from the correspondence of J. L. and Barbara Hammond held there I am indebted to Professor N. G. L. Hammond. Miss Angela Raspin greatly facilitated my work at the London School of Economics, especially on an unexplored section of the Wallas papers and on the manuscript of Beatrice Webb's diaries; I am likewise grateful for permission to quote from these sources. Mrs Jennifer Balme showed great consideration in making some of the surviving papers of her grandfather, L. T. Hobhouse, available to me. I am also grateful to Mr S. S. Wilson for allowing me to use the minute books of the Rainbow Circle. My colleague Melvyn Stokes generously let me partake of the fruits of his own labours in the archives of American progressives; and Mary Chadwick expeditiously extracted the material in the appendix from the probate records at Somerset House. Professors Norman Mackenzie and J. H. Burns commented on early parts of the manuscript to my great benefit. Above all, I am conscious of the help of those friends whom I implicated in the preparation of the final draft. Without Nazneen Razwi, who typed it, the work could not have been finished at all. John Thompson scrutinised it with a keen eye for the nuances of progressivism. Stephen Koss, having earlier directed me to the literary remains of the Rainbow Circle, put me further in his debt by removing blemishes, both scholarly and stylistic. Alan Lee acted with singular magnanimity in drawing on his unrivalled knowledge of J. A. Hobson to such constructive effect. Likewise, I benefited not only from many wide-ranging discussions with Stefan Collini, whose book on L. T. Hobhouse, *Liberalism and Sociology*, will shortly be published by this press, but also from the exact scholarship which he brought to bear upon my manuscript. All of them, to their credit, had different qualms about this book, and its ultimate form is peculiarly my responsibility.

The system of references is something of an innovation. By and large, only the sources of direct quotations are noted specifically; general comments and references to secondary authorities are given in the bibliographical notes. Only in three sections – ch. 3, iv; ch. 5, iv; and ch. 8, i –

where the subject matter has a clear historiographical turn, do I mention the work of other historians in my text. I hope that elsewhere scholars will consult the bibliographical notes before convicting me of a manifest failure to acknowledge my intellectual debts. And most readers will, I trust, find the references supplied on each page of the text an adequate guide. This book will rightly have to be tested by rigorous academic standards, but it is frankly designed also for a wider readership.

University College London
February 1978

System of References

PERIODICALS

A. *Daily and weekly papers (followed by date)*

L	*Listener*
MG	*Manchester Guardian*
M. Post	*Morning Post*
N	*Nation*
NS	*New Statesman (and Nation* after 1930)
S	*Speaker*
Spec.	*Spectator*
Times	*The Times*

B. *Journals and reviews (followed by vol. number and page)*

AM	*Atlantic Monthly*
CR	*Contemporary Review*
ER	*English Review*
Ec	*Economica*
EcH	Economic History (supplement to *Economic Journal*)
EcHR	*Economic History Review*
EcJ	*Economic Journal*
EcR	*Economic Review*
FR	*Fortnightly Review*
IJE	*International Journal of Ethics*
IR	*Independent Review*
NC	*Nineteenth Century*
PBA	*Proceedings of the British Academy*
PQ	*Political Quarterly*
PR	*Progressive Review*
PS	*The Practical Socialist*
PSQ	*Political Science Quarterly*
QJE	*Quarterly Journal of Economics*
QR	*Quarterly Review*
SP	*Sociological Papers*
SR	*Sociological Review*

System of References

REFERENCE WORKS

DLB	*Dictionary of Labour Biography*, ed. Joyce M. Bellamy and John Saville, vols. i–iv (1972–7, in progress)
DNB	*Dictionary of National Biography*

BIOGRAPHICAL WORKS

Autobiog.	*The Autobiography of Bertrand Russell*, 3 vols. (1967–71)
Conf.	*Confessions of an Economic Heretic* (1938) by J. A. Hobson
Memoir	J. A. Hobson and Morris Ginsberg, *L. T. Hobhouse, his life and work* (1931)

EDITIONS AND SOURCES

H–L Letters	Mark DeWolfe Howe (ed.), *Holmes–Laski Letters 1916–1935*, 2 vols., continuous pagination (1953)
H.W.M.	H. J. Massingham (ed.), *H.W.M. A selection from the writings of H. W. Massingham* (1925)
JMK	*The Collected Writings of John Maynard Keynes*, vols. i–x, xiii–xvi (1971–3, in progress)
Men & Ideas	May Wallas (ed.), *Men and Ideas. Essays by Graham Wallas* (1940)
Smuts	W. K. Hancock and Jean Van Der Poel (eds.), *Selections from the Smuts Papers*, 7 vols. (Cambridge 1966–73)
Laurence	Dan H. Laurence (ed.), *Bernard Shaw, Collected Letters*, vols. i–ii (1965–72, in progress)
Wilson	Trevor Wilson (ed.), *The Political Diaries of C. P. Scott 1911–1928* (1970)

The diaries of Beatrice Webb:

MA	*My Apprenticeship* (1926; 2nd edn. 1946)
OP	*Our Partnership*, ed. Barbara Drake and Margaret I. Cole (1948)
BWD, iii and iv	*Beatrice Webb's Diaries* 1912–1924 and 1924–1932, ed. Margaret Cole (1952–6)

Other references to the diary, with date, are to the MS in the Passfield Papers at the London School of Economics

HP	Hammond Papers, Bodleian Library, Oxford
MGP	Scott Papers, *Manchester Guardian* archive, Manchester University Library

MP	Murray Papers, Bodleian Library, Oxford
PP	Ponsonby Papers, Bodleian Library, Oxford
SP	Scott Papers, British Library
WP	Wallas Papers, London School of Economics

Other archives are specified in the bibliographical notes

Where the text identifies the writer and recipient of a letter, merely the date is supplied (in brackets) if the letter is to be found in the recipient's papers. I have tried wherever possible to avoid evisceration or change of tense of quotations. I hope that I have transcribed these accurately, including idiosyncrasies – I do not use *sic* – though I have silently made some transpositions of manuscript into the conventions of printed prose.

At first mention of contemporary published works, the full title (with date) is given in the text and subsequent references are to a shortened version of the title. Works already cited in footnotes are subsequently referred to in the text by the author's name only.

Prologue

Original sin and the modern state

This book is about the relationship between liberalism and socialism in Britain in the late nineteenth and twentieth centuries. It focuses largely on four intellectuals who were, it is held, both liberals and social democrats – Graham Wallas (1858–1932), L. T. Hobhouse (1864–1929), J. A. Hobson (1858–1940) and J. L. Hammond (1872–1949). Barbara Hammond (1873–1961) is hardly less important. Their lifetimes are the time-span of the book. There are other liberals or socialists – notably, Gilbert Murray, Bernard Shaw, Sidney and Beatrice Webb, R. H. Tawney and J. M. Keynes – who receive considerable attention at points where their activities significantly influenced the story. Its central figures, however, were more closely and continuously linked to each other, in their ideas and in their lives. They were recognised as the core of a definite group of publicists, most of whom were associated with the weekly paper the *Nation* under the editorship of H. W. Massingham; and they were perhaps its most academically distinguished members. Wallas spoke for all of them when he said he wished to be remembered by his books. Both their moral commitment and their political leverage was expressed in their published work. 'They went about – or rather they wrote about – redressing human wrongs', was how one obituary put it.[1]

They could be called bourgeois socialists of the sort Marx and Engels warned against in the *Communist Manifesto* – 'economists, philanthropists, humanitarians, improvers of the condition of the working class, organisers of charity, members of societies for the prevention of cruelty to animals, temperance fanatics, hole-and-corner reformers of every possible kind'.[2] They can fittingly be described as reformists, with all that this term implies about their refusal to press change to revolutionary conclusions. Whether they were, as Marx would have held, 'desirous of redressing social grievances, in order to secure the continued existence of bourgeois society' (ibid.), is a more difficult question to answer. If capitalism, or bourgeois society, is an inherently exploitative system; and if it continues to exist so long as the means of production are not in truly common ownership, then it follows that the problems necessarily generated by 'the system' have hardly been tackled, let alone solved, in a country like Britain. All that has

[1] Hamilton Fyfe, 'Almost the Last', *Tribune*, 6 May 1949.
[2] Karl Marx and Frederick Engels, *Selected Works* (1968), p. 58.

happened, according to historians who take this view, is that an 'ideological' necessity to reorganise the state has led to the manipulation of its potential for social control in a different way, *through* social reform. Such reform, then, has been essentially conservative, even though radicals pressed for it at the time.

This is an important criticism but it is also one which verges on tautology, that is to say, it is true by definition. On purely socialist criteria, social democratic reform is always a failure since all it does is invent new devices for strengthening the system, which should itself be attacked. The new varieties of 'capitalism', to be sure, seem to be capable of satisfying welfare criteria in a way that would have made them axiomatically 'not capitalism' to an earlier generation of socialists. This was, indeed, Lenin's trump card against Hobson (see ch. 3, iv). There is, however, a further nuance to the argument. As a generalisation it would hardly be too much to claim that all prospective reform is radical and all achieved reform conservative. It is conservative almost by definition, that is, it is functional from the point of view of the *new* condition of society. The welfare state is thus functional for the mixed economy; it strengthens the workings of the system; it is in this sense that it is a conservative force. But to the generation which helped bring it about, conservatism implied the defence of the *pre-existing* status quo; their position, by contrast, was one of radical innovation. It may be, of course, that what was intended as a radical reform has turned out to be a disappointment.

If prospective reform is radical and accomplished reform conservative, different historical approaches are needed according to what question is then asked. This book is mainly concerned with the history of ideas rather than institutions, and it follows that one of its problems is to recover the intentions of the thinkers with whom it deals. That these intentions were, on the whole, radical is a persistent theme. For, as well as the important distinction between intention and function, there are four subsidiary reasons why early-twentieth-century Liberalism has acquired what I consider a misleadingly right-wing image. The first is that a number of those remembered as 'Liberals' were in fact Liberal Unionists after 1886; that is to say, they were the very people most hostile to the new Liberalism which came to the fore after Gladstone's death. Conversely, prominent new Liberals (and new Liberal influences) have often been assimilated as 'Fabian'. This would apply to several central characters in this book, perhaps especially to the Hammonds. A third point is that, from the time of the First World War onward, those Liberals who remained tended to be the most hidebound – and always had been. Finally, many Liberals who had earlier identified themselves as radicals *became* increasingly conservative in outlook in later years – a point which finds support in the epilogue of this book.

Ideas played a particularly important part in the history of Liberalism. Ideas can, of course, like the institutional reforms which embody them, be regarded in a purely functional way, as subservient to the real interests or motives which governed actions. But this is surely sociologically naive. Ignoring ideas means ignoring men's own understanding of their position and behaviour. It is certainly interesting to ask how men generalise their own position into – or at least reconcile it with – interpretative, evaluative, normative statements of more general bearing. Beliefs may be imparted socially but they meet a need for some understanding of the world which is felt individually. As to *what* is believed, there will doubtless be *some* link between a person's social position and his intellectual bearings, but the problem is to specify what connexions are helpful as explanations. In the most clear-cut case, a person's ideas may be a fairly transparent rationalisation of his material interests or his emotional needs.

The question of the sociological or psychological plausibility of a belief, however, is separate from the question of whether it is true. The first is concerned with why certain sorts of person want to believe something; the second is concerned with the rationality of what they believe. It is difficult to see how the one can consistently determine the other. For one thing, a need to believe is not so doctrinally precise as to specify the content of the belief. There may indeed be a need for the belief which is actually adopted – but this might equally well be satisfied by some functionally equivalent alternative. The test here is whether the belief is functional: whether it copes with either the sociological or psychological problem which gave rise to the need for it. In the case where the formal content of the belief is *sociologically* functional in this way, it can be described as an ideology. There is a verisimilitude about it. It looks like a true map of the world and one which is helpful to particular social groups. Likewise, ideas may have a psychological verisimilitude for individuals. But ideas also have their own force, rules and congruence. Admittedly, there is the logic of a situation; but there is also logic.

It is necessary, therefore, to examine not only the sociological and psychological context but also the intellectual content of ideas that are current. It is the social purchase of ideas in terms of the interests they serve which constitutes their ideological aspect. This is irrespective of whether the ideas are rational in terms of their internal consistency and compatibility with the available evidence. Where these ideas are elaborated into a systematic theory, the question of their rationality can be described as that of their scientific value (in the sense that science constitutes an ordered body of knowledge). The verisimilitude of any world view (*Weltanschauung*) may thus break down for one of two reasons. The first is a weakness in its formal logic; new knowledge makes it implausible and no longer intellectually sustainable; it is shown to be inadequate, or even straightforwardly untrue. The other reason may be a change of context; the world becomes a different place and the old map is no good any more; or the position of an individual or class is altered, needs and interests are changed, and the old ideas no longer fit. The two aspects are, of course, often closely entwined in the psyche of the believer, so that the yearning for belief is naturally taken as evidence for the truth of the desired belief.

It may be argued that the bourgeois socialism of the liberal intellectuals was ideologically constricted to reformist methods by their class interest in maintaining the system as a going concern. But they may, equally, have been opting for a more effective strategy of political change than if they had adopted the revolutionist position. 'False consciousness' is usually seen as being falsely conservative; but it is arguably as often falsely radical. There are two poles of social consciousness. One is to adapt to the world, by understanding it in a particular way, which Marxists regard as a form of false consciousness if it thereby leads to a spurious satisfaction with the status quo. The other is to attempt to change the world – a form of social action which rejects the existing state of society. The dilemma may be posed in an especially acute way for intellectuals since their theories are articulated at a fairly sophisticated level. In Marx's *Theses on Feuerbach* (1845) he concluded: 'The philosophers have only *interpreted* the world in various ways; the point is, to *change* it.'[3] Every individual, however, must come to terms with his immediate environment as the price of his own happiness. The propertied classes may, as Marx argued in *The Holy Family* (1844), represent 'the same human self-alienation' as the proletariat; but in their case they have 'the *semblance* of a human existence' and the not inconsiderable consolations of their economic power (Easton & Guddat, p. 367). What they yearn for is peace of mind. Commitment to a radical critique of capitalism may be quite inappropriate as a strategy of social change, but functional as adaptation for the individual. If it becomes an ethic of ultimate ends it needs no utilitarian justification; and since it will not in fact be realised, it can give the intellectuals not only the material satisfactions of membership of a privileged class but also the psychic satisfactions of rejecting the morality of the system which sustains them. Hobson, for one, was fully alive to the possibilities of what might be called the false consciousness of the radical bourgeoisie.

A further organising concept runs through this book. In assessing what view was taken of the state, I accept that one important dimension can be described as a spectrum running from support of the status quo, through reform, to radical reconstruction and revolution. But in opting for a strategy of change, much also depends upon what view is taken of human nature. There are obvious grounds for associating a belief in original sin

[3] Loyd D. Easton and Kurt M. Guddat (eds.), *Writings of the Young Marx on Philosophy and Society* (New York 1967), p. 402.

with a socially conservative position. But even for revolutionists, it makes a crucial difference whether an optimistic or pessimistic view of human nature is postulated. On an optimistic view progress can be assumed. A moral change, a change of heart, a new consciousness, will be the agent and sanction of a transformation within society. But the revolutionist who takes a pessimistic view has no such confidence; instead he is impressed by the ideological conditioning which has flawed the social consciousness of the very groups who ought to bring change about. Nonetheless, he knows that revolution is correct, and concludes that it must if necessary be made from above if spontaneous forces fail. Mechanical methods have to be substituted instead.

The difference between the moral and the mechanical revolutionist can be illustrated by comparing what Marx and Lenin wrote about the transition to the higher phase of communism. Marx's conception was essentially that of the humanist. Communism was for him the expression of men's real social nature; only overcome the alienation which capitalism imposed upon them and communism would flourish! And there was enough co-operative effort needed even in capitalist society to make this growth of consciousness possible. The vision is obviously that of the young Marx. But even as late as the *Critique of the Gotha Programme* (1875) his argument was that precisely because of the ending of the division of labour, labour would become 'not only a means of life but life's prime want', and 'the all-round development of the individual' was to be the cause of productivity gains which would usher in an age of plenty (*Sel. Works*, pp. 320–1). For the sceptical, tough-minded Lenin, on the other hand, men were creatures of their economic circumstances, and change would not take place until these had been changed from above by the vanguard party. Lenin therefore glossed Marx to mean that 'when people have become so accustomed to observing the fundamental rules of social intercourse', the higher phase would become politically practicable.[4] There is an equally important division between the moral and mechanical reformist; and among opponents of state-sponsored social reform, the moral regenerationist, whose optimistic view of human nature leads him to believe in the possibility of progress, is likewise separated from the pessimistic quietist who believes in original sin. This is, indeed, a leading theme of the rest of this book, concerned more concretely with British history during the past century.

In England the liberal intelligentsia (under the patronage of John Stuart Mill) and the working-class electorate (under the patronage of John Bright) both burst into the political arena in the 1860s. After the second Reform Act the possibility of a dominant working-class movement had to be taken seriously. But the young academic liberals of the day, like T. H. Green,

[4] V. I. Lenin, *The State and Revolution* (Moscow 1965), p. 88.

A. V. Dicey, James Bryce and Leslie Stephen, took the hopeful view that the working class could be safely accommodated within the national community and would make a fruitful response to political leadership of the right calibre. 'The extreme advanced party', John Morley concluded, 'is likely for the future to have on its side a great portion of the most highly cultivated intellect of the nation, and the contest will lie between brains and numbers on the one side, and wealth, rank, vested interest, possession in short, on the other' (*FR*, i, 491–2). This prophecy proved complacent; but it was borne out in unexpected ways. For men like Morley, in the utilitarian tradition, the general problem was that of reconciling democracy with the premium on knowledge: of securing some reverence for ideas (and by extension of their begetters) in a scheme of things where numbers would ultimately carry the day. One way of resolving this difficulty was to stress education, on the view that society would be in its natural state when educated opinion triumphed. The assumed deference towards the best opinions by the uneducated was in practice, perhaps, a more refined version of the assumption on which the Whigs had acted since 1832, that the ties of social deference would keep the poor under control. Either way, Liberalism accepted democracy only when it was tempered by implicitly elitist assumptions.

The Benthamite solution was neater than that of the Whigs. For if the problem was that the many were *poor*, then redistribution of wealth was the natural outcome; but if the many were *uneducated*, their deprivation could be remedied without attacking the economic position of the superior classes. The task was to persuade the uneducated (who happened to be poor) of the essential rightness of classical economics. 'We were not indifferent to the misfortunes of the poor', Bryce reflected to Dicey in 1913, 'but looked on them as inevitable, and did not feel the restless anxiety to remove them, even in defiance of economic laws, which burns in the breasts of modern youth'.[5] Speaking as a socialist in 1886, Wallas made what he called a fair offer to those who took this line: 'If you believe that the more a man knows the less of a Socialist is he, help us to give every man in England a real and thorough education. Then on your showing your position as monopolists will be perfectly safe, though according to our firm belief it will [be] absolutely hopeless.'[6] This problem, however, was not so much confronted as evaded. History dealt arbitrarily with the confident expectations of the academic liberals. They were right in thinking that the new voters would not grasp the state as a tool of class spoliation; but the retarding effect of traditional institutions proved even more effective than they had anticipated and politics fell into a curious impasse. In this situation the Liberal party, innocently or wilfully, produced a different

[5] Christopher Harvie, *The Lights of Liberalism* (1976), p. 159.
[6] Lecture on 'Education' at Kelmscott House, WP 15.

means of persuading the workingmen voters to acquiesce in the prevailing economic dispensation: namely Mr Gladstone. 'I look upon him as the strongest bulwark we have against all the strong socialist doctrine I hate', Morley admitted in 1886.[7]

The greatest achievement of Gladstonian populism was to run a democratic party by keeping class issues out of politics. The sociological basis for this style of politics admittedly depended on a restricted electorate still amenable to the cultural values of Nonconformity. The effect was that Liberal politics characteristically focused on issues remote from the lives of ordinary people. 'To a people without a theatre, without the arts that release the emotions, and bring them into play,' Hammond later argued, 'the great Tsar, with his terrible hand closing over the liberties of peoples at the other end of Europe, the despot at Vienna hunting the patriots of Hungary, the Pope at Rome making his dark religion more obnoxious by his wicked politics, were great stage villains, and men who prided themselves in ordinary life on sticking to business and keeping out feeling were swept away by this dramatic excitement' (*PQ*, ii, 228). Gladstone discovered his power as an orator by beseeching the ordinary Liberal voters to exercise their moral judgment on arcane matters in faraway countries of which they knew nothing. He was prepared to back the masses against the classes because of the unselfishness of the poor, who acted as ragged-trousered philanthropists towards the Italians, the American North, the Bulgarians and even the Irish rather than pushing forward their own class grievances. The Gladstonian style of politics made a transcendant appeal to conscience, but one seldom directed towards social evils at home.

On social questions Gladstone's position was essentially that of the quietist. The quietist sees the imperfections of the world; he attributes them to original sin; and in that case remedies are vain, in this world at least. Gladstone was committed to a view of politics which excluded tampering with social and economic questions. The political economy of his youth made him, to the end of his days, deeply hostile to what he called 'construction'. And he found ample comfort in a creed which made a robust virtue of this fatalism. Thus in 1888: 'I believe in a degeneracy of man, in the Fall – in *sin* – in the intensity and virulence of sin. No other religion but Christianity meets the sense of sin, and sin is the great fact in the world to me.'[8] He acknowledged the civilising role of Christianity in the moral sphere, which he extended to international relations. There remained, however, a vast field where the will of man was helpless to change the world for the better. 'We live, as men, in a labyrinth of problems, and of moral problems, from which there is no escape permitted us', he explained in 1876. 'The prevalence of pain and sin, the limitations of

[7] D. A. Hamer, *John Morley* (Oxford 1968), p. 176.
[8] Janet P. Trevelyan, *The Life of Mrs Humphry Ward* (1923), p. 59.

free will, approximating sometimes to its virtual extinction, the mysterious laws of our independence, the indeterminateness for most or many men of the discipline of life, the cross purposes that seem at so many points to traverse the dispensations of an Almighty benevolence, can only be encountered by a large, an almost immeasurable suspense of judgment. Solution for them have we none.'[9]

In confronting such facts, Gladstone considered that any intellectual difficulties involved in accepting Christianity were as dust in the balance compared to the relief it gave to the moral sense – 'in supplying the most powerful remedial agency ever known, in teaching how pain may be made a helper, and evil transmuted into good; and in opening clearly the vision of another world, in which we are taught to look for yet larger counsels of the Almighty wisdom' (*NC*, xxiii, 787). This was the teaching of Christian dogma. Writers sympathetic to religion who yet could not accept this lesson appeared to Gladstone 'to have a very low estimate both of the quantity and the quality of sin: of its amount, spread like a deluge over the world, and of the subtlety, intensity, and virulence of its nature' (ibid.). This was the world into which Wallas, Hobson, Hobhouse and the Hammonds were born.

[9] Quoted in J. L. Hammond, *Gladstone and the Irish Nation* (1938), p. 544.

I

The passion for improving mankind

(i) EARNESTNESS

'One great reason why clergymen's households are generally unhappy is because the clergyman is so much at home or close about the house', reflects the hero of Samuel Butler's posthumous novel *The Way of All Flesh* (1903); and the fact that he was 'expected to be a kind of human Sunday' made his children into victims of these occupational tensions (chs. xxiv, xxvi). Graham Wallas claimed few happy memories from his childhood. He was born in 1858, the elder son of a clergyman of the Church of England who, for thirty years, successively occupied two Devon livings: first as Vicar of Barnstaple and then as Rector of Shobrooke, a village two miles outside Crediton and about seven miles north-west of Exeter. Graham had four elder sisters and three younger; and there was one brother, three years his junior, who died in 1887. Graham was miserable at Barnstaple Grammar School before being sent on to public school at Shrewsbury. Shrewsbury was the old school of Samuel Butler whose satirical treatment of conventional Victorian values in his novels was to give these a personal resonance for Wallas.

H. W. Nevinson was a contemporary at Shrewsbury and, though their later relations became somewhat chilled, there was much in common in the early experience of the two boys, both sprung from Evangelical homes. In Nevinson's barbed reminiscence, Wallas 'always represented his chance thoughts as direct communications from the Holy Ghost' (*H–L Letters*, p. 1058). Their education at Shrewsbury was in a narrowly classical groove. Their headmaster, who was 'distinguished for his minute and infallible knowledge of all Greek except the beauty of its literature', was adept at preparing boys for university entrance.[1] Between the ages of nine and nineteen Wallas spent hours each day in churning out Latin and Greek verses according to the approved formula, to such good effect that he was elected to a classical scholarship at Oxford. It had not been an education to bring much out of him and, as he later told his wife, he was thankful to think that he had 'changed beyond all recognition from the clever unsatisfactory boy I then was' (22 January 1913). Things started to improve when he began reading Greats at Corpus Christi College, Oxford.

[1] H. W. Nevinson, *Running Accompaniments* (1936), p. 26.

Wallas's father was liberal in outlook and prided himself that his firm Evangelical convictions had not cut him off from developments in modern thought. What his son applauded in his outlook was the belief that it was the duty of the Church to seek the truth and, if convinced of a new truth, to convince others. Doctrine was not to be held lightly. As the son of a clergyman, Wallas had done more churchgoing than most; he maintained a keen interest in ecclesiastical questions and in his later years would read the *Church Times* in bed on Friday mornings. He remembered vividly that when he was seven or eight a churchwarden joined his father and himself 'and told, for my benefit, how a friend of his, who had heard his son swear, lit a bundle of matches and put them, as a foretaste of hell-fire, on the boy's tongue' (*Great Society*, p. 96). In his boyhood home, intellectual life was permeated by a strong theological flavour. He told a friend some years later that the family frequently had a pudding made of rice and currants and was divided over how it was best to eat it. One faction advocated eating the rice first with the anticipated pleasure of the currants to come. The others countered that the Day of Judgment might intervene and the chance of eating the currants be lost. Wallas had the opportunity of escaping into a world where arguments ranged more broadly; his unmarried sisters, of course, remained more closely constricted.

Leonard Trelawny Hobhouse was some five years younger than Wallas. He too was the son of an Evangelical clergyman. The Rev. Reginald Hobhouse was for fifty years Rector of St Ive in Cornwall, a village less than forty miles west of Shobrooke. The Hobhouses were a landowning family, originally Bristol merchants in the eighteenth century, with national connexions and a strong political tradition which Reginald's brother Arthur, later Lord Hobhouse, firmly upheld. The war between Prussia and France was the first public event to impress itself upon Leonard, then six years old, waylaying the postman for the latest news in his enthusiasm for the 'Prooshian' cause. The youngest of seven children, he insisted at the end of his life that the only cloud in an otherwise happy childhood home came from 'the doctrine of eternal punishment with which the air of a Cornish parish at that period was over-charged'.[2] His sister Emily, however, to whom he was closest in age and temperament, recalled this as a period of strain and gloom, from which, as the spoilt youngest of the family, her favourite brother may have come off relatively lightly. Their father was a man of deep but repressed feeling. It was said in the family that he had as a young man been rebuked for reading a novel and that he had never read another. He strictly ruled out all that was modern in thought and science from his reading and was singularly immoveable once his mind was made up. He found it difficult to enter into easy emotional relationships with his children – a barely human Sunday, some might

[2] Ruth Fry, *Emily Hobhouse* (1929), p. 37.

think. Even Leonard, while insisting that he was never untender or unkind, acknowledged that 'he was remorseless in exacting duty and the repair of neglect, and a few mild words of disapproval fell from him with tons' weight, and not on us alone' (Fry, p. 38).

Hobhouse went off to prep school at the age of eight or nine, then at twelve to Marlborough. His schooldays were not untroubled. He had not liked his prep school and at Marlborough he often showed himself difficult. It was only in the Sixth Form, under the influence of the classics master, L. E. Upcott, that he came into his own. Forty years on, he openly sided with Graham Wallas, even in the presence of Mrs Upcott, in maintaining that boys' public schools were an experiment in education which had failed. Part of the trouble was that he was in revolt from the orthodoxy of his home on both religious and political questions. He was a radical before he left Marlborough, reading Mazzini, defending democracy, proposing a republican motion in the debating society. His uncle Arthur and John Morley stood together as the two Liberal candidates for Westminster in 1880 and this can hardly fail to have impressed Leonard, who held his uncle in high regard. His own father was by now uneasy over his unorthodoxy. Balliol, the home of latitudinarianism, was therefore suspect, and in 1883 Hobhouse too entered Corpus Christi College, Oxford, with a classical scholarship.

Wallas and Hobhouse both read Greats and this left a permanent stamp upon their intellectual style, even though both self-consciously broke with this narrow Oxford tradition later. Morley once confided how pleasant it had been to talk to a bishop 'who knows his Aristotle', adding pityingly, 'I suppose Cambridge men have some other sort of intellectual link.'[3] To Shaw, bred outside this coterie, it seemed that 'Wallas brought to bear a wide scholastic culture of the classic type, in which modern writers, though interesting, were not fundamental.'[4] For Wallas, Aristotle was still 'the keenest observer that ever lived'.[5]

The fact that Wallas and Hobhouse were at Corpus was also significant, for the college was egregious in its resistance to the prevailing Oxford school of Idealist philosophy. Thomas Case was the tutor in philosophy at Corpus and he held firmly to the English empiricist tradition. Both Wallas and Hobhouse were influenced by him and both remained lifelong critics of certain aspects of Idealism. Wallas relished the fact that he had been taught by almost the last exponent of the utilitarian system. In a letter to him, Case was still ready to uphold Hartley's theory that all actions can be explained by reference to their indirect association with pain or pleasure as 'the most profound discovery yet made in the psychology of action'

[3] F. W. Hirst, *In the Golden Days* (1947), p. 167.

[4] E. R. Pease, *The History of the Fabian Society* (1916), p. 263.

[5] Lecture on 'Education' (1886), WP 15.

(25 January 1883). Wallas remembered a gibe that was current at the time: 'All bad German philosophies, when they die, go to Oxford.'[6] It is not a gibe that would have been current in Balliol.

At Corpus Wallas became friends with Sydney Olivier, a contemporary reading Greats. Olivier also came from the large family of a clergyman and had enjoyed an upbringing imbued with religiosity. As he reflected, 'the morality is undoubtedly high in such families, at least the standard is, although the result may not be so very different to elsewhere'.[7] He too had bridled at orthodoxy. Olivier and Wallas spurred each other on to read modern works. Wallas introduced Olivier to the writings of Samuel Butler, whose suggestive analogy between sickness and social deviance converted him 'to a belief in the reform of social conditions as a palliative for original sin'.[8]

It was now that Wallas read the *Origin of Species*. It made a great impression upon him. Darwin had wrested truths from nature which were incompatible with the Shobrooke cosmogony. When Wallas later got to know his future wife he pressed her to read the *Life* of Darwin, and she subsequently recorded her conviction that her husband had acquired a personal relation with Darwin's mind of a kind that generally only friendship gave. 'The devotion to truth & the patience month after month & year after year in spite of ill-health with which Darwin worked, & his absolute & abject submission to evidence when it was against a cherished theory – had made on Graham a marked impression' (biog. notes, 9 August 1934). For Wallas there was no higher claim than that of the unfettered play of the objective mind which he saw at work in Darwin and in modern science. The Evangelical Christianity which he had been taught as a boy and the Idealist philosophy which T. H. Green was currently preaching at Balliol both seemed to him to deny this sort of unconstrained intellectual freedom. But what he was rejecting here was the adequacy of a system of knowledge, not the strenuous quest for understanding which in both cases underlay it.

It is tempting but unhelpful to characterise this underlying ethos as a distinctively Evangelical residue. Evangelicalism, of course, had been one influence which helped to transform all religious life in the early Victorian period. But thereafter an intrusion of enthusiasm or earnestness cut across traditional party divisions. A High Churchman like Gladstone exhibited this disposition with as much fervour as a Broad Churchman like Dr Arnold, though neither can properly be classified as an Evangelical. Conversely, many Evangelicals had become complacent adherents of an arid and closed system. In the Oxford of the late 1870s it was, above all, T. H.

[6] Reform Club Banquet, 16 May 1928, Liberal Publication Department pamphlet, p. 31.
[7] Margaret Olivier (ed.), *Sydney Olivier* (1948), p. 67.
[8] Quoted in Norman and Jeanne Mackenzie, *The First Fabians* (1977), p. 59.

Green who transmitted earnestness with a charismatic force. To one sympathetic observer – Arnold's daughter, Mrs Humphry Ward – contact with him brought 'that rekindling of the flame of conscience, that medicinal stirring of the soul's waters, which is the most precious boon that man can give to man' (*Robert Elsmere*, ch. xxviii). The importance of being earnest was that it implied a conscientious search for meaning in the world. Those who were earnest were not distinguished by a common doctrine but by a common seriousness about the dreadful importance of questions of belief as the source of man's vision of the society in which he lived.

Precisely because Wallas was earnest he recognised that he could not himself enter the Church which, recruiting its clergy 'at the age of 24 or so from the general mass of unemployed young gentlemen', was in many respects such an obvious potential career. But, as he explained in 1886, 'a young man of 24 who has lived freely among his fellows is almost certain if he has any wits or earnestness at all to be healthily unorthodox'. So that those who finally did take orders were from this point of view the least desirable clergymen. 'In the time of our fathers,' he acknowledged, 'this was not I believe the case but in those days Darwin had not published his books and many other things had not happened.'[9] Rational inquiry had to be as full and as searching as the present state of knowledge permitted if truth were to rest on a secure foundation.

The intellectual collapse of the Christian world-picture was distressing because its social and psychological functions were left unfulfilled. Nevinson later wrote that no one born after about 1880 could realise how terrible this conflict for faith had been. 'Doubts rent the very being asunder, and deprived existence of its meaning and object' (Nevinson, p. 6). He himself, like other undergraduates, cherished the hope of remedying his shaken religious faith by sitting at the feet of Green, whose extraordinary personal ascendancy was at its peak. But Wallas, as his friend Muirhead later grieved, escaped the Idealist influence 'which eased for so many of us the strain of the loss of our early religious faith'. If only he had been at Balliol, he implied, Wallas 'might have found a new *Weltanschauung* to take its place'.[10] For Green believed that he had found in philosophical Idealism a profound method which enabled him to translate traditional Christianity into terms which would more readily command intellectual assent. In building upon the known facts he thought it natural to begin with the fact of man's consciousness and argue further from that premise.

Wallas later wrote of the great respect in which the Hegelian philosophers were held, invoking the fact that 'those five men alone of all Oxford wore soft hats, and we felt that here indeed were men who knew that their foundations were built upon a rock, and who had strength to stand against

[9] Paper on 'Tithe' (1886), WP 16.

[10] J. H. Muirhead, *Reflections by a Journeyman in Philosophy* (1942), pp. 93–4.

the tide of custom' (*PS*, i, 119). In 1879 he went to hear Green lecture. Green presented an argument for human immortality on the ground that, since we only know of the existence of our bodies from the testimony of our conscious mind, there was no reason to suppose that the dissolution of the body affected the continued existence of the mind. But this left the waters of Wallas's soul medicinally unstirred. 'Green asked for questions', he recalled (*NS*, 25 April 1931); 'I, being fresh from reading Darwin, asked him whether his arguments applied to the conscious mind of a dog, and Green answered that he was not interested in dogs.'

(II) CHARACTER AND PROGRESS

In many respects Green stood for a Gladstonian style of politics, but he showed that the Gladstonian appeal to conscience could be applied to social and economic questions too. He was not therefore a quietist in his social views but a kind of moralist – though whether he should best be described as a moral regenerationist or a moral reformist is less clear. The moral regenerationist acknowledges that society is imperfect; he puts this down essentially to defects in individual conduct and character; the remedy here is the remoralisation of character. Gladstone's own daughter, Mary Drew, is a good example, having transmuted the paternal quietism into a more combative view of the evils of the world. She later considered that the Hammonds' *Lord Shaftesbury* had failed to 'do full justice to the battle with sin, which seems to me infinitely greater, or rather more important, than any social reforms, however noble'. As she explained to Barbara Hammond: 'If we were all *good*, social injustices wd. not matter, as they could not happen' (13 September 1923).

The tension in Green's social philosophy arises from the fact that he worked out his position within an Idealist, and ostensibly Hegelian, framework. This proved helpful in that it firmly located the search for justice within this world rather than postponing it to the hereafter. Morality was essentially the working of reason within a rational world. The rationality of the world was the premise for an unshakeable belief in human progress. Moreover, a man's struggle for self-perfection took place within an actual society, of which he was a part, and its moral ideas were embodied in laws, institutions and social expectations. This embodiment, Green claimed in *The Principles of Political Obligation* (1879), 'constitutes the moral progress of mankind' (par. 6). It is the basis for a political philosophy looking to the fulfilment of the common good. In these matters the Hegelian view may well be thought an improvement upon the mechanistic utilitarian explanation of morality starting with the rational individual. But a problem arises in the further Idealist proposition that a man is only free when he desires and is able to do what he ought to do. There is something evasive, or at least ambivalent, about the argument here, but it allows a very awkward corner to be negotiated. In Hegel it permits the assertion that the State gives true freedom. In Green the thrust of the argument is subtly different since, as a Liberal, he wished to minimise the role of state control; and he therefore stressed instead the agency of the free individual in promoting the good of the state.

So Green's theory provided a language for justifying a wide range of new responsibilities for the state, but it was in fact typically used to emphasise the duties of the individual citizen. The common good was not urged as the rationale of collectivism but was instead applied as an ethical criterion to spur on a more strenuous individualism. Thus in a characteristic passage: 'The reason for not more generally applying the power of the state to prevent voluntary noxious employments, is not that there is no wrong in the death of the individual through the incidents of an employment which he has voluntarily undertaken, but that the wrong is more effectually prevented by training and trusting individuals to protect themselves than by the state protecting them' (par. 159).

This is one face of Green, and it is the face that was seen by disciples like Mrs Humphry Ward and Bernard Bosanquet, who remained essentially moral regenerationists. But the other face was more like that of the reformist. The reformist believes that social defects are systematic; the remedy therefore is to reform the system (and he believes, of course, that the system can be reformed). The moral reformist, moreover, believes that reform will flow from the free will, spontaneous endeavours and democratic efforts of the citizens – it is a moral argument for structural reform.

Green is not thoroughgoing when on this tack. It is certainly a mistake to hail him as a collectivist or an architect of the welfare state. In his lecture on 'Liberal Legislation and Freedom of Contract' (1881) Green did not go beyond an advocacy of a moderate reform of the land laws and – with much more fervour – legislative restriction of the sale of drink. He considered that drink laid a heavier burden on the free development of man's powers for social good than all other preventible causes put together. In seeing it in this light, as the root of other social evils, he was led to override his own principle of relying upon the spontaneous action of individuals. Here he urged prohibition on the basis of local option. On the one hand, he argued that it was dangerous to wait; on the other, that legislation would in itself uplift the national conscience.

This mode of argument, to be sure, was capable of extension, but Green gave no explicit encouragement for this. Where he actually did countenance state action he insisted that this was 'necessarily to be confined to the removal of obstacles' (*Principles Pol. Obligation*, par. 209). The difficulties which this terminology engendered when he was, for example, manifestly proposing *compulsion* in education were evidently compensated by the fact that it avoided repudiating the principle of freedom. To his own objection 'that we are interfering with the spontaneous action of social interests', Green retorted that a law making education compulsory was 'only felt as compulsion by those in whom, so far as this social function is concerned, there is no spontaneity to be interfered with' (ibid.). This seems a rather uneasy resolution of the particular problem, but in general it leaves the onus on 'the growth of capacity' in the individual as the source of progress.

Those who, justifiably enough, took Green to be a moral regenerationist were asserting a vision of society significantly different from that of the quietist. This can be seen in the form of a dramatic confrontation with the publication of Mrs Ward's *Robert Elsmere* (1888), which stirred Gladstone to controvert its spiritual message. For him the theism of Robert Elsmere was 'among the least defensible of the positions alternative to Christianity'.[11] It was helpless when confronted by 'the awful problem of moral evil, by the mystery of pain, by the apparent anomalies of waste and caprice on the face of creation; and not least of all by the fact that, while the moral government of the world is founded on the free agency of man, there are in multitudes of cases environing circumstances independent of his will which seem to deprive that agency, called free, of any operative power adequate to guard against them' (NC, xxiii, 786).

Mary Ward, as a moral regenerationist, had a different view. When she met Gladstone in April 1888, at his request, she pressed him hard about his view of English society in the previous half century, asking, 'in spite of all drawbacks, do you not see a gradual growth and diffusion of earnestness, of the social passion during the whole period?'[12] Gladstone was polite, gnomic, unmoved. Not that Mrs Ward sought to deny the existence of moral evil (any more than Mrs Drew did), but she maintained that 'the more one thought about it the more plain became its connexion with physical and social and therefore removable conditions' (Trevelyan, p. 59). And when she reflected on the conversation, she put it to Gladstone even more succinctly, asking him whether the difference between them was not 'that to you the great fact in the world and in the history of man, is *sin* – to me, progress?...In the life of conscience, in the play of physical and moral law, I see the ordained means by which sin is gradually scourged & weakened both in the individual & in the human society' (15 April 1888).

If sin could be conquered in this world the question of saving one's soul took on a new aspect. For Mrs Ward it led to a strong commitment to the work of spiritual regeneration which was the true answer to the social question. She was much impressed by the personality of Stopford Brooke, who had resigned as a Church of England clergyman and officiated as a

[11] John Morley, *Life of Gladstone* (1906 edn), ii, 597.
[12] Janet Trevelyan, *Life of Mrs. Humphry Ward* (1923), p. 58.

Unitarian at Bedford Chapel in Bloomsbury. He became one of her chief helpers in the foundation of University Hall in Gordon Square. It was intended in some ways to parallel the work of Toynbee Hall in Whitechapel, to which other disciples of Green gravitated, but also aimed to advance religious concerns which, though not formally Unitarian, had an unmistakeable tendency in that direction. The economist Philip Wicksteed, who was also a Unitarian minister, was at first reluctant to become warden but after a personal encounter with Mrs Ward – 'I want to *wrestle* with you!' she proclaimed (Trevelyan, p. 85) – he was duly forced to submit. In fact the institution, which afterwards became the Passmore Edwards Settlement, discovered, as Wicksteed had foreseen, that there was less demand among its clients for a new theology than for more straightforward social work, to which it increasingly turned, and Mrs Ward with it.

In this field the outlook of the Charity Organisation Society seemed to her the true one. In *Marcella* (1894) the heroine is brought to the realisation: 'what is anything worth but *character* – but *soul?*' (Bk. 3, ch. vii). In equating soul with character, salvation was secularised; and conversely, quietism and economic fatalism were abjured. The final message of the novel is explicitly signalled: 'Hold what you please about systems and movements, and fight for what you hold; only, as an individual, *never say* – *never think* – that it is in the order of things, in the purpose of God, that one of these little ones – this Board School child, this man honestly out of work, this woman "sweated" out of her life – should perish!' (Bk. 4, ch. vi).

Bernard Bosanquet was the intellectual leader of those who took this view. Together with C. S. Loch he formulated the characteristic approach of the Charity Organisation Society (C.O.S.). His witness to the revelations of Idealism was also proclaimed in the London Ethical Society. J. H. Muirhead, who collaborated with him there, regarded Bosanquet as the man best fitted to seize on the implications of the philosophy of Green and Bradley and to carry them out in every field of thought and practice. In the hands of Bosanquet and his fellow essayists in *Aspects of the Social Problem* (1895), this made for an approach to social reform which insisted, as he himself put it, that 'character is the condition of conditions' (pp. vii–viii). No doubt there were coercive elements in many political and economic relationships, but he held that the real basis of the state was its commitment as a self-governing body to common values. Nothing must be done to impair the individual's sense of responsibility or to disrupt his socially-learnt pattern of expectations. For these constituted the foundation of rational action. Actions had consequences which grown men could appreciate; their moral sense derived from this; and private property was the concrete expression of their capacity to exercise such a trust.

Through private property men learnt that things did not come miraculously but as the result of effort, and that efficient satisfaction of wants also demanded thrift and foresight. 'Thrift is, for us,' claimed Bosanquet, 'the germ of the capacity to look at life as a whole, and organise it.'[13] This concept of property is far more exalted than that of the utilitarians, for whom property was an expedient device for satisfying the individual's impulses for enjoyment. For Bosanquet the social responsibilities which property enforced and expressed were precisely what differentiated a grown man from a child. 'A man must know what he can count on and judge what to do with it. It is a question of initiation, plan, design, not of a more or less enjoyment' (*Aspects*, p. 313).

It followed as a practical policy implication that individual case-work, as practised by the C.O.S., was the only sure path to progress. Demoralisation was the great danger and any general scheme of state intervention was likely to make matters worse in this respect. It seemed clear to Bosanquet that 'the mere spreading of the vague idea that "something must be done"' was 'in and by itself a potent factor in the creation of the miserable class whose existence we deplore' (*Aspects*, pp. 113–14). Gifts, missions, shelters, doles and, by the 1890s, a prospect of public relief works, all reinforced the demoralising impression that the whole providential arrangement was only a huge wheel of chance. Nothing should be done to undermine personal responsibility to provide for the known contingencies of life. The individual had to recognise that others as well as himself depended on his prudence and that he had to provide not only for the moment but also for the years ahead. State provision of old age pensions would thus infringe this principle as fatally as any other kind of doles. 'We have two paths before us', Loch stated in 1892. 'One seems comparatively slow and laborious. It leads to social independence.' This was the path which the C.O.S. trod in rejecting pensions as any real remedy. 'The other path,' he warned, 'seems quick, though costly. It leads to social dependence' (*Aspects*, p. 165).

(III) THE YEARNING FOR BELIEF

Wallas left Oxford in 1881. He learnt that summer that Olivier had precipitated a religious confrontation with his parents by repeated absence from Holy Communion. Wallas's own loss of faith was finally acted out in the high Victorian manner four years later. His father, as a good Evangelical, clearly did not build his regular ministrations around the Eucharist. But the acceptance of the sacrament once a year had, therefore, all the greater symbolic significance for him. He eventually confided to Graham that, 'as regards our own Communion Sunday at Shobrooke... whenever you are here...it is to me a season most painful to look forward to, and when it arrives it is a day of discomfort and humiliation and sorrow'

[13] *The Civilisation of Christendom* (1893), p. vi.

(24 July 1885). The family stresses which Wallas's lapse occasioned were obviously not lightly taken. It was, according to his father, 'a part of my daily life, an ever present burden, a cloud that never lifts' (ibid.). And his mother, of whom he was fond and who had particularly impressed his friend Olivier, was tearful in her distress.

But Shobrooke also exemplified for Wallas the way in which organised Christianity was tied into the existing class system. The old rectory at Shobrooke stands near the top of a hill, well out of the village but practically at the gates of Shobrooke Park, the seat of the Hippisley family in the late nineteenth century. 'The gentleman who receives nearly all the rent of that parish,' Wallas commented in a lecture in 1886, 'is a young man of dull but not unkind feelings, impervious stupidity, and rather a fine voice. He always reads the lessons in Church' ('Tithe'). He could read the Biblical injunctions, that those with great possessions should give to the poor, without a flicker of compunction. There was no comprehension of the Church's ostensible teaching; services were like communal sleep-walking, with the congregation chanting 'some dreary rigmarole of which the Hebrew must have been nonsense and the translation is gibberish'. Going down from London to witness this spectacle, Wallas claimed, 'one is conscious of a horrible feeling of suffocation' (ibid.).

Wallas had taken a post as a classics master at Highgate School at the end of 1884. In February 1885 his mother died. By Easter the issue had arisen whether he would take communion in the school chapel. He was given the summer term, on leave with full pay, to consider. The promptings from the bereaved household at Shobrooke were affectionate but firmly supported the headmaster's insistence on conformity.

Robert Elsmere is the classic contemporary study of a crisis of conscience of this kind. We know that Mrs Ward drew upon Wallas for some of her later fiction; perhaps he confided in her because she seemed to comprehend the nature of his experience. The most direct models are likely to have been Arthur Acland and Stopford Brooke, both of whom resigned their orders in the Church of England during 1879–80. But it is obviously true, as Mrs Ward later acknowledged, that her most famous novel had a 'suggestive, symbolic character' because by a happy chance 'the generation in which it appeared had spoken through it'.[14] Graham Wallas is a case in point.

Wallas's father held tenaciously to a stern orthodoxy. The Church was the only sure path to salvation among the treacherous sands of the world, which would otherwise suck a man down. It was a stark vision in which Sin and Faith represented themselves as the only alternatives. It is a view which Mrs Ward puts in the mouth of the High Church clergyman Newcome. 'God, Heaven, Salvation on the one side, the devil and hell on the other – and one miserable life, one wretched sin-stained will, to win the

[14] Introduction to the Westmoreland edition of *Robert Elsmere* (1911), pp. xxix, xiv.

battle with. . .*I stand for Christ*, and His foes are mine' (ch. xii). Wallas was upbraided from home less hysterically but to the same effect. His father went as far as he could in sympathising with Graham's doubts. 'The Christian faith,' he explained, 'comes to no one by instinct. The history of almost every Christian's belief is this: viz. first he hears of revealed religion, then he tries it in practice, observes its ordinances and its practical rules; he then finds the fruit of it to be so good, so conducive to strength and happiness of mind and purity of life, that he feels assured that the root must be sound; and so he learns to live upon it. If he refuses to adopt it until all be previously made clear to him his unbelief will continue to the end of time' (24 July 1885).

When Wallas's wife read this correspondence thirty years later it struck her how difficult it was for a Churchman to escape claims urged with such consistency, and in her diary she not unfairly summarised the main theme: 'Accept – do not trouble about believing it – belief will come with conformity even if the forms & the religion were man-made – such men as Temple etc were wiser than you – be modest intellectually' (11 May 1916). But this was where Wallas, like Elsmere, could not in conscience submit to the opinions of others. 'I am content with my Creed', his father assured him. 'I learnt the truth of it experimentally by it preserving me from permanent moral ruin' (24 July 1885). This is an intriguing hint; but the fictional Newcome, of course, was able to draw upon a richer vein of rhetoric when he expanded on this theme (ch. xxv):

> 'Do you think I don't know', and his voice rose, his eyes flamed, 'what black devil it is gnawing at your heart now? Why man, I have been through darker gulfs of hell than you have ever sounded!'

The remedy too was relayed *forte* where the Wallas family had tried it *piano*. 'Trample on yourself!' Newcome enjoins. 'Pray down the demon, fast, scourge, kill the body, that the soul may live!' (ibid.)

Gladstone, in his famous review of *Robert Elsmere*, quoted this passage in a spirit of mixed incredulity and indignation. 'Considered as a medicine for a mind diseased, for an unsettled, dislocated soul, is it less or more than pure nonsense?' (*NC*, xxiii, 770) He hardly found it plausible that such a response should, in good faith, be attributed to the defenders of orthodoxy. Yet clearly the novelist was not at fault. This was the medicine on offer. Gladstone was impatient with what he saw as an unfairly weighted presentation of the whole argument – 'the one side is a paean, and the other a blank' (p. 769). But the effectual points in defence of Christianity which were urged on Elsmere were those which were urged on Wallas, and in fact they were those urged by Gladstone as the crux of his case.

'Once loosen a man's *religio*, once fling away the old binding elements, the old traditional restraints which have made him what he is, and moral deterioration is certain.' Elsmere's heart goes cold within him when he considers this familiar maxim in his hour of doubt. 'What shall it profit a man, indeed,' he ponders, 'if he gain the whole world – the whole world of knowledge and speculation – and *lose his own* soul?' (ch. xxvii) Elsmere's solution was to go to Oxford and seek salvation from the fictionalised T. H. Green. Even had Green still been alive, that recourse would hardly have been open to Wallas; they had long since exhausted their common interest in dogs. His sister Nellie, however, did what she could to fill the breach. 'Gra dear,' she pleaded with him, 'dont leave if you possibly can help it tho' you maynt believe in the divinity of Christianity you cannot help knowing that if any one followed the simple rules of the bible they would lead good & useful lives wh: is your great idea of life isnt it' (n.d. but 1885). Everyone could see that men like Wallas or Elsmere were not out to give countenance to any ethical backsliding. The evidence suggests that it would be a mistake, however, to suppose that by the 1880s social morality and revealed religion were seen as quite dissociated. The upshot of Gladstone's argument against *Robert Elsmere* shows him to be working from not dissimilar premises.

Gladstone summarised Mrs Ward's purpose as that of 'discarding the supposed lumber of the Christian theology, while retaining and applying, in their undiminished breadth of scope, the whole personal, social, and spiritual morality which has now, as a matter of fact, entered into the patrimony of Christendom' (*NC*, xxiii, 777). But this he considered 'a vague and arbitrary severance of Christian morals from the roots which have produced them', *viz.* Christian dogma (p. 781). As regards the historical record, he swept aside the doubts of modern scholarship and inferred the greatness of the truth from the fact that it had prevailed. Basing his claim upon the Christian tradition, he could give it almost a sociological bearing: 'What right have we to detach, or to suppose we can detach, this type of personal character from the causes out of which as a matter of history it has grown, and to assume that without its roots it will thrive as well as with them?' (p. 784).

For Wallas the issue was personally painful but intellectually clear. His favourite sister Mollie wrote: 'I know it is dreadfully difficult for you to be self contained as discussion is as the breath of your nostrils but Billy my darling stay – Can a man be better than by being a *true* Christian – well knowing that it is a good life to lead whether invented by man or coming from God' (10 May 1885). But who had actually invented it seemed to Wallas a point of some importance. The claims of intellectual integrity, as he understood them, were paramount. Gladstone suggested in a final point against Mrs Ward that the Christian doctrines were rejected by thinkers who had not fully had to feel the *need* of them. In this respect, however, the dying Robert Elsmere is hardly remiss in his yearning for God. 'And in life,' he tells his wife, 'He only makes us yearn that he may satisfy. He cannot lead us to the end and disappoint the craving He himself set in us' (ch. li).

Wallas differed from both in scouting this as any ground for belief. In rejecting dogmatic Christianity he did not accept any theistic surrogates. It is true that Ada Wallas's diary records that she and her husband later reflected 'how at first freedom from the indelicacy & stuffiness of Evangelical Xtianity seemed enough in itself; then how one by one we found some form of socialism' (29 October 1916). But in religious matters Wallas's position was one of rationalism like that of his friends Bernard Shaw, J. A. Hobson and Bertrand Russell. Twenty years later Shaw reprimanded him as a 'futile old Anti-Clerical' for 'reeking a parricidal vengeance on the bones of your father' (28 November 1908). Forty years later Hobson wrote feelingly of the general predicament: 'An escape from prevailing sanctities, stamped by early association upon the tender mind, can only be achieved by an emotional struggle in which the combative instinct is engaged so strongly as to leave behind a sentiment of hostility and disgust, often intensified in passionate natures by well-founded fear lest the emotional escape be incomplete.'[15] It was Russell who made the essential distinction most neatly. Ada Wallas records that she once told him that she understood a man's great desire for a religion. 'He said he understood a man's desire for a fortune but the desire for a fortune did not justify a man in forging a cheque' (diary, 6 April 1905).

(IV) THE MANTLE OF GREEN

Hobhouse was an undergraduate from 1883 to 1887. His university career was one of easy academic distinction. He got a First in Greats and was elected to a prize fellowship at Merton. In 1890 he returned to Corpus as tutor in philosophy and was elected a Fellow in 1894. According to Wallas, who was trailing from one unsatisfactory teaching post to the next in these years, 'he had before him the most delightful form of living that can be found in the world' (*Ec.*, ix, 247). Yet already in 1889 Hobhouse was thinking of spending some time in London, finding Oxford 'rather a misty out-of-the-world place' (*Memoir*, p. 26). He was temperamentally unable to accept Oxford as a world in itself. A contemporary later wrote of him as an undergraduate: 'By nature a fearless mind, he took Mill's motto "Follow your intellect to whatever conclusions it may lead", and he was led to the left. In politics he was and always remained a firm radical. In religion he was an (if possible yet firmer) agnostic' (*Memoir*, p. 23).

During this period two of his closest friends were Charles Roberts and Maurice Llewelyn Davies. Both had been at Marlborough, though Roberts then went to Balliol not Corpus; and both were the sons of clergymen.

[15] *Free-Thought in the Social Sciences* (1926), p. 39.

The Rev. John Llewelyn Davies, indeed, was a famous Rector of Marylebone, a Broad Churchman, a Christian Socialist, and father of six remarkable sons and one daughter, Margaret, who became a lifelong friend of Hobhouse. Roberts seems to have been more closely involved than Davies in Hobhouse's political activities at this time. There was no open Liberal society in the university but there were two intercollegiate clubs to which undergraduates could be elected: the Palmerston, which was Whiggish, and the Russell, which was radical. Roberts and Hobhouse belonged to the Russell Club and each in course became president. Another friend was Hubert Llewellyn Smith, like Hobhouse a scholar of Corpus. All three were drawn, probably through Arthur Sidgwick, into the orbit of the formidable Lady Carlisle and stayed frequently at Castle Howard.

Lady Carlisle was a Stanley of Alderley. Her sister had married Viscount Amberley and was the mother of Bertrand Russell, who observed in 1904 that his aunt conducted conversation 'in a way which makes it a game of skill played for high stakes. It is always argument, in which, with consummate art, she ignores relevancy and changes the issue until she has the advantage and then she charges down and scatters the enemy like chaff before the wind' (*Autobiog.*, i, 174). This was life in the ripe, eccentric, egotistic, radical fringe of Whig society. Lady Carlisle's causes were woman suffrage, temperance, Home Rule. Hobhouse was sent out with the other young Oxonians who had shown themselves sound under cross-examination, like Charles Roberts and Gilbert Murray, on temperance propaganda among the villages around Castle Howard. Mary Howard, with whom he was on easy terms, once told her mother that she was selfish – 'You *must* do what *you* want to do *for* other people.'[16] There are, indeed, rich ironic possibilities here which Shaw seized upon in his portrayal of Lady Britomart in *Major Barbara* (1905). 'And my family, thank heaven,' she exclaims, 'is not a pig-headed Tory one. We are Whigs, and believe in liberty. Let snobbish people say what they please: Barbara shall marry, not the man they like, but the man *I* like' (Act 1). It was Gilbert Murray who married Major Barbara; and he later described his mother-in-law as 'the Whig aristocrat in an extreme form, with all the authoritarianism and fearlessness of the aristocrat and the rebellious idealism of the radical' (Henley, p. 147). His marriage to Mary Howard took place in 1889 and in 1891 Roberts married her sister Cecilia. Perhaps it was just as well; Hobhouse's own mother-in-law seems to have been the least of his problems.

All of this is within the ambit of radicalism of a well-understood kind. Even Hobhouse's connexion with Canon Barnett and Toynbee Hall can be seen as flowing in this channel. But there were also new springs to be tapped. Hobhouse and Llewellyn Smith were members of the 'Inner Ring' which met to discuss social and economic questions under the guidance of

[16] Dorothy Henley, *Rosalind Howard* (1958), p. 40.

Arthur Acland. Acland came from a landed family, had taken orders, and become a don. But in the course of the 1870s, along with Oxford friends like Green and the Humphry Wards, his interests had turned to the social question, and in 1879 he resigned his orders. Moreover, he had actually gone out into industrial England to find out about life 'on the workmen's side'. 'In all the good work I have ever done,' he later told C. P. Scott, 'the vigour of the *North* has been with me. And for one brought up amidst the tenacious traditions of an old county family in the South that means well! everything!' (4 July 1898). Acland was, then, the right man to open new doors for Hobhouse.

Acland was elected to Parliament in 1886 but remained in contact with the Inner Ring. When in 1886 the trade unionist John Burnett was appointed Labour Correspondent at the Board of Trade, Acland brought him to Oxford. Llewellyn Smith and Hobhouse were greatly impressed by Burnett. He spoke, with the authority of a former general secretary of the Engineers, in favour of trade unionism as the most effectual means of improving the conditions of the working class. He maintained, moreover, 'that unorganised labour is most dangerous to social order. No stronger barrier to social revolution exists than those which have been erected by the Unions' (*DLB*, ii, 74). From this time on Hobhouse and Llewellyn Smith were to be found investigating social conditions in Oxfordshire villages and encouraging the agricultural labourers to become unionised.

In Parliament in the late 1880s Acland acted with a group of younger Liberal members which included Asquith, R. B. Haldane, Edward Grey, Tom Ellis and L. A. Atherley-Jones. Among these it was Acland's brief to keep in touch with organised labour. They adopted John Morley as the Liberal leader most open to their pressure for a more advanced policy, though Morley himself seems to have been largely impervious to their influence on questions of any real substance. The existence of the group demonstrated the emergence at a parliamentary level of a sort of progressive Liberalism which was seeking a new political formula. It was an article by Atherley-Jones which first established the concept of a 'new Liberalism'. Rather like the ontological proof for the existence of God, reference to a new Liberalism may be taken to imply a felt need for a reformulation of Liberal ideas, even though there was for many years no clear agreement on what the content of the new agenda should be. Atherley-Jones at least confirmed that the new Liberalism was that of the working class, as opposed to the old Liberalism of the Nonconformist middle class, and that its tenor would lay it under the imputation of socialism. In summarising its aims as 'a wider diffusion of physical comfort, and thus a loftier standard of national morality' (*NC*, xxvi, 192), he was seeking to annex a moralistic claim to a demand for legislative regulation. It is a manner of argument, of course, not dissimilar from that of Green.

What did Hobhouse think of Green? Because he became a professional philosopher himself he paid considerable attention to justifying his position in relation to Green. By the time Hobhouse became an undergraduate Green was already dead. His collected works were published between 1885 and 1888. There was, of course, a strong oral tradition in Balliol itself, where R. L. Nettleship, Green's editor, was a tutor. Even so, it is difficult to see how Hobhouse could have become properly acquainted with Green's thought until the late 1880s.

Hobhouse had, however, read works by Mill and Spencer while at school. He later recalled that in the mid 1880s 'the biological theory of evolution was already very generally accepted, and the philosophical extension of the theory by Mr Herbert Spencer was, except in academic circles, in the heyday of its influence'.[17] In academic circles, of course, it was enough to deny an interest in dogs; but Hobhouse was interested in dogs. He seized on Spencer with a naive enthusiasm and set himself, after he graduated, to master the methods of natural science. For six months he worked full time at the Oxford physiological laboratory under Professor J. S. Burdon-Sanderson and J. S. Haldane (uncle and brother respectively of the politician), and his approach was resolutely down to earth. Indeed, Hobhouse's sustained ingenuity over the years in devising practical experiments with animals was to abash many of the philosopher's friends. 'His kindly training of dogs, cats and rabbits would throw, he hoped, some light on the relations of reason, instinct, associative memories, and so on; but I cannot believe that it threw very much.'[18]

One side of Hobhouse's work was an attempt to out-Spencer Spencer in this way. Starting from a commitment to social reform, he was hardly disposed to bow before the scientific credentials which lent authority to Spencer's political views, as pungently expressed in his recent tract *The Man Versus the State* (1884). According to Spencer, surveying the legislation of Gladstone's second government, the Liberals had become exponents of a new Toryism and had 'lost sight of the truth that in past times Liberalism habitually stood for individual freedom versus State-coercion' (Pelican edn, p. 67). Through a confusion in thought it had allegedly gone against its essential nature by inverting the method by which it had previously brought about public good.

At this point, however, the argument shifts back to Green. For when Hobhouse came to read Green on 'Liberal Legislation' he found the matter put the other way around. Green acknowledged that, a generation previously, Liberals had been fighting in the name of individual freedom. But only the appearance, not the reality, was now changed. 'The nature of the genuine political reformer is perhaps always the same', he held. 'The

[17] *Development and Purpose* (1913), p. xv.
[18] J. B. Atkins, *Incidents and Reflections* (1947), p. 83.

passion for improving mankind, in its ultimate object, does not vary' (*Works*, iii, 367). The only change was in the means whereby reformers pressed the same old cause of social good. This claim of Green's rests not on his metaphysics, which Hobhouse rejected as a valid philosophical solution, but on an appeal to temperament, where Hobhouse could recognise an affinity in outlook. It irritated him that those who lectured on Greats should disparage Mill, for whom he was always ready to stand up; but, anticipating a turn from Idealism, he maintained that 'he should set his face against Green being treated as Mill had been' (*Memoir*, p. 32).

In his mature years Hobhouse liked to consider Green in terms of a political tradition which had been carried forward at different times by men of different schools. In this sense he described Green in *Democracy and Reaction* (1904) as Mill's 'true successor in the line of political thinkers' (p. 224 n.). Moreover, he claimed that, like Bentham and Mill, Green had 'a practical situation in view', to which his doctrine was a response.[19] Likewise, in *The Metaphysical Theory of the State* (1918) the judgment on Green is that 'the strength of his grasp lay upon the hard problems of social reform. He was at his best in working through practical issues to the principles guiding them' (p. 122). And right at the end of his life Hobhouse would still defend Green before his students in this spirit: 'I think you're too hard on T. H. Green. He didn't dare say too much in those days, and hid a lot of good material in poor padding' (*Memoir*, p. 79).

When Green is approached in this way – from the point of view of what he dared not say – he emerges as a staunch yet clandestine champion of collectivism. The qualms of the moral regenerationist were thus vanquished. The reformist position here was perhaps best stated in the late 1880s by D. G. Ritchie, who was both explicitly countering Spencer and posthumously interpreting Green. Ritchie was ten years older than Hobhouse; he was a Fellow of Jesus and one of the leading radicals among the Oxford dons; he joined the Fabian Society in the 1880s; and he was a Hegelian. Like Hobhouse, he wished to establish the political congruence of the teachings of Mill and Green. In *The Principles of State Interference* (1891) he alleged that Mill's thinking showed 'a process of transition from the extreme doctrines of individualism and *laissez faire*, in which he was brought up, to a more adequate conception of society' (p. 83). So Mill and Green would often in practice be found on the same platform, and in these practical affairs there was 'no reason why the Idealist, after making clear his objections to Hedonism, should not join hands with the Utilitarian' (p. 145). Ritchie described the changed role of the state in a less tentative way than Green. 'There is a time to break down and a time to build up; and the same men may have to do both' (p. 7). The merely negative work of pruning back mischievous state activities had, according to Ritchie, to

[19] *The Roots of Modern Sociology* (1908), p. 10.

give way to the positive use of government power. In Green himself, of course, this transition is masked by construing the removal of obstacles in different senses.

Hobhouse tackled the problem in much the same spirit. When, in *The Labour Movement* (1893), he came to deal with the supposed rights of the individual – those of the man *versus* the state – he seized on the common hostility of Mill and Green to the idea that there were innate natural rights. So far as it goes, this is indisputable. But Hobhouse then proceeded to put his own gloss upon Green's highly abstract statement of the Idealist postulate that only in a society conscious of its common interest can rights exist. 'A right,' Hobhouse concluded, 'is nothing but what the good of society makes it. . .If, therefore, any right to any form of property or freedom no longer serves a good social purpose, it must go' (p. 90). Ritchie and Hobhouse were not distorting Green's logic but they were arguing in much more robust and sweeping terms from what were in Green little more than agonised and unresolved dilemmas.

Ritchie concluded his account of Green by asserting that 'there is no *a priori* presumption in favour of a general policy of *laissez faire*, because in a vast number of cases the individual does not find himself in a position in which he can act "freely" (i.e. direct his action to objects which reason assigns as desirable) without the intervention of the State to put him in such a position' (p. 148). In Green's original treatment, however, this had remained as a pregnant question. Was it the case, he had asked, that the unlimited accumulation of private wealth 'necessarily carries with it the existence of a proletariate, nominal owners of their powers of labour, but in fact obliged to sell these on such terms that they are owners of nothing beyond what is necessary from day to day for the support of life?' (*Principles Pol. Obligation*, par. 226). Was capitalism itself the cause of the social problem?

2

Good men fallen among Fabians

(I) SOCIALISM

On leaving Oxford, while Wallas had become a schoolmaster, his friend Olivier had entered the Colonial Office in 1882. There he met Sidney Webb who was also a resident clerk living in Downing Street. Calling on Olivier, Wallas met Webb and they moved at once on to terms of intellectual intimacy. Webb had met Bernard Shaw a year or two previously at the debates of the Zetetical Society; Olivier met Shaw through the Land Reform Union, formed in 1883 to further Henry George's ideas. By the end of 1884, if not earlier, Olivier, Shaw, Wallas and Webb all knew each other and they seem to have formed a high opinion of each other from the outset. 'The history of any definite "school" of philosophic or political opinion,' wrote Wallas in *Francis Place* (1898), 'will generally show that its foundation was made possible by personal friendship' (p. 65).

At this time they were all groping around for a soundly formulated radical approach to social problems. Shaw had been greatly impressed first by Henry George and then by the writings of Marx, of whom he became an adherent, defending the value theory in controversy with Philip Wicksteed in the winter of 1884–5. For the others, however, though they were looking for some kind of change on the moral axis, it was by no means clear that socialism would meet their need better than a thoroughgoing commitment to moral regeneration. To Olivier, who was influenced by Comte, it seemed in 1884 that socialism required 'as thorough a revolution in morality as would suffice to obviate the evils of the Capitalist system, which if moralised, I am not *sure* is not economically superior'.[1] Webb too moved within the parameters set by Comte and Mill. He had resisted Shaw's pressure to join the Land Reform Union but he later drafted *A Plea for the Taxation of Ground Rents* (1887) for a committee which included its successor, the English Land Restoration League. The difference was that Webb could here work from Mill's line of reasoning. This consorted well with the tone of the preface contributed by Lord Hobhouse, whose own earlier addresses, published as *The Dead Hand* (1880), argued that 'wealth, in order to be useful, ought continually to be used and controlled by those who have the greatest interest in it' (p. viii). According to that unacknowledged legislator Pope,

[1] Margaret Olivier (ed.), *Sydney Olivier* (1948), p. 64.

'Tis use alone that sanctifies Expence.

This can fairly be dubbed a bourgeois ethic; but rephrased in Lord Hobhouse's stolid prose it was in its day the more radical gloss upon classical economic doctrine.

Shaw's controversy with Wicksteed led to the establishment of friendly relations between them and to an invitation to the monthly meetings of an economic circle where Wicksteed lectured on value theory. Its original nucleus had been a study group organised through the Unitarian Manchester College. Shaw and Wallas both became members of this body, which Shaw claimed as the begetter of the Royal Economic Society. Wicksteed, who was, as he used to put it, often taken for a socialist by friends who were not socialists but generally rejected as one by friends who were, was the ideal man to make the work of Jevons accessible. Shaw at first stuck by Marx. Wallas too can be found talking of the extraction of surplus product in terms which are more easily reconcilable with Marx than with Jevons; for example in the first public lecture he gave, on 'Education', in 1886 at Kelmscott House, Hammersmith, the home of William Morris.

This raises, of course, the question of whether Wallas seriously considered the Marxist challenge to reformism before himself becoming a hole-and-corner reformer. It is important to observe that the manner of Marx's reception in England meant that his moral revolutionism was not a historically available option in this generation. The humanist face of Marx was effectively obscured. What was understood as Marxism was the necessitarian doctrine with its appeals to positive science which Engels actively propagated – with Marx's acquiescence in his last years and with *carte blanche* after Marx's death. Moreover, H. M. Hyndman became the chief institutional mediator of Marxism in the Social Democratic Federation (S.D.F.), and in his hands a dialectical approach was discarded in favour of a mechanistic determinism. More practically, his dictatorial methods reflected an austere certainty that a revolutionary movement could be manipulated by those who possessed the key to history. Whether Hyndman should be characterised as a mechanical revolutionist need not be settled here; but it is clear that his great opponent in the S.D.F. split of 1884, William Morris, was the authentic moral revolutionist voice in England.

The moral revolutionist believes that contradictions in the system are structural and endemic; the remedy therefore is to replace the system; and this can be done by releasing the force of popular will as the workers become conscious of their position and their task. The important question is not whether Morris was a Marxist but whether he was a Morrisist, with a coherent and important vision to communicate. The case for seeing him as our greatest diagnostician of alienation seemed strong at the time and is equally persuasive today. For Morris, like Marx, traced alienation to the division of labour, and this in turn to the class division of society. In socialism he found a possibility of abolishing the age-old contradiction between the unfolding possibilities of life and their negation by class oppression. Capitalism not technology was his ostensible target; under socialism the division of labour could be unwound so as to restore dignity and pleasure to work that was known to be done well and in a good cause. Socialism was thus a *Weltanschauung*, implying a total transformation of social consciousness as the agent, the sanction, and the consequence of a revolution in property relations. 'Socialism,' proclaimed Morris, 'will transform our lives and habits, and leave the greater part of the political, social and religious controversies that we are now so hot about forgotten, useless and lifeless like wrecks stranded on a sea-shore.'[2]

Wallas was, like Shaw, a frequent visitor to Kelmscott House in the 1880s. (Who else could have given a lecture on 'Social Science 2,200 years ago'?) The humanism of Morris appealed strongly to him. Morris acknowledged that the differences between them were not very great. But Morris was a prophet, a communist utopian, who rejected the 'common-sense' values of bourgeois society in his confidence that the education of desire would enable society to liberate itself. Wallas was nothing if not empirical, pragmatic, utilitarian. There was a barrier of scepticism between his temperament and that of Morris. To Wallas it seemed that Morris would not face the fact that one could not eat one's cake and have it. 'Once, while I listened to him lecturing,' he recalled, 'I made a rough calculation that the citizens of his commonwealth, in order to produce by the methods he advocated the quantity of beautiful and delicious things which they were to enjoy, would have to work about two hundred hours a week' (*Great Society*, p. 347). In the tradition of Bentham, the earthbound Wallas sought to specify the costs and benefits of change with as much precision as possible. He believed too that at the end of his life Morris had come to recognise that hard economic analysis was the urgent requirement.

At the end of 1884 a small group had begun meeting every fortnight at the house of Mrs Charlotte Wilson, the wife of a stockbroker, who, being drawn to anarchism, had gone to Hampstead to lead the simple life. Among the members was Professor F. Y. Edgeworth, who was the leading exponent of a mathematical approach to Jevonian marginalism. The group constituted itself a seminar to study Marx's *Capital* and became known as Mrs Wilson's economic tea parties or the Karl Marx Society or, later, the Hampstead Historic Society. Shaw was missing from the first meeting, at which the first chapter was discussed in his absence. Wallas's later impression was that, when he himself joined this group in February 1885, one or two chapters of *Capital* had already been discussed. 'We sat round a table,' he recalled, 'with copies of Karl Marx in front of us expecting to find direction for all our activities. I took my turn in writing an analysis of a

[2] E. P. Thompson, *William Morris* 2nd edn (1977), p. 689.

chapter. I can remember our astonishment when we found that we did not believe in Karl Marx at all' (*M. Post*, 1 January 1923).

This does not altogether tally with the tone of contemporary evidence. Webb wrote to Shaw of the meeting which he had missed, saying that he and Edgeworth had spent the evening 'gaily dancing on the unfortunate K.M., trampling him remorselessly under foot, amid occasional feeble protests & enquiries from Mrs Wilson (who had thrown away her young love upon him)' (4 November 1884). It should, however, be remembered that this is a letter from the most hostile student of Marx in the group trying to goad the most sympathetic into attending next time.

Few of Marx's works were available in English at this time: *Le Capital* was the set book. Shaw remembered going to find it in the British Museum Library. E. R. Pease had his own copy by October 1883 (though he mistakenly thought the original Fabians had not read the work). Webb naturally interpreted Marx as an economist in the classical tradition whose major theoretical achievement had been his concept of surplus value. The importance of the Hampstead group, according to Wallas, was that 'under Webb's leadership, we worked out the Jevonian anti-Marx value theory as the basis of our socialism, and that from our studies of the history of the socialist idea we became consciously "evolutionist" '.[3]

They had already decided that social defects were systematic, and therefore rejected the regenerationist position. The salient question in the mid 1880s was, therefore, as Beatrice Webb put it: 'Were we or were we not to assume the continuance of the capitalist system as it then existed; and if not, could we by taking thought, mend it or end it?' (*MA*, p. 178) For Marx, revolution was the necessary solution because surplus value was what the capitalist stole from the worker, that being how the system inexorably operated; so it could only be restored, once for all, by a successful revolution. But Wallas, following Webb, now came to believe that surplus value was pervasive and protean and that it accrued to other classes apart from the capitalist in the form of different kinds of rent. Ricardo had established a theory of rent for land of differential fertility; the discussions in the Hampstead Historic Society now pointed to the conclusion that this could be extended to all other economic advantages.

The result was, Wallas later claimed, 'that we could treat as questions of more and less problems which the Marxists treated as questions of absolute contradiction'.[4] The tactical corollary was clear. Wallas elucidated it in a paper read at Kelmscott House in the spring of 1886. Revolutionary socialists might 'rejoice at everything which under the present system tends to increase the suffering and helplessness of the working-classes and therefore, they think, to bring the day of Retribution nearer'. Wallas was

[3] Wallas to E. R. Pease, 10 January 1916, WP 10.
[4] Wallas to E. R. Pease, 4 February 1916, WP 10.

dismissive here. 'A man who habitually cherishes such thoughts if he is not a god is in danger of becoming a devil.' His own alternative strategy located revolutionary motive power in moral enthusiasm (as, of course, did Morris); but this came 'neither to the driver who wields the whip nor to the slaves who feel it but to those who are intensely conscious of the smallest as well as the greatest increase of the sufferings of the oppressed and who rejoice at the smallest as well as the greatest improvements in their lot' ('Tithe'). How could such power be harnessed, organised and directed?

Shaw had joined the Fabian Society in 1884, a few months after its foundation. The way he put it later was: 'I chose it for my head quarters. It was nothing until I induced Webb to join' (Laurence, ii, 490). But it had at least rejected the moral regenerationism which had captivated one section of the parent body, the Fellowship of the New Life. The advantage it had over other socialist groups, which aimed at being big working-class organisations, was that it was small, select, undoctrinaire. 'I wanted something in which I could work with a few educated clever men of Webb's type' (ibid., p. 494). Shaw persuaded Webb and Olivier to join in May 1885 after many long discussions late at night, strolling up and down Whitehall outside the Colonial Office. Wallas was away in Germany in 1885–6, following his crisis at Highgate School, and there he eagerly observed the progress of the Social Democrats. On his return to England in April 1886, he joined his friends in the Fabian Society. With adequate opportunity to study the revolutionary socialist movement, they had looked over the brink before staking out a reformist position – a principled reformism which they believed offered a telling critique of Marxist postulates. Wallas was later emphatic about the importance of this aspect of the pre-history of Fabianism. 'We therefore came into the Society ready-made Anti-Marxists, and at once began that insistence on the Ricardian Law of Rent as applied to Capital and ability, as well as to Land which made William Morris say "These Fabians call their noddles their Rents of Ability".'[5]

Two points can be made here. In the first place, there was probably always some difference between the attitudes of Wallas and Shaw towards Marx. In Wallas's later recollection, 'they had the devil's own effort to convert Shaw from Marx to Jevons', for he resisted with every dialectical art. 'And when he eventually surrendered to Webb he protested that they had made out a poor case for Jevons, and that it was the restatement of their case by himself that had overpowered him by its brilliance' (*H–L Letters*, p. 603). Though Shaw came to regard *Capital* as amateurish in its abstract economics he nonetheless thought it a great book. 'It knocked the moral stuffing out of the bourgeoisie, and made an end for ever of middle

[5] MS. review of Pease's *History of the Fabian Society* (1916), WP 12.

class self complacency and optimism' (Laurence, ii, 558). Wallas told a friend in the 1890s that he believed that the non-revolutionary image of the Fabian Society as a whole derived chiefly from himself. 'Aren't you really revolutionary at heart?' he was asked. 'Not nearly so much as Shaw and Webb', he replied.[6] It remains true, however, that Shaw and Wallas alike followed Webb's lead in mastering a theory of rent which became the basis of Fabian economics.

In the second place, then, the form in which Wallas described the theory is worth noting. He can be found blandly expounding it in 1888 as 'what Political Economists call the three Rents,'[7] conferring a perhaps premature authoritative status on Webb's recent article elaborating this theme. Webb had referred to rents of land, labour and capital, and contended that the differential advantages not only of land but of capital too were fortuitous. He denied, therefore, that high profits chiefly represented a rent of *ability* to the employer, and reserved this term for the extra product due to the superior skill of labour. To a larger extent than Webb explicitly acknowledges, this is an analytical rather than an empirical distinction; he is in fact maintaining that 'masters' might receive a rent of ability as part of their 'wages' rather than as part of their 'profits' (*QJE*, ii, esp. 199–200). This is in fact made clearer in Wallas's slight but significant contraction of the argument. 'These three Rents,' Wallas explained, 'are the Rent of Land, of Capital and of Ability' ('Notes'). When labour is redefined as ability in this way, entrepreneurial efficiency is assimilated to an analysis which in effect covers what mid-Victorian radicals liked to call the industrious classes. It is not very far from the distinction between active, productive wealth and the dead hand.

In the mid 1880s, Shaw wrote later, Webb, Olivier, Wallas and himself were the Three Musketeers and D'Artagnan. They were an incomparable threshing machine for ideas which Shaw – 'an amanuensis with a rather exceptional literary knack, cultivated by dogged practice' – could put before a wider audience. 'They knocked a tremendous lot of nonsense, ignorance & vulgarity out of me; for we were on quite ruthless terms with each other' (Laurence, ii, 490). Wallas was equally appreciative and attributed the combination of artistic seriousness and intellectual seriousness mainly to Shaw. 'Truth,' he recalled Shaw as maintaining, 'comes, not from an avoidance of the vulgar vice of lying, but from the agony and sweat in which the professional critic has to approach his work' (*Great Society*, p. 205). Gilbert Murray wrote long afterwards that he had never known anyone 'who lived so vividly the life of the mind and cared so little for that of the mere body'.[8]

[6] Gilbert Slater, 'Reminiscences', WP 32.
[7] 'Notes' for Wallas's debate with Stopford Brooke, WP 16.
[8] S. Winsten (ed.), *GBS 90* (1946), p. 13.

After Oxford Wallas found it refreshing to meet these remarkable men who had not, like Olivier and himself, undergone a gentleman's education. 'What I like about you, Webb,' he once said when he saw him running for a train, 'is that there is no damned nonsense about style' (B. Webb diary, December 1903). An incident from a novel which Shaw was writing stuck in Wallas's mind. The young man from Oxford in a navy blue suit is devoting himself to socialist propaganda; he comes in and throws himself into an easy chair, and says to the beautiful heroine: 'I'm damnably tired. Are you game to address envelopes?'[9] Shaw and Webb gave Wallas a new conception of sustained effort. Webb was unsparing of himself or others in his application to political work, believing that one should find exercise in walking to lectures and amusement in delivering them. He seemed to have read everything and to be master of every argument. Shaw in turn took Webb in hand and cured him of his cockney pronunciation (he used to say political as *plitical*). He called Webb and Wallas amateurs for not taking elocution lessons before undertaking to deliver lectures. Wallas described it as a turning point in his own career when he once explained to the Executive that he had been unable to carry out a promise to draft something, and Webb responded: 'No doubt you had every excuse, but you will observe that the thing has not been done...' (*Men & Ideas*, p. 105 n.). The reproach was never repeated. Beatrice Webb remarked a few years later on Wallas's 'natural sluggishness of nature, turned by his social fervour into a slow grinding at anything that turns up to do' (*OP*, p. 37).

The sheer professionalism of the struggling professional men who formed the nucleus of the early Fabian Society was one of their most outstanding characteristics. They had a respect for the expert and aimed to become experts themselves. They were part of the *nouvelle couche sociale* of the late nineteenth century: an intellectual proletariat claiming the rent of its ability, and hence with little reason to fear the supersession of capitalism by Fabian socialism. They showed real devotion and patent disinterestedness for the common good. As the young H. G. Wells, who observed Wallas and his friends from Kelmscott House days onwards, put it: 'They took the idea of getting a living as something by the way; a sort of living was there for them anyhow.'[10] There was, however, no reason to suppose that the sort of living it was would be any worse when they had remade the world in their own image. In the meantime it was sufficient.

In his letters Shaw writes of walking home from lectures miles away to save the tram fare – 'for years past every Sunday evening of mine has been spent on some more or less squalid platform, lecturing, lecturing, lecturing, and lecturing' (Laurence, i, 216). He and Wallas bore the brunt of the open-air meetings. Little wonder that Shaw fell into hyperbole when the

[9] Ada Wallas, biog. notes (9 August 1934), WP 48.
[10] H. G. Wells, *Experiment in Autobiography* (1934), p. 598.

Fabians actually seemed to be achieving something. 'The fact is,' he told a Liberal editor in 1890, 'Webb & I and half a dozen other men who know their own minds and can live on £150 a year, have out talked you, out written you, out worked you, brought your official ring climbing down in all directions with speeches on "social reform" and then set Radical London laughing at their ineptitude' (ibid., p. 234).

The life which they had undertaken made importunate demands upon their time and abilities. It was possible because they were young and unmarried and ready to pool their talents in a quite unselfish way. This was what impressed Beatrice Potter so forcibly when she met them: 'the charm is in the relations between these men – the genuine care for each other, the trustfulness & practical communism of property & ideas' (diary, 26 August 1890). As Shaw said, they were ruthless with each other; but the candour, of course, rested on camaraderie; and the style might easily be misunderstood by outsiders to whom, as Shaw put it, 'it seemed callous and cynical to be even commonly self-possessed in the presence of the sufferings upon which Socialists make war' (*Tract* 41, p. 127). They no more talked about their desire to promote the general good, Wallas explained, than a soldier on campaign talks of his patriotism. Mrs Ward, who formed her impressions here largely from Wallas, wrote in *Marcella* (1894) that: 'A Venturist [Fabian] is a Socialist minus cant, and a cause which cannot exist at all without a passion of sentiment lays it down – through him – as a first law, that sentiment in public is the abominable thing' (Bk. 3, ch. viii). Rhetoric and emotion were in themselves suspect. Shaw, of course, was a severe critic here, on one occasion telling Wallas, who had a hereditary disposition to preach, that the strained and tearful expressions on the faces of his audience were not due to the pathos of his peroration but to their fear that the pencil he was whirling on the end of his chain would fly off and hit someone in the eye. Wallas respected Shaw's apparent heartlessness as a sign of his deep sincerity of feeling; and in this opinion he persisted even in later years when they were less close politically. He recalled Shaw refusing to speak at an unemployed meeting in the mid 1880s and saying, 'No, as long as I have a watch in my pocket which I do not intend to pawn, I will not pretend sympathy with men who are actually hungry' (N, 11 December 1909). And if Shaw flouted the morality which held that a 'moral' man was one who kept the ten commandments and an 'immoral' man one who broke them, so much the worse for conventional morality.

For Wallas the Fabian hostility to cant – even when expressed as a Shavian hostility to accepted morality – cleared the ground for fresh thinking, uncluttered by establishment attitudes. His sense of what was gained from their close association on these terms, and a suggestive evocation of the timbre of life in his bachelor days, is conveyed in a cameo that must relate to 1890. There used to be an assembly for tea at 4.30 in Sidney Webb's room in the Colonial Office, which Wallas would attend when in town. 'They had a not very fresh tin of condensed milk, and not a very clean teapot and kettle as their possessions, and they used to stand drinking, out of thick teacups, very bad tea. They said precisely – and they were extraordinarily clever men – what came into their minds.' At the time, the Matabele War was brewing and public opinion was full of phrases about honouring the flag. As Wallas recalled it, 'to get behind the conventional feeling that Lobengula was a brutal savage, Sydney Olivier, standing before the window, said "it was not necessary to believe that Lobengula was unlike a British Cabinet Minister: I am not pretending that Loben is a missionary, he did not look like a missionary"'.[11] The incongruity was humorous. The humour brought a new insight.

In May 1888 Wallas suggested to the others that the work of the Hampstead Historic Society should be continued in a smaller group, preferably confined to themselves. 'Four is enough for an efficient dialectic and five is almost too much' (Memo., May 1888). His proposal was that 'since we are the only people in England who are agreed about anything...we should write Tracts for the Times or Epistolae Obscurorum Virorum' (ibid.). This was the origin of the *Fabian Essays* (1889). It was to be, as Olivier put it, a double-barrelled New Testament, with two gospels from each of them; and the volume indeed eventually contained eight essays (two by Shaw). But its structure is in fact based on the lectures given in the autumn of 1888 by the Executive of the Society, which also included three other members. Annie Besant and William Clarke were both familiar figures in the Bloomsbury world of Unitarianism, the Bedford Debating Society and the Ethical movement. Hubert Bland, by contrast, in his frock coat, tall hat and monocle, with a voice like the scream of an eagle, led an outwardly decorous life in Blackheath, and his general political convictions likewise set him apart. 'He was,' Pease wrote afterwards, 'a sound Socialist, but otherwise a Tory, and the rest of us were born Liberals.'[12] Although a member of the Executive from the outset, Bland was never an intimate of Wallas or Olivier or even Webb. It was Shaw who cultivated him as an ally and who – when everyone else was dead – promoted him alongside the others to 'the Politbureau or Thinking Cabinet' which was his later term for the Three Musketeers of the 1880s. This jarring lack of affinity stands out significantly in the case of Wallas, for whom the Hampstead Historic not the Fabian Society represented the days of unsullied unanimity.

Wallas's essay on 'Property under Socialism' sketched a 'tentative and limited Social Democracy' as 'the necessary and certain step to that better life which we hope for' (p. 147). There was here a note of reservation.

[11] 'Conditions of organised purpose', 9 November 1922, WP 13.
[12] Margaret Cole (ed.), *The Webbs and their Work* (1949), p. 19.

'The system of property holding which we call Socialism', he explained, was not such a life 'any more than a good system of drainage is health, or the invention of printing is knowledge' (p. 148). To this William Morris replied in a review that socialism was 'emphatically not merely "a system of property holding", but a complete theory of human life, founded indeed on the visible necessities of animal life, but including a distinct system of religion, ethics, and conduct' (Thompson, p. 548). But for Wallas socialism did not in itself constitute a *Weltanschauung*; it was not 'the only condition necessary to produce complete human happiness' (p. 148). He remembered talking at this time to a middle-aged workman who had fought for the Paris Commune. 'There can be good socialisms and bad socialisms', he told Wallas, meaning that he could imagine radically different situations existing in two countries, in both of which the means of production had been nationalised (*Great Society*, p. 343). For Bland, and also for Shaw, socialism was the essential object which had to be achieved by whatever means seemed promising at the time. For Morris, of course, the democratic ends and means of socialism were so closely intertwined that the problem did not present itself in this light at all. A 'bad' or 'false' socialism would not be socialism at all. So what he excoriated the Fabians for was the confusion of 'the co-operative machinery towards which modern life is tending with the essence of Socialism itself' (Thompson, p. 687).

The question of the relation of humanism to socialism was very much in the air in the 1880s. In an early issue of the Fabian magazine *The Practical Socialist* Edith Simcox considered the relation between socialism and liberalism in terms close to those of Wallas. 'The via media between absolutism and anarchy,' she suggested, 'lies in Liberal Socialism, or Socialistic Liberalism' (*PS*, i, 36). And she argued that there was no need for socialists 'to abandon the conquests of Liberalism for dim visions of a *coup d'état*, or other short cut to social salvation' (ibid., p. 54).

Wallas consistently looked with scepticism on those who found a new religion in socialism. In 1895 he considered disavowing his connexion with the term socialism precisely because of its connotation as 'a cut & dried formula held with theological fervour' (B. Webb diary, 25 September 1895). He had not painfully rejected one theology only to put another in its place and never invested socialism with the omnipotent and providential overtones of a religion. This is a point of some importance in view of recent interpretations. When Wallas asserted in 1886 that 'the social idea is a new religion' ('Tithe'), he did not make this claim, as he so easily could, on behalf of what he understood by socialism. When he told the Fabian Society that 'every step which leads to increased happiness, education and leisure, for our fellow-men is a step forward for our Cause', he was urging a step-by-step policy as against a visionary outlook (*PS*, i, 125). When he tried to define 'personal duty', he did so 'believing, as I do, that the meaning of a word is the sum of the senses in which that word is actually used, and nothing else' (ibid., p. 118). What duty amounted to for the professional man was an obligation to devote his rent of ability to social purposes: preferably through labour, but if he should turn his labour into money the hardheaded advice was that 'he must see that he gets his full pay' (ibid., p. 119). Duty to society was real; but the conception was humanistic not ascetic. 'Remember when you plan your day's work that you are a man, and not a machine', Wallas enjoined. 'Do not refuse to share in the interests, and take part in the politics of to-day' (ibid., p. 125).

In all this Wallas believed himself at one with Webb. Webb was in these days no less ready to expatiate on the personal duty of rentiers under the prevailing system. In a long letter to Haldane's aunt, Jane Burdon Sanderson, he went over the question as scrupulously as Wallas. There was, he insisted, the duty of labour which 'must be the rendering of some personal service to the community, in the way one best can. "From each according to his abilities".' But there was also the duty of economy. 'It appears to me,' he concluded, 'that the maximum justifiable expenditure for anybody is that amount which keeps him in the fullest working efficiency. Everything beyond is selfish waste. "To each according to his needs".'[13] And Webb, of course, like Wallas, also saw collectivism as a businesslike way of transacting the business of society. It was only later that a significant difference opened up between them as to the further implications.

Wallas was cautious in his advocacy of the acknowledged superiority of common ownership on the grounds that more radical extensions, especially in the field of consumption, were 'distasteful to men as they now are' (*Fab. Essays*, p. 134). As a moral reformist, he did not think that collectivism ought to outrun the sanction of a particular community at a particular time. It would not be profitable, in any sense of the word. With a typical recourse to personal experience, he claimed in one of his lectures that 'anyone who has assisted at a London Vestry election will realise that pending a considerable growth of public spirit the advantages of the management of most other industries [than gas and water] by existing public bodies would be for the moment rather ethical and political than economic' ('Morals of Interest'). With the gradual extension of common efforts, however, the prospect of further progress would be opened up. The provenance of socialism was limited in two senses. On the one hand, it was Wallas's position that socialism would fail of its purpose if it went beyond the partial and imperfect ideals of the present. On the other hand, though a fully-fledged socialist system might settle the problems of poverty and over-work, even so, a whole range of other problems would remain –

[13] Webb to Jane Burdon Sanderson, 25 November 1887, Haldane Papers, NLS 6103 ff.131–40.

'we might still suffer all the mental anguish and bewilderment which are caused, some say by religious belief, others by religious doubt; we might still witness outbursts of national hatred and the degradation and extinction of weaker peoples; we might still make earth a hell for every species except our own' (*Fab. Essays*, p. 148).

(II) PERMEATION

The year 1890, in which his father died, was a landmark in Wallas's life. The *Fabian Essays* had just been published; Olivier left for a career in British Honduras; Beatrice Potter appeared; Wallas himself thankfully terminated his career as a schoolmaster. With Webb's assistance he became a university extension lecturer and the fees from this (about £150 a year) supplemented the private income of about £100 which he inherited. The work was congenial and eventually led to his full-time post at the London School of Economics. He and William Clarke and J. H. Muirhead lived in two interconnected houses in Great Ormond Street (Webb was in Camden Town and Shaw in Fitzroy Square). It seemed to Muirhead, who attended some Fabian meetings, that Wallas and Clarke took a broader view than the rest, or at any rate one more congenial to himself. Clarke's argument, presented in 1893, that the sphere of collectivism was confined to the 'great industry' (CR, lxiii, 263–5) brought him closer to Wallas's view than his Fabian Essay would suggest. Muirhead's real allegiance was to Bosanquet and hence the outlook of the C.O.S., Charles Loch and Mrs Humphry Ward. Wallas found no difficulty in working with Mrs Ward, a fellow moralist, despite the divergence of their political views; and indeed she pressed him to make use of the cottage on her estate at Tring, where he and Shaw were able to walk over the downs preaching the virtues of collectivism and Jaeger clothes to her daughter. Wallas was, moreover, sound from the C.O.S. point of view on the issues of outdoor relief and relief works, holding that relief and industrial organisation should be kept apart. This eased the way for joint sponsorship by the C.O.S. of Wallas's extension lectures on citizenship since Elizabethan times, although some objections over his prominent political work evidently had to be surmounted.

Wallas had a stern sense of the requirements of objective scholarship. Like Darwin he felt under a pressing obligation to see where the evidence led. His views on current political issues were another matter. When he was charged with giving a partisan extension lecture in Oxford, he was bitterly stung. At once he called upon the testimony of those in his audience, laid his notes before the Secretary of the Delegacy, and returned his fees until he had been cleared. His interests, of course, were directed and stimulated by his political concerns; but his conviction was that only a resolute effort to discover and communicate how things had actually happened would be of real value. At this time, too, he began the research for his book on Francis Place, who was an almost totally neglected figure in early nineteenth century history. He immersed himself in the extensive and hitherto unexplored Place archives and, indeed, when his sister Mollie was married to Muirhead in 1892 he had to be hauled out of the British Museum and conducted to the church in time for the ceremony.

Shaw saw in his efforts a Fabian willingness to take 'a great deal of trouble to find out how things were really done before we began trying to do them' and considered *The Life of Francis Place* (1898) 'a much later and riper product of that trouble than Fabian Essays' (Laurence, ii, 254). When Wallas wrote that 'the apathy in London continued with that startling completeness which only London politicians know' (p. 288), this was the testament of experience. One can well imagine that the old gang relished his dry description of Place's manoeuvres against the Rotundanists, a sort of S.D.F. of the 1830s – 'if, as was very nearly true, there were no effective politicians among the working-men who were not in sympathy with the Rotundanists, such men must be created' (p. 283). And there is surely a glimpse of the author in the sketch of Horne Tooke who, 'like many moderate men, was supposed to be an extremist merely because he was courageous' (p. 23).

When Beatrice Potter first met Sidney Webb her impression of him was 'somewhat between a London cad & a German professor' (diary, 14 February 1890). And although she liked him she was fully alive to his personal drawbacks. 'His tiny tadpole body, unhealthy skin, lack of manner; cockney pronunciation, poverty are all against him' (ibid., 26 April 1890). To a less strongminded woman, Graham Wallas, to whom she warmed from the outset, would have seemed a more acceptable match in the eyes of her class and her family. (Lord Hobhouse was to win her heart as one of her few upper-class acquaintances to welcome her marriage.) Beatrice Potter was also conscious of the permanent emotional scars which her courtship in the 1880s by the forceful figure of Joseph Chamberlain had left upon her. Poor Sidney was therefore enjoined not to let his mind dwell upon his personal feeling – 'I know how that feeling unfulfilled saps all the vigour of a man's life.' Sidney found it difficult to promise so much but undertook at least 'to look at the whole question from the point of view of Health' (ibid., Whitsun. 1890). Beatrice was, however, before long overwhelmed by his other merits. 'And I am not "in love" – not as I was', she reflected. 'But I see something else in him – (the world wd say that was part of my love) a fine intellect, & a warm heartedness, a power of self subordination & social devotion for the "common good"' (ibid., 20 June 1891). With these considerations in mind, their strenuous regime of joint research on trade unionism was allowed some alleviation – 'while

I have been lying on the sofa he has been busily abstracting & extracting amply rewarded he says by a few brief intervals of "human nature" over cigarettes or the afternoon cup of tea' (ibid., 10 October 1891). Wallas was best man at their wedding in July 1892 and later in the year was 'a constant visitor for Sunday middle day dinner & walks on Hampstead Heath' (ibid., 1 December 1892). Observing the firm of Webb must have given him a new insight into human nature in politics.

To Beatrice Webb, the Fabian junta consisted of Wallas, Webb and Shaw. 'Sidney is the organiser and gives most of the practical initiative, Graham Wallas represents morality and scrupulousness, Bernard Shaw gives the sparkle and flavour' (*OP*, p. 38). When the Webbs moved in to their new house at 41 Grosvenor Road, Millbank, in September 1893 they began a series of 'junta dinners' every Saturday to which Shaw and Wallas had a standing invitation. The junta also took holidays together in these years, especially at the Potter country home in Monmouthshire. It seemed to Beatrice Webb before long that Wallas was being submerged by hard work in his solitary existence. Although able to come and go as he pleased at the Webbs, he had neither 'a beloved Partner' nor Shaw's capacity to live out his own life as drama. 'Graham Wallas grinds,' she noted in her diary – 'making no personal claims – impersonal almost callous in his manner – an English gentleman in his relations with women – to whom a flirtation let alone an intrigue would seem underbred as well as unkind & dishonourable' (25 July 1894). When a hopeful admirer redecorated the Great Ormond Street rooms during his absence, Wallas failed to notice the difference.

The rising tide of Fabian influence was celebrated by Shaw in *Tract 41, The Fabian Society: what it has done and how it has done it* (1892). The tract, which Wallas approved before publication, is a paean to the policy of permeation. 'We have never indulged in any visions of a Fabian army any bigger than a stage army', Shaw claimed (p. 152), and so the Society could only make headway by gaining the confidence of Liberals, trade unionists and Co-operators. Fabianism was to advance by socialising the Radicals. This was a strategy which worked reasonably well in London and, although modern historians have shown many specific Fabian claims to be exaggerated, the Progressive party on the London County Council (L.C.C.) was generally open to Fabian influence. Wallas and Shaw both became active members of Liberal and Radical associations, and the Eleusis Club in Chelsea was particularly important. Connexions with the press were also fostered, and here the key figure was H. W. Massingham. Massingham was close to the Fabians in age: a journalist moving in the same Bloomsbury circles (and squares) in the 1880s – Stopford Brooke's Bedford Chapel, the British Museum, the Shelley Society – and a friend of William Clarke, who later worked with him on the *Daily Chronicle*. His connexion with the evening paper the *Star*, of which he rose to be editor briefly in 1890–1, was often puffed by Shaw as one of the highlights of the Fabian marionette show; but Massingham, who was on the Fabian Executive 1891–3, actually remained very much his own man.

When it came to the recognised leaders of Liberalism, permeation looked less promising. Gladstone was a figure from another world. More important, the prominent men in the Liberal party whom the Fabians recognised as fellow intellectuals were woefully out of sympathy with the new politics of collectivism. The name of John Morley was – along with those of Herbert Spencer and Leonard Courtney – held up as a byword for individualism in Fabian circles. In 1889 Massingham warned of the hopelessness of stirring the apathy of the working-class electorate until 'Mr Morley shows for the East End docker the enthusiasm which he has rightly developed for the Connemara Cotter' (*H.W.M.*, p. 95). When Morley spoke to Beatrice Potter of the social question being the only thing to live for, she commented: 'And yet he has evidently never thought about social questions; he does not know even the ABC of labour problems' (*MA*, p. 262). To Shaw he represented '18th century Rip-van-Winkleism' (Laurence, i, 185), and earned especial opprobrium as the opponent of Eight Hours legislation. Courtney was likewise deprecated as a rigid exponent of the old political economy which persuaded him that '*these evils cannot be cured*' (*OP*, p. 130); and he was, therefore, despite his apostasy over Home Rule, also committed to a Gladstonian conception of politics. To Beatrice Potter it seemed obvious that the Liberal party now lacked a policy. 'Political Democracy achieved, what more is there to do, unless you are prepared for Social or Industrial Democracy?' (diary, 31 December 1890).

The so-called 'progressist Liberals' in Acland's group at least recognised that the new Liberalism would be different from the old. Haldane was on closest terms with the Fabians and in 1891 tried to arrange an alliance between the two movements. Wallas reported unfavourably on a dinner he and Webb had with Haldane and the Greys in January, but a further experiment was nonetheless attempted. 'I think Wallas & Massingham & I would do best for us', Webb wrote to Haldane (30 April 1891), picking his men with care. In fact it was to be Massingham, Clarke, Olivier, Shaw and Webb who met Asquith, Haldane, Grey, Buxton and Acland. But none of this led very far, beyond putting Webb and Wallas under suspicion of too strong an attachment to the Liberal party. Curiously enough, Wallas found that James Bryce, incorrigibly Gladstonian though he was, talked the language of 'social compunction' in a much more forthcoming style.

Wallas resisted attempts to overthrow the policy of permeation, which men like Bland naturally found uncongenial since in practice it was always the Liberal party which was to be permeated. Wallas – 'aspiring fretfully towards a Blandless universe' (Laurence, i, 276) – helped Shaw and Webb to stave off one challenge in 1890, and to damp down enthusiasm for a more visionary socialist commitment. He and Shaw seem to have seen eye to eye on policy in the course of the next couple of years, which saw the return of Gladstone to power. In 1893 Shaw affirmed his intention 'to go uncompromisingly for Permeation, for non-centralized local organization of the Labor Party, and for the bringing up of the country to the London mark by the supplanting of Liberalism by Progressivism' (ibid., p. 377). And Wallas's dictum in this period was 'Postulate, Permeate, Perorate'.

It is thus at first sight difficult to understand Wallas's acquiescence in the manifesto *To Your Tents, O Israel* which appeared in November 1893 as an attack on the Liberal Government and an appeal for an independent party. In later recollections Wallas implied that he was uneasy about it. The explanation probably rests in the internal politics of the Fabian Society where the 'old gang' was facing a challenge from supporters of Hyndman's S.D.F. Part of Shaw's response was, as he told Wallas, to try to 'satisfy the legitimate aspirations of the ardent spirits by getting out a furious attack on the Government' (Laurence, i, 404–5), which, in this context, was to be a diversionary ploy to undercut more radical opposition. Wallas apparently considered that they had been rushed into it by fear of being thought complacent by the recently formed Independent Labour Party. The manifesto provoked the resignation of Ritchie and also of Massingham, who declared: 'I have been a permeator all my days, a Collectivist Radical...And that I remain.'[14] Wallas took a notably conciliatory line in the Executive in urging Massingham to reconsider, but without success. In fact the whole issue was rather inflated. Massingham did not disagree with the substantive criticisms in *To Your Tents*; he did not permanently sever his relations with the Fabians; and the old gang remained firmly committed to the strategy of permeation. Wallas himself was elected to the London School Board in 1894 on progressive lines. His own view of permeation may perhaps be gauged from a favourite passage from Francis Place about reform organisations which 'can only succeed by long-continued steady, patient, liberal conduct, accepting and using every kind of assistance which may at any time, and in every way, be available, making no absurd pretensions to anything and especially not to superior wisdom and honesty, but acting with becoming modesty, but with indomitable perseverance' (*Francis Place*, p. 370).

Wallas certainly did not wish to discount the value of the Fabians' hard-won technical expertise. On the contrary, as Beatrice Webb noted, it was the appeal of 'empirical administration & "untrammelled" thought' which helped make him restive within the Society when he became involved in his School Board work (diary, 25 September 1895). Shaw put a slightly different gloss upon the Fabian position. 'The people want a policy (at least

[14] Alfred F. Havighurst, *Radical Journalist* (Cambridge 1974), p. 50.

about 1/1000th per cent of them do); but they can't make one: they must go to the thinker and tactician for it' (Laurence, i, 389). This was the theory of the Fabian shop. It did not mean that the masses were mere puppets since there were other shops in competition and supply and demand did the rest.

When Beatrice Webb compared the Fabian view with that of her brother-in-law Leonard Courtney, a staunch liberal individualist, she discerned a difference in attitude. 'To Leonard the means whereby you carry through a proposal, the arguments with which you support it, are as important as the end itself' (*OP*, p. 120). She gave Courtney credit for '*faith in democracy* – a quality which covers many sins' (p. 123); indeed she acknowledged that he was possibly more of a democrat than themselves, since the Webbs had little faith in the 'average sensual man' who could only describe his grievances, not prescribe remedies. 'It is possibly exactly on this point that Leonard feels most antagonism to our opinions', she concluded. 'We wish to introduce into politics the professional expert – to extend the sphere of government by adding to its enormous advantages of wholesale and compulsory management, the advantage of the most skilled entrepreneur' (p. 120). At times the metaphor was changed, as befitted the aspirations of the *nouvelle couche sociale*, from that of the Fabian shopkeeper to that of the Fabian doctor. Beatrice Webb wanted to 'continue our policy of inoculation – of giving to each class, to each person, coming under our influence, the exact dose of collectivism that they were prepared to assimilate' (p. 122).

At all events, it was clear in the early 1890s that the Fabian shop had cornered the market in collectivism. The New Unionism and, to a lesser extent, the growth of the Co-operative movement helped to bring labour questions to the fore, and the Fabians were now the pre-eminent authorities here. In Oxford, when Hobhouse organised a conference on trade unionism in 1890, Wallas was one of the speakers invited. They had a mutual friend in Llewellyn Smith who was, with Vaughan Nash, author of a sympathetic account of the London dock strike of 1889. Hobhouse also met Webb at this time and, although he had reservations about Webb's socialism, he was unmistakeably impressed by him in much the same way as Wallas had been some years earlier.

Hobhouse found his closest collaborator at this time in Sidney Ball of St John's, who was perhaps the leading Oxford don to sympathise with Fabian socialism. Ball had himself joined the Society in 1886 and although he considered that an Oxford branch would be premature in the 1880s, the Social Science Club, which he fostered, had much the same objects. Wallas spoke to it in November 1890 and met Herbert Samuel, then an undergraduate at Balliol, in Ball's rooms afterwards. Ball remained firmly committed to the Liberal party; hearing the General Election results night by night in 1895 he 'retired to his pillow quite or nearly mute'.[15] He was a senior member of the Palmerston Club, as well as the Russell to which Ritchie and Hobhouse lent their support. It was the Russell Club which, under Samuel's presidency in 1892–3, imported Fabians such as Massingham to address it. For Ball, like Hobhouse, the root questions of socialism were ethical. 'We got into an argument about "the best formula for the moral ideal" ', he reported of one encounter in 1891 (Ball, p. 55).

The exertion of influence in this way seemed to Beatrice Webb in 1895 a better alternative than trying to browbeat the existing wirepullers of the Liberal party, who would 'rather see a Conservative Government in power than allow the leaders of their own side to push forward social democracy' (*OP*, p. 128). Instead she looked to 'the little group of clever and well-to-do young men' like Charles Trevelyan and Bertrand Russell, about whom she reminisced to Samuel, another of them, some fifty years later, adding with a knowing smile, 'they were all there for some reason...'[16] The Webbs' desire to appear disinterested and above mere political considerations was also furthered by the foundation of the London School of Economics in 1895. This seemed to many a curious – and inappropriate – use for funds bequeathed to further the aims of the Fabian Society. To Wallas the Webbs' scheme, at the inception of which he was present, made good sense, and not only because it gave him a lectureship. Collectivists like himself were outnumbered on the staff; but collectivism, so the School's founders believed, would necessarily flow from scientific inquiry in the social field. The importance of attracting clever men from the universities meant that when Webb and Wallas went out lecturing they made it known that anyone interested in economics would have a welcome at Grosvenor Road. 'Leonard Hobhouse recruits for us at Oxford, the young Trevelyans at Cambridge', Beatrice Webb concluded with understandable satisfaction (diary, Xmas 1895).

Hobhouse's first book, *The Labour Movement* (1893), is permeated by Fabianism. It appeared with a preface by Haldane, whether as the brother of Hobhouse's physiology instructor or the friend of Webb or a member of the Acland group is unclear. The book was an attempt to show that trade unionism and the co-operative movement were similarly actuated in that they subordinated individual interests to common ends, and that municipal socialism was in this respect analogous; furthermore, that the democratic state could claim to be the supreme regulative authority since it alone was not dominated by sectional interests. The conclusion was that these four modes of collective control represented convergent paths to social welfare. The postulate which united them was now manifest: 'It assumes that

[15] Oona H. Ball, *Sidney Ball* (Oxford 1923), p. 224.

[16] B. Webb to Samuel, 11 March 1943, and Samuel's MS note, 4 March 1943, Samuel Papers A 119/6, 8.

intelligence is better than blind forces, and reaches its end more speedily and surely. It holds that the economic well-being of society is the true end of industry, and that this end will therefore be reached better by an intelligent organisation of industry, than by the haphazard interaction of unintelligent forces' (p. 53). In conjunction, therefore, these forces could bring about a better distribution of wealth based on 'the principle that payment should be made for services rendered and to those by whom they are rendered' (p. 76).

Arthur Hobhouse's contention that the dead hand was an insupportable anomaly was extended by his nephew into a Fabian indictment of functionless wealth. The existing system of free competition, Hobhouse maintained, placed liabilities upon society: rent charges, which evoked no service, and interest charges, which were a deadweight from the past. These constituted a surplus which should be communised. Hobhouse was taking up questions which were unresolved in Green, and pushing them vigorously to the next stage. 'Given free Competition enormous inequalities of wealth are inevitable. Doubtless, but suppose we can supersede competition by an intelligent control of industry?' (p. 75) Hobhouse suavely dismissed as pseudo-science the notion that political economy could legitimately speak in favour of the status quo. *The Labour Movement* was thus a thoroughly Fabian document in manner, approach, technique, substance and implications – at least as far as the point in the last chapter where Hobhouse brusquely concluded 'that the economic objections to the collective control of industry are not sound' (p. 88). It was only in the pages that followed, dealing with Green and Mill, that it transparently revealed its Oxford origins.

(III) THE ORGANIC LAW

John Atkinson Hobson was born in Derby in 1858 – 'born and bred in the middle of the middle class of a middle-sized Midland industrial town'.[17] His father owned the local newspaper, from which Hobson later derived a private income. He was brought up as an Evangelical member of the Church of England but underwent a painful crisis of doubt in his adolescence and by 1876, when he went up to Lincoln College, Oxford, he was an agnostic. He began to read Herbert Spencer, his curiosity stimulated by seeing the great man out walking in Derby. In later life he shared with Spencer what is evidently a peculiar local trait: the touchy reluctance of a thinker of profound originality to acknowledge any intellectual debts.

At Oxford Hobson was remembered by his contemporaries as a distinguished high-jumper. He read Greats, regarded it a humane experience, but examined badly. He became a schoolmaster in Exeter, and married Florence

[17] J. A. Hobson, *Towards Social Equality* (Oxford 1931), p. 13.

Edgar, the daughter of an American businessman; they had two children. On his first encounter with political economy, at a Cambridge University extension course in Derby in the 1870s, Hobson was, so he recalled, taught that 'principles and laws governed the production and distribution of wealth which intelligent men and women accepted as belonging to the order of Nature. They established the justice, necessity, and finality of the existing economic system' (*Conf.*, p. 24). He always regarded orthodox economics as an attempt to claim the authority of science to sanction socially conservative attitudes. Only later, however, did he himself seek to challenge that authority. In politics he and his elder brother Ernest (later a Cambridge mathematician) seem to have been influenced by their father's Manchester School Liberalism – hardly a radical outlook by the 1880s and one that led them, like the aged Bright, towards Liberal Unionism after 1886. It must be said that there is a sense in which Hobson never ceased to be a Cobdenite.

At Exeter in the late 1880s Hobson came into contact with A. F. Mummery, a businessman who held the view that the underemployment of capital and labour during periods of bad trade was the result of excessive saving. Hobson became persuaded, and together they wrote *The Physiology of Industry* (1889). Mummery was almost certainly the senior partner. He had, according to Hobson, 'a sublime disregard of intellectual authority' (*Conf.*, p. 30), and the book is subtitled 'an exposure of certain fallacies in existing theories of economics'. It was a combative work which was bound to cause offence among a profession struggling, under Alfred Marshall's leadership, for academic respectability. Hobson and Mummery took little account of recent developments in economic thought. They were out to attack classical political economy 'as it left the hands of Mill some forty years ago' since, as far as they were concerned, its central premise, that saving enriched the community, remained unchallenged (p. iii). But they identified 'the highly extolled virtues of thrift, parsimony, and saving' as the chief causes of prevailing industrial maladies (p. 182). Trade depression was attributed to a deficiency in effective demand, since it was consumption that limited production, not *vice versa*. The amount of savings which the community could usefully make was limited by its level of consumption in the immediate future.

There was, of course, no limit to efficacious thrift on the part of an individual. This was the whole trouble. For it does not follow that what anyone can do, all can do. Hobson seized on this as the individualist fallacy, manifestations of which he was to detect in many aspects of contemporary social and economic thought. Since an individual could always save with advantage, there would be competition to try to do so. Each individual was acting rationally within a free market; yet the overall result for society was a position of underconsumption, or, as it was alternatively described, over-saving. The only solution was through an increase in spending. The state had an ultimate responsibility here since there was no effective natural mechanism. Taxation in England, however, currently encouraged saving and penalised consumption, offering quite the wrong fiscal inducements in an underconsumptionist situation. To Hobson and Mummery it was 'evident that taxation should rightly be directed to check saving, and not expenditure, and should fall on that portion of the individual's income which he refuses to spend' (p. 204).

In collaborating with Mummery (who was killed mountaineering in 1895) Hobson had made himself the author of a remarkable book, perhaps more remarkable than he appreciated. 'This was,' he wrote later, 'the first open step in my heretical career, and I did not in the least realize its momentous consequences' (*Conf.*, p. 30). He had recently come to London as a university extension lecturer. But Professor Edgeworth had read his book and considered it an 'attempt to unsettle consecrated tenets' by 'very paradoxical writers' who were, he implied, deficient in understanding and in scholarship.[18] His influence seems to have been decisive in preventing Hobson from lecturing on explicitly economic subjects. In the United States, which he often visited throughout his life, he found a kinder reception. He explained to the American economist Richard Ely: 'As a lecturer in Economics for the Oxford University Extension movement I find in English economists a considerable reluctance to reconsider propositions which they have been in the habit of building upon' (27 December 1889). Ely in fact made consistent efforts to secure for Hobson's views the sort of serious professional consideration which he thought they merited. Hobson later revealed that he was never invited to apply for a post at any English university; nor elected to the Political Economy Club; nor asked to write for the *Economic Journal*. Although he affected to regard it as 'an inevitable consequence of an early heresy' and to claim that he did not regret his exclusion from orthodox economic circles (*Conf.*, p. 84), the animus does not remain entirely hidden.

It would, however, be a mistake to think of Hobson as an otherwise predestined Professor of Economics, cruelly martyred in the cause of underconsumption. He would in any case have been lucky to establish himself as an academic economist in view of the sheer lack of rigour or respect for academic standards in much of his work. Furthermore, there is the curious fact that many of his books are not really underconsumptionist at all. To some extent this can be explained in terms of common prudence. His friends certainly tried to steer him towards other, safer subjects; this was the origin of his work on John Ruskin. But Hobson himself did not make much effort to conciliate the academics or to live down his heresy. It may be, therefore, that Hobson found himself consumed by one line of inquiry

[18] T. W. Hutchison, A *Review of Economic Doctrines 1870–1929* (Oxford 1953), p. 118.

at a time, and that his thought remained somewhat compartmentalised; so that no explicit mention of underconsumption was needed when he was dealing with other discrete aspects of the economic system. Yet even this is not the whole story. The best answer seems to be that underconsumption was not in fact central to Hobson's economic thought. He himself described it as 'a narrower economic heresy' as distinct from 'the fundamental issues of economic science' on which he worked later (*Conf.*, p. 29). He assimilated many other arresting ideas in the course of the 1890s. If there is a single unifying concern it is the broad assault upon *laissez faire* and the protean individualist fallacy, of which underconsumption was only one guise.

Thus in the *Problems of Poverty* (1891) Hobson's chief remedy for the over-supply of skilled labour was some scheme of 'social drainage' on the lines suggested by Charles Booth. The theme of efficiency showed itself in the use of the language of Social Darwinism, sometimes in extremely curt terms. 'We must try,' he wrote, 'to distinguish curable from incurable cases, and we must try to cure the former while we preserve society from the contamination of the latter' (p. 141). Yet the real thrust of the argument was to characterise poverty as a social problem – 'a national, industrial disease, requiring a national, industrial remedy' (p. 227). An extension of protective legislation was necessary and so was a more positive use of state intervention. This was 'socialism', though all that the word meant here was a vague recognition of wider public responsibilities. But the unskilled worker had little to hope for. 'He cannot organize because he is so poor, so ignorant, so weak. Because he is not organized he continues to be poor, ignorant weak' (p. 227). Hobson saw that the existence of an environmental trap here demolished the hope of voluntary regeneration, but he had little to put in its place.

Hobson later claimed *The Evolution of Modern Capitalism* (1894) as his 'first solid piece of economic writing' (*Conf.*, p. 35) and it is true that he seems here to have acquired a distinctive voice. In the *Evolution* – the title, of course, is significant – we find a sustained analysis of society as an organism. Two lines of thought were brought to bear. In the first place, there was the evolutionary schema, which allowed Hobson to enlist current intellectual fashion behind his plea to treat the economic system as a single 'going concern'. This system, moreover, was clearly orientated towards consumption. 'Life not work, unproductive not productive consumption must be regarded as the end' (p. 214). Here was a second theme. For such views fairly obviously derived from Ruskin, whom Hobson was expounding in his lectures at this time. He wished to establish Ruskin's credentials not only as a prophet but as an economist. Evolution as a mechanism of progress needed a hypothetical goal, which Ruskin's insistence on 'life', 'souls of good quality', seemed to supply. The application of an ethical test was therefore functional from the point of view of evolutionary development. This is a line of argument which Hobhouse later pursued in a more persistent and fruitful way.

'From each according to his powers, to each according to his needs' is the precept upon which Hobson fastened to express this insight. He usually called it 'the organic law' or 'the full organic formula'. Apparently of Saint-Simonian origins, it was a slogan often quoted by socialists in the late nineteenth century. In the *Critique of the Gotha Programme* (1875) Marx proclaimed it as the rationale of the higher phase of communist society. Sidney Webb, of course, was justifying it as an ethical postulate in the 1880s (see above, p. 38). To Herbert Spencer in 1896 it was notorious (though evidently unmemorable) as 'a certain formula of the socialists' for which he asked Beatrice Webb to provide a reference.[19] In employing it, therefore, Hobson was asserting a principle which would be immediately recognised as socialist. In glossing it as the 'organic law', however, he sought to give it not just an ethical claim but an evolutionary provenance.

The concept came to fruition in *The Social Problem* (1901). On the one side, Hobson maintained, what men 'need' must be seen as what they need in order to produce efficiently; and on the other side, their 'powers' will clearly be limited by their efficiency, which is in turn, of course, dependent on how far their needs have been satisfied. So efficiency at once *sanctions* needs and *defines* powers. 'Individual needs endorsed by social utility will tend to vary directly and even proportionately with productivity, which is no more than saying that a larger output of energy requires a larger replacement through consumption' (p. 164). At a simple, homely level this sounds like common sense. Those who do most work will have the heartiest appetites; those who do least will find that their eyes are bigger than their bellies. But as a general statement of functional necessity it has its difficulties. The more conclusively Hobson demonstrates that the organic law is inescapable the less room he seems to leave for changing the way the organism works. In short, the radical ethical principle has undergone such a thoroughgoing reinterpretation that it is on the brink of becoming a conservative tautology which *must* be true of any viable society.

Here, however, Hobson could escape by alleging the existence of an organic disorder – underconsumption. The organism behaved in a self-defeating way because an excessive power to consume was possessed by classes whose normal healthy wants were already satisfied; and it followed from the organic nature of the explanation that they had no desire to consume more, and so piled up excessive savings. The trouble was, as Hobson put it more trenchantly in *The Problem of the Unemployed* (1896), that those who have the *power* to consume do not have the *desire* to do so. And he built upon his organic conception of society to explain this in

[19] Spencer to B. Webb, 11 August 1896, in Shaw Papers, BL Add. MSS. 50513, ff.107–8.

terms of 'the natural relation between production and consumption, between effort and satisfaction' (p. 88). Men who saved out of hard-won earnings were hardly likely to save too much, but where incomes were disproportionate to the output of personal effort the result was an 'automatic "saving" which upsets the balance between consumption and producing-power, and which from the Social standpoint may be classed as "over-saving"' (p. 91).

Hobson acknowledged that this was 'no doubt largely an *a priori* argument' (ibid.). But he claimed that it was the only hypothesis which fitted the facts and it was the premise for his remedial policy. For it pointed to redistribution of income as the way out. By asserting that there was an ineluctable natural connexion between an individual's powers of consumption and production, Hobson ruled out luxurious expenditure by the rich as a practical solution. (Practicable or not, it can safely be assumed that he would not have advocated it.) Instead he asserted that the working class must, through trade unionism, co-operation and legislation, secure a larger share of the national income. Death duties, a progressive income tax, and taxation of land values, all followed from this. By a rather different route, Hobson had arrived at a scheme of reforms closely similar to that urged by Hobhouse.

Hobson later wrote that 'though my opinions and my feelings were beginning to move in the direction of Socialism, I was not a Socialist, Marxian, Fabian or Christian' (*Conf*., p. 29). On coming to London in the late 1880s he resumed contact with Wallas, whom he had known at Oxford, and soon met Webb. Through his extension work he became drawn into the London Ethical Society, that peculiar meeting ground between the Fabians and the C.O.S., and got to know Muirhead and Clarke. Clarke, indeed, became a close friend from whom he took over the writing of *The Evolution of Modern Capitalism*. Hobson had also read the first volume of *Capital* and had found the labour theory of value a stumbling block. Though reacting against Jevons and marginalism, his own concept of the surplus was developed in terms of a theory of rent which is in essentials Fabian.

This is apparent (though it is not acknowledged) in *The Economics of Distribution* (1901), in which Hobson sought to ground his fiscal proposals more firmly in systematic analysis. The distinction he developed was between the costs of subsistence for any factor of production and the rent element. Surplus value could therefore in principle accrue to land or capital or labour. If in practice labour currently came off worst, this was an empirical fact not a theoretical necessity.

In explaining the distribution of the surplus through various rents, however, Hobson went further than the Fabians, who had been content to invoke free exchange as an efficient technical mechanism. Hobson propounded a more radically subversive view of the market. It did not promote perfect exchanges; the stronger party usually got some advantage (a 'forced gain') either for himself or for everyone in the same bargaining position. In the sale of labour this normally worked to the disadvantage of the seller, and of course no moral principle of distributive justice came into it. The true origin of surplus value thus lay in 'the various hindrances to perfect equality of bargaining power' (p. 360). By the same token, forced gains were not secure since they corresponded to no real economic necessity. A greater equality of opportunity would create different market forces, as indeed the Fabians had argued. Moreover, forced gains were amenable to taxation since a tax would be rejected by all necessary or subsistence payments and would 'settle upon the "forced gains" or unearned income' (p. 315). This reinforced the case which Hobson had earlier urged on underconsumptionist grounds for taxing 'unearned' incomes. If they were 'unearned', then taxing them could not deplete any necessary economic function. Since, however, there could be no discrimination between the origins of different forms of incomes, how could unearned elements be distinguished? Hobson rested on 'the supposition that the proportion of unearned therefore economically taxable income varies directly with the absolute size of incomes' (p. 332). It is a recurrent difficulty in Hobsonian economics that some such supposition is in the end always necessary. He could never *prove* that society's 'functionless wealth' was the same as the individual's 'unearned income'.

One problem is that the term 'unearned income' in general parlance was a synonym for investment income. But even if this ambiguity is avoided – and Hobson constantly slipped from one sense to the other – a related difficulty remains which is bound to be present in any explanation based on the Fabian theory of rent. Since all factors of production are treated on equal terms, they all include unearned elements in the form of rent. In the case of labour, everyone except the marginal man draws an income which contains a rent of ability; and the remainder of his income is by definition earned by himself. But this does not apply to the individual who draws an income from land or capital. Although part of his income is a rent, it does not follow that the remainder has been earned by himself. An individual who has never lifted a finger can thus draw an income earned by the social utility of the factor of production which he happens to control.

Hobson believed that these discrepancies between effort and reward were endemic in the free market but he was confident that taxation on the right principles offered an effective reform. He rejected therefore the moral regenerationist approach which he found deeply rooted in the London Ethical Society. Hobson felt that there was too much reluctance in the ethical movement to apply moral tests to social institutions and economic practices. For Bosanquet, of course, social ethics underpinned the philosophy of the C.O.S., with its insistence upon attributing poverty to moral failings of an incontestably individual nature. Hobson increasingly found this analysis not merely fallacious but offensive, especially when allied to a defence of inheritance or to an attempt to obstruct social legislation.

For Hobson the origin of poverty was social in a double sense. First, there was his macro-economic analysis, sometimes couched in underconsumptionist terms, demonstrating that unemployment was a fault of the system. The charity organiser, Hobson maintained, fell into error because it was possible in individual cases to correlate unemployment with imputed moral defects. The fallacy was to conclude that 'character' lay at the root of the problem. 'Personal causes,' as he put it in 1896, 'do not to any appreciable extent cause unemployment, but largely determine who shall be unemployed' (*Problem of the Unemployed*, p. 46). Second, however, Hobson also offered an environmentalist extenuation for the individuals whose moral inadequacies had put them into the unemployed class. No doubt the poor are 'thoughtless and extravagant', but the conditions under which they are forced to live 'themselves furnish an education in improvidence' (*Problems of Poverty*, p. 12). Men in this position can hardly be reproached for their shortcomings in respect of thrift or efficiency. For Hobson it was the bitterest portion of the lot of the poor that they were deprived of the opportunity of learning to work well. 'To taunt them with their incapacity, and to regard it as the cause of poverty, is nothing else than a piece of blind insolence' (ibid., p. 177).

The cry which the C.O.S. raised for moral regeneration, then, offered no remedy, and in the autumn of 1896 Hobson publicly attacked it in stinging terms. Its vogue, he claimed, was the result of the personal vanity of lucky or successful men who did not recognise their own class advantages in the great school of character. But the poor, claimed Hobson, knew in a blind instinctive way that they were 'not fairly matched in opportunity with their "friendly visitors"; they feel "it is all very well" for these well-dressed, nice-spoken ladies and gentlemen to come down and teach them how to be sober, thrifty and industrious; they may not feel resentment, but they discount the advice and they discount the moral superiority' (*CR*, lxx, 725). They were right to do so, for men like Bosanquet, although not hypocrites, were applying a double standard. When Bosanquet condemned doles as a form of property which was demoralising because it came miraculously he was making a reasonable point. 'But why stop at doles?' asked Hobson. 'Are there no other forms of private property which should stand in the dock with "doles" to the poor? How about gifts and bequests to the rich?' (p. 713).

After this, it is difficult to imagine Hobson and Bosanquet amicably hobnobbing in the London Ethical Society, and in fact in 1897 it was reconstituted on a new basis. Wallas had instead for several years been associated with the South Place Ethical Society which, under Dr Stanton Coit, had acquired a more socialistic tone. Hobson now migrated to South Place, and he and Wallas remained pillars of the Society for the rest of their lives. It was in a lecture on 'The ethics of industrialism', under auspices provided by Coit, that Hobson succinctly identified the two profound moral flaws which pervaded modern business. 'Selfishness is inherent in competition; force is inherent in bargaining.'[20]

Hobson turned the moral argument back against its begetters, not as a debating trick, but with deep indignation at the 'almost unparalleled audacity' of an appeal to economic reasoning that was selective and partial in its application (*CR*, lxx, 714). When he complained that 'they never lift their voice to save the characters of the well-to-do which are constantly assailed by the same demoralising forces' (ibid.), he expected to be taken at his word. For he too believed that the social problem had a moral cause but one which put the superior classes in an invidious position and which demanded a change of heart in them for its resolution. 'The work of gradually placing "property" upon a just and rational basis, offering that equality of opportunity which shall rightly adjust effort to satisfaction, is a moral task of supreme importance' (p. 726).

(IV) THE RAINBOW CIRCLE

'As time went on we specialised', Wallas recalled wryly. 'Bernard Shaw wrote plays, and Sidney Webb took the general reorganisation of the world as his province' (*M.Post*, 1 January 1923). The days of the Fabian junta were numbered. From the time of its formation the Webb partnership increasingly dominated the Fabian milieu. Shaw found it hard enough to strike the right note in his relations with Beatrice Webb. When she said to Sidney, during a communal session of self-criticism in 1895, 'I think Shaw regards me as a very useful wife for you', the implication was that she valued him less highly than Shaw did: or at least that she knew that this was Shaw's opinion. At all events, it meant that she and Shaw had to be 'constantly more or less on our guard, and resolutely friendly & remorseful for being unfriendly' (Laurence, i, 555). Because Shaw was prepared to adapt to this role, the Fabian junta could be reconstituted as a new trinity of Beatrice, Sidney and himself. He stayed with the Webbs for the whole seven weeks' summer holiday in 1895; Wallas only went for a fortnight and was, Beatrice Webb observed, 'restless & not quite happy in our company' (diary, 25 September 1895). So while Shaw was 'a perfect house friend', Wallas appeared 'lonely & overworked & wants a little mental coddling – & we are inclined to douche him with cold water!' The fact that, as she put it, 'Sidney & I are odiously self-complacent in our perfectly

[20] Stanton Coit (ed.), *Ethical Democracy* (1900), p. 92.

happy married life' clearly did not make for easier personal relations (ibid.). And when she met the wealthy Charlotte Payne-Townshend that autumn her matchmaking solicitude – 'I thought she would do very well for Graham Wallas!' (*OP*, p. 91) – led to unintended results. Wallas bored Charlotte, and she married Shaw instead.

Wallas's dissatisfaction had a more than personal origin. Closeted with his old friends, it became clear that he was 'getting very uneasy in the bonds of socialism', and there were 'fearful and prolonged arguments & pleadings which had to be steered carefully clear of ending in strained bonds & possibly broken ones' (Laurence, i, 549). While maintaining that he was 'still an economic Collectivist of an empirical kind', Wallas now felt constrained by the formulas and intellectual ties of Fabianism (Webb diary, 25 September 1895). He recognised, of course, the need for specialisation. But, when he looked back later, the root of his unease appeared as the Fabian tendency to make a virtue out of necessity. In *Tract 70* (1896) the Society professed to care nothing 'by what name any party calls itself or what principles, Socialist or other, it professes' as long as 'its own special business of practical Democracy and Socialism' was furthered in the result.[21] Wallas could neither abstain from moral judgments on the world at large nor regard socialism as in itself an alternative ethic.

The real ground of the divergence between Wallas and the Webbs has been obscured by a paradox. From about this time, Wallas came to express scepticism about accepted democratic theory, whereas Beatrice Webb developed a consistent description of him as less democratic than themselves. By this she meant that he was less 'objectively' democratic, in the sense of *Tract 70*. The Webbs were increasingly ready to define socialism as what the masses ought to want – what may be called their ascribed class consciousness – as disclosed by their own theory; and to substitute manipulation as a better means to it than the faltering efforts of spontaneous forces. The democratic goal remained the same and hence Wallas was guilty of backsliding in questioning it. The paradox lay in the fact that his scepticism arose precisely from looking at democracy as a system for securing what people actually (subjectively) wanted. It stemmed from observing the manifest failures of the majority to seek their true interests effectively. Beatrice Webb's terminology, in which Wallas was by definition less democratic, meant that the implicit subjective and objective senses were never distinguished. These differences of view were only beginning to emerge in 1895. For the moment, Wallas decided not to continue on the Fabian Executive and he became more committed to his work for the London School of Economics.

The kind of doubts which Wallas harboured had surfaced earlier and more irascibly in his friend Clarke. Barely a year after the *Fabian Essays*

[21] See E. R. Pease, *The History of the Fabian Society* (2nd edn, 1925), p. 252.

had been published Clarke was complaining about 'his isolation among men who have no "ultimate aims", or whose ultimate aims differ from his' (Laurence, i, 275). Clarke was, as Shaw shrewdly recognised, 'an ethicist & moralist to the backbone; and the dawning of Ibsenism & Nietzscheanism & "Shavianism" seemed to him the coming of chaos' (ibid., ii, 496). Throughout the 1890s Clarke's personal misfortunes gave a fierce animus to his increasingly sombre view of events. His life savings had been lost when the Liberator Building Society collapsed; his health became uncertain as he drove himself against strenuous journalistic deadlines; his insomnia became chronic as a result of the city life which he detested; and a general mien of irritability and fatalism suggested disillusion. 'The slowness of the march of progress seemed at times almost to chill his blood', wrote his friend, the socialist Herbert Burrows.[22]

Burrows, Clarke, Hobson and Ramsay MacDonald, together with J. A. Murray MacDonald, M.P., and the city merchant Richard Stapley, were the nucleus of the small group which organised the meetings of the Rainbow Circle in 1894 as a rallying point for social reformers. They sought to place 'the so-called "New Radicalism" or Collectivist politics of to-day' upon a broad ethical, political and economic footing.[23] This was to attempt a more ambitious and wide-ranging synthesis than the Fabianism of *Tract 70*. Herbert Samuel, whom Hobson had met through an interest in land reform, was soon drawn into this initiative, developing his own approach here under the rubric of the New Liberalism.

The aim of the group was to discover the common ground between progressives of various political colours; though its name derived from a prosaic and short-lived connexion with the Rainbow Tavern in Fleet Street, where its initial meetings took place in November and December 1894. At this point a dispute arose with the Tavern, which some remembered as over the inadequate consumption of alcohol and others as over a dinner of 'boiled cod so poor & watery that even philosophers turned against it'.[24] Stapley thereupon stepped in and offered his own house in Bloomsbury Square, which became the meeting place of the Rainbow Circle for thirty years. Stapley's patronage clearly contributed much towards its stability. Among the early members of the Circle were Olivier, the Rev. W. D. Morrison, C. P. Trevelyan and J. M. Robertson. Wallas was a member during 1899–1901, proposed by Samuel, and remained associated with it thereafter. Hobhouse was elected, on Hobson's nomination, at the end of 1903 but never attended a meeting; his name was erased within a year.

At first the Rainbow Circle had considerable success in forging a common

[22] Herbert Burrows and J. A. Hobson (eds.), *William Clarke* (1908), p. xix.
[23] Circular proposing the revival of the Rainbow Circle (1894), Samuel Papers A 10/1.
[24] MacDonald speech, 5 March 1924, Rainbow Circle minutes (cited below as 'minutes' with date).

identity. Among the papers during the first year were those by Hobson, 'Economic deficiencies of the Manchester School', and Clarke, 'Political defects of the old Radicalism', which formed the basis of later published writings. It was accepted in discussion on Hobson's paper that the Manchester School had 'a historical justification which does not hold good now under changing social circumstances' (minutes, 5 December 1894). At the end of the session, Ramsay MacDonald was able as secretary to report 'agreement on the following main positions: that the conception of the individual as independent of society is false; that economics of the quantitative kind must be supplemented by economics of the qualitative kind; that formal political democracy is not sufficient in itself to secure good government; that Trade Unionism cannot be made the basis of a great political movement; that cooperation is equally narrow; & fundamentally that the politics of the past correspond to the economic problem of production & in the future that they must correspond to the problem of use' (minutes, 19 June 1895).

By February 1895 the proposal had been made for a monthly review to do for the public what the meetings did for the twenty members of the Rainbow Circle. The *Progressive Review* was eventually launched some eighteen months later. The capital of £1500 was raised chiefly among the members; Olivier made an unavailing appeal to the trustees of the Hutchinson bequest to the Fabian Society; and Stapley, Samuel and Hobson, who became directors, clearly put up much of the money themselves. William Clarke had always been intended as editor (though an outside journalist had also been approached). But at the beginning of 1896, only weeks before the projected publication date, Clarke withdrew, stating not only the difficulties in obtaining money and writers but also, more ominously, 'the interest being taken in foreign politics' as his reasons (minutes, n.d. January–February 1896). For the moment the differences were patched up. Publication was postponed until September, more shares were sold, and Clarke agreed to resume the editorship with Hobson – at least nominally – in joint control. They were aided chiefly by Samuel and MacDonald, and contributions were enlisted from Fabians (the Webbs, Henry Salt), rationalists (J. M. Robertson), Christian Socialists (H. Scott Holland), and Liberals (Robert Wallace, Haldane, C. P. Trevelyan).

The professed intention of the *Review* was to 'give due emphasis to the new ideas and sentiments of social justice and of a clear rational application of those principles in a progressive policy and a progressive party' (*PR*, i, 3). It was acknowledged that no such principles, policy or party existed at the time. But the fact that they were 'but imperfectly explained and understood' was blandly put down as the cardinal difficulty.[25] Herein lay the task of the *Review*. While there was a fair degree of consensus over policy,

[25] *PR* prospectus, Aug. 1896, Samuel Papers A/10/5.

however, the justifying principles were divergent and there was consequently little agreement on the question of party. Stapley and Murray MacDonald were official Liberals who stood for parliament. Samuel clearly wanted a reconstruction of Liberalism and a repudiation of the Gladstonian heritage. 'Above all', he told the Rainbow Circle when explaining the New Liberalism, 'we must frankly accept democratic methods; & embrace our Imperial opportunities' (minutes, 6 November 1895). This position came to be identified as Liberal Imperialism. Ramsay MacDonald was a member of the Independent Labour Party (I.L.P.). Clarke and Hobson were formally unattached to any party but, when their apparently Fabian surface was scratched, they turned out to be Gladstonian, or at least Cobdenite, underneath.

Pragmatic collectivism was presented as the unifying theme in policy. Three strands were woven together here. The first was the evolutionary argument. Not only was the Spencerian thrust parried, but social evolution was seized upon as itself a validation of progressive proposals. Hobson, of course, had discovered the organic law. But Clarke too argued, in a way that anticipated the more fully developed conceptions of Hobhouse, that now was the time to supersede the blind, unconscious efforts of the past by giving the operations of the social will a higher, conscious purpose. Confronting Social Darwinism more directly, Salt argued that as a social prescription 'survival of the fittest' begged the question of who the unfit were. It was as obvious to Salt as to Hobson that if the residuum were an incubus on society then so – and with less excuse – were the idle rich who lived in luxury upon the misery and exploitation of others. Here were two manifestations of an unjust system which perpetuated 'those two correlative classes of the "unfit" – the so-called "lowest type" of the useless pauper, and what I regard as the equally low type of the useless plutocrat' (*PR*, i, 461).

A second strand was the redefinition of liberty in the sense of T. H. Green. It was part of Clarke's case that those who still wished to call themselves Liberals had to accept that liberty 'must no longer signify the absence of restraint, but the presence of opportunity' (*PR*, i, 4). Haldane, who quoted and endorsed Green, acknowledged that his principles had not yet received 'a real as distinguished from a notional assent from the majority of Liberals' (*PR*, i, 137). In a less indulgent view, perhaps this was another way of saying that Green's shafts 'glance harmlessly from the tough hide of common prejudice' (*PR*, ii, 119). But those who spoke in terms of a New Liberalism used the language of Green to describe society and the state. Thus for Samuel their object was 'to provide the fullest opportunities for every person who forms part of them to attain the best and amplest development of his life' (*PR*, i, 258). More specifically, in considering industrial legislation, the *Review* claimed that it might be directed 'not against the individual's self-dependence, but against the economic necessities which restrict that self-dependence' (*PR*, ii, 121–2). But this was an argument which could as readily take a Utilitarian as an Idealist turn. There followed, indeed, a frank recognition that the legislative establishment of 'freedom from economic pressure of the many is often accompanied by an invasion of the freedom from legal restrictions of the few' (p. 123). This awkward corollary was not evaded as it tended to be in a thoroughgoing Idealist formulation. Instead, coercion was acknowledged, but defended on the ground that the liberty of the minority to act as they wish must be restricted because if they transgress the majority will find it necessary to follow suit against their will.

The third strand was Fabian. The emphasis upon the state as 'the organised intelligence and will of the community' was the justification of a collectivist approach aiming directly at the common good (*PR*, i, 6). But this was a rather nebulous aspiration. It was not a guide to political tactics, and here the progressives diverged. Clarke spoke for one camp, holding the purest democratic view. 'Faith in ideas and in the growing capacity of the common people to absorb and to apply ideas in reasonably working out the progress of the Commonwealth forms the moral foundation of democracy', he proclaimed (*PR*, i, 9), without specifying the mechanics of this process. The importance of ideas was undoubted. But whom was the *Review* seeking to persuade? In recognising that many honest men opposed progressive proposals 'with all the energy that a conscientious conviction inspires' (*PR*, ii, 119), it was putting a high value on winning that moral fervour for a better cause by securing intellectual assent to its own views. Were Fabian tactics indicated? 'The policy of permeation has been a success', Haldane concluded, rather complacently (*PR*, i, 138). If it had, it followed that the Liberal party had become the agent of progressivism. But, on this reading, it could still not move too fast since it was fallacious to suppose that the working-class elector was 'a human being *sui generis*, with a single purpose concentrated on social change' (p. 139). Haldane's argument pointed to a neo-Fabian opportunism and it laid him open to the charge that his New Liberalism, with its condescending attitude to democracy, was seeking to substitute an academic aristocracy for a patrician or plutocratic one. Indeed, Wallace alleged that it was anti-democratic in seeking to manipulate the system in favour of a reform programme for which there was no insistent popular demand.

This sober view of the limited expectations of the electorate, however, also provided the ground for an emphatically democratic affirmation of the reformist position. When socialists directed criticism at the Liberal party for not achieving a vast programme of reconstruction, so Samuel argued, they were making it a scapegoat for their own faulty analysis of democracy. 'Blame if you like the moderation and short-sightedness of the electorate, blame the democracy', he chided them (*PR*, i, 258). Not that Samuel was in any case likely to favour nationalisation of the means of production, of which his reiterated criticism was that it was an 'unproved theory of State capitalism' (p. 256). The economic case against it was that it would not transform the system to the benefit of the working class. The political case was that it impeded the feasible palliative reforms which actually would do some good. It was wholly in keeping with this strategy that the progressives should direct attention to the land question. A case could be made over land which was consistent with socialism while not necessarily leading to it. It allowed them to bypass the problem of whether the landowner or the employer exercised the stronger economic tyranny over the working class. For the injustice of private property in land could be 'made manifest to most persons of tolerable understanding, who are apt to be confused and unconvinced by the more subtle reasoning required to disclose the tyranny of the capitalist employer over labour' (*PR*, ii, 486).

There were always differences of emphasis among the progenitors of the *Review*. At the outset they undoubtedly regarded it as part of the Rainbow Circle's task of reconstruction to establish harmony among progressives of different traditions, as politics began to settle upon its new axis of social reform. The emergent consensus, however, came under strain in an unexpected way. In 1897, when an article in the *Review* asked 'Is Democracy a Reality?', it was thinking of foreign policy, and its conclusion was that imperialism and democracy were inconsistent. 'At the present time the movement is wholly towards empire with all its burdens and special problems, and therefore away from democracy' (*PR*, ii, 29). This was the view of Clarke, supported by Hobson, but it not only set them at odds with Samuel but also reflected a suspicion of the Fabians (including, it must be said, Wallas). 'The real crux of politics', declared Clarke, 'is not going to be Socialism & anti-Socialism, but Jingoism and anti-Jingoism.'[26] Here lay the reason for his reluctance to assume the editorship. Here lay the seeds of the *Review*'s collapse. And here lay the explanation for the failure of the Rainbow Circle to forge a deeper unity from its disparate elements.

By the summer of 1897 Hobson's health had broken down. In Clarke's view MacDonald was irremediably inefficient; and he himself was left to fulfil his editorial tasks during crowded days in London before rushing for the last train to the peace of mid-Sussex. There alone, he told Samuel, could he hope to combat 'this terrible insomnia which at times almost threatens my reason' (12 July 1897). Samuel was consequently unable to call upon Hobson, or to consult properly with Clarke, or to mollify MacDonald; and he too was ready to acquiesce in the *Review*'s demise. The incipient policy dispute removed its rationale.

The continuing discussions in the Rainbow Circle revealed the extent of

[26] Clarke to MacDonald, n.d. (1896) in Bernard Porter, *Critics of Empire* (1968), p. 165.

the differences. When Samuel spoke on 'The Progressive Party' in 1899 he defined its policy as a sort of compromise with socialism but added that it must also have 'a policy of rational patriotism' (minutes, 3 May 1899). Hobson, speaking to the same title a month later, claimed that the principles of such a party were 'already in existence in the form of intellectual affinities which as a matter of fact place the leaders of the Radical, the Socialist & the Labour groups much nearer to each other than their followers imagine'. It was his proviso which marked him off from Samuel. 'The yielding of certain progressives to Imperialism is one of the worst features of present-day politics', Hobson warned (minutes, 7 June 1899). By the time Clarke gave his paper on 'Imperialism and Democracy' later in the year, the Boer War had begun. To Clarke imperialism was clearly incompatible with democracy because, above all, it sapped 'that moral freedom that gives sanction to political freedom' (minutes, 1 November 1899). Samuel remained unmoved. In his analysis, disloyalty to the Empire was electoral suicide – 'The "Little Englandism" of many Progressives stands in the way of Social Reform' (minutes, 7 January 1900). The Rainbow Circle came to pride itself on the fact that civilised relations could be maintained between men of fundamentally dissimilar outlook, but their intellectual affinities as progressives had manifestly failed to eclipse other issues. The Rainbow Circle survived but its high ambitions withered.

3

Imperialism

(I) HOBHOUSE

By 1896 C. P. Scott had been editor of the *Manchester Guardian* for nearly twenty-five years, and when in November of that year Hobhouse first made it clear that he was interested in journalistic work, the circumstances were propitious. Scott was a Corpus man too, and since Arthur Sidgwick recommended Hobsouse as 'quite the ablest of our younger "Greats" men, and a strong Liberal and progressive of the best type' (20 November 1896), Scott was duly impressed. He was accustomed to go to Oxford for recruits to the editorial corridor. In 1879 W. T. Arnold, Mrs Humphry Ward's brother, had become a leader-writer, chiefly on the strength of his study of Roman provincial administration; and in 1890 C. E. Montague came from Balliol. Neither of them had actually got Firsts in Greats but in the case of Montague, who married Scott's daughter, the editor virtually refused to acknowledge the fact – 'He never ought to have got a 2nd!'[1] Hobhouse had gilt-edged Oxford credentials and, although he had originally envisaged sending special articles for the paper from London, by coincidence Scott just then found himself a man short on the corridor because of the collapse of Arnold's health. A brief trial brought an unwontedly warm response from Scott, and Hobhouse was persuaded to settle in Manchester in 1897.

From his point of view the move offered a reputable and financially rewarding escape from the crabbed environment of Oxford. He said that Oxford did not suit his health, an early hint of the psychosomatic difficulties which had first afflicted him in the late 1880s. Hobhouse's current philosophical work certainly did not suit Oxford; he was bruised by the unfavourable response – real or imagined – to his recent book on the *Theory of Knowledge* (1896). At least from the age of thirty, references to his periodic moods of despondency are common and his friends learnt not to take the gloomy prognostications of the moment as his settled opinion. In this connexion it is revealing to observe what he and Scott wrote in obituaries about each other. Scott wrote that Hobhouse's 'deepest instinctive belief and hope was in human progress', yet recognised of course that 'his temperament was not sanguine' (*Memoir*, p. 8). If there was a psycological reason for his belief that the wellsprings of progress had not run

[1] W. P. Crozier to Hammond, 17 December 1933, HP 24.

dry it was clearly not one manifested in a sunny disposition; he thought, rather, as he dug away despairingly, that eventually he must reach the water table. Hobhouse concluded his assessment of Scott by saying simply, 'I never knew a happier man'.[2] This also struck J. L. Hammond who thought that 'what made him such a power was that he had the happiness of a wonderful tranquillity of mind which reflected his outlook, his faith and his own interpretation of life'.[3] Scott achieved this enviable state partly by closing his mind to inconvenient facts. Living on raw fruit in his draughty unheated house he often evoked the image of John the Baptist; but, enabled by his wealth and power to wash his hands of irksome responsibilities, he sometimes seemed more like Pontius Pilate. Hobhouse, with his upper-class background, never felt any uncomfortable sense of social distance with Scott and was from the outset admitted to the privileged sanctum. He found in Scott as redoubtable a Liberal standard-bearer as his uncle Arthur, and one more open to new ideas.

Scott was fifty in 1896, eighteen years older than Hobhouse. He had moved considerably to the left in the previous ten years. Arnold had played a crucial role in bringing the *Guardian* behind the Home Rule policy in 1886, since when the paper's politics had been warmly Gladstonian. When Scott invited Hobhouse to join the staff he gave as his reason the belief 'that the relations of Liberalism and Labour must govern the future of politics, and that the problem was to find the lines on which Liberals could be brought to see that the old tradition must be expanded to yield a fuller measure of social justice, a more real equality, an industrial as well as a political liberty' (*C. P. Scott*, p. 85). Scott had been working along these lines since at least 1891, when he had first stood for Parliament. He was in close touch with the secretary of the National Reform Union, A. G. Symonds, another old Corpus man, who advised him on matterns of political organisation. It was Symonds who gave him the clearest warnings that the democratic claims of the Liberal caucus were fallacious. In practice, as he told Scott, 'the working men won't come to Ward Meetings to elect representatives' and in any case 'they appreciate fully the fact that the money is in the hands of a few men who wd. refuse to subscribe for the election expenses of a working man'. Symonds advocated 'going to the working men if they will not come to us', and, in order to give substance to Liberal professions about the priority of Labour questions, urged that they should 'treat Liberal Candidate & Labour Candidate as practically synonymous terms' (28 June 1894). This was broadly what Scott understood as the policy of progressivism and it permitted, of course, an active Liberal commitment alongside a sympathetic response to an independent Labour movement.

[2] C. P. *Scott 1846–1932* (1946), p. 90.
[3] Hammond to Murray, 4 February 1933, MP.

Hobhouse's role was to make the *Guardian*'s commitment to this approach clearer and more consistent, while not needlessly affronting traditional Liberals. He worked amicably with Montague, who had previously dealt with labour questions, and with Arnold too, until his premature retirement at the end of 1898. Hobhouse, indeed, practically stepped into Arnold's shoes. For Arnold had led a strenuous life, combining leader-writing six nights a week with scholarly work in the mornings. Although his history progressed slowly, his journalism was thrown off in haste with, as Montague put it, 'no painful crushing of the desire to bevel and inlay the phrase'. This Arnold justified on the theory that rapidity in composition induced a sympathetic relation between the writer and the newspaper reader, who read it quickly. So he 'wrote as fast as the pen could move'.[4] Hobhouse proceeded on the same principles. He maintained his philosophical work and wrote *Mind in Evolution* (1901) while on the paper. Admittedly he only went to the office on certain nights of the week, which meant that Montague always took precedence over him in Scott's absence. Hobhouse's facility in composition became as legendary as Arnold's had been, and achieved the same effect, that of good talk rather than fine writing. He liked journalism. 'The smell of the printer's ink is sweeter to me than the smell of violets', he declared (*L*, 22 April 1931). In the end he decided that he could not sustain the double work, partly because he chafed in the subordinate position to which it condemned him. This was to be the main reason for his resignation in 1902.

Hobhouse satisfied not only his editor but John Edward Taylor, the proprietor, who was Scott's cousin. Taylor was an older man (b.1830), much more obviously enmeshed than Scott in the family's Unitarian tradition; a Gladstonian Liberal for whom the drink trade was the root of all social evils. 'If the Liberal Party be not true to its Temperance Programme let it pine for ever in the cold shade of opposition!' he once declared to Scott (22 January 1898). When Beatrice Webb enthused about the *Manchester Guardian* as 'practically our organ' at this time (*OP*, p. 145), she presumably meant that it represented a wholly different outlook than this. Yet Taylor took to Hobhouse strongly and, despite qualms about the increase in editorial salaries since his appointment, he was soon proposing him for a pay rise. 'Hobhouse continues to do admirable work', he told Scott. 'I am extremely pleased with him' (1 February 1899). Part of the explanation is no doubt that *Guardian* progressivism, a creature of liberal compromise, aimed to satisfy the Webbs and the Taylors of the world. Hobhouse had earned his temperance laurels at Castle Howard; he knew that many of Taylor's allies on this issue were sturdy radicals; and indeed it was Leif Jones, Lady Carlisle's secretary, who was introduced to Man-

[4] Mrs Humphry Ward and C. E. Montague, *W. T. Arnold* (Manchester 1907), pp. 70, 73.

chester in this way as the anti-war candidate in a famous by-election at Mafeking time. Hobhouse was ready to humour the old Liberals as long as they had the root of the matter in them.

In this connexion Beatrice Webb's comment is overstated, if not actually misleading. For Hobhouse was already deprecating the 'temptation to hail any and every extension of State authority, whatever its principle or its object, as a triumph for socialism' (*IJE*, viii, 142): which is a pretty clear rebuke to the Fabians. The point he adumbrated here was to take on increasing significance in his later writings. He attacked 'the dreariness of the mechanical schemes of Socialism which from time to time appear' (p. 141), a blanket criticism which covered both Marxism and Fabianism. By the time of *Liberalism* (1911) he had more precisely distinguished his Marxian target, which he termed Mechanical Socialism, from his Fabian target, which he termed Official Socialism. What Hobhouse understood by Official Socialism corresponds, in the terminology of this book, to mechanical reformism; and Mechanical Socialism to mechanical revolutionism. The mechanical reformist takes a pessimistic view of human nature; he has little faith in the capacity of the people to effect the necessary reforms of the system; but he knows on a scientific basis what progress ought to be; and he thinks that it can be achieved by substituting a mechanical for a moral means, to achieve what the people are incapable of doing for themselves.

Hobhouse, as a moral reformist, declared that ends and means could not be divorced in this way. 'Neither a diminishing nor an increased regimentation is an end in itself' (p. 142). The democratic control of the machine was all important. And he added, meaningly: 'Some Socialists, it would seem, have yet to learn that their synthesis must include all the elements of value represented by the older Liberalism' (p. 143). It is significant, too, that when he tried to interest Scott in two of the Fabian Essayists as potential contributors to the *Guardian*, he picked on Wallas, who was admittedly only good for occasional pieces, and on Clarke. Both of them were moving decidedly away from the Webbs. The connexion with Clarke was evidently through Leonard Courtney and was founded on a common anti-jingoism.

Hobhouse continued to call himself a collectivist in a rather self-conscious way, and in his journalism in the late 1890s he was ready to take issue with the ethical individualists on their chosen ground of old age pensions. This was to continue his tussle with Bosanquet for the mantle of Green. To the apostles of the Charity Organisation Society, Hobhouse acknowledged, 'thrift may represent the sum of human virtues and the supreme object of every social institution'. But this he termed a 'curious and not very lovely form of fanaticism' and concluded that 'to maintain an artificial school of thrift by withholding necessaries that might otherwise be granted is to mistake the means for the end' (*MG*, 25 March 1899). The language of means and ends was to take him a long way in defining his mature attitude to questions of individualism and collectivism, liberalism and socialism.

Hobhouse based his social economics on the proposition that under the conditions of modern industrialism a great proportion of the increased wealth of the community – 'all that is known as "economic rent"' – went to a small class and that 'this element of wealth is due not so much to the exertions of any assignable individual as to the general growth and energy of the community'. For the state to appropriate a share of this fund for old age pensions was 'not so much a matter of benevolence as of justice' (*MG*, 23 February 1899). Its most obvious manifestation was in the ground rents of towns. Hobhouse therefore urged the Liberals to espouse the heavy taxation of the future increment on urban land values to provide the financial basis for pensions and also for housing. As he confided to Scott: 'Practically this union of measures is what I beg to propound to you as the social programme for the party!' (25 February 1899). These proposals were, as his *Guardian* leaders admitted, 'undoubtedly socialistic in character in the sense that all socialists except those who are for immediate barricades would accept them as an instalment of what they want. The principle on which we have based them would also be accepted by many socialists as a fragment of their belief' (*MG*, 23 February 1899). It was, in short, attenuated Fabianism, rendered, in Hobhouse's version, unobjectionable to old Liberals like Taylor and, even more significantly, John Morley.

For Morley was the spokesman for a view on foreign policy which, in 1899, united the Cobdenite tradition of non-intervention with the Gladstonian emphasis upon morality. Scott and Hobhouse shared Morley's outlook; and they wished to be sure, as Scott put it, 'that he wd. be right on both sides of our policy' (14 July 1899). Morley satisfied Hobhouse, when he met him in July 1899; and Hobhouse reported that 'he will go with us in our "social programme", i.e. Old Age Pensions, Ground Rents (if a good scheme can be devised) & the extension of the Compensation Act with probably some form of National Insurance to relieve the employers. He is also keen for Local Control rather than pure Veto' (21 July 1899). This was the agenda which Morley in turn impressed upon the young men who were taking on the *Speaker* when he gave then editorial guidance the following month.

The original Fabian policy of permeation had in practice been a tactic for engineering the conversion of the Liberal party to collectivism. But in the late 1890s a more marked element of manipulation manifested itself, and with it a greater readiness to work with the Conservatives. Since the growth of collectivism would in any case be opportunistic, it was argued, 'the most effective reformers have reason to prefer the affable frankness of the Conservative Minister who laughs at his own ignorance and is willing to be coached through his Bills, to the unteachable Liberal who feels bound by the Cobdenite tradition to affect the doctrinaire in political science and economics without genuine knowledge of either'.[5] The voice is the voice of Shaw but the hands are the hands of Webb. Hobhouse was ready enough to admit that the old tradition of political democracy and the newer movement for social reform were often at present hostile; but by the summer of 1899 he was stating the problem as one of discovering the possible synthesis between them.

'Our "practical men,"' he commented scathingly, 'tell us that it does not matter how you get a reform providing that you get it.' He was now ready, in effect, to lecture the Webbs on this fallacy. Reform had to come as part of an orderly scheme not a hand-to-mouth concession with no conviction behind it. There was 'all the difference between benevolent officialism setting the world in order from above, and the democratic Collectivism which seeks not to restrict liberty but to fulfil it'. So the claims of social reform were urged as 'a legitimate outgrowth and development of the older Liberal principles. To throw over these principles in the name of Socialism is to turn towards reaction in the search for progress' (*MG*, 7 July 1899). Having, as he hoped, persuaded the Liberals to acknowledge socialism as their child, Hobhouse was now admonishing the socialists against filial inconstancy.

Imperialism is the word hitherto missing from this story. Hobhouse believed that since 1895 collectivism had suffered an eclipse because attention had been diverted elsewhere – to the Far East, to the Sudan and, above all, to South Africa. By 1899 the Unionist Government was deploying overwhelming pressure against the two Boer republics. Hobhouse regretted that to many collectivists 'opposition to aggression seems to savour of Cobdenism, and whatever Cobden did must undoubtedly be wrong' (*EcR*, ix, 199). For all those of a socially conservative outlook imperialism had an attraction of which they were fully aware: it displaced the divisive issues of social reform from the centre of the stage and fostered national unity. But collectivists seemed oblivious of this, as also of the fact that it ate up those very revenues on which they had designs. Old age pensions had been preempted by increased naval estimates which ruled out 'anything but the most namby-pamby measure for encouraging thrift among fairly prosperous artisans' (p. 210). There was no compensating gain, at least, not for the poor. Hobhouse asserted instead 'the ultimate identity of human relations' as the ground for a collectivist policy that was 'consistent, so to say, inside and out', as much guided by ethical appeals in external as in domestic policy (pp. 212, 214). A debased standard in this respect towards other races had inevitable ramifications at home. 'The essence of aristocratic, anti-

[5] G. B. Shaw (ed.), *Fabianism and the Empire* (1900), p. 14.

popular sentiment lies in the belief that people of a different class do not bleed when they are pricked, as the aristograt bleeds' (p. 213).

For Hobhouse the Boer War became 'the test issue for this generation' (*N*, 30 March 1907), just as to Clarke in 1896 'jingoism and anti-jingoism' had seemed now the real crux of politics.[6] 'More and more one feels that foreign policy is the touchstone of all policy' chimed in C. P. Scott in September 1899 in a letter to Leonard Courtney.[7] It was around Courtney, of all people, that the anti-war forces were first mustered. As Canon Barnett told him in August 1899, 'no one of any consequence except yourself has made a protest'.[8] To Clarke, Courtney became 'the real moral leader of the Opposition' as he rekindled the Gladstonian torch. ('A glorious light has been extinguished in the land', Clarke had written on Gladstone's death.)[9] It was through Courtney that Scott and Hobhouse were able to cajole Morley into speaking at a great meeting in Manchester in September, called to protest against the drift into a unjustified war. 'It will be wrong', declared Morley in perhaps the best-remembered speech of his career.

Hobhouse, who had earlier been 'vexed and depressed by Morley's vacillations and postponements' recanted his earlier doubts and said that the speech was 'worth months of ordinary life'.[10] By appearing on the platform together in the crisis hour Courtney and Morley had vindicated the old Liberalism in his eyes. When F. W. Hirst, who had been devilling for Morley's *Life of Gladstone*, met Hobhouse that summer for the first time since Oxford days, he noted how much his views had changed. 'He speaks and thinks very differently now of Cobden and Bright' (Hirst, p. 174). Taylor assured Scott that he gave full credit to 'the staunchness of the *M.G.*' in upholding this tradition of Liberalism (4 September 1899). The men whom Hobhouse now regarded as the salt of the party included some very old Liberals indeed. His respect for his uncle, Lord Hobhouse, was reinforced; and the old man reciprocated by making significant changes in his will. In what was probably a letter to Leonard himself, he insisted on the maxims that needed to be maintained: paramount being 'that precisely the same moral laws and sanctions apply to nations as to the individuals that compose them'.[11] Another octogenarian, the former Permanent Secretary to the Board of Trade, Lord Farrer, also stood firm, upholding to the last the precepts of his hero Cobden. Hobhouse had evidently meant to encourage Scott when he told him that 'Morley, Lord Farrer, & my uncle all spoke as though you were now recognised as having an influential, if not leading, position among the peace Liberals, & it is evident that men

[6] See above p. 60.
[7] G. P. Gooch, *Life of Lord Courtney* (1920), p. 372.
[8] H. O. Barnett, *Canon Barnett* (1921 edn), p. 517.
[9] *William Clarke, a selection of his writings* (1908), pp. 273, 281.
[10] F. W. Hirst, *In the Golden Days* (1947), pp. 180, 184.
[11] Ruth Fry, *Emily Hobhouse, a memoir* (1929), pp. 65–6.

like Farrer are beginning to look to you as the most resolute exponent of their ideas' (7 April 1899). But his statement did little to suggest that their cause had the future on its side.

Those who opposed the war were in an exposed position, especially in 1899 and 1900. The *Guardian* became very unpopular in Manchester. But on the corridor there was no wavering. Montague, always the connoisseur, made a scrapbook of press cuttings reviling the anti-war element. Arnold, too, though out of the firing line by this time, fully supported the stand taken by the paper. 'Truly it is a case of Imperium *aut* Libertas, not "et",' he wrote to Hobhouse (N, 8 June 1907).

Their opponents labelled them pro-Boers and they took up the name themselves. It is natural to think that, like Old Contemptible, it was an abusive nickname, defiantly adopted, and thereby drained of its pejorative content. But, though largely true, this should not be allowed to conceal the fact that many of them actually were pro-Boer. It is quite clear from Hobhouse's instinctive reactions to the fortunes of war whose side he was on. Emily Hobhouse, according to the tribute which Smuts contributed to her *Memoir*, 'lies buried in the hearts of a grateful people' (p. 11) – the wrong people, of course, from the point of view of a liberal reputation nowadays. Morley had shown himself more aware of this snag. 'Courtney went awry in comparing Kruger to Lincoln, & he lays himself open', he told Hobhouse after the great meeting; 'the Boers are the worst nigger-drivers now left' (18 September 1899). Hobhouse's first connexion with Morley, indeed, had been over the protection of native races during 1898, and at this time he had acknowledged the beneficent effect of Imperial responsibilities if they provoked among collectivists 'genuine shame, for example, at the denial of justice to our black fellow-subjects in South Africa' (*EcR*, ix, 215). But while jingoism at home was daily assaulting Hobhouse's sensibilities, to bring up such considerations seemed more like an example of Imperialist cant.

The dilemma is faced explicitly in Hobson's reports, collected as *The War in South Africa* (1900), which influenced all the pro-Boers. Hobson fully recognised that the position of the Kaffirs ('who do the work and don't count') was the real root difficulty (p. 61). South Africa was a serf-civilisation in which the white race coerced the black; and he maintained that this parasitic life led to 'the mental and even physical degeneracy which develops in all slave-owning communities' (p. 294). He further acknowledged that the 'Boer treatment of natives in the Transvaal has never been enlightened or humane' (p. 233) and that redress of their grievances had been widely urged in England as a reason for the war. At this point, however, Hobson alleged that the argument was doubly flawed. First, because the prospect for the African labourer was 'the new tyranny of the mining capitalist' (p. 285); second, because the 'humane policy, commonly styled

"Exeter Hall", is denounced and repudiated quite as vehemently by the great majority of British colonists as by the Dutch' (p. 283).

Armed with this appraisal, pro-Boers like Hammond satirised the utterances 'from rather unexpected quarters of our duties to the black man in the Transvaal' in contemptuous terms: 'Love your neighbour's black men as if they will one day be your own'.[12] Hobson seems to have seen ahead at least as clearly as any of his contemporaries, arguing that the common hostility of all white South Africans to British efforts on behalf of the natives 'furnishes the not improbable bond of future union of the now disrupted races which will eventually sever South Africa from the control of Great Britain' (p. 291). 'Let us get rid at all hazards,' he concluded bleakly, 'of the cant about the righteous war for the redress of native grievances' (ibid.).

Scott had little respect for the official Liberal leaders, and Hobhouse even less. Feeble was the word for Campbell-Bannerman throughout 1899. Morley was 'now the only effectual voice on our side', according to Scott.[13] The National Reform Union was the only mass Liberal organisation which was, as its secretary, Symonds, kept reminding Scott, 'backing you & the *Guardian* up in your crusade against aggression & Militarism & Imperialism' (22 October 1900). Under the circumstances, things could easily have turned out worse in the Khaki Election of 1900. After initial Liberal setbacks, it seemed to the *Guardian* 'at last as if the better mind of the country as a whole were asserting itself' (MG, 3 October 1900), which sounds like the better spirits of Hobhouse. And the paper now proclaimed that Campbell-Bannerman had 'materially strengthened his hold on the leadership of the Liberal party by a service which will not readily be forgotten' (13 October 1900).

This impression was decisively reinforced within a year. Emily Hobhouse, in consultation with her brother and with Courtney, went to South Africa that winter and came back in May 1901 with first-hand reports of the effects of the British resort to farm-burning and 'concentration' camps. The information she brought back was disseminated by the Courtneys and by Hobhouse, who wrote on it for the *Speaker*. In June 1901 she had an interview with Campbell-Bannerman and formed a deep impression of his wisdom and humanity. The same week he was guest of honour at a dinner given by the National Reform Union, and this was the context for his denunciation of the British tactics as 'methods of barbarism'. From the time of this speech, according to Hobhouse, 'a man with no marked genius but that of character and the insight which character gave into the minds of his followers acquired in his party the position of a Gladstone'. It represented 'the reinstatement of the idea of Right in the mind of Liberalism'

[12] F. W. Hirst, Gilbert Murray and J. L. Hammond, *Liberalism and the Empire* (1900), pp. 182–3.
[13] Scott to Hobhouse, n.d. (May 1900), MGP.

(*Liberalism*, p. 222). Hobhouse continued to believe that the influence of his strong-minded sister – 'the Missis' since nursery days – was highly salutary in goading Campbell-Bannerman out of his indolence. As their mutual friend Margaret Clark put it to Smuts in 1906, '*Methods of Barbarism* made the personality which is now Premier; and it was the Missis who created the situation in which C.B.'s native worth could not choose but commit itself' (*Smuts*, ii, doc. 308).

The Fabians, alas, showed themselves immune from such appeals. The tract which Shaw drafted, *Fabianism and the Empire* (1900) was anathema to a moralist like Hobhouse. Shaw's bland discovery that 'there were better grounds for taking back the Rand than we were conscious of' (p. 30) seemed cynical and, in every sense, wrong. It showed him that 'to a certain kind of Socialism the great capitalist presents himself no longer as an enemy, but as an ally' (*S*, 11 January 1902). The Fabians' fatal flaw now appeared to him as their illegitimate opportunism – the attempt 'to force progress by packing and managing committees instead of winning the popular assent' (*N*, 30 March 1907). Thus they had fallen prey to the catchwords of efficiency. He saw this as a distortion of socialism and, he maintained, 'as the expert comes to the front and "efficiency" becomes the watchword of administration, all that was human in Socialism vanishes out of it'.[14] The Fabians had been led through their anti-democratic attitude to a worship of bureaucracy. 'The creation [as Hobhouse put it] of a highly centralised machine, so delicately specialised in structure and so intricate and secret in working as to be incapable of any real control on the part of the electorate, appears to be the conscious purpose of Mr Webb and his associates' (*N*, 30 March 1907). Scott had agreed with Hobhouse in 1899 that it was 'sad about the Webbs', adding: 'They have been raking about among statistics too long' (3 June 1899).

But it was Shaw who really alienated the pro-Boers. MacDonald had reproached him in 1897 from the point of view of 'Those of us who stand where you used to stand, who still believe in the making of public opinion as a necessary preliminary to any real progress' (7 December 1897). Insofar as Shaw was tempted from mechanical reformism it was towards mechanical revolutionism. In *Fabianism and the Empire* his insistence on the need for 'a Labor Policy, whether the laborer wants it or not' catches this tone (p. 62). A more friendly critic, Gilbert Murray, warned Shaw that he gave the impression 'that you are saying more than you can possibly mean; therefore you do not mean what you say' (30 September 1903). The Shavian mask, the fund of brilliant paradox, left Hobhouse unamused; it was putting decency, conscience and sincerity at risk. His private Hell had Balfour, Shaw and Milner in it and his lifelong dislike of Shaw became a byword among his friends. 'I was with LTH,' J. L. Hammond later recalled

[14] *Democracy and Reaction* (1904), p. 228.

to Murray, 'when the news that GBS had been lost on the Welsh mountains was followed by the news that he had been found. LTH took it as hardly as if it had been a Boer defeat' (16 August 1947).

In this, as in other ways, there are close affinities between the outlook of Hobhouse and that of Clarke. 'He had a profound moral horror of me', Shaw wrote of Clarke in 1905: 'I was to him *monstrum horrendum*, a moral anarchist' (Laurence, ii, 495–6). Clarke left the Fabians in 1897. Dragged down by ill health and prone to pessimistic doubts, the final years of his life present a dispiriting picture. It is easy to depict his break with Fabianism as a disillusionment of socialist hopes whch had never had a secure foundation. But this negative view is incomplete and misleading. For Clarke's writings of the 1890s, fragmentary as they were, provided some of the building blocks for the theories of which his friends Hobson and Hobhouse became protagonists in the next decade. They too were rejecting Fabianism under the pressure of the Imperialist issue; if they had died in 1901, as Clarke did, their work would have seemed to end on a note of pessimism about contemporary tendencies. In short, there are as good grounds for seeing Clarke as a forerunner of the New Liberalism as for suggesting that he had come to the end of the road intellectually because he had the bad luck to die young. This interpretation is reinforced by his posthumous article, 'The Decline in English Liberalism' (*PSQ*, xvi), which seems to have been generally overlooked. In it Clarke offered an analysis of the electoral weakness of the Liberal party as a victim of its own success in terms currently being developed by Hobhouse, a description of imperialism congruent with a Hobsonian view, and an asserveration, common to both, that, as Cobden had long since demonstrated, there was an inner consistency between foreign and domestic policy.

In *Democracy and Reaction* (1904) Hobhouse drew these themes together in a more comprehensive and positive way. In the imperialist reaction, he maintained, progressives had seen 'the whole circle of the Cobdenist ideas turned, as it were, inside out' (p. 55). And this led to the conclusion 'that the teaching of our recent history appears to be not that the older liberalism is "played out", but that the several elements of its doctrine are more vitally connected than appears on the surface' (pp. 164–5). He alleged that 'true socialism is avowedly based on the political victories which Liberalism won, and. . .serves to complete rather than to destroy the leading Liberal ideals' (p. 229). This, of course, was too much for Morley, who entered the caveat that 'a bare logical show of latent identity of principle hardly carries us far enough' (*NC*, lvii, 541), and suggested that Hobhouse was too readily inclined to suppose that improvements were made on the strength of abstract principles. Nonetheless, those of Morley's persuasion recognised Hobhouse's credentials as (to quote Hirst) 'a good Socialist and a good Liberal', because he understood 'that Cobdenites and Socialists should unite to check militarism and imperialism' (*IR*, v, 383). This reflected Hirst's view that 'the true progressive is the old *and* the new Liberal, who has had principles and who keeps them still in use'.[15] Hobhouse himself warmly espoused the view 'that the differences between a true, consistent, public-spirited Liberalism and a rational Collectivism ought, with a genuine effort at mutual understanding, to disappear' (*Democracy & Reaction*, p. 237). Such, he held, was the logic of the political alignments which the Boer War had precipitated: an analysis largely reciprocated on the Labour side by Keir Hardie.

Clarke had concluded that class divisions within the progressive forces were fatal but that if only Liberalism would overcome its 'administrative nihilism' they were needless. Hobhouse agreed. Only develop Liberalism and its apparent dissonance with democracy would turn to harmony. Hobhouse's general theory of social evolution came to his aid here in grounding progress on a surer sociological footing. Intellectual progress, which was essentially ethical, was the basis for social development, which could be measured in material terms. The moral appeals which Liberals had too often been afraid to make would not remain lonely cries but, pitched in the right way, would lead a swelling chorus. Hobhouse was not merely trying to establish the new Liberalism as a legitimate extension from the old but to affirm that all along it had been immanent within it. The re-discovery of the liberal tradition, and particularly of Bentham, is a new concern of these years. Wallas's *Francis Place* (1898) had helped, Leslie Stephen's *The English Utilitarians*, vol. i (1900), did more. It is clear that at some time between 1902 and 1904 Hobhouse read Bentham, who was promptly pressed into service as an opponent of war and came forward as the father of English Radicalism.

Conversely, Hobhouse now took the field as a committed critic of philosophical Idealism. This was the part of his analysis which old Liberals like Morley enjoyed most. Hobhouse acknowledged a lasting debt to Clarke for identifying Hegel as the chief philosopher just as Bismarck was the chief statesman of the counter-revolution. Idealism now seemed to him 'one expression of the general reaction against the plain, human, rationalistic way of looking at life and its problems' (*Democracy & Reaction*, p. 78). Its effect had been 'to sap intellectual and moral sincerity' (ibid.), and to give an ideological cover to Bismarckian *realpolitik*. One might not guess from Hobhouse's treatment that, of the leading Idealist philosophers, not only Muirhead and Caird but also Bosanquet (who differed here from Loch) were strongly pro-Boer in sympathy.

Hobhouse was speaking here as a philosopher, perhaps too ready to believe that in the end the real problems were ones that a stiff tutorial could sort out. He was also speaking as a critic of his own class, believing

[15] *Essays in Liberalism by Six Oxford Men* (1897), p. 54.

that the rot had set in at the top, in 'the world of high finance or of high officialdom' (p. 169). In South Africa the highest official – for all that he had sat at the feet of T. H. Green as an undergraduate – was the notorious pro-consul Milner. When Hobhouse observed sarcastically that there was no reason to suppose that the corruption of opinion would be 'corrected by a government of select Balliol men' (ibid.), he no doubt had in mind Milner and Liberal Imperialists like Asquith, Grey and Samuel. Thinking of his own associates – Scott, Symonds, Wallas, Olivier – he may have considered a government of select Corpus men a more wholesome alternative.

(II) HAMMOND

John Lawrence le Breton Hammond was born in 1872. His father, who came from a Jersey family, was Vicar of Drighlington in Yorkshire: a village, to be sure, but one set amid the great industrial towns of the West Riding. Bradford was only four miles away and Leeds, Halifax and Huddersfield all within ten. From 1885 Drighlington was part of the Spen Valley constituency, with its redoubtable Liberal commitment (Gladstonian by more than two-to-one in 1886) and the Vicar matched the political enthusiasm of his flock. He made Gladstone, as Lawrence later put it, into a sort of fourth person of the Trinity. This may have contributed to the family's local popularity, on which Lawrence was still able to draw in 1935 when he sent a letter of support to the Labour candidate. He was deeply attached to his father and considerably shaken by his death in 1897.

Lawrence Hammond was educated at Bradford Grammar School and won a classical scholarship to St John's College Oxford. His elder brother went to Cambridge and became successively a schoolmaster and a priest; two younger brothers also became schoolmasters; but the Vicar could not afford to give this sort of education to all his sons and Lempriere, later Suffragan Bishop of Stafford, did not go to university. There was an undercurrent of feeling in the family that the elder brothers had made their way in the world as the result of great family sacrifices which they were under a permanent obligation to recompense – 'this (to me) vile family octopus like feeling' was how Barbara Hammond later described it to Lawrence (25 October 1915). He himself evidently decided not to become ordained at some point in his undergraduate career.

At St John's Hammond was a pupil of Sidney Ball, whose Fabian Tract 'The Moral Aspects of Socialism' (1896) was a response from another disciple of Green to Bosanquet's *Aspects of the Social Problem*. As strongly as Hobson, Ball accused the C.O.S. of applying its moral arguments in a one-sided way to the working class. 'The poor man's poverty (it would seem) is his moral opportunity', he commented mordantly (*IJE*, vi, 311). The Socialist emphasis on reconstruction, he claimed, did not mean that character was to be ignored, but only that 'machinery is a means to an end, as much to a Socialist as to any one else' (p. 292). To Ball Socialism was a *Weltanschauung*; he defined it as the end to be sought, not as the means to be employed in reaching it. He therefore took up a similar position to that of Wallas's Fabian essay, but using the word socialism more in the sense of William Morris. 'Mere nationalisation, or mere "municipalisation", of any industry is not Socialism or Collectivism', he therefore asserted; 'it may only be the substitution of corporate for private administration; the social idea and purpose with which Collectivism is concerned may be completely absent' (p. 300). Collectivism, he maintained was 'not machinery, but machinery with a purpose'; it emphatically implied 'ideas' and could only operate through 'will and character' (p. 305). Ball thus defined the claims of socialism in rigorously moral terms and threw upon those who defended the existing organisation of society the responsibility for thwarting the advance of ideas and character. Socialists, he claimed, 'do not believe that grapes can grow upon thorns: they believe that things make their own morality' (p. 306).

Hammond was personally impressed by Ball – 'I cannot imagine what my Oxford life would have been like without him', he wrote later[16] – but in his own politics at this time he was more influenced by his contemporaries. From about 1892 collectivism was on the wane among undergraduates and there was a distinctively Liberal revival in which Hilaire Belloc took the most striking part. Belloc was elected President and Hammond Secretary of the Oxford Union in November 1894. Together with J. S. Phillimore they ran the Palmerston Club, while F. W. Hirst and J. A. Simon, both of Wadham, were rising to take over the supposedly more advanced Russell. Hammond's closest friend here was his fellow Yorkshireman Hirst. The Liberalism which these young men adopted was 'unadulterated with any tincture of Socialism' (*PR*, i, 213) and a society was later formed under Belloc's leadership to take propaganda on these lines into industrial England. Their efforts were welcomed by Morley and by the new Liberal Chief Whip, Tom Ellis; and the radical industrialist Sir John Brunner was induced to subscribe handsomely. On going down in 1895, with a second in Greats, Hammond had succeeded Ellis as Brunner's political secretary and may well have been the vital link here. His friends Hirst and Simon, who both got Firsts, were evidently considered by Scott for the vacancy on the *Guardian* which Hobhouse ultimately filled.

At the end of 1896 Hirst persuaded Hammond, Simon, Phillimore, Belloc, and also P. J. Macdonell, to join him in the production of a volume of essays. Morley, to whom *Essays in Liberalism by Six Oxford Men* (1897) was ultimately dedicated, would not go so far as to write a preface; and Asquith shied away because of its evident polemical thrust against a

[16] Oona Howard Ball, *Sidney Ball* (Oxford 1923), p. 263.

section of the party with which he was popularly associated. But the aged Gladstone publicly endorsed their efforts 'on behalf of individual freedom and independence as opposed to what is termed Collectivism' (p. x). With credentials like these, the volume naturally held an unsympathetic view of socialism. The *Progressive Review*, equally naturally, found the essay on foreign policy (by Phillimore) most congenial, since here the Cobdenite tradition, to which Hirst and Simon appealed elsewhere, was more acceptable to men like Hobson and Clarke. Belloc's essay had the hardest words for Collectivism, which would 'dissolve thrift, and self-control, and the personal honour which keeps a contract sacred, and replace them by a State reserve, by State control, and by a State system, releasing men from the burden of private rectitude' (pp. 4–5). Hirst made a vigorous defence of individualism, which could be taken in the same sense, though he backed it also by an advocacy of a graduated income tax.

From the first page of Hammond's essay on education, however, the tone is subtly different. In maintaining that it was 'the purpose of the State to develop the conditions of civic activity, and to promote the growth of individual character' (p. 176) he was employing language of a Greenian ambivalence. That he was nearer to Ball than to Bosanquet in the way he glossed it seems perhaps less obvious from his formal proposals, which represented a general progressive view, than in the manner of his treatment of the question. When he comments that 'the rich man who had enjoyed all the facilities which the country can provide, cuts a contemptible figure when he grudges his contribution to the cost of supplying elementary instruction for the poor, who have no other resource to fall back upon' (p. 188), the modern reader recognises the Hammond he knows. Hirst later reminded Hammond that 'I very early perceived in you a dangerous and heterodoxical strain', which was blamed upon the influence of Ball (27 September 1923). But at the time of publication it would have needed remarkable discernment to suggest that Hammond was out of kilter with his fellow essayists.

At the beginning of 1899 Hammond, who was at the time contributing two or three leaders a week to the *Leeds Mercury* in addition to his work for Brunner, approached the *Manchester Guardian* through Hirst and through Ball. He probably already knew Hobhouse from Oxford days, but their intimacy dates from this time. In fact Hammond's journalistic career was to develop under other auspices. Brunner had for ten years sustained the *Speaker*, a weakly weekly paper intended to rival the *Spectator*. He now handed it over to Hammond and his friends. Hirst was able to drum up funds on the strength of the 'excellent character as a Cobdenite' which Morley gave him (Hirst, p. 203). At first they only approached Liberals known personally to them for promises of literary contributions; these included not only Hobhouse and Wallas, but also Gilbert Murray, with whom Hammond embarked upon a lifetime's friendship. He assured Murray that he was taking care to avoid the overtones of strident individualism by excising references in the prospectus to '"liberty & independence" which rather savoured of the Duke of Argyll or Lord Wemyss' (5 April 1899). For the outlook of the *Speaker* was really defined by an opposition to imperialism rather than by domestic policy. So, whereas in December 1898 Hirst, Simon and Hammond had gone to the Chief Whip 'to tell him that the youth of England demanded that Asquith shd be Liberal leader', six months later, as Hammond wryly recalled to Murray, 'the youth of England were singing a very different tune but with equal confidence' (24 March 1933). All the *Speaker*'s preliminary policy discussions in the summer of 1899 were conducted under the cloud of the Transvaal situation. Just as this crisis led men like Hobhouse to rediscover the virtues of the old Liberalism, so, conversely, it induced the youthful Cobdenites to extend their intellectual sympathies towards the collectivist opponents of imperialism.

It used to be Hirst's style to taunt Wallas about Francis Place's individualism – 'How cld he manage to drag on political life without the illuminating conception of the State as a social organism or Bureaucratic God?' (29 January 1898) – and to deride Ball's social visions as 'founded on sand' (*Essays*, p. 72). But, brought to the test, he formed a different view of his fellow moralists. His autobiography speaks of the Fabian Society 'losing several prominent members like Graham Wallas and Sidney Ball' through its support of the war (p. 193), and in a sense this is more of a truth because it is incorrect. The diary extracts from 1899, which he also printed, show that he and Hobhouse now found themselves 'in agreement on most questions of foreign and home politics, including rating reform and anti-bureaucracy, and the right methods of dealing with natural monopolies and municipalisation' (p. 174). The comment that 'Both of us have moved, but he, I think, the most' is very revealing coming from Hirst, always a self-conscious and unrelenting man of principle.

Hobhouse warmly supported the plans for the *Speaker* and he assured Scott that Hammond had 'the root of the matter in him tho' he does not look a very strong man' (17 June 1899). Morley also formed a high opinion of Hammond's judgment and character when he met him at this time through Hirst, and the curious fact has already been observed, that it was Morley who broached Hobhouse's social programme as the agenda for the *Speaker*'s domestic policy (see p. 66). Hirst, indeed, declaring himself 'impressed by your way of putting the Old Age Ps' and 'delighted by your dicta on rating', was soon pressing Hobhouse to pursue this line of thought in the *Speaker* (30 August 1899).

The first issue of the refurbished *Speaker* appeared in October 1899. The paper was edited from a small room, at the top of a flight of dark, dusty, carpetless stairs, in Henrietta Street, Covent Garden. There Hammond sat at one table with his valued assistant, Arthur Clutton-Brock, at another. Hammond's valiant editorship of it throughout the war years gained it and him a formidable reputation untainted by prosperity. Hirst stood by it to the end but Simon and Belloc soon faded out of the picture. Hirst was also instrumental during the winter of 1899–1900 in the formation of the League of Liberals Against Aggression and Militarism. He and Hammond became active committee members and their colleague R. C. Lehmann chairman; Hobson and Clarke were also on the committee, as were Scott and Lloyd George. This was the nexus for the younger and more active pro-Boers who claimed Morley, Courtney and Bryce as their champions in an older generation.

In March 1900 Hammond, Hirst and Murray decided to collaborate on the book published some months later that year as *Liberalism and the Empire* (1900). Hammond tried to get Hobhouse to contribute to it as well, asking him for a discussion of 'the probable future of the Labour Party, & not least the rally of the Trades Unionists against Imperialism & the effect of Imperialist policy on Labour prospects' (4 April 1900). Hobhouse was unable to join them; but even so, the three Oxford men of 1900 were not half so anti-collectivist in tone as the six of 1897. Both Hirst and Hammond had benefited from Hobson's recent book *The War in South Africa* and held to his hostile view of the role of financial imperialism. Hirst analysed the bloated military expenditure which imperialism caused and invoked by contrast the financial tradition of Cobden and Gladstone. Moreover, he defended increased municipal spending on health and education against Tory attacks, on the ground that it constituted a social investment; and he further proposed the taxation of land values which had hitherto 'been let off scot-free by a sympathetic Legislature' (p. 83). This critique, however, differed from that developed by Hobhouse when it adumbrated the alternative fiscal policy; Hirst put both retrenchment on the naval estimates and the product of land taxation in the context of reducing income tax 'to a reasonable figure' (p. 90), rather than that of financing old age pensions. He even seems to have hankered after lowering the income-tax threshold to include well-to-do working men who would thereby also be made responsive to the need for economy.

Hammond offered a suggestive endorsement of Hobhouse's argument that domestic reform depended on the reassertion of the language of morality in external affairs, but, in an essay on foreign and colonial policy, he had no scope to be more specific. Whereas Hirst held to the Cobdenite doctrine of non-intervention, Hammond – like Hobhouse and newer friends like G. P. Gooch – revealed himself an adherent of the Gladstonian view that the demands of morality might on occasion demand an active foreign policy. 'It is not a question of weakness against firmness,' was how Hobhouse put it, 'but of the occasions upon which firmness is most necessary' (*EcR*, ix, 215–16). Gladstone's principle of international morality, being at once simpler and fuller than Cobden's view, could on occasion override the practical policy of non-intervention. Events in Armenia and Crete had presented recent opportunities to rally international morality in support of oppressed nationalities; but the Powers' inaction here had demonstrated to Hobhouse the moral bankruptcy of European statesmanship. Gladstone, explained Hammond, 'recognised one code of honour for nations and for men' (p. 165), and his respect for nationalism and his responsiveness to European feeling both derived from this.

In Hammond's hands the argument from Liberal tradition acquired two idiosyncratic points of emphasis. One was Francophile. Belloc's influence is possible here; likewise the family's Channel Island connexions. For Hammond the liberal alliance was a civilising force which he invested with a deep and permanent emotional commitment. Secondly, he was distinctive in tracing the Liberal tradition to Fox (another champion of France); Hammond's conviction, as he expressed it to Murray (12 October 1903), 'that he was a great man & a heroic liberal' was one which few of his friends shared. Coming down from Oxford in what he later regarded as an appalling state of ignorance, Hammond had begun to read Morley's books and had been led on to study the eighteenth century himself. His first book, *Charles James Fox: a political study* (1903), was the outcome. References to 'Fox and the little band of liberals' throughout a lifetime's anonymous journalism are no mean help in tracking down Hammond's work.

Both Hammond and Hirst saw democracy as the means of overthrowing the imperialist policy. Democracy was 'open to intellectual and, still more, to moral conviction' (p. 3); it had a 'capacity for grasping and acting on simple moral principles' (p. 161); and since the strength of the Liberal party lay in moral enthusiasm this gave ground for hope.

As a result of the *Speaker*'s role, Hirst and Hammond found themselves in contact with the leading pro-Boers. Courtney and Bryce were among their habitual visitors and, although Morley himself avoided close co-operation, the paper sought to support his line on the war, with a view to bringing Campbell-Bannerman round to the same point of view. Morley's own opinion was that Hammond, as he put it to him, did not 'think sufficiently of the S. as a journal endeavouring to *attract* a public' (15 December 1900). It is true that although Hammond was personally mild-mannered, with a talent for conciliation, he saw the *Speaker*'s role as that of bearing witness to unpopular truths. To Morley, hamstrung by fears for party unity and by his own irresolution, matters often seemed less simple. One gathering at Morley's house in January 1901, called to consider future policy, broke up, as Hammond told Hobhouse, 'with the sort of feeling that nothing could be done & that J.M. would scarcely make things better for us if he spoke'.[17] Courtney, who had been present, had turned to Hammond and Hirst and called out, 'I look to these young men' (Hirst, p. 217). This was a pleasing tribute, if not much of a lead, and it suggests how far the *Speaker* group felt that the initiative was passing into their hands. Courtney, with his outspoken pleas for a negotiated peace, for the recall of Milner, and against the annexation of the republics, was closest to the *Speaker* policy. But after 'methods of barbarism', the importance of sustaining Campbell-Bannerman seemed to demand more finesse than previously. 'We have got to do all we know to get the party round to him in his present position,' Hobhouse cautioned Hammond, '& it wd. be a misfortune if the stalwarts on our side raised a frank attack on him' (7 December 1901).

In April 1901 Hammond became engaged to Barbara Bradby. She was a daughter of the Rev. Dr E. H. Bradby, a former headmaster of Haileybury, who had then gone with his family to live in the St Katharine's Dock House in order to help the Barnetts with the work of Toynbee Hall. Until her father's death in 1893, when she was twenty, this was the milieu of Barbara's early life. She took a First in Greats at Oxford, where she was taught by Hobhouse as one of the tutors most sympathetic to feminist claims. For a while she was a Fellow of Lady Margaret Hall and, with her own income of £150 a year, might have made a comfortable academic career. But she had an active desire to wrestle with the evils of the world. She was an ardent pro-Boer and spent much time in helping Emily Hobhouse on her return from the camps. The Balls were mutual friends and may have been instrumental in bringing the Hammonds together. Lady Mary Murray was also already a friend of Barbara's through their common involvement, with the MacDonalds, in the women's industrial committee. Indeed Barbara warned her not to think 'that Mr Hammond is anti-woman; I have hopes of the Suffrage – he acknowledges that there are no arguments against it!' (12 April 1901).

On questions like these Barbara seems to have shared Hobhouse's views, and even at the outset Hirst confessed to Lawrence that 'there must be just a little anguish in the very thought of your felicity' (9 April 1901). This hint turned out to be fully justified. The Hammonds' marriage was extremely close and this new partnership displaced the collegiate comradeship of Lawrence's youth. Apart from its personal aspect, this constituted part of Lawrence's political education. The divergence between his path and Hirst's became more apparent. 'With regard to Womens Suffrage,' Barbara told Mary Murray a couple of years later, 'converts need gentle handling, &, as you surmise, there are difficulties in the way of the *Speaker* taking any line. Mr Hirst is already somewhat suspicious of my malign influence (which as a matter of fact is *nil*) & informed me sententiously

[17] Hammond to Hobhouse, 20 January 1901, HP.

the other day that the best thing he had ever heard on Women's Suffrage was Mr Phillimore's answer to the question "Are you in favour of women voting", which was "I do not think that either women or children should have votes" ' (8 December 1903).

The Murrays and, more significantly, the Hobhouses were better able to accept Barbara on her own terms. Hobhouse was drawn increasingly into the affairs of the *Speaker*, and clearly exerted a strong influence upon Lawrence Hammond. Hammond received a dedicated copy of the second edition of the *Labour Movement*. By the end of 1901 Hobhouse was restive about his own appointment on the *Manchester Guardian* and envisaged regular work for the *Speaker* as an alternative platform if he came to London. As it was, he remained for another year in Manchester but continued to supply Hammond with articles; *Democracy and Reaction* began as an eight-part series starting in December 1901. The *Speaker* too had an unsettled time since its finances were so precarious.

A major scheme of reconstruction was mooted in August 1902 which looked like the end of Hammond's editorship, and his own proposal was for Hobhouse to succeed him; but in fact the paper managed to ride out this crisis. Hobhouse was fully apprised of the Hammonds' difficulties and was able to sustain both their morale and their bank balance. In 1902, when he finally moved to London, it seems clear that he made a sizeable gift to them, the acceptance of which was eased by a letter from 'Aristotle', arguing that 'he who refuses to receive is in defect, & does not perform his function as one of a community: for it is by exchange of gifts that the community is kept together: & he is nameless because among Pro-Boers he does not at all come into being, but only among Jingoes, for the Jingo is an unfriendly animal' (15 November 1902). On the death of his uncle in 1904, Hobhouse chose Hammond as his collaborator in producing *Lord Hobhouse: a memoir* (1905). This gave Lawrence congenial employment and most of the book is apparently his; moreover, since Hobhouse insisted that a great deal of his own part of the work had in reality been done by Barbara, he insisted that the Hammonds receive the lion's share of the honorarium. With the legacies that came to him after Lady Hobhouse's death, it was a gesture which he could now well afford.

When Hammond took over the *Speaker* its editorial raison d'être was a Gladstonian view of foreign policy; within five years it had become identified with a progressive approach to domestic policy. As with Scott and Hobhouse, Hammond's tactical support for Campbell-Bannerman warmed into loyalty. 'I think he is doing extremely well', he told Murray (1 December 1903). His own statement of the Liberal case remained more traditional in form than Hobhouse's and, when he considered standing for Parliament at the end of 1903, he had no difficulty in satisfying the Dover Liberals of his soundness on such issues as education, licensing and free trade, which were the staple of the old Liberalism. While he reaffirmed his Gladstonian commitment against imperialism, he also explicitly urged the restoration of the legal immunity of trade unions and supported the rating of ground values.

The land, indeed, remained the starting point for the development of a social programme. It was part of Hirst's Cobdenite zeal to claim the land question as one which the great man's 'keen eye had foreseen and marked out for solution'.[18] So Hirst appeared, alongside Hobson and Hobhouse, among the nine contributors to *Towards a Social Policy* (1905) which Hammond edited as a *Speaker* venture. The polemical advantages of giving the land this priority lay in its susceptibility to analysis from the standpoint of both the new and the old Liberalism. 'Upon this question,' it could be asserted, 'the disciples of Henry George make common cause with the disciples of Richard Cobden; at this point the Liberal tradition and the Socialist movement converge' (p. 44). Hammond himself had moved towards such a perspective as a result of a consideration of the morality of imperialism. A far-reaching social policy at home, so he now believed, consorted naturally with a liberal and civilised policy abroad; and, conversely, he maintained that 'no article in our faith is more definite than the belief that we pay, in our own unredeemed and unliberated proletariate, for the crimes we commit against the freedom of other peoples' (preface).

(III) WALLAS

'Real married life,' Shaw declaimed in 1901, 'is the life of the youth and maiden who pluck a flower and bring down an avalanche on their shoulders. Thirty years of the work of Atlas; and then rest as pater and materfamilias. What can childless people with independent incomes, marrying at forty as I did, tell you about marriage?'[19] In 1898 Graham Wallas married Ada Radford. He was forty; she was two years younger and had an independent income of three or four hundred pounds a year. She too had had a Devonshire childhood in which the importance of religious belief had been deeply impressed upon her. But her family's Nonconformity had become less strict since the day of her grandfather, who once confessed to her that the play house had been his besetment – 'So much so, my dear, that even after my conversion I have stopped in the street and read the play bills.'[20] Her family tradition was strongly Liberal. She herself was a graduate of Girton, with marked literary and aesthetic commitments, running to a taste for greenery-yallery clothes and decor.

'I do not take to her', Beatrice Webb confided to her diary, while

[18] F. W. Hirst (ed.), *Free Trade and other Fundamental Doctrines of the Manchester School* (1903), p. xii.
[19] Bernard Shaw, *Sixteen Self Sketches* (1949), pp. 53–4.
[20] Ada Wallas, *Daguerrotypes* (1929), p. 34.

acknowledging that she was 'obviously a good woman – sweet natured (Graham says humorous) with decision & capacity'. Beatrice's brisk conclusion was that 'she has just enough money to make marriage – with no prospect of children – prudent if not actually desirable for Graham. I doubt whether we shall be much of friends' (21 January 1898). On the whole they were not, though Beatrice's respect for Audrey (as she was often known) increased over the years. Her prediction, however, was wrong in one respect. The Wallases had a daughter, May, to whom they were devoted, and there is plenty of evidence of a very happy family life. Beatrice, by contrast, was sometimes disposed in the following years to wonder whether the books she and Sidney had written were worth the children which – 'rightly or wrongly' – they had decided against having (diary, 1 January 1901). Moreover, the unmistakeable snubs of Charlotte Shaw remained branded in Ada Wallas's memory for thirty years. While such considerations do not account for the divergence of Wallas from the Webbs and from Shaw, they may have made the breach easier to bear.

Wallas's experience of practical administration satisfied him that his sort of collectivism had irresistibly gained ground and he remained attached to what Shaw called 'that foolish democratic mistake, the adhocious School Board' (Laurence, ii, 100). In this respect he was revealing himself more conservative than Shaw who roundly declared that his contempt for the status quo grew from year to year. This is the interpretation which Shaw would have endorsed of their ensuing policy differences. When the pro-Boers in the Fabian Society threatened to disrupt its unity by bringing forward the war as the great issue, he was contemptuous of the fact that 'in the absence of any alternative the Fabians fall back on Cobdenism, recruited by pure Humanitarianism'. Such a view was 'only possible to a Gladstonian of the sixties, not to socialists educated by Marx' (Laurence, ii, 119). Not that Wallas was a pro-Boer. He seems to have accepted the war once it had been declared, which would have been consistent with the position of his Liberal Imperialist friend Samuel. It was left to Ramsay MacDonald and Sydney Olivier to take up a strong anti-imperialist position, with Sidney Webb somewhere in the middle. The Webbs spent several weeks in Manchester in the autumn of 1899 and were fellow-guests in Liverpool with the Courtneys the weekend after the great Transvaal protest meeting; so it is quite possible that they had the benefit of Hobhouse's views face to face. At any rate, he was to Beatrice an example of those who thought the times looked black, and, she added feelingly, 'the fact that those they are accustomed to agree with, look upon them as suffering from a kind of hysteria does not raise their spirits or improve their temper' (diary, 4 December 1899). The bitter division was felt by Fabians and Liberals alike, and perhaps most keenly by persons who were both. One could say that the social democrats became divided over liberalism.

Beatrice recognised that 'this friction is made more deepseated by this cleavage transversing that on social questions' (diary, 20 February 1900). She and Sidney, Shaw and Wallas, each felt different pressures on their opinions and pulls on their loyalties.

To Shaw the role of the Fabians had always been essentially anti-Gladstonian. The reason why they had never previously extended their criticism from domestic to foreign policy was, he maintained, sheer neglect, which 'in the hour of trial, left us nothing to fall back on but the most miserable 1880 Radicalism' (Laurence, ii, 121). This neglect he now set out to remedy. 'The Socialist,' he claimed, 'has only to consider which dog to back; that is, which dog will do most for Socialism if it wins' (ibid., 122). Put in this way, the claims of the Boers were not very strong. To Shaw it seemed that the struggle should be viewed through the eyes, not of a moralist, but of a natural historian, and, in an equivalent simile, 'the knocking over of a Krugerite theocracy by a Milnerite plutocracy leaves me as cool as the extinction of the stage coach by the locomotive' (ibid., 369). His refusal to make any protest stemmed precisely from the fact that, as he put it, 'I am an old Socialist, inveterately anti-Liberal, anti-Individualistic, anti-Jehovistic, anti-Independence–Liberty–Nationality and all the rest of it' (ibid., 168). Whereas the Transvaal represented a purely reactionary cause, he warmed to an imperialist war which 'had put a fourpence on the Income Tax which will never come off if the Fabian can help it; so that Old Age Pensions will be within reach at the end of the ten years repayment period, if not sooner' (ibid., 153).

The aim of *Fabianism and the Empire* (1900) was therefore to give imperialism a socialist rationale. Wallas was staying with the Shaws while it was being drafted and realised from the first that he would not agree with it. 'It is interesting,' he wrote in extenuation to Ada, 'and shows that he is thinking on the Imperial question but is a bit bumptious in tone and hasty in statement' (22 August 1900). In it a series of domestic measures aiming at efficiency was suggested. Annexation was justified on the ground that 'a Great Power, consciously or unconsciously, must govern in the interests of civilisation as a whole' (p. 23). The more limited objectives of the Chamberlain policy were a makeshift on the road to internationalisation. Wallas remained unhappy with the tone of this document and considered its ostensible appeal to a spirit of imperial trusteeship vitiated by its lack of consideration for the non-white races.

Sidney Webb's attitude to the war was really a non-attitude. From the first he tried to avoid committing himself on a question which he regarded as extraneous to his own field of competence. He refused to read the blue books and Beatrice considered him pro-Boer by sentiment. 'Sidney,' Kate Courtney recorded, 'has adopted the formula "the war was *wholly* unjust but wholly necessary", & though I would not for the world have been guilty of making it yet now I don't see why we should not reap the benefits.'[21] This is a hostile report yet it captures his agnostic opportunism on the issue. 'It is not my show', he would say (*OP*, p. 218). To some extent this explains Beatrice's attitude too. These new issues were not the work they had undertaken or were trained to consider. They would leave them to others. They would co-operate with people of any opinion about them as long as there was a chance of smuggling in Fabianism by the back door.

Yet this does not wholly explain the intensity of Beatrice Webb's response nor the fact that she exhibited as consistent a natural bias towards Unionism as Sidney towards Liberalism. Her retort to the Liberal chief whip, Herbert Gladstone, that 'as far as I am concerned I have never been a Liberal & my husband is not in Politics but only in local administration' (diary, 10 June 1904), is a purely formal description of the position. In fact the Transvaal crisis coincided with, and may have contributed to, a personal crisis for Beatrice. The link was Joseph Chamberlain, with whom her stormy love affair had ended in 1887. In the autumn of 1899, after meeting the Courtneys, she was 'puzzled to try & resist the atmosphere of hostile criticism to his actions in Sidney's & Leonard's minds'. She recognised that her feelings were not impartial having 'suffered years of pain, possibly from the same coarse inconsiderateness which others say he has shown towards the Transvaal. I am a prey therefore to an involved combination of bias & counter-bias' (diary, 10 October 1899). For at least three years she had been seeking to repress persistent fantasies about her relationship with Chamberlain. 'I sometimes wonder whether certain illusions will ever pass over', she had written (diary, 8 November 1896). In 1897, the tenth anniversary of the proposal, the fretful tone is the same – 'there is melancholy in the stillness of the mid-summer air – life is a struggle of vivid hope with desperate fear' (diary, 22 June 1897). In June 1899, as the prospect of war loomed nearer every day, 'my cursed habit of sentimental castle-building leads me to harp back on the past...Oh! the mysteries of human feelings!' (diary, 15 June 1899). This state of 'chronic daze' (diary, 16 March 1900) was recurrent in the following months. She found her thoughts 'constantly wandering to the great man & his family, watching his career with sympathy & interest & desiring his welfare' (diary, 22 May 1900). Then, in July 1900, at a party of Haldane's, just as Beatrice was 'explaining to Mr George Windham that "a Tory was a man without prejudices" (compared to a Liberal) I became aware that Mr Chamberlain had joined us'. It was their first meeting for thirteen years. Beatrice reflected afterwards that 'there is a bond of sentiment between us – he for the woman that loved him, I, for the man that I loved – loved but could not follow' (diary, 4 July 1900). Indeed she later dramatised this meeting so far as to imagine that Chamberlain and his wife had separated as a result

[21] Kate Courtney diary, 19 January 1900, Courtney Papers, vol. 29, f.153.

of it. None of this implied a repentance of her marriage with Sidney. What remained of her former passion for Chamberlain, she wrote at the turn of the year, was 'only a tenderness for the man I loved & an almost exaggerated desire for his success & happiness' (diary, 1 January 1901).

Within a year or two Beatrice Webb found herself no longer plagued by her romantic imaginings. She submitted herself to a strict and abstemious regime, to which she attributed her good health and spirits. By 1903 she had become a vegetarian and hankered after giving up tea, coffee and tobacco – 'all poisons – but the appetite overcomes my better will' (diary, 29 April 1903). All was well. Meanwhile, the Fabians had become committed to imperialism.

The Webbs and Shaw found it fairly easy to accept the Unionist hegemony, which the war reinforced, as the inescapable context for political action. 'The social enthusiasm that inspired the intellectual proletariat ten years ago has died down and given place to a wave of scepticism about the desirability, or possibility, of any substantial change in society as we know it', Beatrice Webb wrote in January 1900 (*OP*, p. 195). In this chastened spirit, the Fabian aims became not only more cautiously reformist but, equally significantly, almost entirely mechanical in their reformism. 'It is a tiresome fact,' Beatrice acknowledged, 'that to get things done in what one considers the best way, entails so much – to speak plainly – of intrigue' (*OP*, p. 259). Shaw's plea to the Webbs to 'handle' Rosebery, who being 'a peer & a political pillar, is necessarily a political tool', is an expression of this view (Laurence, ii, 230). Since the Liberal Imperialists were at least ashamed of their Gladstonian old clothes, there was room for Sidney Webb, a latter-day Francis Place, to offer himself here as the collectivist tailor of Millbank. His widely-read article 'Lord Rosebery's Escape from Houndsditch' – in fact a joint production with Shaw – appeared in September 1901. Instead of Gladstonianism, with its inveterate tendency to 'think in individuals' (*NC*, l, 369), it offered Rosebery a policy of National Efficiency buttressed by the legal enforcement of a National Minimum. Indeed, with this sort of appeal, the chief problem which Shaw foresaw was 'to avoid any appearance of going back on our Socialism' (Laurence, ii, 232). At the end of 1901, therefore, while Beatrice Webb celebrated their close partnership with Shaw, 'based on a common faith & real "good fellowship",' she noted too their strained relations with Wallas, who now distrusted the expedients by which the Webbs sought to further what they understood as Democracy (diary, 9 December 1901).

For Wallas was by no means so eager as Webb to escape from Houndsditch. It was, after all, the birthplace of his hero Bentham. Like Hobhouse, with whom he remained in contact, he was reassessing the liberal tradition in a more favourable light. His associates at the South Place Ethical Society (S.P.E.S.) were largely pro-Boer in sympathy. It was at South Place that he gave an address in October 1901 strikingly similar in theme to the articles on the fate of Liberal ideas which Hobhouse published a few weeks later in the *Speaker*. The old Liberalism, Wallas admitted, had even at the beginning displayed a tendency to simplify problems. But what had shattered Liberalism was not the original failure to see all the conditions but rather a change in the conditions of the problem. Some of these changes were economic, creating a world market and a complex industrial system in which Cobdenite ideals of free contract were meaningless. Empire had undermined confidence in democratic nationalism. There was also a change in knowledge, stemming from Darwin. A new emphasis on racial distinctions and the unconscious led to a 'shaken insistence on rationality'. Men had fallen back, therefore, from abstract ideals like Humanity, Freedom and Democracy to the more specific ties of loyalty, patriotism, religion and common sense. The effect which this made upon Wallas is vividly summarised in his notes: '*drift* instead of *steer* and in *unknown seas*'.[22] His prescription remained firmly that of the moralist. They must insist again on the return to reason: not as all human motive, nor as offering easy solutions; but as a call to a difficult duty demanding constantly renewed effort in face of painful discouragement. The scathing comment in the Webb–Shaw article, that ' a Liberal reform is never simply a social means to a social end, but a campaign of Good against Evil' (*NC*, l, 370), could well have been directed against their old friend.

Whatever his earlier leanings towards the Liberal Imperialist view on the origin of the war, therefore, Wallas found it impossible to accept the inferences drawn by the Webbs about the political future of collectivism. The Khaki Election of 1900, with its revelation of the mass appeal of jingoism, might have been designed to demonstrate the persistence of those 'outbursts of national hatred and the degradation and extinction of weaker peoples' of which Wallas had written in his Fabian Essay (see p. 39). And his further warning there that questions of religious principle were similarly not amenable to the panaceas of collectivism also now exemplified itself in current politics.

The Webbs were eager to co-operate with the Government in reforming the structure of public education and were content to pay the price for enlisting Conservative support: namely that the Act must also extend financial aid to the Church schools. Wallas did not, like the Nonconformists, spring to the defence of the existing system. 'Abolish the School Boards outright', he had asserted on administrative grounds in 1900.[23] This was done by the Education Acts of 1902 and 1903. But he was as fervent as any Nonconformist Liberal in opposing the use of public funds to support religious teaching in the schools. Ada Wallas not unnaturally shared his

[22] 'The Decay of Liberalism', MS notes of lecture at S.P.E.S., October 1901, WP 16.
[23] Lecture on 'Education', 26 March 1900, WP 16.

view, and it is interesting that some acquaintances consequently supposed Graham's background too to have been Nonconformist. Beatrice Webb discovered the real basis for his position during a long discussion in June 1902. What Wallas deplored was the growing tolerance of, if not sympathy with, religious teaching on the part of confessed agnostics – people who accepted the church's teaching, not because it was true, but lest worse should befall the child's mind in the form of a crude materialistic philosophy. 'I cannot see the spirit of genuine reform,' Wallas maintained, 'if there is no portion of the church's teaching which you object to more than any other; if you cease to discriminate between what you accept and what you reject, denying all and accepting all, with the same breath, denying the dogmas as statements of fact, accepting them as interpreting a spirit which pleases you' (*OP*, p. 242). For Wallas this was the continuation of a very familiar argument. Only the idiom has changed since the letter which he had received from his sister Mollie at Highgate School: 'Don't think me a Silly Prig for talking so,' she had written, 'but I do think the simple way in which the Moral Law is put in the New Testament is beautiful for boys and it is beautiful enough for me all my life' (10 May 1885). Beatrice Webb, seventeen years later, was unable to shake Wallas here. 'I admitted there was much in his contention', she noted. 'I could only shelter myself by the argument that the reform of the Church was not the work I had undertaken to do, or which I was trained to consider' (*OP*, p. 242).

To Wallas, then, it seemed illegitimate to gain administrative reforms at the expense of ecclesiastical control of the schools. To Sidney it seemed almost incomprehensible – 'I cannot but believe that we both want the same thing' he wrote (4 September 1903) – that they should be opposed. But the fact that by early 1904 'our old friend G. Wallas is left in the cold' was more easily accepted by Beatrice. 'One has [she continued], in this ruthless world, to accept uncomfortable facts & act on them' (diary, 27 February 1904). And to Shaw it seemed that having 'kicked Wallas out of the Fabian Society' over the London Education Act (Laurence, ii, 408–9), Webb might as well openly show gratitude to the Conservatives for passing it. In fact this overstates the issue since the gulf between Wallas and Webb was not unbridgeable and within a year or two they were able to co-operate once more over educational matters. But that a serious breach had occurred could hardly be denied.

H. G. Wells suggested two reasons why Wallas was now suspicious of the Webbs. First, that Sidney was too 'foxy' and fond of displaying his 'tactics'. Second, that the Webbs were a 'combination', assiduously working together but from rather different motives – that, as Beatrice recorded it, 'I was regarded as a "reactionary" with an anti-Radical creed, and it was suspected that Sidney would eventually veer round to my side' (*OP*, p. 289). As an account of Wallas's views this certainly tallies with what he later told Ada of the 'elements of greatness' which Sidney had displayed in his youth. 'G. thinks the "we think" fatal to intellectual sincerity,' she noted in her diary (21 May 1916). As to the substance of the charge, he had had ample opportunity to observe the Webbs at work in London politics. Beatrice conceded that the Progressives would 'unconsciously resent having situations "prepared" out of which there is only one way – i.e. ours!' (*OP*, p. 268) She knew that there had been a 'slump in Webbs' among them as a result. 'They have not the wit to see that, if a Government is in power with an overwhelming majority, it is no use fighting it', she complained in March 1903 (*OP*, p. 261). This is a fair statement of the opportunist case for bowing to necessity in face of adverse political realities. Yet it hardly explains why, before the 1904 L.C.C. elections, when Wallas was for the first time a candidate, the Webbs should actually hope for the defeat of the Progressives. Nor does it explain why, when that defeat did not materialise, Beatrice Webb should find it 'perturbing' that ecclesiastical influence was so small (*OP*, p. 284). It is clear that her own spiritual yearnings, which led her by 1905 to identify the Church of England as the local representation of the spirit of religion, rendered her particularly susceptible to the claims of the established order.

It was on the issue of tariffs that Wallas finally left the Fabian Society. The Webbs, while welcoming the new ferment of the Tariff Reform campaign, had no more use for protection than for what they regarded as Nonconformist fanaticism. Both were equally irrelevant to their new policy enforcing a national minimum. 'It is open to us to use either or both parties' Beatrice Webb concluded in July 1903 (*OP*, p. 272). Nonetheless the rally of 're-actionary enlightenment' to the Liberals (Mrs Humphry Ward, for example) disgusted her, and she observed that 'we find ourselves far more sympathetic to the present Government than those who 10 years ago wd have considered us rank rebels' (diary, 6 January 1904). And to Shaw, a fortiori, here was a new opportunity to build on the insight that the British workman was not interested in Socialism. 'We are necessarily anti-Free Trade, anti-Manchester, anti-laissez-faire, anti-Cobden and Bright, anti all the Liberal gods', he claimed.[24] His policy was really to test the Tories by making them see the true implications of their proposals. When Shaw was allowed to draft the tract *Fabianism and the Fiscal Question* (1904) Wallas found that 'All the turns of phrase and all the underlying assumptions are Protectionist.' Shaw's treatment, equating Cobdenites with Whigs, Protection with factory legislation, free trade with laissez faire, Liberalism with reaction, and so on, seemed to Wallas 'insincere and mischievous'. 'On the questions which divide the Liberal and Conservative Parties,' he affirmed, 'I am a Liberal.'[25]

[24] Shaw to Pease, 30 September 1903, Shaw Papers 50557, ff.71–3.
[25] Wallas to Pease, 21 February 1904, copy in WP.

As far as the Webbs were concerned, the revival of Liberalism which Free Trade consummated was depressing. They were, as they well knew, completely out of touch with the followers of Campbell-Bannerman, whom they regarded as hopeless from the point of view of social progress. In the previous eight or ten years, Beatrice reflected in 1904, many of their old comrades had become 'indifferent or even hostile to our ideas – Graham Wallas, Llewellyn Smith, Hewins, Leonard Hobhouse, C. P. Trevelyan & Herbert Samuel & Billy Phillimore are no longer, for one reason or another, habitués of Grosvenor Rd. Massingham, Vaughan Nash, H. Spender have become distinctly hostile.'[26] Wallas's retirement was more amicable and he continued to be a friend of his old collaborators. He found himself more in tune with the ideas of H. G. Wells, who knew him well at this time, and who was just beginning his own struggle to remould Fabianism from within. Wells knew from conversation with Wallas of his growing conviction that the key to progress lay in a better understanding of social psychology rather than in an obsession with the mere mechanism of administration. This was, as Wallas subsequently recognised, the origin of his study of *Human Nature in Politics*. It arose, Ada Wallas recorded, from 'the urgency of his own difficulties' in reconciling his work in London politics with his membership of the Fabian Society: 'G. says where to differ in opinion means to lose friends – or even an election – it sharpens your analysis of the causes of your differences' (A. Wallas's diary, 21 September 1918).

(IV) HOBSON

Hobhouse did not meet Hobson until the summer of 1899 but he knew enough about him to suggest to Scott that Hobson should go to South Africa as a special correspondent for the *Manchester Guardian*. There can be no doubt that he was chosen as a committed opponent of imperialism. He had, as Hobhouse knew, already formulated a critique of what has since become known as the Imperialism of Free Trade – 'the policy of forcing doors open and forcibly keeping them open' (CR, lxxiv, 167). He sought to show that Britain's expanding foreign markets were in the advanced industrial countries, with whom she was on peaceful terms, whereas the enormous tracts of territory added to her possessions in the late nineteenth century had yielded little commercial advantage. It followed that the heavy expenditure on armaments necessary to force new markets was unprofitable. He further argued that expansion of foreign trade was unnecessary if – on an underconsumptionist analysis – effective demand could be increased at home. That the upper and middle classes at present held an excessive share of national wealth was proved by the export of

[26] Beatrice Webb diary, n.d. but May 1904 (runs on from OP, p. 291).

capital for which they had no other use. 'It is possible, indeed,' Hobson added at this point, 'that the growing pressure of the need for foreign investments must be regarded as the most potent and direct influence in our foreign policy' (p. 178).

Here was the germ of a new theoretical development, but for the moment Hobson was content to appeal to an old doctrine. Significantly enough, he bypassed the Gladstonian moral imperatives which appealed so strongly to Hobhouse and Hammond and claimed that the choice between external expansion and internal reform was 'the plain and very practical issue which Cobden and his friends strove to place before the Liberal party half a century ago' (ibid.). Koebner and Schmidt make the point that Hobson's analysis transfers the motive to another historical level by identifying the parasites as an outgrowth of capitalist society rather than a privileged remnant of feudal society.[27] But the transition here appeared natural and continuous to adherents of a theory of rent which identified many other incomes as well as those from land as 'unearned'.

Hobson went to South Africa watchful and suspicious, but without a necessitarian view on how the situation would develop. There is no need to accept literally his account in *The War in South Africa* (1900) of the apprehension with which he looked forward to his stay in Johannesburg – 'I pictured in my mind the oppressed helot of Sir Alfred Milner's famous telegram, continually harried in the peaceful pursuit of his calling by extortionate officials' (pp. 52–3). Even so, it is clear that he was strongly influenced by what he observed on the spot. His range of contacts admittedly left something to be desired from the point of view of impartiality – to a fellow journalist he was 'a dismal fellow sent out on purpose to take the Boer view of things'.[28] Through his brother Ernest he had an introduction to Smuts and spent much of his time in Pretoria staying with the Smutses, to whom he soon became 'onze oude vriend Hobson'. He quickly dismissed the outlanders' grievances or an Afrikaaner plot or a concern for native rights as adequate reasons for hostilities. He looked, however, with grim disfavour on the conduct of the British authorities. 'I regard Milner as bent on war', he told Scott early in his stay (n.d., ? August 1899). Milner struck him as 'a strong-headed bureaucrat, extremely capable in the autocratic conduct of affairs', but unable to achieve his objectives by conciliation and consent (CR, lxxviii, 544). As late as the middle of August 1899 Hobson affirmed to Scott that 'I still disbelieve in war' (15 August 1899). If war came, then, it was because powerful interests desired objectives which only war could achieve. Here his attention was persistently drawn to the activities of certain financiers and to the ramifications of their

[27] Richard Koebner and H. N. Schmidt, *Imperialism: the story and significance of a political word* (Cambridge 1964), p. 254.

[28] J. B. Atkins to Hammond, 15 January 1900, HP.

political influence. For South Africa did not have the sort of bright economic future which might have supplied a general motive for annexation. 'We are fighting,' Hobson claimed, 'in order to place a small international oligarchy of mine-owners and speculators in power at Pretoria' (*War in S. Africa*, p. 197). Their business interests forced them into politics because they needed the State to secure them control over cheap labour and to make privileged fiscal provisions for them.

Hobson has sometimes been accused of anti-semitism in pointing to the prominence of Jews in South African financial circles. Some of his despatches admittedly contain passages searching for evidence of Jewish connexions. He acknowledged that 'the ignominious passion of Judenhetze' might easily be aroused (p. 189), and he made a firm distinction between, on the one hand, the great majority of South African Jews – 'a rude and ignorant people, mostly fled from despotic European rule' (p. 190) – and, on the other, 'the class of financial capitalists of which the foreign Jew must be taken as the leading type' (p. 189). This class represented 'the most highly organised form of international finance yet attained' (*CR*, lxxvii, 3). Hobson wanted to confute twice over the patriotic claim that the interests at stake were 'national': once by showing that they were sectional, and again by showing that they were cosmopolitan. His contentions here were empirical; in a Marxist or an anti-semitic theory they would have been axiomatic. To Hobson, it was an unfortunate fact that Rhodes and the German Jews of the Rand manipulated British policy to their own advantage; it was not in the nature of things that this must be so.

A central problem remained in Hobson's analysis. The interest of Rhodes was clear enough. But to enlist British power on his side 'it was above all things necessary to apply an adequate motive-power to the minds of the British Government and the British people' (*War in S. Africa*, p. 207). How was the trick turned? Here Hobson pointed to 'the press conspiracy which has successfully exploited the stupid Jingoism of the British public for its clearly conceived economic ends' (p. 217). Once more he tried to document the personal and institutional connexions. At this point his conspiracy theory on the origin of hostilities was complete. The war had been caused by 'a small confederacy of international financiers working through a kept press' (p. 229).

Hobson *needed* a conspiracy theory because he believed in liberal democracy. There could be no imperialism without public support. This had to be explained in terms of Jingoism. Why, after all, was war waged enthusiastically not only against the Transvaal but against the Orange Free State, where there was no gold and no pretence of Outlander grievances? 'I can find no other explanation,' wrote Hobson, 'save the sheer lust of domination, which resents the claims of other people to freedom and equality with Englishmen' (p. 144). This was the 'one powerful secret ally which ever lurks in the recesses of the national character', ready to respond 'with eager frenzy' when summoned by its financial masters (*CR*, lxxvii, 16). On his return from South Africa it was this phenomenon, not the financial aspects, which Hobson chose for closer analysis: an option which may puzzle modern readers in hot pursuit of the 'economic theory of imperialism', but which seemed perfectly understandable at the time.

Professions of belief, Hobson held, had to be taken seriously. Rational argument depended on their having a substantive content, amenable to formal rules of logic and consistency. And yet he fully acknowledged that there were important ideological and psychological influences at work. Surveying the development of classical economics he readily acquitted such men as Ricardo, Senior and James Mill of any conscious intellectual dishonesty. But there were, he thought, strong forces working on intellectuals to build convenient systems, and 'generally the steady and persistent secret pressure of class bias, working through "the spirit of the age" is successful in getting what it wants'. It was clear to him how this had happened in the case of classical economics. Adam Smith's 'policy of social progress' had become one of 'despotism and degradation' as expounded by 'a subsequent generation of mill-owners, financiers, and their intellectual henchmen'.[29] Much of Hobson's animus against orthodox economics arose because he saw in it (as Brailsford later put it) 'a defensive outwork of the capitalist system'.[30] He always insisted that thinkers were not so disinterested as they imagined and retained a sardonic scepticism about even his own intellectual position as a heretic. The sort of bias he had in mind was as much the product of psychology as of economics.

The next stage in Hobson's theoretical refinement of his South African experience was, logically enough, a book on *The Psychology of Jingoism* (1901). Drawing to some extent on the suggestions of writers like Le Bon, Hobson sought to assess the motivation of the Jingo crowd. It manifested the mentality of the spectator or the inciter and was 'a collective or mob passion' (p. 9) where 'the pulsation of the primitive lust which exults in the downfall and the suffering of an enemy' broke through the veneer of convention (p. 31). His phrase 'the mob-mind' became a stock category for political analysis by such friends as Hobhouse. Observing it at work, of course, was 'an experience calculated to stagger any confidence one might have held in man as a rational and moral being' (p. 33), and a public which had succumbed to brutality and credulity in this way 'could surely afford no more convincing proof of its mental collapse' (p. 70).

This collapse into irrationalism was discouraging for Hobson; yet because he also believed that it had not been spontaneous his analysis took on a further dimension. The real lesson of the war had been 'its revelation of the

[29] J. A. Hobson, *The Social Problem* (1901), pp. 22, 24–5.

[30] *The Life-work of J. A. Hobson*, Hobhouse Memorial Lecture (1948), p. 11.

methods by which a knot of men, financiers and politicians, can capture the mind of a nation, arouse its passion, and impose a policy' (p. 107). The channels through which public opinion had been formed were the music halls and, above all, the press. Jingoism was rooted in social psychology; but its manipulation for certain ends was the result of a wholly rational policy. 'The businessmen who mostly direct modern politics require a screen', Hobson epitomised his argument; 'they find it in the interests of their country, patriotism. Behind this screen they work seeking their private gain under the name and pretext of the commonwealth' (p. 131). In paraphrasing a favourite quotation from Sir Thomas More, Hobson drew attention to the historical persistence of the sort of conflict of interests which he saw at the root of the problem. The role he attributed to speculators in promoting imperialism was, indeed, similar to that which Adam Smith had attributed to merchants in sustaining mercantilism.

Hobson wrote in his autobiography of his 'distinctive attitude in social thinking, viz. the testing of all political and economic conduct by the criteria of human welfare' (*Conf.*, p. 70). But he maintained there that he had not achieved this intellectual synthesis at the time he wrote his famous study *Imperialism* (1902). It is true that it was only after his return from South Africa, when he was over forty, that he first became drawn into active political commitments. 'Hobson is a careful thinker but no politician', Wallas wrote to his wife (25 November 1901). Hobson himself commented on his partisan involvement in controversy that 'by enlisting my combative instincts in defence of my heretical views of capitalism as the source of unjust distribution, over-saving, and an economic impulsion to adventurous imperialism, it led me for a time to an excessive and too simple advocacy of the economic determination of history' (*Conf.*, p. 63). By 1938, when he wrote this, *Imperialism* had gone through several revisions; and Hobson had just contributed a new introduction to the third edition clarifying the connexions between underconsumption at home and colonial expansion abroad. This twenty-page introduction has been taken by some writers as in itself the authoritative statement of the theory. On this basis it then becomes natural to stress the affinities of Hobson's theory with that of Lenin, which had in the meanwhile revivified the whole subject. It was the reputation which his book had acquired in this context for which Hobson was apologising in 1938; but the book he had published in 1902 cannot properly be characterised in this way.

Imperialism takes up where *The Psychology of Jingoism* left off. Part 1, on the Economics of Imperialism, began as a series of articles in the *Speaker* at the end of 1901, though conceived from the first as chapters in a projected book. Gilbert Murray read the proofs for Hobson. Hobson's analysis of imperialism, like his analysis of underconsumption – 'the taproot of Imperialism' (p. 86) – rested on what he saw as a variation of the individualist fallacy, in the familiar form of the opposition between the interests of one class and those of the community as a whole. For there was no profit to the nation from empire. The real question was: 'How is the British nation induced to embark upon such unsound business?' (p. 51)

It was unfortunate but characteristic that Hobson should initially overstate his case in terms of some clearly specious assertions. His *Speaker* articles got off to an inauspicious start, provoking a correspondence in which he was clearly worsted. It may have been this which led Hobhouse to tell Hammond that he found them 'just a little disappointing' (7 December 1901). The issues raised here, moreover, led Courtney to temper his general approval of Hobson's analysis – 'Its main thesis seems to me abundantly proved' – with the qualification that 'in his zeal for his end' Hobson had in one respect been led astray from his neo-Cobdenite path (*NC*, liii, 806).

All three editions of *Imperialism* contain the estimate, following Giffen, that British profits on external trade in 1899 stood at £18m, taken at 2½ per cent on a turnover of £765m (p. 62). These profits, Hobson maintained, could not yield 'an economic motive-power adequate to explain the dominance which business considerations exercise over our imperial policy'. Only when set against 'some £90,000,000 or £100,000,000 representing pure profit upon investments' could the economic impulse be explained (p. 63). This is clearly a fair point since it explains why, for the capitalist class, foreign investments bulked larger than foreign trade. But the first edition also contains another prominent argument on apparently similar lines. Hobson stated national income at £1700m for 1898 and the value of foreign trade as £765m. 'If we were to take the very liberal allowance of 5 per cent as profit upon this turnover of trade,' he continued, 'the annual income directly derived from our external trade would amount to a little over £38,000,000, or about one forty-fifth part of our total income' (pp. 30–1. No explanation is offered as to why Giffen's estimate of the profit margin has been doubled). From this Hobson drew the conclusion that external trade played only 'a small part in the total income of Great Britain' (p. 31). Little wonder that when this contention had appeared in the *Speaker* (in an even balder form) it had drawn the comment that Hobson's message was 'Perish our foreign and colonial trade!' (*S*, 16 November 1901). Moreover Hobson had quite properly been taken to task for stating that only 'profit' entered into national income. What Hobson had done was to pass off the capitalists' profit margin as the total gain to the community from foreign trade. As a piece of slipshod legerdemain it ranks with his propositions about 'unearned' income. It was only in the second edition of 1905 that he withdrew from his untenable position and based himself instead on the proportion of the labour force working for export.

The dispute, however, served to clarify Hobson's argument, and perhaps to modify its thrust, in two important respects, both of which have been the focus for much subsequent debate. In the first place, Hobson was led to reinstate underconsumption more prominently. Only in August 1902 was his article 'The economic taproot of imperialism' published – the coping stone not the foundation stone of the theory. It is a coherent part of the theory because underconsumption *permits* imperialism. The domestic market for consumer goods was chronically depressed, according to Hobson, but Lichtheim distorts his meaning completely by saying that: 'The implication was that such markets could be built up in the dependent tropical empire'.[31] The capitalists might indeed strike gold in the Empire, but it would remain 'bad business' for all that. For Hobson, of course, the real crux of the problem was the distribution of wealth at home, since this was in turn the economic taproot of underconsumption. By stating the principle that whatever goods were produced in the country could be bought and consumed in the country, Hobson was able to extricate himself from some of his earlier difficulties; for the dispute about the exact scale of current benefits from foreign trade was now overshadowed by the argument that in any case equivalent gains could be generated at home. But *Imperialism*, of course, as Courtney was quick to warn, now contained an argument which 'could easily be used by those who hanker after protection in support of their propositions' (*NC*, liii, 811).

Hobson himself turned the reasoning in another direction. The distribution of wealth, he maintained, evidently did not correspond to the organic law, and here, of course, he had long been brooding over the corrective measures necessary. The key lay in democratic politics and the choices polarised neatly. 'Imperialism is the fruit of this false economy; "social reform" is its remedy' (p. 93).

This is where the ideological bearings of the Hobson and Lenin theories are diametrically opposed. When Lenin came to read this chapter, Hobson's position struck him as ludicrous: 'ha-ha!! the essence of philistine criticism of imperialism', he scribbled in his notebooks.[32] Modern Marxists like Kemp have been similarly unwilling to take Hobson's proposal seriously, arguing that he wanted to change the capitalist relations of distribution without altering the relations of production on which they rested.[33] These are valid responses so long as Marxist postulates are accepted as axiomatic. Lenin acknowledged in his *Imperialism* (1917) that the reformist proposals of Hobson (with whom he lumped Kautsky) would indeed cut the taproot. 'But if capitalism did these things it would not be capitalism', he asseverated (*Works*, xxii, 241). To Lenin 'the system' was capitalism, which

[31] George Lichtheim, *Imperialism* (Penguin, 1974), p. 172.

[32] V. I. Lenin, *Collected Works* (1960–70), vol. xxxix, *Notebooks on Imperialism*, p. 414; commenting on pp. 86–7.

[33] Tom Kemp, *Theories of Imperialism* (1967), pp. 35–6.

would always control democracy; whereas to Hobson the system was democracy, which could be used to control capitalism. When he wrote that imperialism 'can only be overthrown by the establishment of a genuine democracy' (pp. 381–2), Lenin's marginal comment was 'petty-bourgeois democrat!!' (*Works*, xxxix, 432). In a sense Lenin summed up the implications of the argument rather neatly. Hobson was indeed working for a sort of 'not capitalism'.

In the second place, the *Speaker* controversy led Hobson, almost in spite of himself, to bring out the more telling side of his case on external trade and finance. 'My main argument,' he explained, 'was concerned, not with the smallness of foreign and colonial trade as compared with home industry, but with the utterly insignificant part played by our trade with territories acquired under the new Imperialism' (*S*, 16 November 1901). These overseas territories had nothing to contribute to British prosperity. Trade was minimal. 'No effective demand can come from the Soudan or Uganda, or even from Rhodesia', William Clarke had written (*CR*, lxxviii, 861); and Hobson's analysis followed the same path. Investments were certainly important *for the investors* but not for the nation. Economically, therefore, imperialism was a drain on resource. There are passages in *Imperialism* which, again taking up a favourite point of Clarke's, amplify the theme of parasitism. This was where Lenin found most to build upon; and quotation from these passages allowed John Strachey, for example, to expound 'the Hobson–Lenin Explanation'.[34] Hobson, of course, strenuously denied that the system needed imperialism, which, far from sustaining it, was a drain upon resources.

Kiernan poses the theoretical alternatives perceptively in a modern context: 'whether America's behaviour in the world is dictated by basic requirements of American capitalism as a whole, or by sectional interests able to manipulate irrational factors, from private corruption to public hysteria'.[35] The choice here is really *between* the theories of Lenin and Hobson. It follows that while it might be possible to test Lenin's contentions by measuring the net economic gain to the metropolitan country, Hobson's quite different hypothesis is less easily disposed of. It is not the case, as Fieldhouse asserts, that this 'remains critical for his explanation of tropical colonisation'.[36] Hobson did not suppose that a large share of investments went to tropical colonies. He contended, moreover, that such gains as did accrue went to a small group and did not offset the costs, which were borne by others. Imperialism was thus marginal and peripheral for Britain. But at the periphery, of course, the perspective was different; there it was of intense concern to the financial interests concerned. It is ironical

[34] John Strachey, *The End of Empire* (1959), title of ch. vi.
[35] V. G. Kiernan, *Marxism and Imperialism* (1974), p. 67.
[36] D. K. Fieldhouse, *Economics and Empire 1830–1914* (1973), p. 493.

that these distinctively Hobsonian insights should find impressive empirical support from Fieldhouse, a modern historian ostensibly countering Hobson.

Perhaps the most important part of Hobson's analysis was his account of the weight of imperialist sentiment which had no money behind it. Baran is at least correct in seeing that this is what is problematic for Hobson and that he does not move on to the Marxist solution in terms of real dispersed benefits to the ordinary man in an imperialist country.[37] Indeed, when Hobson returned to this point twenty-five years later, he explained imperialism as 'the expression of two dominant human instincts', and of the two he assigned primacy to self-assertion rather than acquisitiveness. He politely distanced himself from Leonard Woolf's attempt to demonstrate the opposite in Africa.[38] In *Imperialism* Hobson had depicted the capitalists who used their political power to promote an aggressive policy as 'employing their own genuine convictions to conceal their ill-recognised business ends' (p. 102). He allowed the businessmen and the politicians credit for their sincerity in linking high motives with the financial benefits in prospect. He surmised that this 'genius of inconsistency' was 'perhaps peculiarly British' (p. 222). There is irony here; but also a consistent application of Hobson's view of ideology. The mass support for imperialism he explained in terms of the psychology of Jingoism, to which he had already given close attention. 'The dangers of Imperialism to the Imperialist state are many', he had told the Rainbow Circle: 'Revolt, envy, stagnation at home are the most important' (minutes, 30 May 1900). Knitting together his various studies of the subject, he concluded that an alliance of vested interests was able to take advantage of the less attractive features of mass politics in order to promote a policy which it found congenial. Imperialism was rationally desired by privileged elements in society because as an economic system it brought profits to a narrow class of investors and because as a political diversion it sustained the general cause of conservatism. It followed that imperialism was best attacked, not by lopping off branches, but by cutting the taproot.

Once more, therefore, Hobson returned to the political choices at stake. Identifying himself now with the pro-Boer wing of the Liberal party, he was less troubled by the party's lukewarm attitude over the social policy to which he was committed than by its 'gross palpable betrayal of the first conditions of liberty' (p. 151) when confronted with the war issue. (Lenin's mirth, of course, could no longer be contained at this point.) No more than Hobhouse could he accept the Fabian plea for riding the imperialist tiger. The heterogeneity of Empire, he alleged, gave its government an increasingly mechanical character, whereas a 'moral basis of union' was to be

[37] Paul Baran, *The Political Economy of Growth* (Penguin, 1973), pp. 244–5.

[38] J. A. Hobson, *Free-Thought in the Social Sciences* (1926), p. 192; and p. 193n. on Leonard Woolf, *Empire and Commerce in Africa* (1920).

found above all in small nations (*IJE*, xii, 54–5). He found the same contrast in domestic affairs, where the Fabians seemed to rely 'more and more upon the wire-pulling and intriguing capacity of an enlightened few' (*CR*, lxxxi, 105).

The tide of imperialism left Hobson with an unhappy experience of the mob mind and an equally distasteful revelation of the elitist character of Fabian socialism. With invincible resilience he sought to restate a more positive view of democracy which was tempered to experience. Social psychology was pressed into service to buttress a view of the general will, which owed something to Bosanquet. Undeterred by the Jingo crowd psychology, Hobson seized on social proximity to explain 'a force of neighbourhood which for good or evil is a restraint upon all its members' (*CR*, lxxxi, 265). This common consciousness – a spirit of the hive – could as readily become a constructive force as an outlet for ignoble passions. It was the organic view of society in its political rather than its economic form. And the most essential task was now 'the welding of public intelligence and morals into an effective general will' (p. 272). But though Hobson banished elitism through the front door of the hive it kept creeping in at the back. The inequality of men's abilities was what vitiated individualist democracy. Following Ruskin, he was ready to acknowledge that 'Reverence naturally, necessarily, follows any recognition of superior powers' (p. 110). The fact that reverence was to attach to functions rather than classes did not entirely dispel the hierarchical overtones here. The formal equality of a democratic franchise was robustly defended; otherwise it would not be apparent where the shoe pinched. And the claim that more political power should go to the educated class because they were better able to use it was likewise rejected by Hobson. The argument he used against it, however, was that their amateur knowledge was irrelevant once evolution had given the democratic organism 'a specialised "head", an expert official class' (p. 271), which could act as the tool of the general will. At this stage – whether far in the future or not is unclear – Hobson surmised that 'laws, like hats, will be made by persons specially trained to make them, the people "ordering" these laws, directly or through their accredited representatives' (ibid.). This is virtually the theory of the Fabian shop, resurfacing after ten years: a more liberal theory, to be sure, than its begetters had subsequently espoused but bearing, for all that, the marks of its origin in the *nouvelle couche sociale* of the late nineteenth century.

4

The State and the Nation

(I) THE EPIC OF A JOURNALIST'S CAREER

'How I wish I could get some public work to do!' was Harold Spender's lament to Wallas (28 July 1902). 'How tired I am of this perpetual underground life of anonymous journalism! How I envy you on your School-board!' Spender had been a contemporary of Hobhouse's at Oxford, and later his lodger in Manchester when forced to take refuge as a leader writer on the *Guardian* after the *Daily Chronicle* shed its pro-Boer members of staff. Now on the *Daily News*, his aptitude for self-dramatisation made him at once a slave to journalism and an unreliable witness to his servitude. To Wallas, too, the grass often seemed greener on the other side of the hill; not so much, it must be said, in the field of journalism but in the more scholarly pastures which he was discovering. He could, as he acknowledged to Shaw, have written more books if he had regarded himself as a professional writer. They would, he supposed, have been 'about as good as J. A. Hobson's', but he was by no means sure that he would have 'got more done by means of them than by direct administration' (13 December 1908). At any rate, he remained on the London School Board until its demise in 1904 and then served for three years on the L.C.C. before making his academic post at the London School of Economics (L.S.E.) his paramount commitment. He acquired a reputation as a lecturer of effortless gifts by Shavian methods: relentless practice in front of the mirror. He made one serious effort to secure a post at Oxford in 1909, but his life in London gave him the compensation, as he once told Ada, of feeling that 'I have kept my end up in the real world, which is bigger and more important than the closed easy world of the professions or the old universities' (22 January 1913).

Hobhouse's career unfolded in a closely similar way. On leaving the *Guardian* he became secretary of the Free Trade Union, which involved him more closely than at any other time of his life with the Liberal party organisation. There was a time when he wished to become secretary to a cabinet minister and he may still have been toying with this idea. But in 1907 he too took up an established post at the L.S.E. when he became Martin White professor of sociology. The friendship between Hobhouse and Wallas grew in these years. They saw eye to eye on the education question and shared a distrust of Webb on this score. It was the Hobhouses rather than the Webbs whom the Wallases now saw on their summer holidays. They had children of a similar age; Nora Hobhouse and Ada Wallas had much in common in their cultural and political outlook. The Wallases had been living in Putney until 1906 and then in Holland Park; the Hobhouses had gone from Manchester to Wimbledon where they lived in some style. In 1911, however, the Wallases moved in to 58 Southwood Lane, Highgate, a semi-detached, late-Victorian slab of a house with room for servants at the top. And Hobhouse began house-hunting in Highgate the same year, eventually finding 7 Broadlands Road, a mock tudor mansion in an opulent, leafy road, only a few minutes away. As a close neighbour as well as a colleague, Wallas would take Hobhouse on long walks designed to improve the temper while their families rehearsed amateur theatricals. Wallas's deep discernment, long patience and broad tolerance made him the ideal friend. He wrote afterwards that Hobhouse, 'with his very human restlessness and fits of depression, was the kind of saint which modern civilisation most requires' (*NS*, 25 April 1931).

In the two years before Hobhouse went to the L.S.E. he made a further sustained effort at daily journalism. 'It is strange,' he told Scott, 'but I think I have realised the influence of the *M.G.* more since I came to London than when I was in M/c. The other Liberal papers are so futile' (18 June 1905). The proposal for a new quality daily paper, the *Tribune*, therefore caught his imagination. And though he at first supposed that he would be too socialistic for its proprietor, the Lancashire businessman and single-taxer Franklin Thomasson, he was in fact engaged as 'political editor' at £1000 a year, responsible for the leaders to Thomasson alone. As Hobhouse prophetically confided to his sister Emily, 'I am not sure that we shall always agree & there will be the eternal question of the ethics of compromise' (28 August 1905). He had some responsibility for the appointment of other leader writers and was able to engage Hammond for three nights a week, at £350 a year. These special terms, including six weeks holiday, were to obtain so long as Hammond continued to edit the *Speaker*. H. N. Brailsford became the third leader writer. Hobson, who had spent much of 1905 in Canada, was summoned home to help them.

Hobhouse was in some ways in an awkward and ambiguous position since at the end of 1905 recruitment for the *Tribune* was conducted under the shadow of the *Manchester Guardian*'s impending dissolution as a result of John Edward Taylor's death. More than one appointment to the *Tribune* was contingent on whether Scott would be able to buy the *Guardian* from the trustees. In the end he was successful. The *Guardian*'s gain may have been the *Tribune*'s loss. But the outcome was to assure Hobhouse of a privileged relationship with at least one newspaper proprietor, Scott himself, who had discovered him to be 'the best of friends'[1] during what was potentially an embarrassing crisis.

[1] Scott to Hobhouse, 18 December 1905, MGP.

For Hammond the launching of the *Tribune* was even more traumatic. In August 1905 Barbara Hammond became seriously ill, and for a month Lawrence was sleepless with anxiety. An operation revealed that the trouble was tubercular. The medical advice was that they should leave their present flat in Battersea and move to the country. This prescription of the outdoor life was something of a shock for the Hammonds, whose highly metropolitan existence was geared to Lawrence's journalism and Barbara's committee work. As things turned out, however, the opportunity for a different sort of fulfilment was opened up. 'Barbara's illness seemed a great catastrophe six years ago,' Hammond told Murray later (9 November 1911), '& yet it has enabled her to find the work & life that are most congenial & most suitable.' Plans were mooted with the Murrays to move to Guildford or to Boar's Hill, but the disadvantages, if Lawrence were to be away half the week on the *Tribune*, were appalling. With Barbara's rapid progress by the end of 1905, however, the doctors relented and decided that Hampstead would do instead. 'If you are condemned to live as a vegetable,' Barbara reflected to Mary Murray, 'then, *ceteris paribus*, it is better to be planted in a country garden than in a suburban back patch, but if you are a vegetable with a race horse chained to you, you feel that you have no business to keep him away from the races' (21 December 1905). The Hammonds found a semi-detached house, Hollycot, in the Vale of Health, an enclave on Hampstead Heath. It stood slightly apart from the other houses and had a moderate-sized garden, though not as sunny or secluded as it might have been. For it was recommended that Barbara should sleep out of doors in a shelter.

This was the beginning of the Hammonds' distinctive penchant for fresh air. Barbara was soon telling Mary Murray that 'Lawrence is, or pretends to be, most enthusiastic for open air, & wages a brave but futile war against fug at the Nat. Liberal Club' (12 November 1905). 'I wonder whether you have ever slept out in a shelter', she asked Gilbert a little later; 'it is really delightful, for you wake up naturally with the birds & dont feel cheated of sleep as you always do indoors. Also it is much warmer than sleeping under an open window. Lawrence gallantly sleeps out with me & in the small hours of the morning I hear him muttering through chattering teeth, "How *can* anyone sleep indoors?" ' (23 November 1905). Barbara's medical needs became the basis for a developing life style in which open windows, *al fresco* meals, gardening, pets, and country walks, led on to their eventual pursuit in a more authentically bucolic setting. For the moment, Hampstead Heath – 'a very good imitation of country'[2] – was the centre of their world. H. N. Brailsford, H. W. Nevinson, Vaughan Nash, Ramsay MacDonald, were all friends and colleagues living nearby. In the Hammonds' later years in the Vale of Health Hobhouse and Wallas were both within

[2] Barbara Hammond to Gilbert Murray, 24 May 1906, MP 23b.

easy walking distance. And in 1914, just after they left, Hobson moved from Surrey to the house at 3 Gayton Crescent in the centre of Hampstead where he spent the rest of his life.

The life of the *Tribune* was fraught and unhappy: likewise life on the *Tribune*, though, at least in Barbara Hammond's letters to Mary Murray, it attained moments of distinction as black comedy. She could see that the atmosphere of the editorial office was not improved by 'L.T.H.'s unfortunate way of treating fellow workers as "the dirt beneath his feet"', even though there might be extenuating circumstances to plead. 'Isn't it odd that thin skinned persons rarely realise that other skins can be thin as well?' she remarked (2 August 1906). Hobhouse had a difficult temperament at the best of times, which 1906 was clearly not. Hobson quickly discovered that he was ill-fitted for daily journalism and withdrew. Nevinson was proposed by Hobhouse for employment but vetoed by the management. Hobhouse, Hammond and Brailsford therefore constituted a highminded trio of leader writers and there were inevitable clashes between them and Thomasson's business manager, all too conscious of the losing battle for circulation. 'I left Hobhouse writing his resignation' was Lawrence's familiar report when he returned home in the small hours (ibid.). Thomasson, by his own acknowledgement, knew that he was 'an awkward fellow'; he knew this because Hobhouse had told him so (ibid., 12 August 1906). His gaucheries would provoke Hobhouse into composing a letter of resignation; Brailsford would follow suit; and Hammond would wearily join them. Then, to Hobhouse's chagrin, the difficulties would be ironed out and the pretext for resigning disappear. The 'extra special bad epidemic of Tribunitis' in November 1906 lasted so long, reported Barbara, 'that both Mr Brailsford & Lawrence are growing thin. Mr Hobhouse, who came up to talk the wretched thing over the other day seems to thrive on it for he is plumper than ever. But then I think he wld be unhappy without some sort of a crisis on' (ibid., 30 November 1906).

To Hobhouse, for whom the Hammonds retained a sardonic affection, the experience of 'the trials of journalism to a nervous temperament' seemed more immediately painful. It formed the basis for his subsequent bitter comment to Barbara that 'Journalism is a profession which may be carried on (a) by people with independent means, (b) by people without convictions' (4 September 1907). Part of the trouble, of course, was the 'double load'. There is a feeling remark in Wallas's *Great Society* – 'Hardly any man, for instance, can give six hours a day to journalism and follow it with four hours of concentrated thinking' (p. 197) – which may well draw upon the confidences of those long walks round Hampstead Heath. There was, at any rate, ample warning of the final debacle on the *Tribune*. At the beginning of January 1907 Thomasson gave the new editor, S. J. Pryor, who had become an able practitioner of the new journalism in his time with the Harmsworth press, complete control of the paper, including leaders. This was a breach of Hobhouse's contract and he resigned – as was, perhaps, intended. This left Hammond in an invidious situation since he had always held that 'the circumstances under which we agreed to work together bound us more than any ordinary agreement to consider each other's position'.[3] With Hobhouse gone, Hammond would succeed him as chief leader writer, with a larger salary. But he was, as he later put it to Thomasson, 'a politician first and a journalist afterwards'.[4] He knew that Thomasson commended Pryor for holding the opposite view; and he discovered also that the sinking *Trbune* was to be baled out by an offer of American capital. This was Hammond's breaking point. Despite Hobhouse's view that he was straining at a gnat, he felt that he had to resign too. He persuaded Murray – 'the friend whose good opinion I value more than that of anybody else outside this house' – that this was the only possible course for him to take. 'It is all drip, drip, drip', Hammond told him (30 January 1907). In 'this world of mercenary journalism' there was 'much less danger of men strutting too much than there is of their crawling too much' (ibid.).

The Hammonds found that many of their friends regarded them, so Barbara admitted to Gilbert Murray, as 'foolish cranks quarrelling with our bread and butter' (30 January 1907). They had very little to fall back upon. Lawrence got a discouraging answer from Morley when he asked about openings in the civil service. Hobhouse was better placed, with what was virtually a standing offer from Scott to return to Manchester; and this he did not need since, by the time he stopped contributing to the *Tribune* in March 1907, his academic appointment was already in prospect. Nonetheless, the months before he clinched the offer of the Martin White chair in September were for Hobhouse a distressing period, during which, as he revealed to Barbara Hammond, 'all the psychophysical trouble has deepened' (4 September 1907).

Fortunately for the Hammonds, Barbara was soon able to report to Mary Murray that 'the next book of the Epic of a journalist's career opens more cheerfully' (13 February 1907). Apparently at Hobhouse's instigation, A. G. Gardiner of the *Daily News* arranged with Hammond for him to write leaders four nights a week at £600 a year; and Brailsford was engaged on similar terms. Hammond acted as Gardiner's deputy and in the six months he was with the paper became a highly prized member of staff. His principal new colleague was Charles Masterman; and Hammond found it 'a great relief to be on a paper where people are Liberals' (ibid., 1 March 1907). The only difficulty was the air conditioning which had been installed in the offices. At the *Tribune* Hammond was often recalled sitting in the

[3] Hammond to Hobhouse, draft, n.d. (probably August 1906), HP 34, ff.95–7.
[4] Hammond to Thomasson, draft, 29 January 1907, HP 34, ff.116–17.

draught with his beard flowing and his feet muffled in straw to keep them warm. 'The *Daily News,*' Barbara observed to Mary Murray, 'talks a grt deal abt the tyranny of the squire & the parson, but the tyranny of shutting people's windows & forcing them to breathe germproof air is far worse' (ibid.). Lawrence was consequently allowed to write his leaders in a friend's chambers in the Temple nearby.

What, then, of Hammond's own health? The regime seems valetudinarian. In later years it was usually supposed that he too had had some tubercular trouble. In August 1907 he accepted the post of secretary to the Civil Service Commission at £800 a year, rising to £900. 'The work connected with the post is by no means arduous', he was assured by his friend Arthur Ponsonby (24 August 1907), who, as Campbell-Bannerman's private secretary, had plainly had a hand in the appointment. The Hammonds, as Lawrence admitted in reply, were strongly tempted 'to retreat into the haven which has been so unexpectedly offered' (27 August 1907). But, as he told Murray, there were other considerations; not only would it be 'a great sacrifice to throw away one's polemical pen, & to silence ones tongue on the controversies of the moment', but it would also be 'very unpleasant from every point of view to be treated as a Minor Scandal' (27 August 1907). This point cannot be overlooked. Was it a job of work, or merely a 'job'? When the Royal Commission on the Civil Service (of which Wallas was a member) had to consider evidence on patronage in 1912, Hammond's case was raised and the damaging imputation was made that the Liberal Government had pensioned off an invalid at a comfortable salary in recognition of services rendered. Hammond thereupon had to collect medical certificates from his friends. Both Hobhouse and Lehmann testified that Hammond had not suffered a breakdown of health in 1906–7, as had been alleged. Hammond could point to the difficulty of combining night work with sleeping in a shelter outdoors as a sufficient reason for wishing to leave the *Daily News*.

This explanation was a sufficient defence in 1912. The charge was withdrawn; an apology was made. But in 1907 he had also told Ponsonby that he was going to see his doctor 'about some nervous symptoms wh. have been rather alarming me' (27 August 1907), and he used his health as a reason in his resignation letter to Gardiner. Barbara, indeed, wrote to Mary Murray of the doctor's advice as 'the thing that really decided us', since its import was that Lawrence could hardly 'go on for many years without a serious breakdown, & he doubted whether he wld have the physique to get over it' (30 August 1907). Her comment that 'Lawrence's eyes are like saucers & what cheek remains is ashy white & people kindly tell him that he looks like a corpse' (ibid.) would have made embarrassing reading before the Royal Commission.

As he took up his new duties, therefore, Hammond was well aware that 'in all the circumstances it is a remarkable piece of good fortune'[5] More time was henceforth available for Hammond's historical work – and in this Barbara now became fully implicated. Lawrence withdrew from active politics; he was less often seen at the National Liberal Club. But, as Murray rightly predicted to him, 'There is no chance of your losing interest in politics – much less in progressive causes: you will always carry your liberalism about with you' (28 August 1907). Hammond expected, as he told Ponsonby, that 'though I shall not be able to wield a pen in controversy I shall still hope to conspire with you & Nash & Charley [Buxton] & other plotters against the governing classes' (4 September 1907). That his participation proved in the event to be less clandestine and peripheral must be attributed to the emergence of the *Nation*.

The crises of the *Speaker* and the *Tribune* had interlocked, like the commitments of the men who ran them. In August 1906 Hirst got the Rowntrees interested in financing and rejuvenating the *Speaker* and secret negotiations dragged on for the rest of the year. Hobhouse was apparently considered for the position of editor but it was Massingham who was eventually selected. In February 1907, when Hammond went to the *Daily News*, he gave up the editorship of the *Speaker*, which he had held for seven years, and on 2 March the first issue of the *Nation* appeared, in much the same format, to take its place. Massingham took over a going concern. The Oxford men who had seen the *Speaker* through the South African War stayed on. Hammond, Hirst, Hobson and Hobhouse were all on the staff; Brailsford became a regular writer on foreign policy; Nevinson contributed unsigned 'middles' whenever he was in England. And the Cambridge element became more prominent.

'Is it not amazing to find the way the Cambridge people stick together?' Barbara Hammond demanded ingenuously of Mary Murray (6 May 1906). It was true that the group responsible for the essays on *The Heart of the Empire* (1901) retained some kind of corporate identity. Charles Masterman was the leading figure here; a contributor to the *Speaker*, he became a pillar of the *Nation*. 'How I hate High Church slime', was Barbara Hammond's comment on him (ibid.). P. W. Wilson who, like Masterman, was elected to parliament while working for the *Daily News*, was equally out of favour. Yet the Hammonds' closest friends at the time were Charles Roden Buxton and his wife who also moved within this ambience of Cambridge Christian Socialism. Hammond was active in campaigning for Buxton as Liberal candidate for East Herts. in 1906. G. P. Gooch was another Trinity man whom they found congenial from *Speaker* days onward. But it was, above all, G. M. Trevelyan whom the Hammonds admired. Trevelyan, as Bertrand Russell found at this time, 'though he

[5] Hammond to F. S. Marvin, 19 September 1907, Bodleian MS Eng. Lett. d. 258, f.149.

maintains that the world is better than I think, maintains it with an air of settled gloom' (*Autobiog.*, i, 175). Accustomed to Hobhouse, the Hammonds found the Trevelyans easy company, and spent long walking holidays with them in Italy. Trevelyan's example was a direct spur to the Hammonds' historical ambitions.

In the Surrey village of Limpsfield, where Hobson had lived since 1899, he and Sydney Olivier were moving spirits in the socialist society which on occasion Scott attended. Hobson's daughter Mabel was to marry Scott's son Ted in 1907; and Ted Scott, who had come to Limpsfield to study economics at the Hobsons, went on to become Olivier's private secretary for a couple of years. Hobson was by all accounts a man of captivating charm, his earnestness alleviated by a mordant appreciation of the absurdities of humanity, including himself. 'It is his personality, as you say, which impresses one most,' Scott told Wallas, '& that unfortunately cannot be conveyed in the written word, though it is unforgettable for any one who has known him' (8 October 1926). On a visit to America Hobson wrote, in a bread-and-butter letter to Mrs E. A. Ross, that he hoped his friend had 'not lapsed into the sinful path of industry from which I extricated him', because 'I intended the smoke and beer cure to be finally efficacious but I have felt some doubt at times – the possibilities of back-sliding in a University are serious' (13 April 1903). Florence Hobson, an American herself, held sterner views – not least on matters of proper diet – as her tract *Ideals. True and False* (1917) makes abundantly clear. Her message was that 'the task of the reformer, simply stated, would appear to be *the substitution of true ideals for false in the hearts of the people*' (p. 28). But she felt some sense of grievance that the world did not rightly prize the thinkers who should be its natural leaders. 'Thinking is at a discount,' she asserted, 'and the most difficult, delicate and essentially valuable intellectual work, is the least appreciated and the most inadequately rewarded' (p. 10). The wives of most heretics have probably nursed similar feelings. Hobson's categorical exposure of the evils of unearned income would hardly have been possible but for his own unearned income, a fact of which he was well aware. As he told Scott, 'if I gave the whole of my working time to reading and writing notices of review books, I could not earn more than £200 per annum' (26 April 1905). Work on a daily newspaper was plainly no answer for Hobson, as he and his friends quickly recognised, and his precarious health would not have stood it. 'I do not blame you for getting out of journalism', he told Hammond with feeling (19 September 1907). Moreover, Florence Hobson's tubercular condition, necessitating 'the open air business', was a further difficulty. Hobson's hankering was for the editorship of a periodical, and the *English Review*, for which he drummed up contributions, seems to have been nearly within his grasp in 1909; but it eluded him. The universities remained closed to

Hobson, and he looked to the clubable life of journalism for a stimulus which others got from an academic environment.

The *Nation* lunch, which Massingham inaugurated, was not a meal but a seminar. It was held every week on Monday or Tuesday, often at the National Liberal Club, though sometimes at favoured restaurants outside. All members of staff were expected to attend and selected guests were brought in. Nevinson, who was piqued at not being invited until the middle of April 1907, initially found the lunch 'depressing & irritating & a waste of time' (Nevinson diary, 16 April 1907), but he, like the rest, mellowed as the lunch developed into a famous institution. The regular attenders were Massingham, Hammond, Hirst, Hobhouse, Hobson, Masterman, Brailsford and the Rev. W. D. Morrison. Massingham took the chair; failing him, Hobhouse; and when both were away, Hobson. It was generally acknowledged that when the editor and 'the 2 Hobs' (as Barbara Hammond termed them) were all absent the occasion was inferior.

These three saw eye to eye on general policy; Hirst, Nevinson and Brailsford were all snubbed when from time to time they disagreed, which happened chiefly over woman suffrage. When Hobhouse on occasion found himself out of sympathy with the agreed line, he would sulk in his tent and only reappear weeks later. Hobson's absences, on the other hand, were chiefly the result of illness. When Nevinson returned from a foreign trip in 1910 he found Hobson 'very frail & suddenly old' (Nevinson diary, 27 September 1910), and in the autumn of 1911 he nearly died from heart trouble. (On this occasion Wallas cheered him up by giving him a list of books on Biblical criticism to take his mind off his work.) When Hobson was present he could delight everyone with his illuminating shafts of wit.

Delicate nuances of style and feeling reinforced affinities and aversions here. Lowes Dickinson, a guest at the lunch one day, was still 'a little "Cambridge" ', despite the favourable impression he made (ibid., 19 December 1910). P. W. Wilson fared less well, being memorably denounced by his *Daily News* colleague G. K. Chesterton in a poem which ended each verse with the refrain: 'Wilson's the man that I could do without.'[6] Facing the double handicap of his Cambridge and ecclesiastical connexions, Masterman's jokes would merely make Hobhouse lose his temper. Hobson's ironically anti-clerical pleasanteries found a better audience:

> Hobson hearing proposal to transfer Bish. of London to Archbish. of York said 'Dick Turpin rode from London to York'. Morrison said that after what he had heard at the Pan-Anglican Congress he wd believe anything, & Hobson corrected him, 'You mean you would believe something' (Nevinson diary, 16 June 1908).

This captures something of the tone of the weekly gathering. (There was also, once a year, a *Nation* dinner at which the whole staff and wives

[6] Hammond to Ponsonby, 2 January 1928, Bodleian MS Eng. hist. c 668, ff.124–5.

played Progressive whist – clearly a more ponderous occasion.) The *Nation* lunch made a deep impression upon those who attended it and the high opinion which they formed of it testifies to the value of the searching discussions which took place. It is evident from reading the leading articles week by week that a common approach to a topical question had been thrashed out. Massingham's strength as an editor lay in his ability to distil coherent journalism from what might otherwise have been an obscure academic wrangle. 'Very often he said little himself,' Hammond recalled, 'and the debate would close without any definite conclusion, but its effect was apparent when his article appeared' (*H.W.M.*, p. 21).

(II) THE NEW LIBERALS AND THE LIBERAL PARTY

When Hobhouse looked back in 1908 it seemed clear to him that Liberalism had reached its ebb in 1902 and that within a year the tide had begun to flow the other way. The Tariff Reform campaign gave renewed strength to the Liberal party, which could rest its case on the received wisdom of Free Trade. Campbell-Bannerman asserted an unshakeable grip upon the leadership. The Radicals rather than the Liberal Imperialists were ascendant. Labour was brought within an electoral arrangement which was now 'progressive' rather than 'Lib–Lab' in form. All this was welcome so far as it went. But to those progressives who were in earnest about social policy the rally of traditional radicalism had a disturbingly conservative character. Masterman and William Beveridge evinced 'no hope of the Liberal Party' in the summer of 1905 (*OP*, p. 309). Even Gilbert Murray confessed himself 'unexcited about the change of Government' to Hammond when Campbell-Bannerman became prime minister (5 December 1905). The landslide electoral victory in January 1906 swept some likeminded figures into Parliament – men like Masterman, Gooch, Charles Roberts. But, remembering 1880, Wallas saw that a failure to capitalise on this victory would mean the annihilation of Liberalism. 'The modern artisan voter has shown in France and in New Zealand continuous loyalty to a progressive Government that legislates', he warned; 'he has apparently no use for a progressive Government that merely talks' (*S*, 27 January 1906).

After more than a year in office the Government had given little encouragement to such hopes. 'The Liberal Party', Hobhouse asserted, 'stands on the power which it claims to carry out the great social reforms which are twenty years overdue, and if the event shows it has not that power it must fall, and fall beyond hope of final recovery' (*CR*, xci, 6). If it failed this test of life and death, serious social reformers would clearly have to join the Labour party instead. The Government had, to be sure, shown considerable willingness to conciliate Labour; but it had spent most of its energies on an Education Bill ostensibly designed to placate its Nonconformist supporters, only to find it rejected by the House of Lords. There was no sign of a coherent strategy in its work here, still less of a firm commitment on social policy.

The king's speech in 1907 heralded legislation on Ireland and on temperance. These were, with education, the very subjects to gladden the hearts of traditional Liberals; they were also the very subjects which had stultified the Liberal party for twenty years, and, not coincidentally, the very subjects on which the House of Lords was least afraid of popular disavowal. This was a discouraging prospect. 'The true battle ground for a struggle with the Lords is the land which is so largely in their hands', Hobhouse asseverated in March 1907 (ibid., p. 317). This, it was argued, was the master question which could 'bring all the forces of democracy into line' (N, 9 March 1907). The tactical appeal of this course became a leading theme for the *Nation* that summer. The constitutional issue of the Lords' power could only be pursued by giving it a social and economic dimension. The land was a subject close to the hearts of many old Liberals; but when approached by the new Liberals as the paradigm case of a theory of unearned income it embraced a view of society which approached socialism. When Hammond wrote that it was 'impossible to touch on any of the social perplexities of modern England without coming back to the Cloaca Maxima of feudalism' (N, 6 April 1907), he was taken to task for seeming to suggest that 'the riddle of the village' was all that was meant by the land question. That the *Nation* was in any way disparaging its urban aspect was firmly denied and its relevance to progressive unity was reiterated. Such unity had in the past manifested itself 'under the dictatorship of a great cause, or the magic of a great leadership, or the menace of a great danger' (N, 20 April 1907). But such conditions were, at best, only latent in 1907.

The Government's most promising move here was in the field of finance. The *Nation* sketched a Hobsonian Budget proposal which would give provision for old age pensions a higher priority than retrenchment; and further proposed a move towards graduation of income tax by combining what was called a surtax with some remission for the 'many thousands of hard-working men, who, without taxation are hard pressed to make both ends meet' (N, 30 March 1907). This was a plea to relieve not only the social conscience of the progressive professional man but also his pocket. Here at least the Government fulfilled its supporters' hopes. Asquith's 'brilliant Budget' of 1907 set aside revenue for pensions; it made the rates at which death duties were paid more steeply progressive; and it reduced the rate of income tax on incomes under £2000 a year provided that they qualified as 'earned' rather than 'unearned'. 'The man who earns £500 a year by teaching, or writing, or in business,' the *Nation* explained (20 April 1907), 'is in a totally different position from the man who draws £500 a year from the funds.' Even so, attempts at differentiation between sources of income were not the core of the Hobsonian doctrine on ability to pay, which rested on a more categorical assumption that all high incomes contained large elements which had been 'earned' by the community rather than the individual recipient. 'Once identify "unearned" income with publicly created income, the fiscal policy of a progressive State becomes clear' (*N*, 27 April 1907). At this point the *Nation* sought to integrate old age pensions with the land and the Lords as the triple problem which the Government should solve. It now seemed clearer that 'the road to political democracy in England lies through what, in a broader sense than is usually given to the term, we may call social democracy' (*N*, 25 May 1907).

It was, therefore, 'the new Liberal finance typified in Mr Asquith's Budget' (*N*, 27 April 1907) which went some way towards redeeming what was otherwise an uninspiring Government record – 'we shall not use the word failure in connection with it' (*N*, 1 June 1907). The term Radical, which had happily covered not only Campbell-Bannerman but also pro-Boers like Morley and John Burns, now proved itself an inadequate analytical tool. The *Nation* preferred to assert that the Liberal strength came from its Left. Campbell-Bannerman had ample claims to the ambiguous encomium of the 'first Radical Prime Minister' but it was 'the much more powerful and serious Left' to which the *Nation* was really looking (29 June 1907); and in these terms it had to be acknowledged that Asquith 'identifies himself with the dominant left wing' (31 August 1907). Campbell-Bannerman had immense reserves of good will upon which to draw. He could be accounted 'with the advanced guard of Liberalism, and in the van of his Party, and, unfortunately, ahead, by no mean interval, of his cabinet'. But few of the measures of his administration went 'straight to the heart of any of the great social issues' (*N*, 12 October 1907).

Liberalism was safe with Campbell-Bannerman; but social democracy seemed as distant as ever. The challenge to the Liberals from independent Labour and socialist candidates in the by-elections of 1907 therefore pressed the *Nation* very closely. It held that Labour politicians were mistaken to think that 'their mission is to replace Liberalism and capture the modern British State'. Since the general elections had shown that 'the Labour Party waxes with Liberalism and wanes with it', it believed that 'sharp limits are set to the progress of a body so largely divorced from middle-class brains and middle-class sympathy as is the Independent Labour Party' (*N*, 6 July 1907). The insurgent socialist vote which carried Victor Grayson into Parliament in July 1907 implied, therefore, 'not a break-up of a powerful and sincere party of progress, but at the most a change in its constitution and balance of power, and a reinforcement of its more vigorous and uncompromising elements' (*N*, 27 July 1907). Socialism was a missionary movement; it occupied 'about the same relation to Liberal politics as the

Salvation Army to the regular churches' (ibid.). The moral was that in face of what was 'partly a competitive and partly a co-operative idea', Liberalism must be made more attractive (*N*, 3 August 1907). It must act as a Government of the Left by releasing the moral and intellectual force with which it was charged.

A sanguine view of events came easily to Hobson. It already seemed to him in October 1907 that for the first time the party leaders had 'committed themselves with zeal and even passionate conviction to promote a series of practical measures which, though not closely welded in their immediate purport, have the common result of increasing the powers and resources of the State for the improvement of the material and moral condition of the people' (*N*, 12 October 1907). Admittedly he tempered this claim with the warning that this was 'the last chance for English Liberalism', for unless the 'centre' of the party could be won over it was doomed. Hobson asserted that 'a small band of "righteous men"' were insufficient to save the party; but he affirmed also his belief that the real difficulties of the centre were intellectual (ibid.). Presumably, with enough articles to the *Nation* to disentangle these knotted questions the situation might yet be saved. His own strategy was to take up the charge of socialism, which would in any case be levelled at the Liberals, and show that there was much to be said in favour of socialistic schemes which brought effort and reward into a more equitable relationship.

Hobhouse's temperament was at the opposite pole. As the Government's electoral unpopularity mounted in the winter of 1907–8 his gloom deepened. When the Hammonds met him on Hampstead Heath with the news that their friend Charles Roden Buxton had lost the Mid-Devon seat, Barbara Hammond told Mary Murray that 'in ¼hr he had got the Liberals out in 3 months, & the Tories in with Milner as Colonial Secretary' (2 February 1908). He was afraid that the Liberals would not even go down with their colours flying. Campbell-Bannerman's health made his retirement imminent. To Hobhouse the prospect of an Asquith premiership was still repellent. But, as he told Scott, when the possibility of a protest was discussed at the *Nation* lunch, 'they were all against me' (n.d. but February 1908). His colleagues had, like himself, been supporters of Campbell-Bannerman. When he died in April Hammond felt that politics were suddenly the poorer – 'one feels today more than ever how much their reality during the last few years was bound up with his leadership', he wrote to Ponsonby (23 April 1908). But Hobhouse was isolated in regarding Asquith as an unacceptable successor. In March 1908 he staged a Foxite secession from the *Nation* lunch to register his anger.

Despite the introduction of the Old Age Pensions Bill the Government failed to capitalise on the new approach to social policy which Hobson had detected; he admitted that 'the zeal of Liberalism is everywhere chilled by doubts and difficulties' (*N*, 2 May 1908). To Hobhouse the twin problems of social reform and the House of Lords remained soluble but unsolved, and in passing Resolutions against the Lords in 1907 without giving effect to them, the Government had adopted 'a course which must surprise even those who took the least favourable view of their capacity' (*CR*, xciii, 354). The problem of raising finance for old age pensions, however, helped to interlock welfare issues with the established party controversy over tariffs. 'The problem of Free Trade finance,' the *Nation* concluded, 'is to show that the burden can be placed where it ought to rest – on the vast surplus wealth of the community' (20 June 1908). This in turn had a direct relevance to the electoral appeal of the Liberal party. The decision of the Miners' Federation to join the Labour party in June 1908 hammered home the message that 'Liberalism will have to fight for working-class support, to earn it, and to pay for it' (*N*, 13 June 1908). There was a long list of major reforms which could only be achieved if Liberals and Labour worked together. 'The ideas of Socialism,' Hobhouse maintained, 'when translated into practical terms, coincide with the ideas to which Liberals are led when they seek to apply their principles of Liberty, Equality and the Common Good to the industrial life of our time' (*CR*, xciii, 353). Arthur Ponsonby was strongly supported when he deprecated talk of precipitating a breach with Labour. 'It is important to remember that there is no distinct line of cleavage among the Progressives', he averred. Left-wing Liberalism shaded off into Socialism: 'Socialism is not our enemy' (*N*, 15 August 1908).

The trouble was that the Government was not socialist enough; and this in one respect for a paradoxical reason. John Burns had been appointed to the Local Government Board as a gesture to Labour but he had made it 'the most conservative office in the Government' (*N*, 24 October 1908). By compensation, Lloyd George and Winston Churchill had been given key posts in the Asquith Government and were plainly more open to argument from the Left. Churchill had announced his commitment to a wide-ranging programme of social reform in a letter to the *Nation* in March 1907. Lloyd George had the more immediate problem of framing a Budget. The *Nation* struck early with a succession of articles urging a Hobsonian attack on high (and therefore unearned) incomes by means of a more progressive scheme of direct taxation. What the *Nation* was urging upon the Government took an increasingly specific form. The distinctive part of its work should be fiscal. By employing the instrument of direct taxation more drastically, the Government should embark on a policy which would be called socialist; in a sense it would be socialist and could be defended as such; but it would also be the means of defending Free Trade. It would, too, vindicate the reformist belief that the existing economic system could be readjusted so as to work more equitably. Furthermore, if the House of Lords was thereby provoked to intervene, so be it.

There remained a tantalising gap between the intellectuals' aspirations and the Government's actual course. Hammond sardonically observed to Murray that the principle which united all reformers was 'that the panacea for all abuses is to vote against a Liberal Government' (15 October 1908). For themselves, they continued to give it the benefit of the doubt. Up to the end of 1908 the intractable problem of education continued to fix the Liberals' attention upon increasingly ill-defined principles of religious teaching. The new Education Bill, a creature of weariness and compromise, offended Wallas because it '*requires* us to teach something, and we do not know what it is' (*MG*, 1 December 1908). Designed to appease the Church, it failed even in this objective and was ignominiously withdrawn. Bertrand Russell's comment to Wallas – 'Let us hope Christianity will suffer as much as Nonconformity will' (5 December 1908) – was a despairing epitaph on the Liberals' doomed attempts to satisfy their traditional supporters during their first three years in office.

Yet feeling at the *Nation* was still that the Liberals held the master-card, if only they would play it. At the lunch on 8 December 1908 there was 'doleful debate on evil plight of Liberals who, as Masterman said, have turned every cheek in their body!' (Nevinson diary) Three days later Asquith declared that the House of Lords was the 'dominating issue', but, as the *Nation* complained, although the gun was now loaded, 'the electric spark is still wanting and the shot is not fired' (19 December 1908). Hobson confided to Smuts at this juncture that 'some of us are trying to incite them to dissolve after the Budget is got through and a Veto Bill has been put up to the Lords and rejected. But it is unlikely our attempt will be successful' (*Smuts*, ii, doc. 414). Hammond agreed with Ponsonby that it was 'really ludicrous to swear away at the Lords over our champagne & then let them kick the [Miners'] Eight Hours Bill into a cocked hat' (21 December 1908). They therefore concerted plans for Ponsonby to put down an amendment to the Address in January 1909, calling for the Government to deal with the Lords on the lines of the 1907 Resolutions. Hammond urged him on with the argument that 'if the Government *are* going to settle down to the policy of stagnation, the sooner & the more emphatically the standard of revolt is raised the better' (1 January 1909). The *Nation*'s view was that the Government would once more dissipate enthusiasm if it sought excuses for timidity. 'Socialism will then be left as the one fearless, combative party in the State, sucking up the flower of its serious youth and moral force' (20 January 1909).

The *Nation*'s complaint through the first quarter of 1909 was that the House of Lords issue 'was only dominant in the sense in which it long has been, and long will be, dominant; that is to say, in the sense that it reduced Liberal legislation to a nullity and Liberal promises to a farce' (27 February 1909). To Hobson it seemed that 'not only the fortunes of the Liberal Party.

but a far more important stake – the principles and practice of Liberalism itself lie in grave jeopardy' (*N*, 27 February 1909). True, social reform measures were now being put forward. Churchill's Trade Boards Bill was judged to contain 'in embryo, the boldest and most far-reaching of all the social reforms which separate modern constructive Liberalism from the older policy that bore that name' (*N*, 3 April 1909). Yet Churchill and Lloyd George seemed prone to regard activity in this untrodden field as an alternative rather than a prelude to a battle with the Lords. Churchill's argument, as he put it privately to Massingham, was that the constitutional attack upon the Lords, 'however vigorous, must be backed by some substantial political or social demand which the majority of the nation mean to have and which the Lords cannot or will not give'.[7]

Only with Lloyd George's Budget was the *Nation* convinced that the Government's strategy was right. Everything suddenly fell into place. Week after week the lunch was devoted to the Budget. Its various provisions were given detailed and vigorous defence. 'Under it,' the claim went, 'no man can lose any fruit of labour or organisation; the State will merely aim at detecting and applying forms of wealth which cannot be traced to individual effort at all' (*N*, 8 May 1909). The doctrine of the 'surplus' was, of course, by now familiar to readers of the *Nation*, as it exultantly pointed out; and by a happy coincidence Hobson's book *The Industrial System* was published only a fortnight after the Budget speech. It was greeted as 'a theoretical exposition of the principles of democratic finance at the very moment at which Mr Lloyd George has been administering a practical demonstration' (*N*, 29 May 1909). In attacking the Budget as socialist its critics succeeded in drawing attention to Hobson's crucial contention 'that there are elements of "social value" in almost every form of wealth' (*N*, 12 June 1909). The Budget therefore represented an economic vindication of Hobson and a political vindication of the Liberal party. 'We have not always agreed with Mr Asquith', the *Nation* confided as it now welcomed his qualities as those which the situation demanded (19 June 1909). For Hobhouse it was the Budget's foundation upon a 'new political doctrine, passing for the first time clearly from theory into practice, that frightens the rich by making politics "real"' (*N*, 26 June 1909). For Hobson, likewise, the Budget had put 'a new spirit into English politics'. He admitted modestly that 'No conscious theory of taxation but sheer political necessity has driven the Liberal party along the road which many of its members treat reluctantly' (*ER*, ii, 794). But he predicted that, even for the sceptical, 'party loyalty and hatred of Protection will secure their adhesion to the revolutionary Budget' (ibid., p. 795).

If the Budget passed then Tariff Reform would receive a body blow; this

[7] Churchill to Massingham, 22 January 1909, in Randolph S. Churchill, *Winston S. Churchill*, companion to vol. ii (1969), 872–3.

was, as the *Nation* had purposefully stated, 'the point of tactics on which the chancellor of the Exchequer will fix his eyes' (15 May 1909). By the end of July the connexions had fully sunk in. The *Nation* surveyed 'a country so changed that politicians hardly know it for the same'. The Budget had 're-heated the force out of which all Liberal triumphs grow, the enthusiasm of the main body of the party'. The campaign against it had merely advertised its class character. 'Rich men have simply wept in public on rich men's shoulders' (*N*, 31 July 1909). The popularity of the Budget arose because it had 'struck a deep vein of social injustice' (*N*, 7 August 1909). When the House of Lords lumbered into action against the Budget, the circle was complete. They had chosen 'an ideal ground of conflict for us', the *Nation* exulted (11 September 1909). 'For years every progressive combatant has prayed that the issue might be joined on the joint question of the Lords and the Land.' Lloyd George's Budget – 'the most popular Liberal measure of our generation' – had given substance to what for a generation had been merely a pipe dream (ibid.).

It was a new, and to some an unexpected, configuration of politics. Beatrice Webb had had ample warning from Halford Mackinder that, with a confrontation looming between Tariff Reform on the one side and socialism on the other, the Conservatives would prove unable to sponsor the sort of welfare measures in which she was interested. By the autumn of 1909, 'now that the cleavage between parties is chiefly a cleavage with regard to the ownership of property', she realised that he was right (*OP*, p. 433). She saw now that 'the welding together of old Radicalism and modern Socialism, which this pro-budget-anti-Lords movement means', had made it impossible to ignore party politics as an irrelevance (ibid., p. 437). Lloyd George and Churchill had intermeshed social reform with partisan manoeuvres specifically Liberal in character. In attacking laissez faire in the name of socialism, the Fabians had judged that the Tariff Reformers were more promising allies than the Cobdenites of the Liberal party. But this analysis no longer held. When the Webbs approached a sympathetic Tariff Reformer like Hewins, Beatrice recorded that, like John Morley twenty years previously, he 'talked vaguely & grandiloquently about "social reform" without being in the least aware what social reform he desired' (diary, 6 March 1911). Each particular reform was 'socialism', which was, of course, abhorrent. Conversely, for a Free Trader like Mrs Humphry Ward, suspicion of this same socialism underlay a conversion to Tariff Reform, as the drift of her *Letters to My Neighbours* (1910) makes evident. To say that protection was the last refuge of the moral regenerationists would not, however, do justice to the firm Liberal commitment of both Bosanquet and Muirhead.

The *Nation* applauded Lloyd George's Budget and at the end of October 1909 gave him its leading article to defend it. It was, however Churchill who voiced the intellectuals' concerns most effectively, and this because he had evidently taken the trouble to understand their arguments. When his collected speeches were published as *Liberalism and the Social Problem* (1909), Massingham contributed the introduction. Churchill's Leicester speech of 5 September 1909 was almost purely Hobsonian. It proclaimed 'the new attitude of the State towards wealth' and justified the Chancellor in asking not only 'How much have you got?' but also 'How did you get it?' (p. 377). The *Nation* naturally backed up this arresting proposition with a full explication. Churchill's book was hailed by Hobson as 'the clearest, most eloquent, and most convincing exposition' of the new Liberalism (*N*, 27 November 1909).

Churchill, of course, was a man of fundamentally conservative outlook though combative temperament. The question of his 'sincerity' is hardly a profitable issue. But it is interesting that Hobson distinguished between 'the strictly conservative element in the new Liberalism', which was its policy for a national minimum, and the 'creative or progressive policy', which was concerned with developing those properties of the nation's land and labour 'which private enterprise is not adapted fully to evoke and utilise'. The distinction, however, did not turn essentially upon the principle of public ownership since Hobson also endorsed Churchill's discrimination between Liberalism and Socialism. He too rested upon the concept of a 'moving equilibrium of the forces of collectivism and individualism, not a contradiction or a compromise, but a harmony' (ibid.). His own book *The Crisis of Liberalism* almost immediately went to press. Taken together with *Liberalism and the Social Problem* it is a striking indication of how closely the arguments of the politicians and the intellectuals now coincided.

The *Nation* was therefore an unqualified partisan of the Liberal party in the first General Election of 1910. 'The difficulty,' according to Hobhouse, 'has been to turn the minds of social reformers from the direct practical objects which engaged their energies to the destruction of the obstacle which confronted them all' (*CR*, xcvi, 651). But the issues were now 'larger and cut deeper than any which the country has been called on to decide since 1832' (*ER*, iv, 359). 'We may never again get so clear an issue to fight on', maintained Wallas (*N*, 11 December 1909), who thought that the Budget had been a bold step in the right direction. Hobhouse found himself giving wholehearted endorsement not of some abstraction like 'the better mind of Liberalism' but of the actual Liberal party with Asquith at its head. 'Few things,' he reflected, 'are more remarkable than the way in which a practicable social policy commanding wide agreement has crystallised itself in the last two or three years' (*ER*, iv, 369). Hobhouse was as persistently led by his intellect to hope as by his temperament to despair. Hobson's more equable outlook had proved a more reliable pointer to trends in politics which gave the intellectuals not only a political doctrine but a political party. Perhaps some sense of this led Hobhouse to write of 'the beginnings of a reconstruction to which Mr Hobson's writings have contributed more than any single intellectual cause' (*N*, 8 January 1910).

(III) THE ROLE OF THE STATE

For the moment the apostles of the new Liberalism were triumphant. They believed that they had given to party what was meant for mankind. This euphoria was transient. Within a couple of months Asquith's tactics had apparently led the Liberals into an impasse, and Nevinson recorded that demands for 'his death or resignation for breach of trust' dominated the *Nation* lunch (diary, 22 February 1910). But such vicissitudes could not obscure the revelation of the Liberal party's potential. It had emerged as the agent of what Hobson had defended as socialism in 1907 and what he claimed as the new Liberalism in 1909: a change in terminology partly to be explained by the *Nation*'s tactical view that there was 'nothing to be gained by waving the Socialistic red flag in the sight of an easily-roused John Bull' (6 February 1909). What, then, was the conception of the state that was endorsed? In a perceptive comment on his 1907 articles, which Hobson approved, E. O. Post advanced the distinction between two aspects of socialism. He argued that if the Liberal party adopted the first, a programme of anti-capitalism, it would no doubt break up; but adoption of the other, anti-destitutionism, would force 'a clear vital issue between Progressives of all kinds and Conservatives of all kinds' (*N*, 19 October 1907).

This is the issue which the Royal Commission on the Poor Law faced from its earliest days. It had been set up at the end of 1905 and the commissioners included Beatrice Webb, Helen Bosanquet and C. S. Loch. Already by May 1906 Beatrice Webb noted Loch's anger over the fact 'that the enquiry is drifting straight into the *causes of destitution* instead of being restricted to the narrower question of granted destitution is inevitable, how can we best *prevent pauperism?*' (*OP*, pp. 341–2) By the end of 1907 she herself had come to see the necessity of a double scheme of reform. This involved, in the first place, the break-up of the Poor Law; and by May 1908 a hundred copies of her proposals had been printed and distributed to politicians and journalists. Secondly, she also proposed a 'more revolutionary' scheme for dealing with unemployment, and this she hoped to circulate through Churchill at the Board of Trade.

From an early stage, therefore, Beatrice Webb was committed to producing a minority report. Her tactics had precipitated a breach with the C.O.S. element in the Commission. 'Mrs Webb comes here, to drive wedges between us', Helen Bosanquet reportedly complained (Webb diary, 13 January 1908). So Beatrice Webb took to staying away, preferring to cultivate the interest which the new Prime Minister and Churchill were taking in her plans. The tendency of the Webbs' thinking was becoming known at a time when the Government was highly receptive to well-formulated ideas on social administration. But party considerations dictated that reforms would also be judged by two political considerations: congruence with Liberal principles and acceptability to the working class. The *Nation* held a brief to speak on the first and the Labour representatives on the second.

In the summer of 1908 the Webbs' scientific penchant for using the 'expert' was already exciting the disquiet of the *Nation*. 'Officials secure of their posts,' it growled, 'sitting in the remote recesses of an intricate system, even when chosen for special abilities, tend to become arbitrary, slow, mechanical, unduly conservative, and not infrequently corrupt' (13 June 1908). The Liberal party was warned, therefore, to scrutinise with the utmost closeness any proposal to remove Poor Law administration from representative bodies to paid officials. 'The expert official is a god out of the machine to some social reformers', the *Nation* hinted (4 July 1908). The piecemeal disclosure of the Webbs' plan was taken a stage further in August 1908 when a version of the first part, for the break-up of the Poor Law, was published in *The Times*. This leak marked the final separation between Beatrice Webb and her colleagues. It permitted the *Nation* to comment more specifically on what is glimpsed behind the veil; its reaction was hostile and it hoped for 'something rather more human and less mechanical' in the Commission's final report (22 August 1908). Crompton Llewelyn Davies's surrealistic allegation that the Webbs employed a pauper with a wooden leg to drill holes for potatoes catches this mood.

The second part of the Webbs' scheme, for the organisation of the labour market, also met with political objections. As finally drafted, the plan had four main aspects, to be co-ordinated through a Ministry of Labour. First, labour exchanges should be established. Second, the demand for labour should be regularised by a ten-year programme of public investment, applied in an anti-cyclical way. Third, a voluntary system of unemployment insurance should receive state aid. Finally, for the residual class of unemployed, maintenance should be offered, but only on condition that the men submitted to such remedial training as proved necessary. For those in default, detention colonies were to be established. In October 1908 Churchill made an eloquent plea in favour of 'that necessary apparatus of insurance and security' needed to deal with unemployment (*Lib. & Soc. Prob.*, p. 198). To Beatrice this suggested that 'he has mastered the Webb scheme' (*OP*, pp. 416–17); but, as she discovered, while labour exchanges might be instituted without too much difficulty, the same did not hold of the rest of the plan. The insurance principle was all too liable to divert the Liberals away from what she regarded as essentials. When Lloyd George talked of extending national insurance to cover invalidity as well, Beatrice Webb was vehement that any such grant 'ought to be conditional on better conduct and that any insurance scheme had the fatal defect that the state got nothing for its money – that the persons felt they had a right to the allowance whatever their conduct' (ibid., p. 417). She began to realise how deficient Liberal conceptions were in these matters; at least 'there would be no nonsense about democracy' if the Tories had to implement the scheme (diary, 15 November 1908). The dependence of maintenance upon submission to conditions laid down by the state was the crux of the Webbs' proposals. They discovered, however, that this notion was scouted by the Labour representatives who went so far as to suggest 'unemployment benefit paid by the state *with no conditions*' (OP, p. 419).

The Webbs' Minority Report was in proof by January 1909 and they took care that it was in the hands of sympathetic reviewers before publication. Wallas was sent a copy. The *Manchester Guardian*'s copy went to Hobhouse, who may also have been briefed by Webb. Both of them weighed in against the Majority Report, with its elaborate arrangements for buttressing Poor Law institutions with voluntary committees. To Wallas it was evident that 'public assistance should have less and not more of the traditional atmosphere of English "charity" – organised or unorganised'. He deprecated 'the spectacle of "well-to-do" ladies who have never earned a shilling in their lives' having a further opportunity to play Lady Bountiful.[8] To Hobhouse it seemed that the Minority were 'working towards a different conception of the duty of the State in relation to poverty' (*MG*, 18 February 1909). The central idea was that of anticipating and preventing destitution. He paraphrased the remedy of the Minority as 'to get rid of the conception of destitution as the basis of relief, to recognise that there are many distinct forms in which, without sinking to destitution, without the slightest degradation or the least forfeiture of independence, individuals may stand in need of public assistance' (*MG*, 1 March 1909). This was the side of the recommendations which he urged most warmly.

But the Minority Report, having broken up the Poor Law, proposed to stick it together again through the co-ordinating agency of a Registrar. He was to be 'an officer of high *status* and practical permanence of tenure' (Cd 4499, iii, 410). To Hobhouse he must have sounded rather like a Balliol man: just the thing to trigger off his deepest suspicions of Fabianism. It may be a mark of how efficiently Webb had nobbled him, or of how much he detested Lady Bountiful, that Hobhouse restrained himself here to a moderate amendment of the Minority Report. The Registrar, he insisted, should be responsible to the local government representatives who appointed him. This was his chief reservation. He did not cavil at the Webbs' plan for submitting the able-bodied unemployed to compulsory retraining as a

[8] Letter to *Morning Post*, 20 February 1909, WP 33.

condition of maintenance. Hobhouse acknowledged that commitment of the obdurate worker to a detention colony would have to be 'very carefully scrutinised', but he firmly defended the principle on the ground that 'the more the State is ready to assist him in real need the more unhesitatingly it can demand of him that he should respond with an effort of his own' (*MG*, 15 March 1909).

This brisk and bracing conclusion in fact reflects a rather fine distinction. The new Liberals were engaged in an assault upon laissez faire and the shibboleths of individualism. Thus they asserted that it was no use preaching thrift to the working man as a remedy against the contingencies of life. 'But what about his "character", the splendid stimulus such effort of saving will apply?' it was asked rhetorically. 'Well, our answer is that just now he cannot afford this character' (*N*, 2 January 1909). It was the unrealistic nature of the demand, and therefore its hypocrisy, to which objection was taken. It was rather uncritically accepted that indiscriminate outdoor relief before 1834 had led to a situation in which it had been necessary 'to preach the virtue of industry, thrift, and self-reliance', whatever the cost. 'As compared with the flesh-pots of dependence, the bread and water of economic freedom was worth winning, though it meant a hard struggle and a spare life' (*N*, 4 July 1908). This appeal to history, of course, was extremely indulgent to the old Liberalism. The issue was better resolved by making the claim hypothetical – to say that the principles of 1834 might have been the best course 'under certain imaginable economic circumstances' which did not in fact exist (*N*, 6 March 1909). On either reading the explanation for the change of course was the same. 'The newer methods of the State towards poverty have arisen because none of these conditions are fulfilled, nor are they in a fair way to be fulfilled' (ibid.). As things stood, therefore, such measures as old age pensions implied 'a sensible addition to the self-respect of the poor, and a spur to their self-dependence' (*N*, 9 January 1909). Hence the real presumption is that, although character cannot be expected to triumph against overwhelming odds, once the odds have been adjusted the expectations can be reimposed.

The Minority Report was not a socialist document and the Majority Report did not speak for the C.O.S. Even so, the issues between them were argued in terms of a familiar debate, going back to the 1890s, over the priority of 'economic' and 'moral' reform. The moral reformists stood ranged against the moral regenerationists. What Hobhouse had done for the *Manchester Guardian* Muirhead did for the *Birmingham Daily Post*, and his articles were republished under the title *By What Authority?* (1909). To him the hypotheses of the two Reports seemed 'to differ from one another in merely laying the emphasis on opposite but complementary sides of the truth' (p. 71). But where they differed, as in the analysis of drink as a cause of pauperism, the Majority seemed to him to have a decided advantage. Their psychology was better. They saw that it was 'fatally easy by our methods of public as well as private assistance to undermine individual energy and self-respect, and *thereby* weaken the forces that make for social solidarity' (p. 32). Predisposed against the Minority Report, then, he found himself suspicious of 'such short cuts to efficiency as are represented by the "Registrar"' (p. 79), with his 'almost sultanic powers over the lives and liberties of those whose cases are submitted to him' (p. 74). Muirhead was by no means averse to Poor Law reform; in fact his emphasis on the amount of common ground reflected not only the Idealist quest of the higher synthesis but also a shrewd political judgment. 'I rather grudge having to differ among ourselves just now', he told Wallas (24 October 1909). But when his tract was reissued, he reiterated in a postscript that there was 'no way of escaping the conclusion that the defects of a social organisation rest in the last instance on defects of character' (p. 88).

So long as the argument was put in those terms, the new Liberals were bound to stand on the other side. Beatrice Webb wrote to Wallas at the end of April 1909 broaching the idea of a committee in favour of a crusade against destitution on the lines of the Minority Report. 'Do you think Leonard Hobhouse & J. A. Hobson would join?' she asked. 'It seems rather an opportunity of drawing together forces which are, at present, split up & even unnecessarily hostile to each other' (24 April 1909). This was the beginning of what Beatrice described as their 'campaign of forcing public opinion' (diary, 15 May 1909), and it got off to a promising start. By June Beatrice could record that 'many progressives who have shunned both us and the Fabian, are trooping in to the National Committee [for the Break-Up of the Poor Law] – Hobhouse, Hobson, Gooch, Wallas, Gilbert Murray & H. G. Wells & others' (ibid., 18 June 1909). In this company, it would be surprising if Hammond's name is absent for any reason other than his officially non-partisan civil service status. Beatrice Webb perceived three forces behind the opposition they encountered. There was the vested interest of some doctors; there was 'the busy-body relief-of-distress philanthropist' to whom the Majority Report gave an honoured role; and finally there were 'the Hegelians, led by Bosanquet, clinging to the "category of the destitute"!' (*OP*, p. 432)

The most insidious enemy of the Minority Report, however, was the Government. Reform of the Poor Law was not formally removed from its agenda but the reasons for tackling it were systematically undercut. Instead of compulsory labour exchanges and voluntary insurance, Churchill pledged the Government to voluntary labour exchanges and compulsory insurance (in certain trades at first). He claimed the two systems as complementary since the labour exchange established a test of willingness to work. 'If I had to sum up the immediate future of democratic politics in a single word I should say "Insurance",' he said (*Lib. & Soc. Prob.*, p. 309). It was a word which chilled the Webbs' hopes. There were good, sound, pusillanimous reasons for the Government to avoid implementing the Minority Report. But insurance was not only less socialist than the Webbs' proposals: it was also more liberal. It is an ironical reflection on Churchill's successful assimilation of liberal principles – on which the *Nation* kept congratulating itself in 1909 – that it was left to him to state this case. Not only did he demonstrate his complete intellectual independence from the Webbs but also his ability to break through any purely tutelary relationship. His 'Notes on Malingering' of June 1909 offered a justification of the insurance principle because it gave an *entitlement* to benefit to a man who had qualified through his own contributions. It avoided 'mixing up moralities and mathematics'.[9] Churchill was pressing for the application of this principle to certain aspects of administration. On these he lost the battle: under the National Insurance Act workmen dismissed for misconduct or leaving 'without just cause' were disallowed benefit for a six-week period. But he had won the war in the very adoption of an insurance scheme.

Beatrice Webb was not so churlish as to refuse to acknowledge this. Through some process which she could not fully comprehend, her scientific schemes had fallen foul of the vulgar imperatives of party politics. Social reform had become enmeshed with the Lloyd George Budget and this in turn with the House of Lords issue and the fate of the Liberal party. 'What the Government shirk is the extension of *treatment* and *disciplinary supervision*', she commented scathingly on the National Insurance Bill (OP, p. 468). She had to face the fact that 'public opinion has got firmly into its silly head that insurance has some mystical moral quality' (ibid., p. 470). Sidney Webb found it easier to reconcile himself to this alternative approach than did his wife. 'Hitherto,' she reflected, 'Sidney and I have kept ourselves almost exclusively for the work of Expert guidance of the Expert' (diary, 12 March 1911). Perhaps the time had come to reconsider.

Hobhouse retained a preference for the 'Ghent scheme' rather than that finally adopted, which smacked to him of 'the old patriarchal conception of the duty of the employer'.[10] He was accordingly half inclined sometimes to dismiss the National Insurance Act as a 'big measure of essentially conservative social reform', which had found the workers 'not altogether indisposed to sell their birthright for a mess of pottage'.[11] But while remaining critical of the Act's finance, which threatened to tax employment rather than the unproductive surplus, by the time he prepared a third edition of *The Labour Movement* (1912), he came to think that the other side of the Insurance scheme 'deserves more praise than it has received'.

[9] See Bentley B. Gilbert, *The Evolution of National Insurance in Great Britain* (1966), p. 272.
[10] Introduction to I. G. Gibbon, *Unemployment Insurance* (1911), p. vi.
[11] *Questions of War and Peace* (1916), pp. 9, 105.

By securing 'certain definite benefits as a matter of indefeasible right' it was 'the true break-up of the Poor Law' for the great majority. 'To assure them a certain definite provision, small as it may be, as their own is to treat them as independent citizens', Hobhouse proclaimed. 'To send them to plead their case before inspectors of committees, be these never so benevolent, is to reduce them to dependence' (pp. 139–40).

The outcome was less galling to those who shared the Government's general outlook and priorities than to the Webbs. Churchill's public adoption of compulsory insurance in May 1909 was greeted by the *Nation* 'not, indeed, as a radical cure, but as a medicine operating on some of the most distressing symptoms of the disease' (29 May 1909), despite its previous advocacy of a voluntary system. By the autumn of 1909 the whole position was viewed as 'indissolubly bound to the enforcement of the new taxation to which the Government is committing the nation' (25 September 1909). To Wallas it seemed that the coincidence of the Poor Law Report and the Budget created a peculiarly good opportunity for 'a really fruitful discussion of social economics' which might illuminate the whole question of 'ability to pay'.[12] In naturally transposing the problems of the Poor Law in this way, Wallas showed the way his mind had been working since the turn of the century. For the Webbs the Fabian theory of rent had led to an increasingly institutional approach to collectivism; but for Wallas it pointed to fiscal solutions. 'The problem of "rent" is ultimately the problem of the right incidence of taxation', he affirmed in 1903.[13] The framework he had adopted was no longer Fabian but Hobsonian.

The four recommendations of the Minority Report for dealing with unemployment had been labour exchanges, which were enacted; insurance, which was extended; conditional maintenance, which was evaded; and regularisation of the demand for labour. This was in some ways the most intriguing of the Webbs' proposals. At the time it was occasionally suggested that the Government's Development Bill was functionally equivalent to it. It has also understandably caught retrospective attention with the fashion for hailing any hint of a counter-cyclical policy as an anticipation of Keynes. This claim is also, of course, often made for the work of Hobson, with special reference to *The Industrial System*.

The Minority Report, to be sure, raised the possibility that government capital expenditure might be concentrated unevenly in the years of cyclical trade depression. This was not a novel proposal and it was hedged about with disavowals of relief works. 'All that the state would do would be to steady the market for efficient labour', Beveridge had explained in advocating this step in 1906 (*SP*, iii, 329). The Minority Report improved on his argument by suggesting that if the expenditure were financed by loans

[12] 'Holiday thoughts on ability to pay', *Clare Market Review* (October 1909), pp. 3–6.
[13] Wallas to Shaw, 'Credo', draft, n.d. (probably January 1903), WP 10.

there could be no corresponding loss of employment elsewhere through increased taxation. What captivated the Webbs was the bargain that could be gained for the nation because it was cheaper to execute public works during a depression. 'It is in the lean years of the trade cycle, when business is depressed, that most capital is Unemployed, and the Bank rate is at its lowest.' Borrowing became cheap. If the Government, 'when no one else is willing to embark in new undertakings, borrows some of the capital that is lying idle and unused', it could produce 'a real addition to industry' (Cd 4499, iii, 661–2). This interesting comment on the cost-effectiveness of public investment might well have been generalised into some insight about the relation of saving to investment in the economy as a whole. But it was left at that point, and the Webbs did not really suggest that public expenditure would have more than a once-for-all impact upon the economy. Their analysis lacked a dynamic dimension.

This is where Hobson had the advantage. He always maintained that the economy should be studied as 'a going concern'. Beveridge only seemed to him to understand the problem 'up to a certain point', while Beveridge in turn acknowledged that Hobson 'possesses a peculiar economic theory which I am unable to follow' (*SP*, iii, 332, 341). In his major work, *The Industrial System* (1909), and in the popular version, *The Science of Wealth* (1911), Hobson was concerned with the economics of growth; and in dealing with unemployment he restated his view on underconsumption. Thus, while he sympathetically commended the proposal of the Minority Report, there was a real gulf between the thinking that underlay it and his own. To him the crux was that rising consumption by wage-earners was 'necessary in order to take out of the industrial system the increasing quantity of consumables which its growing powers enable it to produce' (*Sc. of Wealth*, pp. 115–16). The consistent idea here is that consumption must 'validate' the amount of saving in the economy. As he once put it in a private letter to Samuel, 'if an attempt is made to persist in over-saving, all markets are glutted and unemployment of capital and labour ensues' (n.d., ? 1903). Hobson usually argued the proposition that there was an *actual* excess of capital, taking the form of overproduction; or alternatively that '"savings" which lie idle in banks' were responsible for unemployment (ibid.).

In chapter xviii of *The Industrial System* Hobson went further by claiming that idle balances were also irrelevant. Instead he suggested that when an economy in equilibrium attempted to over-save, although some part of the excess capital might be hoarded, most of it would be accounted for otherwise. Reduced consumption would reduce all real incomes, diverting some existing savings into an attempt to maintain living standards. So the new 'saving' was absorbed – but from the standpoint of the community it represented no additional saving at all. The desire to save more would merely reduce aggregate income until automatic checks came into play.

The resultant unemployment was 'due to the attempt to save a larger proportion of the general income than the present state and prospects of the industrial arts render feasible' (p. 294). The desired over-saving would thus not actually be accomplished because 'any attempt at over-saving will be checked when it has gone a certain way, by means of the under-production and shrinkage of income it inevitably produces' (ibid.). Read in the light of Keynesian economics it is naturally tempting to jog Hobson's elbow here and to convert his hints and suggestions into a rigorous theory. His ideas certainly have a macro-economic sophistication wholly lacking in the Webbs' account; but even so they hardly amount to an anticipation of the *General Theory*, or even the *Treatise on Money* (see below ch. 7, iii).

Hobson's concerns were different. Unemployment, he held, could certainly be attacked through state action insofar as taxation succeeded in 'converting surplus income, either into wages spent in raising the standard of comfort of the workers, or into public revenue spent in raising the standard of public life' (*Ind. Sys.*, p. 297). Hobson preferred to analyse this 'surplus' in relation to underconsumption, but it was the surplus not underconsumption that was the central organising idea. He distinguished the 'productive surplus', which was organically necessary, from the 'unproductive surplus', the distribution of which accorded with no organic principle. The productive surplus covered the costs of the maintenance and replacement of the factors of production; and it was needed, too, to provide the necessary stimulus for growth. The unproductive surplus was the unearned income of the community. It alone disrupted the natural harmony of the industrial system. 'The only true bone of contention,' he alleged, 'the only valid cause of conflict between capital and labour, land, ability, is the unproductive surplus' (*Sc. of Wealth*, p. 82). It trenched upon the costs of growth and robbed other factors of production of their due reward. Trade unionism and redistributive taxation pointed the way forward. The fiscal emphasis of the new Liberalism was again reinforced.

In 1914 Wallas admitted that he was unable to accept Hobson's theory of underconsumption. In 1911 the Hammonds acknowledged a heavy debt to the *Industrial System*, also without showing any taint of this famous heresy. Even Hobhouse, who had read the book in proof, found this part of the analysis questionable – it was the Hobsonian doctrine of the surplus which he seized on as the indispensable contribution of 'this most original and independent of our economists' (*Lab. Mov.*, 3rd edn, p. 7). In *Liberalism* (1911) Hobhouse based himself squarely upon it in asserting 'the equation of social service and reward' as 'the central point of Liberal economics' (p. 209). The surplus was truly a social creation and the proper function of taxation was to secure for social use all wealth that did not owe its origins to the efforts of living individuals. Conversely, 'the share of personal initiative, talent, or energy in production' needed adequate recognition (p. 212).

For Hobson the rationale of the industrial system was primarily as 'a great co-operative society of consumers' (*Sc. of Wealth*, pp. 54–5). Its incipient harmony was bedevilled by problems of distribution. Too much wealth was unearned. It was the task of Liberalism to effect a redistribution which would give appropriate incentives for useful work. Hobhouse hoped that 'a Socialist who conceives Socialism as consisting in essence in the co-operative organization of industry by consumers' would be led by his consideration of 'the psychological factors in production' to much the same conclusion (*Liberalism*, p. 212). Under socialism or capitalism the problem was the same: to discover a distribution of rewards which would be accepted as fair. Assent and consent were crucial. So the economic problem merged into the political. 'Liberalism condemns all Socialism that is not truly Liberal in the sense of being a genuine expression of the popular will', wrote Hobson in commending Hobhouse's book (*MG*, 13 June 1911). In propounding this principle they hoped to show that 'the growing co-operation of political Liberalism and Labour, which in the last few years has replaced the antagonism of the 'nineties, is no mere accident of temporary political convenience, but has its roots deep in the necessities of Democracy' (*Liberalism*, pp. 212–13).

5

Human nature in politics

(I) FURTHER INTERVALS OF HUMAN NATURE

Hobhouse's son Oliver later wrote that 'Father was immensely conservative in some ways, and would not take up with a reversal of the old order of things' (*Memoir*, p. 90). One example was his hostility to motoring. This was a favourite grievance on the *Nation*, and opposition to the Road Board was its main reservation over Lloyd George's constructive approach to national finance. Motor cars manifested an intrusion upon the amenities of the countryside by an unfeeling privileged class; it was only after Hobhouse bought one himself that he was able to contain his outrage. On bloodsports he felt so strongly that it precluded the temptations of taking up hunting. The Hammonds were passionately committed on both these issues, and indeed concern for animals seemed to them an indispensable part of a humane outlook upon society. As Samuel put it to Wallas, 'the same temperament which makes a man a really sincere social reformer often also makes him abstain from "sports" which involve suffering to animals' (31 January 1917). There was an incident in 1911, in which Shaw was supposed to have boasted of running over thirteen dogs in his car, which seemed to make all the connexions explicit. 'Mr Hobhouse came over yesterday afternoon in a white heat of indignation about it', Barbara Hammond wrote to Gilbert Murray. 'I suppose all motorists lose their moral sense but very few acknowledge it so openly & brutally as Mr Shaw' (12 March 1911).

In the field of literature Hobhouse had a special admiration for the novels of George Eliot. He discerned in her work 'the moral conservativism of the Victorian age, with its exaltation of self-sacrifice and all the traditional virtues as means not to salvation in another life but to social harmony in this life'.[1] It seemed to him to reflect no credit upon his own generation that her reputation should have declined. At the time Hobhouse saw current literary developments as an insidious threat to his values, yet in retrospect the almost hegemonic liberalism of Edwardian men of letters is more striking. The three novelists above all who touched on the concerns of the *Nation* group were John Galsworthy, Arnold Bennett and H. G. Wells.

It was of Galsworthy that Massingham once announced to the *Nation*

[1] *The World in Conflict* (1915), pp. 43–4, cf. 34–5.

lunch: 'I have found a man, a big man, a writer on the grand scale!' (H.W.M., p. 155) The Hammonds were personally closest to him and he dedicated one of his novels to them. They had taken a strong and immediate liking to the first and most astringent of the Forsyte books, *The Man of Property* (1906), with its indictment of the myopia of the possessing class. A 'Forsyte' was diagnosed as a man who was a slave of property to an unusual degree. 'He knows a good thing, he knows a safe thing, and his grip on property – it doesn't matter whether it be wives, houses, money, or reputation – is his hall-mark' (Pt. 2, ch. x). *In Chancery* (1920) retrospectively raised the Boer War to the status of myth in working out this theme. It was used as an analogy to the relationship between Soames and his estranged wife Irene, who was repudiating his legal suzerainty. Soames of course, defended the war by saying 'a contract is a contract', whereas in his presence young Jolyon felt himself 'boxed up with hundreds of thousands of his countrymen' and revolted by 'their intense belief in contracts and vested rights, their complacent sense of virtue in the exaction of those rights' (Pt. 1, chs. xii, xiii). 'Domination of peoples or of women!' he reflects. 'Attempts to master and possess those who did not want you!' (Pt. 2, ch. xii) For the Forsytes, with their instinctive support of the war, there could be no 'rape' of the Transvaal because it had once acknowledged suzerainty, and likewise no 'rape' of Irene because she was married to the man of property.

Literary acclaim came to Bennett with *The Old Wives' Tale* (1908). Massingham considered it one of the really great novels of the previous thirty years and asked him to become a contributor to the *Nation* at the end of 1909. Fond of calling himself a socialist, Bennett found his political niche with the new Liberalism of the 1910 elections, which he sat out in a mood of partisan anxiety in the dissonant surroundings of a Brighton hotel, 'obsessed by the thought that all this comfort, luxury, ostentation, snobbishness and correctness, is founded on a vast injustice to the artisan-class'.[2] It was here that he wrote the early section of *Clayhanger* (1910), including the fiercely ironical account of the boyhood of Darius Clayhanger in the potteries in the nineteenth century. This episode drew a warm allusion from the Hammonds when they published *The Town Labourer*, and Bennett, in turn, when he read their book, regretted that he had not been able to make use of their chapter on child labour in his novel. 'I'm reading *Clayhanger*', Ada Wallas wrote to Graham. 'It would interest thee to begin it. The boy's sudden revolt from the acceptance of the second rate standard in all his provincial surroundings, is so well done' (28 August 1911). This was a theme close to Wallas's heart. He was always moved by the struggle of the underprivileged for the sort of intellectual liberation which he had fought for as a young man. When he saw copies of the new

[2] *The Journals of Arnold Bennett*, ed. Newman Flower, i (1932), 350.

Home University Library series, of which Murray was an editor, in the shops in industrial areas he took heart from these signs of vigorous mental life and felt his feet upon a firm foundation. Edwin Clayhanger asserted himself against a community that scorned intellectuality by attending the young men's debating society which met at 'the preposterous hour of 6 a.m.' on Sundays. 'They considered themselves the salt of the earth, or of that part of the earth. And I have an idea that they were' (Bk. 1, ch. xv). Wallas too had an idea that they were.

The impact of Wells's novels stemmed not merely from the fact that they were close to life but that they were unnervingly close to his own life and that of his immediate circle. *The New Machiavelli* (1911) sketched the world of the publicists through the thinnest veil of fiction. Willersley (Wallas) is one of the few sympathetic characters, and one of the central episodes is a version of the walking holiday in Switzerland which Wells took with Wallas in 1903, when they discussed the problems of democracy. To some extent Wells took up in the Fabian Society where Wallas had left off, but his own vague schemes for its reform were promulgated with little tactical aptitude or, indeed, consistent sense of direction. When he sent the Webbs his *Modern Utopia* (1905), with its elitist supersession of democratic methods, he claimed with justice: 'The chapters on the Samurai will pander to all your worst instincts' (*OP*, p. 305). Yet this mechanical conception of progress found no place in *In the Days of the Comet* (1906), where social transformation rested upon the change of heart and mind which the comet had wrought. It is not surprising that his challenge to the old gang in 1906–7 was parried with nonchalant ease, and the professionalism of Shaw and Webb earned his rueful respect. 'They are the least diabolical of men', he wrote in their defence against Hobhouse. 'To regard Webb, for example, as a Machiavellian statesman is ridiculous' (*N*, 6 April 1907). This disclaimer reads ironically from the author who most compellingly portrayed the Webbs in just this light only three years later.

'Year by year', Wells had once told Wallas, 'my Christian training scales off me & I get more & more purely physiological with regard to sexual intercourse' (19 September 1902). In *The New Machiavelli* the hero's sexual adventures provoke Willersley's impatient disapproval. '"When we found that League of Social Service we were talking about," he said with a determined eye upon me, "chastity will be first among the virtues prescribed"' (Bk. 2, ch. i, 13). Wallas was in fact not overtly censorious of Wells. While he thought *Tono-Bungay* (1909) very good, however, to Barbara Hammond it left 'such a nasty taste in yr mouth quite unlike his other books'. The reason was, as she explained to Mary Murray, that 'like so many other "advanced" writers Wells has taken to treating all the phenomena of love à la Tom Cat' (13 March 1909). The evidence for this is hard to find. 'For all that is cardinal in this essential business of life she had one inseparable epithet – "horrid"' (Bk. 2, ch. iv). Was this enough to trigger Barbara Hammond's revulsion? Beatrice Webb had some time since discovered that *In the Days of the Comet* ended 'with a glowing anticipation of promiscuity in sexual relations' (*OP*, p. 359). In some quarters, then, the ground was well prepared for the iniquity of *Ann Veronica* (1909). The shock here, however, derived less from the actual story than from the fact that it was true. It was too transparent an apologia for Well's seduction of the daughter of two well-known Fabians. 'Ann-Ver-onica. Am-ber-reeves', Beatrice Webb observed incredulously (diary, 4 October 1909); and she acknowledged that 'the damning review of his book in the *Spectator*' was really 'an exposé of his conduct under the guise of a criticism of a "Poisonous Book" written clearly with knowledge & intent' (27 December 1909). After this, Wells's work could hardly sink lower. With an orthography which she would have resented being described as Freudian, Beatrice Webb noted that he was 'now engaged in satyrising us in *New Machiavelli*' (diary, 4 October 1909).

In Beatrice Webb's eyes the Wells escapade only brought out the worst in Shaw, whose dramatic progression from *Mrs Warren* to the 'almost farcical impression of the Rabbit-Warren as part of human life' in his latest work had often displeased her (diary, 27 December 1909). By standing outside the Victorian conventions Shaw and Wells put themselves in touch with a younger generation of iconoclasts. Keynes's image of them was as two schoolmasters: Wells was the stinks master, while Shaw taught divinity. In the Cambridge to which he returned in 1908, indeed, sexual liberation and socialism were two sides of the same coin. The booming support for the Fabians took a form which was not altogether to Beatrice Webb's taste when she observed the Cambridge contingent at the summer schools of 1908 and 1910, and closer inquiry would have disconcerted her even more. When Keynes attended a Fabian meeting he reported that 'the paper was chiefly about sodomy which is called "the passionate love of comrades"' and asserted gleefully that 'these Fabians talk about nothing else'.[3]

John Maynard Keynes was twenty-five in 1908 – half the age of Hobson, whose brother Ernest had taught him mathematics at Cambridge. His father, J. N. Keynes, was one of Marshall's closest associates in founding the Cambridge 'school' in economics, with its severe formal rigour and its pre-eminent professionalism. The intellectual relationship of Maynard Keynes to Marshall was thus curiously similar to that of John Stuart Mill to Bentham – Father, Son and Holy Ghost. The young Keynes broke free from the cultural moorings of his respectable, conventional, Congregational family, with whom he nonetheless remained closely affectionate, and instead moved into a milieu of hedonistic high aestheticism spiced with the forbidden joys of homosexuality. Undergraduate friends like Lytton

[3] Keynes to Duncan Grant, 28 July 1908, B.L. Add. MSS. 57930.

Strachey were joined by avant-garde artists like Duncan Grant. It is likely that words spoke louder than deeds here. As Keynes admitted when he told Grant of the 'volcano' of Cambridge life: 'Even the womanisers pretend to be sods, lest they shouldn't be thought respectable' (11 February 1909).

Cambridge Fabianism did not, then, take after that of the parent body; indeed a rejection of the parental style was intrinsic. Keynes was quite ready to read a paper to the Fabians although he himself was clearly committed to the Liberals. These were not important distinctions within Edwardian progressivism. In February 1911 Keynes was one of the paper speakers, along with Sidney Webb, in favour of the motion before the Cambridge Union: 'That the progressive reorganisation of Society on the lines of Collectivist Socialism is both inevitable and desirable.'[4] There was no inconsistency between this and his strong support for the Liberals in 1909–10. He defended the Lloyd George Budget, as indeed, more discreetly, did Marshall. In December 1909 he wrote publicly that he attached 'unusual importance to a Liberal victory in the forthcoming election' (*JMK*, xv, 40). He took an active part in both election campaigns in 1910. He told Grant that 'we go to the Union every night to cheer the results – where it appears that all Tories have bass voices and all Liberals tenor' (6 December 1910). Nor can Keynes's excitement be explained away on the ground that the audiences in his political meetings were entirely male. There is, in short, unmistakeable evidence of an earnest political commitment to the new Liberalism, notwithstanding the often-quoted later comment about 'having a religion and no morals' as the constituent of his early beliefs (*JMK*, x, 436).

Wallas addressed the Cambridge Fabians at this time, and when Hobhouse went up to give a lecture he stayed with Keynes. 'He's very nice, I think', Keynes told Grant (17 February 1909). But there were, of course, formidable barriers in the way of any personal intimacy. It was, in a way, the difference between Hampstead and Bloomsbury, where Keynes's own friendships lay. Virginia Stephen had actually moved into the same house in Fitzroy Square which Shaw had vacated on his marriage; and after her own marriage to Leonard Woolf in 1912 Tavistock Square and Gordon Square recaptured the sort of topographical significance they had had twenty years before for an older group of left-wing intellectuals. 'Strange,' Virginia Woolf once observed, 'what a stamp Hampstead sets even on a casual gathering of 30 people; such clean, decorous, uncompromising & high minded old ladies & old gentlemen.'[5] Barbara Hammond had equally firm views about Bloomsbury. When she read Virginia Woolf's *The Voyage*

[4] *The Cambridge Union Society Debates, April 1910–March 1911*, ed. Gilbert E. Jackson and Philip Vos (1911), pp. 79–87.

[5] Anne Olivier Bell (ed.), *The Diary of Virginia Woolf* (1977), i, 83 (3 December 1917).

Out she told Lawrence that it was 'unutterably boring' and 'amazingly prurient too'. It seemed to her 'to pass the bounds of decency & to be quite pointlessly coarse' (25 December 1915).

Maybe this should not be taken too seriously – decrying Woolf was an easy game. But experimental literature, post-impressionist painting and the Russian ballet, let alone suggestions of sexual unorthodoxy, were clearly not to everyone's taste. Lawrence Hammond did at least later admit to Barbara that he had 'a less horror of an invert or pervert or Lesbian or whatever that type of lady is called than I have of people who can endure to see otter hunting' (28 August 1928). And it should be said that the Wallases were more open-minded. Ada Wallas recorded in her diary their view of 'sex dreams which are as natural as measles' (29 October 1916), though also that she was prejudiced against Edward Carpenter 'by his defence of the cultivation of unnatural passion' (27 November 1916). Her reading included such works as Joyce's *Portrait of the Artist as a Young Man*, and the Wallases even approached Hobhouse for help in that quintessentially Bloomsbury good cause of trying to get T. S. Eliot a job.

The differences in outlook between Keynes and Hobson cut deeper since they involved matters of scientific disagreement. It was Marshall's achievement to establish economics as a discipline with recognised professional standards and agreed methods of inquiry. Partly because of his own temperament, authority and tradition were exalted at the expense of controversy and originality. Maynard Keynes's conception of the subject was, at least until Marshall's death in 1924, essentially Marshallian. He took pride in the self-conscious superiority of the Cambridge school. In *The Social Problem* (1901) Hobson had used Ruskin to reproach Marshall for constricting the scope of economics, though he also conceded in a rather backhanded way that Marshall's 'hankerings after humanity continually break the rigour of his mathematical proclivities' (p. 58). Hobson's basic position was that economics needed to be transformed into a science of human welfare by introducing ethical considerations. Neville Keynes, on the other hand, had written a classical statement of the view that political economy must insist on a distinction between what *was* and what *ought* to be. Hobson denounced this as 'only another instance of the protean fallacy of individualism, which feigns the existence of separate individuals by abstracting and neglecting the social relations which belong to them and make them what they are' (p. 67). The Cambridge emphasis upon monetary theory seemed to Hobson a consequential failing of the method adopted – a conclusion which was congenial since this was certainly never his strong suit.

Hobson sent Marshall friendly criticisms of his *Principles*; Marshall sent Hobson comments on *The Social Problem*. 'There is an immense deal that is most fascinating about him,' Marshall admitted; 'and he is certainly very able. But he is in a hurry: and so he disappoints me whenever the only good work is slow work.'[6] Marshall's ponderous methods and his search for an academic consensus made him unreceptive to the insights of a wayward outsider. Conversely, Hobson's lack of rigour and his journalistic short cuts made him the wrong thinker to breach the self-contained Cambridge tradition. His slight treatment of *Gold, Prices and Wages* (1913) served to demonstrate this. 'One comes to a new book by Mr Hobson with mixed feelings,' Maynard Keynes began his review, 'in hope of stimulating ideas and of some fruitful criticisms of orthodoxy from an independent and individual standpoint, but expectant also of much sophistry, misunderstanding, and perverse thought' (*EcJ*, xxiii, 393). Keynes thought this a poor effort, a mythology of money, riddled with fallacies which he went to great lengths to demonstrate. If Hobson chose to venture upon such ground, he would clearly be judged by the severe standards of Cambridge; and on the whole he kept clear in future. He admitted to Ponsonby that his next book had turned out 'much heavier and more formal than I had intended. I attribute this in part to an unconscious desire to "hedge" against academic criticism' (22 June 1914).

(II) DEMOCRACY

Wallas was lecturing at Harvard University, with considerable success, during the first half of 1910. He suddenly rediscovered a great interest in English politics when a copy of the *Nation* reached him in May. 'I suppose that things are going fairly well', he wrote to Ada; and the prospect of 'a rather revolutionary epoch like that from 1832–36' meant that 'a good deal of hard thinking towards reconstruction' would be required (4 May 1910). He himself was clearly ready for duty. In 1910 there was a union of hearts between the progressive intellectuals and the electorate. They were 'all rather jubilant over elections' at the *Nation* lunch on 18 January (Nevinson diary). Then came the 'awful day', as Barbara Hammond recollected to Murray, when 'the counties began to go wrong'; and it was only after going through 'different strata of gloom' that the Hammonds became 'more cheerful again' (6 February 1910). In December they felt a personal sorrow at Buxton's loss of Mid-Devon. 'Otherwise the elections have been extraordinarily good', Hammond wrote to Ponsonby. 'London is remarkable' (16 December 1910). The big cities, where the mob mind of Jingoism had revealed itself in 1900, had come to repentance.

Within London, according to Masterman, the Liberal strength rested upon the skilled artisans; among unskilled labourers feeling was less intense either way; and it was 'villadom' which gave the Conservatives their

[6] Marshall to Ely, 11 July 1901, *Ec.*, n.s., xxviii, 191.

strength (*N*, 8 January 1910). Elsewhere the social division showed itself as a geographical division. While the south was reverting to Toryism, the industrial north, with the exception of Birmingham, was, as Beatrice Webb thought, 'going Radical-Socialist, self-conscious Radical-Socialist' (*OP*, pp. 443–4). The class character of the results seemed unmistakeable. 'If we save our liberties, we have the artisan classes to thank for them', commented the *Nation* (22 January 1910). But in claiming that it did 'not ignore the work of the isolated thinkers and leaders in the professional and business classes, or the enthusiasm which the new Liberalism has generated among them' (ibid.), it touched on an awkward question. The cleavage was, as Hobson summarised it, 'organised labour against the possessing and educated classes, on the one hand, against the public house and unorganised labour, on the other' (*SR*, iii, 114). But if elections could indeed be explained in such clear-cut terms, did it not suggest that social forces rather than reasoned argument prevailed?

In *Human Nature in Politics* (1908) there is a well-known description of the closing half-hour of polling in Wallas's last contest for the L.C.C. in 1904, as the stragglers were rounded up. 'A few were drunk, and one man, who was apparently a supporter of my own, clung to my neck while he tried to tell me of some vaguely tremendous fact which just eluded his power of speech. I was very anxious to win, and inclined to think that I had won, but my chief feeling was an intense conviction that this could not be accepted as even a decently satisfactory method of creating a government for a city of five million inhabitants' (pp. 229–30). Wallas brooded on this problem for many years before publishing his book, which, so Shaw chaffed him, 'contains 77,552 words, the fruit of 3,650 days labor' (13 December 1908). It is a polished exposition, in the discursive style, designed to carry its learning lightly. There is, too, almost a suggestion that the responsibility for resolving its problems lies as much with the reader as the author. It was the seminal critique of the liberal democratic prospectus of the nineteenth century. Its ambition was to ground the democratic faith upon a more realistic sociological basis. G. M. Trevelyan told Wallas that he liked his 'steady gaze at the terrors near ahead, and ultimate hope dawning beyond and general attitude towards the coming ages' (19 November 1908). But, though this is fair comment on the tone and intention of the work, most readers will feel that Part I, examining the 'Conditions of the Problem' has a more convincing ring than Part II, on the 'Possibilities of Progress'.

Wallas knew from the inside what an election was like. In terms of its important functions for the political system – choosing a set of governors – it seemed curious. By these criteria the electors were inadequate for their task. Yet Wallas did not depart from his Benthamite faith that there was 'no other way than democracy of securing that the "end" of the State shall be the good of all and not the good of some'.[7] He demonstrated indeed that in terms of the values of ordinary life it was the candidate who was behaving in an anomalous way; the 'good-natured tradesman who says quite simply, "I expect you find politics rather an expensive amusement"', undeniably had his feet upon the ground (pp. 43–4). The disjunction was, of course, due to the fact that political commitments were not, by and large, matters for lengthy intellectual consideration. Instead, 'most of the political opinions of most men are the result, not of reasoning tested by experience, but of unconscious or half-conscious inference fixed by habit' (p. 103). The interpretation of politics in terms of an 'ideal' citizen – intelligent, patriotic, disinterested – was wholly misleading. Wallas accused Victorian Liberals like James Bryce of adhering to the intellectualist fallacy here. Bryce's 'ideal democracy' seemed to be 'the kind of democracy which might be possible if human nature were as he himself would like it to be, and as he was taught at Oxford to think it was' (p. 127).

Wallas had a dual prescription for the ills of democracy. The individual elector should be strengthened and the strains upon him minimised. He laid considerable emphasis, as might be expected, upon the extension of a fuller education. He also suggested some changes in electoral practices: using more dignified public buildings and polling booths, closing public houses on polling day, perhaps introducing Sunday voting. The number of constituencies might be reduced, the alternative vote might be adopted. But in general he brushed aside proposals for tinkering with the representative system.

To a greater extent than he cared to acknowledge, the argument pointed to the role of an elite as the real problem. An explicit avowal of this would no doubt have seemed undemocratic, illiberal and opportunistic. It would, in short, have been redolent of the sort of Fabian tactics which Wallas had recently renounced. There is thus a subterranean argument in *Human Nature in Politics* which is never clearly articulated. For it would have knitted together so many loose ends *if only he had said*, without any room for misinterpretation, something like this: that a progressive working-class force was increasingly providing a new dynamic in democratic politics and that its direction and shortcomings could to some extent be modified by the application of intellectual expertise. As it was, there was no neat concatenation of the argument, even though Wallas forged the five necessary links in the chain.

In the first place, he maintained that the political problem turned on taking human nature as it was. Politics had to rest on 'facts in the psychology of the electors, which will change very slowly if they change at all' (p. 242). As Lowes Dickinson pointed out to him, 'people who talk

[7] 'Credo', notes for Shaw, n.d. (?1903), WP 10. All otherwise unidentified page references in this section are to *Human Nature in Politics*.

about human nature being immutable are usually people opposed to all reform' (7 January 1909). Dickinson acknowledged that 'if "human nature" means biological inherited qualities', Wallas was no doubt right, though he himself preferred the term 'animal nature' (ibid.). He interpreted Wallas as meaning that to improve environment was 'to improve, if not human nature, yet its manifestations in actual life; and that is all a reformer wants as a basis of action' (N, 12 December 1908). Yet Wallas's own way of putting it does suggest that democracy has to be made to work with citizens as they now are. So party justifies itself as 'something which can be loved and trusted, and which can be recognised at successive elections as being the same thing that was loved and trusted before' (p. 83). Since the divine oracle here was all too often only the tired householder it followed that 'proposals are only to be brought "within the sphere of practical politics" which are simple, striking, and carefully adapted to the half-conscious memories and likes and dislikes of busy men' (pp. 171–2).

On his first proposition Wallas took a more jaundiced view than some progressives; but on his second they were all agreed. Progress was real. The masses were becoming better able to exercise a far-reaching and beneficent power. There were signs – 'as the social question in politics grows more serious' – that more people, especially among the working class, were becoming interested and actively involved in politics (p. 233). To Hobson this new development was the central theme of electoral history. He had, he recalled, 'no idea, as a boy, that politics had anything to do with industry or standards of living' (*Conf*., p. 18). He came to regard this fact as highly significant because so long as this situation prevailed the control of the upper class was secure. In a spirit of half-conscious connivance, both parties had kept social reform out of politics by inflating other questions – 'those stage monsters of foreign or imperial policy, the menace or the misdeeds of France, Russia, Turkey, or Germany kept for the purpose'.[8] Hobhouse explained the weakness of the working class in the nineteenth century by saying that 'social forces are not cheated by political forms'. There was no 'equality, or equalitarian tendency, in the general structure of social life' to make political democracy a reality (ER, iv, 360).

Hobson made a detailed analysis of how all this came to an end with the General Election of January 1910. Distractions had been swept aside. The contrast between North and South meant that a Producer's England, which was Liberal, confronted a Consumer's England, which was Conservative. Two different social structures were revealed. The political position in the industrial North was held by an organised working class which simply did not exist in the south. 'This new force of associated labor has been slow and reluctant to adopt the machinery of party politics as a necessary instrument for the attainment of its ends', he admitted. But having done so, it

[8] *Traffic in Treason* (1914), pp. 8–9.

could overawe the deferential South – 'parasitism is, from its very nature, timid' (*N*, 26 February 1910).

In 1901 Hobson had explained the origins of jingoism by reference to the 'crowding of large masses of work-people in industrial operations regulated by mechanical routine', which helped 'to destroy or impair independence of character, without substituting any sound, rational sociality such as may arise in a city which has come into being primarily for good life, and not for cheap work' (*Psychology of Jingoism*, pp. 6–7). Capitalist exploitation had apparently made the city into the breeding ground of the mob mind; it seemed, as he put it in 1908, 'as if the close contact of modern city life generated a sort of social consciousness definitely hostile to reason, shifty, irritable, credulous and violent' (*N*, 1 August 1908). Yet in 1910 it all sounded so different: 'where masses of men are thus associated for work and life, there exist the best conditions for the emergence and the operation of that sane collective will and judgment which, in the sphere of politics, constitutes the spirit and the policy of progressive democracy' (*SR*, iii, 116). Hobson in fact recognised the ambiguity here. His basic position was, like that of Marx, that exploitative modern industrialism produced the popular consciousness which would remedy it. In the meantime the democratic problem was to comprehend 'the processes by which the horde-mind can be raised into a collective rational will' (*N*, 1 August 1908). So in 1910, although Hobson claimed to find 'a larger play of rationalism and of conscious individual judgment in this election than in any former one', his chief hopes were based upon the 'half-instinctive, half-conscious drive of collective wisdom, set up by the associated working class life which the needs of modern capitalistic production have established' (*SR*, iii, 116–17).

This acceptance of the class dimension in the struggle for social democratic reform helps explain why men like Hobhouse were so strongly opposed to the aims and tactics of the suffragettes, who were ready to breach the sex exclusiveness of the existing electorate even at the price of accentuating its social exclusiveness. The major cause of personal friction at the *Nation* lunch was invariably woman suffrage. Brailsford and Nevinson displayed a single-minded devotion to the militant position and resigned from the *Daily News* on this issue in October 1909. Apart from a running feud with Masterman, they were frequently at odds with Hobhouse, who was usually supported by Hammond, Hobson and Massingham. Barbara Hammond, who told Murray that 'a few more years of suffragette methods will ensure the franchise not coming till we are all in our graves' (22 November 1908), was an early supporter of the efforts of Margaret Llewelyn Davies for complete adult suffrage. In the autumn of 1909 the newly formed People's Suffrage Federation, with Emily Hobhouse as Chairman, attracted the support of Hobhouse, the Buxtons, Beatrice Webb,

Massingham, Gardiner, Lary Mary Murray, Galsworthy, the George Trevelyans and the Bertrand Russells. Its basic objections to the proposals of the Women's Social and Political Union were that they would not give the vote to 'the great body of working women (trade-unionist & married)' and that 'the present men's electorate – already unfair to the workers – would be still further weighted agst. them'.[9]

The third proposition argued in *Human Nature in Politics* is that as a political force Labour has the defects of its virtues, both deriving from the conditions of working-class life. An easy-going solidarity and tolerance was socially inculcated; in its local context it was generous, ungrudging and attractive. But when transferred to the official sphere it opened up a prospect of sectionalism and laxity degenerating into corruption. On this point Wallas was in effect generalising from existing practice in the parts of East London which he knew best. Hobson saw the danger of a sort of self-interested sectionalism in equally graphic terms. If the routine industries were to be taken into public ownership, as he hoped, there would be new scope for electoral log-rolling by public employees; and here both he and Hobhouse claimed that proportional representation (to which Wallas was opposed) was 'the only method by which the "tyranny of Socialism" can be averted' (*Crisis of Liberalism*, p. 155). They were all hostile to the development of purely trade-union, syndicalist, vocational or professional claims. As Beatrice Webb noted, Wallas held 'in his heart of hearts, that all groups based on economic interests, are conspiracies against the Public' (diary, 6 July 1916).

The Parliamentary Labour party had been called into existence in the early years of the century to defend trade unionism from the hostile trend of case law. 'That which no Socialist writer or platform orator could achieve was effected by the judges', Hobhouse commented (*Lab. Movement*, 3rd edn, p. 12). Its policy was that of 'Labourism'; its characteristic activity was as a trade-union pressure group. It did not have what Wallas called 'a Socialist clergy, such as the German social democrats had created, charged with the duty of thinking for the working class' (*SR*, v, 249). The English working class, he thought, might conceivably be forced to build up a nation within a nation in the same way, fencing it off from all outside influences; though he deplored the danger 'both to the general intellectual life of the country, and to the possibility of peaceful social change' which this involved (*N*, 11 December 1909).

As Hobhouse saw it, there was a real division in the Labour party between doctrinaire socialism and the practical collectivism of the trade-union leaders. But the Liberals were also divided. On the right were those who regarded Liberalism as 'the more enlightened method of maintaining the

[9] Margaret Llewelyn Davies to C. P. Scott, 4 September (1909), MGP.

existing social order' (*CR*, xciii, 353). The group with which he himself was identified had, by contrast, formulated a theory which, he wrote in 1912, 'appears to me, even more clearly than before, to express the real mind of the Labour Movement and the possible lines of social regeneration better than the more familiar forms of socialistic theory' (*Lab. Movement*, p. 5). It followed that there was 'no division in principle or method' between the main body of the Labour party and the advanced Liberals (*CR*, xciii, 353). Progressivism was the ideology which united them.

The new Liberals were, in effect, volunteering for some of the clerical duties in this broad church. Defending the policy of the *Manchester Guardian* in 1914 against Margaret Llewelyn Davies, who was more closely identified with the views of the Labour party and the *Daily Herald*, Hobhouse acknowledged that Labour was 'presumably suffering from the wrong of unequal distribution, and in all its efforts commands, therefore, a certain sympathy'. But he could not accept that Labour was 'always and necessarily in the right', and therefore commanded uncritical support, which seemed to be the viewpoint of the *Daily Herald*. 'Our object, on the other hand,' he explained, 'is to address people of all views, and to try to reason with them. We may not make many converts, but we make some, and we mitigate opposition' (*Memoir*, pp. 64–5). This may suggest that Liberalism was a rather conservative influence, mediating Labour's demands. But the essential claim was on behalf of the trained and critical intellect, and this could be given a different twist. The British Labour party was a genuinely working-class movement – as Massingham put it, a 'class-party' not a 'policy-party' (*H.W.M.*, p. 96). Wallas held that its representatives were therefore liable to be overawed by the permanent officials (for whom in themselves he had a high regard). The enthronement in office of John Burns lent credence to this suggestion. 'No pure workman's party can go very far', the *Nation* insisted. 'Middle-class brains and training are indispensable to it' (13 June 1908). The Liberals therefore claimed a continuing role, and a radical one at that.

Moreover, even when the failure of the Liberal party to match up to this standard was recognised, it did not imply that Labour was a better alternative. In Hammond's case the admiration which he expressed to Murray for Asquith's 'incomparable coolness & judgment' over the constitutional crisis (9 August 1911) turned to apprehension over his equal coolness towards woman suffrage. At the beginning of 1913 he noted that 'my enthusiasm for the Govt is severely restrained' and that he was 'gloomy about the Suffrage' (ibid., 7 January 1913); and by November, with the imprisonment of the Irish labour leader, Larkin, his mood was one later described as 'cold disillusionment'.[10] He found some consolation in the reflection that 'when the Liberals are routed in the towns at the next

[10] Jason, *Past and Future* (1918), p. 109.

election we shall feel it is deserved' and added: 'It is the class war from above.'[11] Yet even now Barbara Hammond was confessing to Lawrence that 'I really *dont* like the *Daily Herald*' (11 November 1913); and he was writing to Murray of the Labour party's 'curse of respectability' (2 November 1913) and its extraordinary lethargy in this situation. 'Why do they leave it to Liberals always to defend the rights of working men?' he demanded (16 November 1913). His subsequent statement to Ponsonby that 'I ceased to be a Liberal when the Govt took to prosecuting workmen & broke faith with the women' (24 May 1915) should be read in this light. His comment some twenty-five years later was that 'in the early years of the century the Liberal leaders had recognised that this new force was a progressive force and that if it were treated in an ungenerous spirit and combated as an enemy there would be little hope of making an effective fight against the strength of wealth and rank' (*MG*, 29 April 1938). Looking back, the cardinal mistake seemed to be the Liberal failure to implement proportional representation, so as to mobilise the full force of progressivism. Likewise in 1914, Scott told Hobhouse that he was beginning to agree with Hobson's recently expressed view 'that the existing Liberal party is played out'; but what they envisaged instead was 'a full union of progressive forces', since the political inadequacies of Labour were equally manifest (19 June 1914). 'This left wing of Liberalism (for in spite of its distinct party organization, it has been nothing more)', was how Hobson described it (*Traffic in Treason*, p. 63).

Hence – fourthly – for Wallas 'the problem' was one for the elite. When he had a chapter called 'Political Morality' it was the morality *of the politician* with which he was concerned. In 1903 he had stated his primary aim as that of 'making politicians realise that they are not the servants of an eager public but a small and responsible minority who have to force an absorbed and indifferent public to realise its own opportunities' ('Credo'). Wallas's utopia – when 'much in politics which is now impossible will become possible' – is one in which 'the politician will be able not only to control and direct in himself the impulses of whose nature he is more fully aware, but to assume in his hearers an understanding of his aim' (p. 198). In the meantime, presumably, his superior insight would have to work unaided. So Wallas put great emphasis, especially in private, on the need for representatives to lead and for the initiative of permanent experts to be strengthened. For him the real constitutional check in England was the centralised, impartial knowledge of a permanent civil service, 'the one great political invention in nineteenth-century England' (p. 249).

Thus the effectiveness of progressive reform relied upon a blind democratic force from below combined with enlightened direction from above, or what Hobson called 'a concessionaire policy of the owning classes'

[11] Hammond to Ponsonby, n.d. (?Nov. 1913), Ponsonby Papers, C.683 f.15.

(*Conf.*, p. 102). Both responses could be expected; both were functional from the point of view of society as a whole. Hobson sometimes wrote of 'the inevitable logic of events' which would drive society along the path of collectivism. But if, in the future, social progress were to be 'swifter, safer and more effective' it had to become 'the conscious expression of the trained and organised will of a people not despising theory as impractical, but using it to furnish economy in action' (*Crisis of Liberalism*, p. 132). To Wallas the educated man played a key role because 'the history of human progress consists in the gradual and partial substitution of science for art, of the power over nature acquired in youth by study, for that which comes in late middle age as the half-conscious result of experience' (p. 153). For Hobhouse, too, the role of the intellectual was an important one: 'the thinker is no recluse but a man with a living and practical function' (*N*, 8 January 1910). True, he made 'no figure on the platform and is little spoken of in the Press' but it was nonetheless the case that 'all the great movements, from the French Revolution onwards, have been made under the direct inspiration of organic social ideas' (ibid.).

'We do not believe in ideas as we believe in force', was one of Hobson's wry *obiter dicta* (*Crisis of Liberalism*, p. 110). A favourite phrase of Wallas's was 'the intolerable disease of thought'. For them politics was about hard thinking. Wallas asserted that Liberalism stood for 'the belief that the unbribed [unbridled?] love of knowledge and beauty leads the elect to the love of mankind, that Heine's "Ritter des heilegen Geistes" are recruited not only in the workshop but in the study' (*Men & Ideas*, p. 153). The demands of science (in Wallas's sense) were heavy: 'a combination of moral earnestness and intellectual concentration, without the promise and inspiration of revolutionary change' (*N*, 6 February 1909). One of the leading tasks of the twentieth century was to effect a permanent alliance between science and democracy – 'between the movement towards greater social equality and the new conception of intellectual duty that inspires modern students and thinkers' (ibid.). Clearly this ought to take place in the university. Yet few Liberals held a very high opinion of the existing state of Oxford and Cambridge: as G. M. Trevelyan put it to Wallas, the collegiate system was 'one of the few good points of those institutions' (7 December 1906). Wallas considered that admission to Oxford was too easy for public school 'dolts', too difficult for candidates from a different background. At present, therefore, higher education was far from guaranteeing progressive sympathies, as the 1910 elections made clear. But the *Nation* was able to find comfort in the reflection that the most eminent men of letters and science spoke otherwise. It confidently claimed that 'the best intellectual culture of the nation severs itself from the definitely reactionary policy to which the larger "educated" classes commit themselves' (22 January 1910).

The final proposition advanced by *Human Nature in Politics* is really the converse of this faith in the power of the superior intellect. For the possible manipulation of the masses by an elite in turn constitutes a major peril. Wallas warned that the politician might 'cease even to desire to reason with his constituents, and may come to regard them as purely irrational creatures of feeling and opinion, and himself as the purely rational "over-man" who controls them' (pp. 173–4). Evidence survives showing that Wallas had explicitly concerned himself with the arguments of Shaw's Nietzschean play *Man and Superman* (1904). He was ready to concede that such manipulation, common enough in the past, might become more prevalent in the future. Lowes Dickinson told Wallas of his reaction on reading *Human Nature in Politics*. 'I said "This man is the Machiavelli of Democracy". Then, in Part II, appeared the *other* Wallas' (26 November 1908).

A strong faith in democracy shines through the book. Indeed this seemed rather naive to Webb who was content to justify elections to Wallas on the ground that it was 'necessary (or convenient) to get popular consent i.e. popular consciousness that they consent' (23 July 1908). If the real point was the 'feeling of consent', rather than the decision made, the defects of the system hardly mattered. But it followed that the Referendum was not a hopeful device. For Hobson, on the contrary, the Referendum was a logical extension of the organic conception of popular government. From 1907 he took every opportunity to advocate it, on the ground that 'the theoretically "good" law must be stamped with the sort of "goodness" required to secure the approval of the people' (*Crisis of Liberalism*, p. 65). This was to follow through the logic of the moral reformist position and to accept, if need be, that there was 'a certain inertia of the popular will that will retard the rate of progress, a conservatism if you will' (ibid., p. 46). Still, it was better to proceed in this way than by 'faking' progress. Mechanical reformism stood condemned. To Hobson Liberalism implied 'that the people knows what it wants, and that it is better to give it what it wants than something "technically" better which it does not want' (ibid., pp. 40–1) – an argument which would have justified National Insurance over the Minority Report. Beatrice Webb, herself came virtually to admit this point: 'By no other measure could any statesman have raised 25 millions to be spent on sickness. The fact that it is going to be wastefully collected & wastefully spent condemns it both in the eyes of sane socialists & carefully minded conservatives – but to the stupidity of broad-minded Englishmen it makes no difference because he is too unintelligent to see it' (diary, 1 December 1912). Hobson also advanced the further claim that because the Referendum allowed the people 'not merely to make mistakes but to recognise that they have made them', it fostered a process of social learning (loc. cit.).

Wallas did not go so far as this; but he remained confident that democratic solutions would prevail. He attributed most of the deficiencies of democracy to the apathetic, under-informed electorate – a dog with eyes like saucers. The remedy, Wallas implied, is to invoke the power of his intellectual master, who understands him, and can therefore use the tinder-box to control him, and who may turn out to be an anxious do-gooder (like Wallas himself); or who may turn out to be a man of a different stripe who will use the tinder-box for quite other purposes. In that case we will be confronted with a dog with eyes like windmills. It is not clear why 'the other Wallas' should prevail over Machiavelli. Did Wallas really comprehend the magnitude of threats to representative government from powerful irrationalist ideologies? He gave a long description of how a mass agitation might be organised (pp. 246–8). He cited the hypothetical example of a campaign for currency reform, with a virulent propaganda effort to back it, preying on paranoia and promising panaceas. It was a graphic adumbration of fascism. Wallas presented it as an account of how a fraudulent agitation might take hold – *if* official statistics did not exist.

The danger from the mob mind lay in its openness to manipulation by vested interests. Even under formal democratic conditions the forces of conservatism could find powerful and effectual backing. 'The power of organized capital is the standing danger of democracy', Hobhouse had written in 1898.[12] In 1912 he reaffirmed that 'the influence of wealth does not diminish' (*Labour Movement*, p. 125). To Wallas the money-power, highly organised and without scruple as to the means it employed, was 'the central problem of Democracy all the world over' (*N*, 11 December 1909). To Hobson it was 'for popular Governments the most constant source of danger, worse than ignorance, worse than apathy, worse than faction, worse than demagogism' (*MG*, 27 December 1909). As in other respects, he felt that there was a great deal to be said for Marx. 'His intellectual penetration, persistency and honesty were wonderful', Hobson once told the Rainbow Circle (minutes, 9 April 1902). The Marxist case was that only such democratic progress would be permitted as did not threaten the position of the capitalist class. He was ready to admit the difficulties in bringing the people to a realisation of their true position when 'the machinery of education is in the control of interests opposed to popular progress' (*Crisis of Liberalism*, p. 181). He also admitted that it was 'not easy to disprove' the contention that the apparent liberties of the citizen were 'concessions of the ascendant classes', permitting a more subtle but no less effective form of control. But Hobson regarded this argument as containing 'an admission of positive progress, for the elevation of the nature and instruments of domination is itself progress' (ibid., p. 182). The true metaphor of progress was not the vicious circle but the spiral.

[12] Stefan Collini, 'Liberalism and Sociology' (Cambridge Ph.D. 1977), p. 92.

Democracy rested on the ideologically flawed perceptions of the citizens of an imperfect society. But in the end the cause of the people would prevail. The paradox was that 'the very conditions of modern profitable exploitation favour the physical and intellectual solidarity of the people: modern capitalism makes directly for moral democracy'. And in this contest the masses would find that 'justice is a great ally' (ibid., pp. 189–90). For the struggle was continually being raised to a higher level. Hobson appealed for confirmation to 'the fact that the vested interests base their defence more and more upon appeals to the supreme court of reason and of morals' (ibid., pp. 182–3). This again threw the problem back upon the intellectuals who would have to get up the brief for the people. It was their task to counter the ideologies of conservatism in science (Social Darwinism), economics (laissez faire), philosophy (Idealism) and religion (quietism).

In June 1914, in his pamphlet *Traffic in Treason*, Hobson returned to a question which he had raised earlier: whether the armed forces were not the final arbiter. Surveying the situation in Ireland after the Curragh incident, he accused the Conservatives of bringing the Army into play as a last card when they had been defeated by every constitutional means. Their property was threatened by socialism – 'not the revolutionary Socialism of the "reds", but the more insidious policy of "levelling", which they identify correctly with the new Liberalism' (pp. 58–9). Hobson raised the spectre of a last-ditch resistance to the democratic onslaught. But having done so, his own trump card was the prospect of a General Election. Like Wallas, he could only envisage threats to liberal democracy of a kind which were susceptible to liberal democratic remedies.

(III) HARMONY

In an address on *Industrial Unrest* (1912), delivered to the National Liberal Club, Hobson pointed the novel and explosive character of current discontent. 'The sentiment of severance between rich and poor, the spirit of class hostility, has grown more conscious and more acute', he acknowledged. 'This is not a popular thing to say in a middle class audience, but it is true' (p. 2). Yet he also claimed that the British people 'are not by temperament or by history anarchistic. Now strikes and lock-outs are anarchy' (p. 12). Declining real wages explained spontaneous unrest but use of the state offered the rational remedy. Two years later Hobson's perspective was altogether more comforting and he insisted on 'the fact that the number of actual conflicts between capital and labour is constantly diminishing'.[13] The unproductive surplus, to be sure, remained a source of discord between capital and labour. But when it came to the division of the productive surplus, 'there exists a harmony of interests between the

[13] *Work and Wealth* (1914), p. 277.

two groups of claimants, which is more clearly recognised with every improvement of the general standard of intelligence and information' (*Work & Wealth*, p. 276). Rather like the *Daily Express*'s headline on European peace after the 1938 Munich pact, Hobson evidently assured himself each morning that there would be no class war in 1914 or the next year either.

Wallas, working throughout these years on what he hoped would 'turn out a good book with a kind of passion in it',[14] was hardly less hopeful. The complex social arrangements which went with advanced industrialisation – the Great Society – brought a sense of alienation to many, which mocked the Aristotelian ideal of the mean. In *The Great Society* (1914) he therefore suggested that the 'master-task of civilised mankind' was to examine the conditions of a good life. Though this was no easy challenge, it was 'hardly possible for any one to endure life who does not believe that they will succeed in producing a harmony between themselves and their environment far deeper and wider than anything which we can see to-day' (pp. 71–2). For Hobhouse the concept of harmony was central to his theory of development. When, in *Social Evolution and Political Theory* (1911), he postulated 'a possible harmony between the claims of different persons', he added: 'that such a harmony can be found is, I think, the fundamental postulate of social ethics' (p. 86).

The form of these statements, with their constant reference to harmony, prompts the question whether this sort of liberal thought was not, in the end, a conservative theodicy. Harold Laski gave the best expression to this criticism in his Hobhouse Memorial Lecture, *The Decline of Liberalism* (1940), claiming that Hobhouse and Green 'believed in the necessary unity of society; they did not see that we have deliberately to plan institutions and processes through which this unity is achieved' (p. 13). The Hobhouse whom Laski knew as an older colleague at the L.S.E. in the 1920s cast himself rather convincingly for the character part of Liberalism in Decline. But though this extenuates Laski's charge it does not absolve him from the counter-charge that he could not have read what Hobhouse actually wrote in his prime. For what Hobhouse reiterated was that the conditions of social justice had to be created in society before harmony could be realised. In *Liberalism* (1911), while he conceded that there had to be 'some elementary trace of such harmony in every form of social life that can maintain itself', he firmly rejected the idea that there was 'an actually existing harmony requiring nothing but prudence and coolness of judgment for its effective operation' (p. 136). True harmony was for him 'an ideal which it is perhaps beyond the power of man to realize, but which serves to indicate the line of advance' (p. 129). 'Regard the harmonic conception of society as an ideal and you give us something to work for,' he put it later, 'regard it as some-

[14] Graham to Ada Wallas, 28 August 1911, WP 44.

thing actually realized and you confuse every issue of practical reform and theoretical right.'[15] Hobhouse's postulate may indeed be an unproved utopian assumption, as has sometimes been alleged; but in this form it is one which underpins most theories of progress. It is attractive to moral reformists like Hobhouse and indispensable to moral revolutionists like Marx.

Laski, of course, recognised that Hobhouse's system hinged on progress. But he again bracketed him with Green in maintaining that they divorced 'the process of history from the deliberately willed effort of individuals to plan social change in a wholesale way. . .Given goodwill, they tended to believe that history made itself, and beneficently, if it was only left alone' (loc. cit., p. 12). Here too this seems to be flatly contradicted by Hobhouse's repeated and emphatic statements. 'The theory of continuous automatic inevitable progress is impossible', he wrote (*Soc. Ev. & Pol. Theory*, p. 160). In *Democracy and Reaction* he subjected Idealist philosophy and Social Darwinism to hostile scrutiny precisely because they seemed to him the chief intellectual supports of a view of 'destiny' which paralysed the moral consciousness of society. And yet, Laski's comment is not without psychological insight. The true ground for this can be gauged from an examination of Hobhouse's own formal theory of evolution, which made certain concessions towards a teleological view; and the point would find further support in the work of Hobson. For one who wrote so much, Hobhouse was an unusually rigorous and systematic thinker, seldom caught off guard even in his ephemera. There is a high degree of consistency throughout his works. Hobson's ostensibly similar view of progress, however, is presented with an engaging and revealing innocence of such pedantries. Keynes returned the manuscript of Hobson's *Work and Wealth* (1914) unopened to Macmillans, declaring that he had 'so much prejudice against what I regard as his sophistries' that he could not fairly report upon it[16] – forebodings which a reading of the work would hardly have dispelled.

In the 1880s Hobhouse had found himself confronted by starkly different intellectual traditions: in the closed world of Oxford, philosophy, Idealism and T. H. Green; in the secular world outside, science, positivism and Herbert Spencer. Spencer was not interested in God, Green was not interested in dogs. By the time of *Development and Purpose* (1913), Hobhouse's conviction 'that the philosophy of the future must make its account with science' (p. xvii) had borne fruit in a comprehensive statement of an evolutionary sociology. The methods of science were a very good way of assessing the state of *development* which a society had reached, as measured by certain empirical criteria. Only philosophy, however, could provide the ethical standard by which *progress* could be assessed. By making this

[15] Hobhouse, *The Metaphysical Theory of the State* (1918), p. 97.
[16] Simon Nowell Smith (ed.), *Letters to Macmillan* (1967), p. 282 (25 October 1913).

distinction, Hobhouse sought to escape the tautologies of Social Darwinism, where 'survival of the fittest' merely imputed fitness to those who survived and defined fitness as survival value. Evolution was no testimony to morality. 'The fact that a thing is evolving is no proof that it is good, the fact that society has evolved is no proof that it has progressed' (*Soc. Ev. & Pol. Theory*, p. 8). Social development and natural selection operated in different ways and on different time scales. 'Progress is not racial, but social', he maintained (ibid., p. 39). This progress rested upon the growth of self-consciousness within society, and with this assertion of control the brutal and haphazard struggle for existence was superseded. This process, to which Hobhouse attached the name 'orthogenic evolution', comprised 'a series of advances in the development of mind involving a parallel curtailment of the sphere of natural selection' (*Dev. & Purpose*, p. xxi).

Hobhouse's subsequent sociological standing might well have been higher if he had cut loose altogether from the terminology of evolution. He had a viable theory of social development of which his pupil Morris Ginsberg offered an able defence in later years. Hobhouse once wrote that Ginsberg 'knows my mind as well as I know it myself' (*Memoir*, p. 48). But even Ginsberg was clearly hampered by reservations over the 'cosmic bearing' of the theory. In itself Hobhouse's theory of social development rested on a view of the 'social mind', which is analogous to some of the insights for which his illustrious continental contemporaries have received so much credit. Hobhouse clearly specified that the concern of sociology, as distinct from biology or psychology, was with the *interaction* of individuals – with the social *as such* (to adopt Raymond Aron's expression). By the social mind Hobhouse meant 'something essentially of psychological character that arises from the operations of masses of men, and molds and is in turn remolded by the operation of masses of men' (*Soc. Ev. & Pol. Theory*, p. 98). He invoked history to show that there had been a real advance; he gave an affirmative answer to the question whether there was a tendency 'to realise the conditions out of which when complete a harmony would emerge' (ibid., p. 152). But this conclusion was not surprising in view of Hobhouse's method; and the reason for this also throws light upon his resolute commitment to the evolutionary schema.

Harmony was Hobhouse's ethical test for social progress. It manifested itself in rational control, co-operation and social justice. These manifestations, however, were also the mainsprings of development. This, to be sure, is a happy coincidence; it is almost too good to be true. Orthogenic evolution meant that at a certain point the best had become the strongest and thereafter harmony became 'the touchstone of social development' (ibid., p. 204). Ethical progress was still not assured but its *prospects* were assured. 'Its possibility,' Hobhouse claimed, 'rests on the facts of evolution' (p. 205). He had explained development in terms of the growth of the social mind, which in many respects suggested the analogy of the organism. But the existence of the social mind also implied purpose. Hobhouse took a further – and strictly unnecessary – step. *Development and Purpose* showed that he had made his peace with Idealism to the extent of interpreting all organic growth as the realisation of purpose. He thus made social development a special case of cosmic evolution. Natural selection was a constant condition but, he commented gnomically, 'the start of the whole process, and we may say of every new development within it, has still to be set down to an unknown factor' (*MG*, 13 October 1913). If, he now concluded, 'a purpose runs through the world-whole, there is a Mind of which the world-purpose is the object' (*Dev. & Purpose*, p. 365). One feels at this point that Paley is owed an apology. The providential overtones were to some extent mitigated by the argument that 'the central mind' was itself conditioned by development. But the teleological interpretation of progress was now explicit, and took on an almost Hegelian assurance. 'The human mind is a germ for whose maturity provision is already made' (ibid., p. 371).

As compared with Hobhouse, Wallas was more sceptical and Hobson less critical. Wallas's belief that in the Great Society conscious, directed thought was more necessary than ever was urged on a mundane, utilitarian level. He refused to adopt the term social organism, with its suggestion 'that the arrangement itself has a "super-life" or "super-consciousness" of its own' (*Great Society*, p. 250). Hobson saw in this refusal 'a reluctance to recognise the evidence of facts attesting to a collective consciousness which often counterworks, perhaps injuriously, the efforts towards rationalisation of the individual will' (*MG*, 10 July 1914). Wells commented that Wallas did 'not appear to comprehend the nature of that large discussion between the species and the individual which has been, and is, the subject matter of metaphysics, and which supplies the underlying conception of this idea of a collective mind' (*N*, 4 July 1914). But Wallas's scepticism did not stem from ignorance either of social facts or philosophical theory. Muirhead made persistent efforts to keep him abreast of the latest developments in Idealist thought. Wallas's own thrust against Hobson was that acceptance of the doctrine of the social will would not only encourage 'what I hold to be the bad habit of believing things without evidence, but would also be likely to lead to that sort of easy-going optimism which one detects in some of the followers of Hegel. If a super-brain is thinking for us the necessity of undertaking the intolerable toil of thought for ourselves seems less urgent' (*N*, 27 June 1914).

Hobson himself was organically incapable of resisting this allure. He bridled at the statement – in effect Hobhouse's – that society exists in individuals and insisted that it had instead to be conceived 'as a collective organism, with life, will, purpose, meaning of its own, as distinguished from the life, will, purpose, meaning of the individual members of it'

(*Work & Wealth*, p. 15). His view of social evolution was more clear cut than Hobhouse's since he was less afraid of the implications of the organic metaphor. So the evidence he found for 'the ascent of human society towards a larger and closer complexity of human relations and a clearer intellectual and moral consciousness' (ibid., p. 350) pointed to its political manifestation in the general will, a term which Hobhouse abjured as leading 'to the most inhuman torture of evidence to prove that there is a generality of will where there is none' (*Soc. Ev. & Pol. Theory*, p. 97n.). This view of the state, as Hobson acknowledged, had found its best expression in English in the work of Bosanquet. For Hobson the language of Idealism provided the most persuasive reconciliation of organic conceptions with the standards of rationalism.

Hobson found in the social will a means of overcoming the alienation to which work of a merely routine character gave rise. There was no problem over the creative work which he called art, in which individualism and free enterprise were living ideals. In the great industry, based upon the division of labour, things were different, as Marx and Morris had rightly maintained. Wallas considered that Morris, Ruskin and Rousseau 'had something very real to say when they talked about a "natural" life' but that the real problem was 'how to live an unnatural life in such a way as to afford that satisfaction to our inner nature which is called happiness'.[17] His own stern conclusion was that, however the Great Society was reformed, 'we must submit to the Division of Labour; and the Division of Labour will involve, if it is to be effective, a certain degree of compulsion' (*Great Society*, p. 391). This is a long way from Marx's vision. But Hobson, ready like Marx to proclaim the slogan, 'From each according to his abilities, to each according to his needs', as the supreme principle, also sketched a more roseate view of the future. He did not suggest that the division of labour could be ended; but he held that the 'free-will and voluntary enterprise' of society provided a spontaneous, self-directed power which could be brought to bear upon the routine industries. 'For once conceive Society as a being capable of thought and feeling, these processes have an interest for it.' So for Hobson, hardly less than Marx, labour can become 'a truly social function, the orderly half-instinctive half-rational activity by which society helps itself and satisfies its wants, a common tide of productive energy which pulses through the veins of humanity, impelling the individual members of society to perform their part as contributors to the general life' (*Work & Wealth*, pp. 305–6). This was an evasive account, however, which served to conceal the iron fist of coercion beneath the velvet glove of Idealist phraseology. Continuing his description of social labour, Hobson commented: 'Whether those individual actions are strictly voluntary, pleasurable and interesting in themselves to those who perform

[17] Wallas to A. E. Zimmern, 16 March 1909, copy, WP 10.

them, as in the finer arts, or are compulsory in their main incidence upon the individual, and accompanied by little interest or social feeling on his part, is a matter of quite secondary importance as viewed from the social standpoint' (ibid., p. 306).

The organic metaphor described what was functional in social evolution; the Idealist overtones turned this into a supposition about purpose and destiny. Hobson moved from the one conception to the other with great nimbleness, and seized on analogies throughout nature to reaffirm the coherence and comprehensiveness of his view. He found forms of co-partnership in his Surrey garden which offered 'the rabbit, the thrush, the bee, the worm, the cabbage, the rose' grounds for appeal against man to 'the wider cosmic order' (*N*, 16 October 1909). Parasitism gave him ample opportunity for elaborating detailed analogies between its biological and social modes. Paley's remark, 'It is always an agreeable discovery, when, having remarked in an animal an extraordinary structure, we come at length to find out an unexpected use for it',[18] captures the spirit of Hobson's inquiries. Although it was unfortunately 'almost or quite impossible to put to Nature the question of Free Trade or Protection' (*N*, 22 January 1910), numerous object lessons on other matters were turned to account. In particular, the paradigm of the hive allowed an imputation of purpose to order, whether as a social, natural or universal principle. 'This sense of "manifest destiny" is surely no illusion', Hobson concluded. 'It is the evolutionary method by which all organic process is achieved, whether in the growth of an oak tree from its acorn, of a motor-car from the earliest hand-barrow, a musical symphony from a savage tom-tom, or a modern federal state from the primitive tribal order' (*Work & Wealth*, p. 355).

Harmony had the wings of a dove; it could soar off in a breathtaking way; and in its beak it held an olive branch. The testimony to an emergent harmony which Hobhouse invoked buttressed his confidence in the efficacy of rational aspirations as against the rule of blood and iron. The support for tariffs, armaments and efficiency of a man like Mackinder, whom Zimmern described to Wallas as a 'Bismarckian Darwinist of the purest Milnerian water' (12 March 1908), epitomised everything that was anathema to the new Liberals. They believed that war was immoral, irrational and unnecessary. This did not prevent Wallas from lying awake at night worrying about its likelihood. Ada Wallas had to tell him not to talk about it so much at home in front of their young daughter; and Walter Lippmann was one of those who later wrote to him of 'the foreboding of this war' which haunted the pages of the *Great Society* (5 October 1915). War meant the disastrous triumph of the policy of blood and iron; and so did class war. It seemed to Wallas that the success of *Capital* in helping divide Germany into two mutually intolerant camps had meant that it was

[18] William Paley, *Natural Theology*, 2nd edn (1828), ii, 12.

'the camp of Bismarck and not that of Marx which has so far gained thereby' (*Great Society*, p. 90). If he were convinced that nothing could be got except through force, wrote Hobhouse impatiently to Margaret Llewelyn Davies in 1914, he would 'shut up shop as a radical or socialist or anything reforming, because I shall be convinced that human nature is hopeless', and he affirmed that 'if it comes to a class war, the class in possession will win hands down' (*Memoir*, p. 65).

It took two to make a fight. In Britain there was no obvious basis for the class war, but this condition did not necessarily hold elsewhere. 'In Prussia,' the *Nation* explained, 'the Marxist doctrine seems reasonable and self-evident, for the middle-class itself acts on the assumption of an inevitable class war, and was, indeed, the first to proclaim it' (19 September 1908). Much of the work that socialism stood for in continental Europe was the work of Liberalism in England; conversely, in a country like Germany progress was represented by Social Democracy. This analysis was in effect reciprocated by Eduard Bernstein who was a friend of Wallas and Massingham and a regular contributor to the *Nation*. He revised the German edition of *Human Nature in Politics* to which he contributed a preface. On the eve of the 1910 elections he wrote an open letter on 'The Electoral Policy of German Social Democracy', arguing that where conditions were appropriate the party had 'by no means been so Doctrinaire as is generally believed' and that in Prussia it was 'not the unwillingness of the Social Democrats, but the unreadiness of the Prussian Freisinnige which stood in the way' of a policy of honourable co-operation for progress (*N*, 11 December 1909). Bernstein knew perfectly well that the German revisionist crisis had made virtually no mark in Britain. 'There are very few people in England who know that there is such a person as Bernstein' he had assured an inquirer in 1899.[19] But in the following decade his own reading of what revisionism implied in an English context is unmistakeable.

Wallas, Hobson and Hobhouse held a virtually identical view of syndicalism. Insofar as it rested upon methods of direct action they condemned it as anti-intellectual and counter-productive; they did not accept that organised violence could produce construction. And, insofar as it aimed at putting industries under the control of particular groups of producers, it exemplified their worst dreams of sectionalism. But syndicalism was certainly understandable as a protest against the cumbersome slowness and bureaucratic proclivities of orthodox collectivism. In the 1880s, Wallas confessed, collectivism had seemed the only alternative to the individualist conception of property; but since then its defects as a comprehensive alternative had become more apparent. The Guild Socialist ideas associated with the rising figure of G. D. H. Cole were at least addressed to this problem. Cole was, so Murray explained to Hammond, 'very clever, handsome,

[19] Eduard Bernstein, *My Years of Exile* (1921), p. 251.

austere, ferocious and young, and his views are violence personified' (2 January 1914). But though his eyes would 'flash fire at the mention of Peace or Prudence or Liberalism or Ramsay MacDonald or the Insurance Act', and he regarded the *Nation* 'much as we regard the *Church Times*' (ibid.), his revolt against Fabianism struck a sympathetic chord. For the new Liberals, it was the old story.

When Laski came to remedy the deficiencies of Liberalism in 1940 he declared that what was required was 'a new conception of property in which social ownership and control replace individual ownership and control' (*loc. cit.*, p. 22). This is hardly very different from the agenda which Hobhouse, Hobson and Wallas had been proposing in the years immediately before the First World War. For Hobson the co-operative feeling in society could only be evoked 'by setting Property upon an intelligible moral and social basis' (*Work & Wealth*, p. 297); while for Wallas the disadvantages of individualism, collectivism and syndicalism as exclusive principles demonstrated the need to replace the 'rights of property' with more adaptable conventions (*Great Society*, p. 331). Hobhouse sought a way forward here by distinguishing 'the control of things, which gives freedom and security' from 'the control of persons through things, which gives power to the owner'.[20] Property for use, in this sense, could be defended in Aristotelian terms as an expression of the human personality; but such a defence could not extend to property for power. Hence, 'Ethical individualism in property, carried through, blows up its own citadel' (ibid., p. 29). It was a Liberal principle that property for use should be guaranteed to the individual; but property for power – what on a different analysis would be called the ownership of the means of production – rightly belonged to the democratic state.

At the turn of the century, Hobhouse acknowledged, Liberalism had had 'the air of a creed that is becoming fossilized as an extinct form, a fossil that occupied, moreover, an awkward position between two very active and energetically moving grindstones – the upper grindstone of plutocratic imperialism, and the nether grindstone of social democracy' (*Liberalism*, p. 214). But, writing in 1911, he claimed that it was 'now sufficiently clear to all parties that the distinctive ideas of Liberalism have a permanent function' (ibid., p. 224). Liberalism as a permanent principle was to transcend any particular expedients of property-holding. It was founded upon the idea of growth and the goal of harmony. It was the humanistic vision of a state of society in which the spontaneous fulfilment of capacities became possible for all its members. 'The heart of Liberalism,' Hobhouse maintained, 'is the understanding that progress is not a matter of mechanical contrivance, but of the liberation of living spiritual energy' (ibid., p. 137). What Hobson called 'this illimitable character of Liberalism, based

[20] Charles Gore (ed.), *Property: its rights and duties* (1913), p. 10.

on the infinitude of the possibilities of human life' (*Crisis of Liberalism*, p. 95), could not be restricted to the moral reformist position which he and Hobhouse took up; by definition it applied to the moral revolutionist as well. When Hobhouse wrote of 'a Liberal Socialism, as well as a Socialism that is illiberal', and specified that this must be founded upon democracy and individual liberty, his argument worked on two levels (*Liberalism*, p. 165). Its immediate context is that of the British Liberal party in the years around 1910. It is a Critique of the Limehouse Programme. But the form in which he cast his argument was designed to give it a wider provenance. On his own principles, liberalism ought to be capable of extension into the socialist future: but it had to be socialism with a human face.

(IV) THE USEFULLER LIFE

'What, under modern conditions, constitutes history?' Wallas suggested in 1906 that there was a need for a fresh approach to this question now that the modern reader was 'as dissatisfied with a history consisting in the main of parliamentary debates and newspaper events, as his grandfather was of the "drum and trumpet" style' (*IR*, viii, 230). The Hammonds came up with their answer in a book some five years later. There had been many histories of the English governing class in the eighteenth and nineteenth centuries, their preface acknowledged, but what they proposed was 'to describe the life of the poor during this period'. This project was very largely Barbara's doing. She would spend three days a week at the Public Record Office or the British Museum doing the research for it and she also took on the major problems of organising its exposition. She had, Lawrence told Murray, 'a really remarkable talent for putting great masses of fact & detail in order, seizing their significance & seeing how they should be set out' (9 November 1911). A bulky manuscript took shape during the summer of 1910, following their return from holiday in Italy with the Trevelyans. They refused all social engagements that autumn in order to press on with it, seized now 'with an unreasoning panic lest someone else should anticipate our main points!'[21] Unfortunately the strain began to tell on Lawrence. In December 1910, with three chapters still to go, his recurrent symptom of writer's cramp was diagnosed as 'cerebral exhaustion', and, under doctor's orders, the Hammonds went on holiday to St Jean de Luz with the Murrays. But by the end of January 1911 the manuscript had been accepted for publication by Longmans, whose reader pronounced it 'sound historically though written from the Radical point of view'.[22]

The Hammonds' travails were not over. In June the printers discovered that the book would run to 560 pages. This was unthinkable; it would be

[21] Barbara Hammond to Gilbert Murray, 19 October 1910, MP 23b.
[22] Lawrence Hammond to Gilbert Murray, 24 January 1911, MP 23a.

unreadable. 'For some hours we were in despair,' Lawrence told Gilbert Murray, '& I as usual at the end of my resources' (16 June 1911). When he went off to the office in the morning, the problem seemed insoluble, but when he returned in the evening he discovered that 'by a Herculean effort Barbara [had] devised a scheme for breaking the book into two. The first on village condit^{ns}: the second on town conditions' (ibid.). This day saw the creation of the *Village Labourer* (1911) and the *Town Labourer* (1917) was made from its spare rib.

The authors of *Towards a Social Policy* – principally Hammond, Hobson, Hobhouse, Masterman, Vaughan Nash and Charles Roden Buxton – had devoted no less than ten of their eighteen chapters to the land. When Hammond left journalism in 1907 he felt somewhat rueful at leaving the political firing line with 'a long fight for the land' in prospect.[23] But Buxton, who had just been reading the first of Trevelyan's volumes on Garibaldi, offered him the pregnant reflection that its author 'had chosen a really usefuller life than the political' (22 September 1907). And in 1911, after a spell in Parliament, he wrote to the Hammonds again to say: 'I wish I could think that I had spent 4 years of such constant & well-directed labour as you have' (12 November 1911). Their book was, so John Masefield assured them, 'one of the really big things in liberal thought of recent years' (16 January 1912); or, as another correspondent (A. M. D. Hughes) put it, 'a pushing at the cart which has to be got forward, albeit by the back wheel, but then again that is the most effective place to push at' (25 October 1911).

The theory of the back wheel was axiomatic in the liberal view of progress as the growth of rational understanding. Propaganda had its place. But the *Village Labourer* was welcomed by Liberals not so much because parts of it could be incorporated in the leaflets which the Committee for the Taxation of Land Values proposed to shower upon unsuspecting Wiltshire farmworkers, as because it spoke with the authority of proper documentation and reasoned judgment. When Wallas had published *Human Nature in Politics*, William James had predicted to him that it would have 'a powerful effect, being *real* political philosophy' (19 December 1908). In the same way, what pleased the Hammonds most was that Morley told them their book was 'real history' (29 October 1911). To Murray, both it and the final volume of Trevelyan's trilogy were 'books that make a permanent difference in one's outlook' (7 November 1911).

The *Village Labourer*'s subtitle – dropped in modern editions –is 'a study in the Government of England before the Reform Bill'. It was, as the preface to the second edition reiterated, 'a study in government, a discussion of the

[23] H. C. Bradby to Hammond, 29 August 1907, HP 16. All otherwise unidentified page references in this section are to the first edition of the *Village Labourer* (1911).

lines on which Parliament regulated the lives and fortunes of a class that had no voice in its own destinies'. In England the old village community, as a relic of feudalism, had survived into the eighteenth century. The fact of its break up was an agrarian necessity: the manner was a landlords' policy. The measures of enclosure showed how a House of Commons representative only of the landed interest naturally behaved.

Was this inevitable? The Hammonds suggested that it was not, because alternative courses existed at the time, chiefly in the form of land apportionment and a statutory minimum wage. A minimum wage fixed by magistrates in response to public opinion 'would have given the village labourers a bond of union before they had lost the memories and the habits of their more independent life' (p. 237). The 'great mutual fidelity' which the labourers finally showed in their rebellion might have been differently channelled if they had had 'a right to defend and a comradeship to foster from the first' (p. 239). This was to counter 'inevitability' on one level, by sketching an alternative version of what might have been. The difficulty with this sort of argument is that so many historical variables have to be accommodated. How much is, as it were, renegotiable? Are, for example, the Combination Laws still to be assumed? What, then, about the pervasive assumptions and entrenched interests of which they were symptomatic? To what extent were the Hammonds projecting an anachronistic humanitarianism by inviting their readers to re-imagine the history of the late eighteenth century as it might have been remade by the men of the early twentieth?

In some ways they had a whiggish sense of the strong continuity between the political world which they described and their own. Barbara Hammond's comment to Murray that at one point she had become so immersed in her research 'that the Whig Govt of 1830 & the present Govt are quite mixed up in my sentiments & I expect that a good deal of the disgust I feel for the latter is due to the behaviour of the former' (29 September 1910) may show her more sceptical here than Lawrence. 'Fox's wisdom,' he had written in 1903, 'lay in a spacious and large-hearted liberalism, such as is to be found a century later in very few of the men who lay claim to that quality' (*Fox*, p. 11). The *Village Labourer* remained faithful to this vision. The politics of the oligarchy, which come in for so much criticism, were nonetheless 'illuminated by the great and generous behaviour of individuals' (p. 329). Samuel Whitbread, who introduced the minimum wage bill in 1795, was 'one of the small band of brave Liberals who had stood by Fox through the revolutionary panic' (p. 139). But he was almost alone in being right, as Scott would have put it in 1899, on 'both sides of our policy'. When the Hammonds wrote that 'in glancing at the class whose treatment of the English poor has been the subject of our study, it is only just to record that in other regions of thought and conduct they bequeathed a great inheritance of moral and liberal ideas' (p. 330), they made Fox's statement of the Liberal doctrine on nationality the chief ground of their extenuation.

Subsequent historians have been less ready than the Hammonds to suppose that with a different throw of the dice at Westminster things would have turned out so differently. But the other level at which the Hammonds suggested that the process was not inevitable turned the argument from the past to the present. They were challenging the view of the past as the authoritative sanction of arrangements in the present, by showing their historical relativity and by testing received opinions against alternative hypotheses. A critical examination of the ideology of the governing class was not the least of their objectives and, like Hobson, they had a sophisticated view of the play of self-interest in the realm of ideas. To some extent the Hammonds were drawing aside the veil of cant with which the upper class had concealed its motives and actions from the gaze of history. But they also recognised that this class was a victim of its own ideology (in its case, of course, a position not without its material compensations). The whole structure of politics and the law and the church constituted a great interlocking system of class government which denied the poor not only a parliamentary voice or vote, but also a fair trial if apprehended and, not least, a spiritual comfort or understanding. The aristocracy and their hangers-on ruled England in this way, and robbed the poor of their patrimony with arrogant contempt. A favourite quotation from Galsworthy summed it up: 'if we go, the whole thing goes' (p. 35). The landlords saw their own rule as the only possible way for society to function and they imagined their own property rights to be absolute wherever they chose to enforce them.

Against this, the Hammonds sought to show that the landlords and the Church were 'two classes who had both contrived to slip off their obligations to the State' (p. 167). They were not, in the eye of history, absolute owners. The *Village Labourer* sought to establish this as fact and drew upon the *Industrial System* for analytical support. Guaranteeing a decent standard of life to the labourer was the first charge on the Hobsonian surplus and any increase here would be shifted back on to rent, just as the poor rate was under the Speenhamland system. But at the time, of course, the governing class 'never conceived the problem as one of distribution' (p. 171). Instead, discussion in the contemporary House of Commons was sealed in by its own assumptions. 'All the interests and instincts of class were disguised under the gold dust of Adam Smith's philosophy' (pp. 142–3). Like Hobson, the Hammonds did not hold the actual writings of Smith responsible; the trouble was that a class with great possessions 'had learnt a reasoned insensibility from the stern Sibyl of the political economy in fashion, that strange and partial interpretation of Adam Smith, Malthus and Ricardo which was then in full power' (p. 207). For an economic discussion less strange and less partial other interests would have had to be represented in Parliament. 'A different kind of House of Commons', the Hammonds speculated, would have put the whole business on another footing (p. 47).

The Hammonds' upper-class readers, like Lady Courtney, found their fears that the book would reveal 'a sad story of wrong if unconscious wrong' amply borne out. 'You and Barbara,' she wrote, 'will have made some restitution for your & our forbears by throwing a searchlight into the past' (30 October 1911). She went one better than Wallas, who read it 'with an overmastering sense of dramatic force greater than any which a novel has ever given me' (N, 11 November 1911), and kept hoping that like a novel it was not true. Other correspondents worried away at this theme. To Buxton it 'burned upon me the sense of the irremediableness of past wrong; and I think of the refrain of Greek tragedies – "the blood spilt on the ground cannot be raised up again"'. (12 November 1911) And yet the need for restitution and remedy could not be overlooked. The revelation of 'how blind the whole upper & middle class can be to the condition of the poor, & how helplessly inarticulate the poor themselves' prompted Murray to wonder 'if we are even now doing something of the same kind' (7 November 1911). To Charles Trevelyan it was 'a terrible exposure of the quality and results of the aristocratic rule in England' (29 November 1911); and Arthur Clutton-Brock drew out this implication by saying that he had 'never heard so powerful an argument for democracy in all institutions in my life' (3 June 1911).

The *Village Labourer* made this impact because Lawrence's prose style, at once lucid and evocative, brought before the general public the fruit of Barbara's cultivation of a largely untilled field of research. The story of the labourers' rising of 1830, with which the book culminated, came as a revelation. As the Hammonds later explained, here lay the accidental origin of the labourer books: 'One of the authors, when playing with the idea of writing a Life of Cobbett, dipping in a desultory way into the "Political Register" was startled to come upon a series of events quite new to him: the rising in the southern counties in 1830' (QR, cclii, 290). In their modern reworking of this topic, Hobsbawm and Rudé point out that the early volumes of the *Victoria County History* had virtually ignored it; and their claim to supersede the *Village Labourer* is in itself testimony to its classic status.[24] The Hammonds were wrong about the revolt, which was more widespread and lasted longer than they supposed. But since it was their work which called attention to it in the first place there is scant cause for lamentation here. They were also deficient in their account of poor law administration, depicting Speenhamland principles as more systematic than subsequent research has allowed.

[24] See E. J. Hobsbawm and George Rudé, *Captain Swing* (1969).

Where the Hammonds' work was from the first most controversial was in its treatment of enclosures. Lawrence acknowledged to Murray that they had not made it 'clear enough that we were not discussing enclosure as a policy wh. is one question but the actual measures of enclosure wh. is another' (4 March 1912). They were partly to blame, therefore, for laying themselves open to J. H. Clapham's complaint that there was 'nowhere any suggestion as to how common-field agriculture was to meet the needs of England' (*EcJ*, xxii, 249). Even so, this missed the Hammonds' point entirely. The fate of the village labourer was their subject. The greater the progress in agriculture during this period, 'the greater appear the perversity and injustice of the arrangements of a society under which the labourer became impoverished' (2nd edn, p. x). W. J. Ashley, it must be said, told the Hammonds that he accepted their account as 'substantially true' (12 March 1913): a measure of accord between political opponents which they reciprocated in later editions. Clapham also accused the Hammonds of bias against the governing class, as illustrated by their unfair use of the story of George Selwyn's attempt to enclose Sedgemoor to pay off gambling debts as an example of how things were done. Modern historians have established that in general the rules of the game were observed more strictly than the Hammonds suggested; but the main question for them was: 'Were the poor sacrificed or not in the enclosures as they were carried out?' (2nd edn, p. xi) Their own view was that enclosure 'was fatal to three classes' (p. 97). These were the small farmers, where they were probably wrong; secondly, the cottagers, where even their critics acknowledge that there is 'a great deal of truth in the Hammonds' brief summary';[25] and, thirdly, the squatters. These occupiers of common-right cottages admittedly came off badly. As Chambers and Mingay put it, they 'received no compensation because they were not, of course, the owners of the rights' (p. 86). This distinction helps to absolve the commissioners of complicity in 'a gigantic swindle' (which is what the Hammonds are supposed to have alleged). But it was, of course, precisely their own point that those without strict legal right were not treated 'even outwardly and formally as having any claim to be consulted before an enclosure was sanctioned' (p. 52). This did not make their loss any less real in a period when ancient custom was being replaced by new conceptions of property rights. The Hammonds' historical treatment was subversive of the very idea that such titles were absolute or that a landowners' Parliament was an appropriate body to enforce them. The conclusion of their modern critics – 'This was not perfect justice, but in an age of aristocratic government and exaggerated respect for the rights of property, it was not a bad approximation to it' – would have left them unimpressed (Chambers and Mingay, p. 88).

[25] J. D. Chambers and G. E. Mingay, *The Agricultural Revolution 1750–1850* (1966), p. 97.

The break-up of the medieval village was their theme. The chief modification which subsequent work would suggest is, as R. H. Tawney put it, 'to lengthen the perspective in which innovations formerly assigned to the later eighteenth and early nineteenth centuries must be seen' (*PBA*, xlvi, 275–6). His own book *The Agrarian Problem in the Sixteenth Century* (1912) was an early contribution to this shift in perspective. His historical interests were closely related to those of the Hammonds – he and Wallas took a major part in the preparation of the *Town Labourer* – and this can be explained in terms of their closely similar social views.

Tawney was thirty-two in 1912; he called himself a socialist; he remained a Christian. After Balliol and Toynbee Hall he had taken a post under the Workers' Educational Association teaching in Lancashire and the Potteries. In July 1912 he became director of the Ratan Tata Foundation, affiliated to the L.S.E.: an appointment in which both Hobhouse and Wallas took a hand. It is easy to see from the commonplace book which he kept in these years why they would have been attracted by his outlook. He wrote at this time of 'the stages of thought about social affairs through which I, and I suppose other people, have passed'. The first stage was that of individualism – the Charity Organisation Society view. This gave way to theoretical socialism as a general analysis. The third stage, however, represented a reversion to a view of the State as composed of individuals, while recognising that it was only through collective action that salvation could come.[26] No quietist, he firmly believed 'that our present (though not all) inequalities are the creation of man not of God' (ibid., pp. 52–3). The prevailing social assumptions were the real corruption and the first priority was to change these. 'There *is* no creative force outside the ideas which control men in their ordinary actions', he insisted (ibid., p. 76).

Tawney was staking out a position somewhere between that of the reformist and the revolutionist – but firmly on the moral axis rather than the mechanical. The Fabians, he thought, erred because they wanted to take short cuts – to trick statesmen into doing what was needful. He condemned this as strongly as Hobhouse: 'No amount of cleverness will get figs off thistles' (ibid., p. 46). Tawney's opinions often had an uncompromising ring to them. He claimed not to see how economic privilege could be attacked 'except by a large transference of property rights, by the adoption of the principle that economic "rent" is not to be left in private hands' (ibid., p. 52). It was his moralism which accounted for this, and this was a kind of extremism which the new Liberals found it easy to tolerate. In Tawney's view the causes of poverty were to be found in 'the existence of economic privileges which give those who enjoy them a lien or bond on the labour of those who do not' (ibid., p. 37). When he came to specify the

[26] J. M. Winter and D. M. Joslin (eds.), *R. H. Tawney's Commonplace Book* (Cambridge 1972), p. 45 (2 December 1912).

actual reform programme necessary to give substance to his often visionary language, it turned out to comprise the public ownership of land, nationalisation of coal-mines, railways and pubs, the democratisation of higher education, and heavy taxes on property incomes. None of this strayed outside the parameters of progressivism.

The *Village Labourer*, after a slow start, sold over a thousand copies within six months and did better in the second year than the first. By May 1913, eighteen months after publication, the Hammonds had received about £110 in royalties, as compared with Lawrence's annual salary of £900. But during 1912 it became clear to him that, with the growing responsibilities of the Civil Service Commission, he would have to give up either his post or the writing of history. The Hammonds had hoped to publish the *Town Labourer* before considering such a step, but it now seemed that the book would never be finished until Lawrence was free. He therefore planned to resign in June 1913. They had been saving for ten years; Barbara had an allowance; and they thought that Lawrence's journalism might bring in £300 a year. If they could find a house in the country, they could sleep one or two nights a week in London while Barbara went to the Public Record Office and Lawrence to the *Nation*. In December 1912 they settled on the house at Piccotts End, near Hemel Hempstead, which was to be their home for the rest of their lives. 'Oatfield' was high up a lane, with fine views and no houses near; the eponymous meadow of three acres, where the Hammonds took in broken-down horses, adjoined a garden of an acre. The house had been built as a rich man's hobby and was a bargain at £45 a year. 'In some moods,' wrote Barbara to Gilbert Murray, 'it seems the height of folly to chuck up £900 a year, and in other moods the only possible course' (2 January 1913).

The Hammonds received a cruel confirmation of the wisdom of their choice when Barbara suffered a recurrence of tubercular trouble in February 1913. She went with the Ponsonbys to a cottage in Dorset to recuperate and, although she did not need an operation, she was out of action until April. Eager to get back to work on the *Town Labourer*, and telling Mary Murray that she was 'quite willing to avoid going under any roof that is not a Temple of the Winds' (15 April 1913), she attempted to go up to London from the country one day a week to work in the Public Record Office where Lawrence tried to find a room with an open window. Even this arrangement proved too exacting. In October Barbara handed over the unfinished research to Molly Hamilton, whose friendship she had made while convalescent: a delegation of responsibilities with subsequent scholarly repercussions. She decided to work at Oatfield, hoping that 'perhaps when I no longer reduce myself to pulp once a week I shall be able to do more than 3 hrs a day' (ibid., 12 October 1913). Lawrence continued to go up one day a week to the *Nation* lunch; but Barbara admitted to Gilbert Murray that she now accepted the doctor's message 'that I am a Ticket of Leave man, & shall be clapped into prison again if I don't lead a very vigorous life' (11 December 1913). When the snow came that winter it kept the Hammonds awake in the shelter and after Christmas even Barbara acknowledged that working out there was 'not unmitigated pleasure at present, but I manage it by means of frequent breaks & get warm by violent exercise'. It was, under the circumstances, a congenial life, with friends like the Marvins and the Trevelyans a trifling four-mile walk away at Berkhampsted; and for the benefit of sybaratic visitors like the Murrays the Hammonds put in grates which gave out 'immense & to us unbearable heat, so that we sit in the French window while guests toast at the fire' (ibid., 11 December 1913).

The *Village Labourer*, raking over the ashes of traditional radicalism, is dedicated to Gilbert and Mary Murray. The *Town Labourer*, projecting its analysis of the evils of landlordism on to industrial capitalism, is dedicated jointly to Hobhouse and Hobson. The books can not unfairly be regarded as historical prefaces to the Rural and Urban Reports of Lloyd George's Land Enquiry Committee, published in October 1913 and April 1914. Charles Buxton was the secretary of the committee and Molly Hamilton was for a time employed as assistant secretary, though Seebohm Rowntree seems to have done most of the work. In the summer of 1913 he and Hobhouse were briefing Lloyd George as part of his effort to 'convince the thoughtful men in the Party'.[27] In the sixty-page introduction which Arthur Acland, as chairman, contributed to the first report, the only historians mentioned by name were the Hammonds and Tawney. Dealing with enclosure, he asseverated that 'it was in no sense an economic necessity that this change should be carried through in such a way as to impoverish the poor while enriching the wealthy, or to convert the peasant into a despairing, crushed, and dependent labourer' (p. lxxix).

Perhaps the most striking feature of the first report was the central importance given to the proposal for a minimum wage for farmworkers. Hobhouse's own experience epitomises the shift of view here. Twenty-five years earlier he had worked for agricultural trade unionism; but this had failed to raise wages; and his own recent membership of trade boards in other fields where low pay was normal showed what could be done by legislative methods. The second report was half as long again as the first, and by far the largest part of it dealt with the housing problem. It proposed that municipal responsibility be enforced here by direct enactment. But so that the normal family could be decently housed, the committee exceeded its terms of reference and, capitalising on the Government's acceptance of its agricultural recommendations, proposed a statutory minimum wage for all low-paid wage earners. It asked, too, for a start to be made on site value

[27] Lloyd George to Scott, 4 September 1913, copy, Lloyd George Papers C/8/1/9.

rating so that future increases in land values should go to the community. The theme of the Land Reports was the justice of making the general welfare the first charge on the one indisputably monopolistic factor of production.

It should be obvious by now why, when the new Liberals were confronted by the problems of industrial capitalism in the early twentieth century, they went back to the land. Many historians of Liberalism have taken this as axiomatic evidence of evasion, atavism and obsolescence. There is a tactical point here. Hobhouse was always anxious to give the old Liberalism a fair chance of living up to its professions. He recognised, in the series of articles he wrote about the land and labour in 1913, that there was a school so enamoured of the taxation of site values that they could see no other problem. But he thought it would be possible for land reformers like himself to co-operate with such Liberals so long as they did not stand in the way of the interventionist side of the programme. He himself preferred to develop the question from the historical principle of a living wage, drawing on the Hammonds to suggest that 1795 was a parting of the ways, when 'a Government, which did not hesitate to use repression when the rights of combination were in question, refused to see anything but the blessings of liberty when the defence of the poor man's standard of living was proposed as a legitimate object of its efforts' (*MG*, 2 October 1913). He went on to cite recent experience of minimum wage regulation and to bring out its link with acceptable standards of housing.

A consideration of taxation was the complement to this analysis of earnings and needs, costs and surplus, earned and unearned: problems which were fundamental to advanced industrial societies. Starting in the 1880s, a theory of 'rent' had been generalised by those who called themselves socialists from land to cover all functionless wealth; by 1914 this analysis had been accepted as the economic theory of what was now called the new Liberalism. The means of implementing the necessary changes had been revised in the light of experience. To some extent collectivist appropriation had yielded priority to fiscal intervention. In this respect the new Liberalism was not proto-socialist but revisionist.

6

War

(I) THE MISJUDGING OF SIR EDWARD GREY

'It was quite characteristic of the state of mind of England in the summer of 1914 that Mr. Britling should be mightily concerned about the conflict in Ireland, and almost deliberately negligent of the possibility of a war with Germany.'[1] The years before 1914 were hardly a golden afternoon of placid contentment. Threats and challenges to Liberal assumptions bristled at home and abroad. Grey's foreign policy, based on a Triple Entente which included Tsarist Russia, seemed to men like Hobson to be 'radically discordant with the essentials of Liberalism' (*MG*, 18 July 1912). The division here, as in the Boer War, was between Radicals and Liberal Imperialists. In Parliament a Foreign Affairs group was set up under Ponsonby and Noel Buxton in November 1911. Its work was complemented by an outside Committee, organised by Hobhouse, of which Courtney became President. Within six months, however, the Committee's initial funds had been exhausted to little effect and it seems to have expired before the end of 1912. Persia was a particularly sore point since here Britain seemed not only to be thwarting nationalist aspirations but to be doing so in collusion with Russia. 'The situation is unspeakably humiliating', Hammond confessed to Ponsonby (31 December 1911). The Foreign Policy Committee confidently characterised such evils as 'the work of a secret diplomacy which committed the country to lines of policy that it did not approve' (*CR*, ci, 471). Here, as elsewhere, Radicals diagnosed the problem as one for which they had a standing remedy: more democracy.

'To the eye of a thorough-going Liberal,' Gilbert Murray was to admit in *The Foreign Policy of Sir Edward Grey* (1915), 'there is something sordid and even odious about the ordinary processes of Foreign Policy' (p. 41). There was the suspicion of intrigue, of vested interests, of secret class pressures. Neither Hobson nor Norman Angell nor Brailsford suggested that war could benefit business interests, still less the nation as a whole. But whereas Angell's message that war was the great illusion was directed to the enlightened capitalist, Hobson's analysis usually stressed the power of the classes who might gain from at least risking war. It therefore followed that 'the problem of peace is nothing less than the problem of democracy, in its political, industrial, and moral aspects' (N, 1 August 1908). Liberal

[1] H. G. Wells, *Mr Britling Sees It Through* (1916), Bk. 1, ch. v.

democracy itself lay at the root of the foreign policy question – as it did of so many questions. Hobson looked at Ireland through the same eyes. 'Unless the organized working people of the country in the Labour Party, and their trade unions, can be brought in to stiffen, and if necessary to direct, Liberalism, there is little hope of victory', he wrote in *Traffic in Treason* (p. 62). To Hobhouse and Scott, who largely shared his view, the Government's weakness here was only encouraging the prevalent appeals to strength rather than persuasion or justice. Ulster came off better than the women, and the women better than the strikers, because Asquith was ready to cave in to the more powerful elements within society. Liberalism was being betrayed. To Hobhouse in May 1914 this looked like 'the beginning of the end of the Liberal Govt & a good job too if only the others weren't as bad!' Yet, from the perspective of wartime, such challenges to Liberal doctrines appeared 'annoying and ridiculous rather than a source of vital danger'.[2] The solution still lay in a more thoroughgoing application of democratic principles. The problem was not whether progress would triumph but how and when. Even the prospect of a continental war presented itself to Scott in much the same light. 'It ought,' he told Hobhouse, 'to sound the knell of all the autocracies – including that of our own Foreign Office' (29 July 1914).

Wallas had for some time been haunted by the possibility of a European war which might smoulder on for thirty years. By Tuesday 28 July 1914 his fears were taking tangible form in the international crisis and he rang up Hobson to arrange to meet. Wallas was worried that the Triple Entente was coming to be regarded as a binding alliance. On 30 and 31 July he and Hobson conferred at the National Liberal Club and copied out from *Hansard* Asquith's and Grey's declarations that Britain was free from ties. Hobhouse, somewhat to his subsequent regret, left them to it while he went on holiday to Scarborough. They began collecting signatures, at the House of Commons and elsewhere, for a letter urging British neutrality, and took an office as the headquarters of the British Neutrality Committee. The historian Basil Williams joined them as a third full-time instigator. Another effort under Angell's guidance was proceeding on parallel lines. On Sunday 2 August the Committee's letter was sent to the press over the signatures of Courtney, MacDonald, Murray, Gardiner, Wallas, G. M. Trevelyan, Hobhouse, Hobson, Hirst, Hammond and Williams. When the Webbs called at the National Liberal Club in the afternoon, Sidney fetched down from the smoking room not only their old friend Massingham but also Hammond, who was evidently unfamiliar to Beatrice (she called him Drummond). They were, she noted in her diary (5 August 1914) 'bitter & depressed', but they vehemently denied that a violation of Belgian neutrality meant

[2] Leonard to Emily Hobhouse, 5 May 1914, Hobhouse Papers; Hobhouse, *The World in Conflict* (1915), p. 54.

that Britain had to go to war. Hammond, along with Trevelyan and Murray, sent congratulations to Gardiner for the firm support for neutrality which he had given in Saturday's *Daily News*. The *Manchester Guardian* too was standing firm for righteousness against the cries of the warmongers. 'The Jingoism of the *Times* clique baffles the imagination & we are evidently in the greatest danger', Leonard Hobhouse wrote to Emily (2 August 1914).

But this was almost the last moment at which the Radicals were united in knowing their own mind. Hammond, Gardiner and MacDonald were already having second thoughts about the neutrality declaration, as more news of Belgium's plight came through. (MacDonald was soon to have third thoughts.) On Monday, Hobson and Wallas were in the lobby of the House of Commons during Grey's speech which won general assent for a decision to support France. When Murray, who had heard it, met them afterwards he told them that it had converted him. (In his later published account he had to do violence to the known chronology in order to stretch this conversion over a full week). That evening it seemed pretty certain to Hobson that there would be war. He accepted that there was a British obligation to defend the French coast but thought that this could have been met by accepting Germany's undertaking not to cross the Straits of Dover. Instead, Britain had by her insistence made the preservation of Belgian neutrality into the *casus belli*. 'This I personally regard as indefensible,' he told Scott, 'though Germany's brutal behaviour to Belgium merits every reprobation' (Wilson, pp. 94–5).

A meeting at noon on Tuesday 4 August formally consituted the British Neutrality Committee. Among those present were Hobson, Wallas, Hammond, Lowes Dickinson, G. M. Trevelyan, Bertrand Russell, Basil Williams and Charles Roden Buxton. Some of these, including Russell and Wallas, went on to the *Nation* lunch. Massingham was, according to Russell's autobiography, still vehemently opposed to British participation in the war. Wallas, however, learnt there that Germany was certain to invade Belgium. He realised, of course, that this made war inevitable. But, as he recalled in a private memorandum a few weeks later, in all the rush of interviewing and telephoning, 'I had no time to decide whether I desired to fight for Belgian neutrality or not. If Belgium were invaded I should be unable to influence events' (6 October 1914). During the two or three bewildered hours before the British ultimatum was announced that afternoon, the rump of the committee reconvened. Russell was apparently present but not G. M. Trevelyan. They had walked the length of the Strand quarrelling, since Trevelyan too had now swung round in support of Grey. 'During the meeting,' Russell recalled, 'there was a loud clap of thunder, which all the older members of the committee took to be a German bomb. This dissipated their last lingering feeling in favour of neutrality' (*Autobiog.*, ii, 16).

At 11.00 p.m. on 4 August the British ultimatum to Germany expired; at 11.00 a.m. the next morning the British Neutrality Committee met and agreed to dissolve. Barbara Hammond was still commending the outspoken Ponsonby for his attacks on Grey. 'I wish we'd gone into it, if we had to go, with clean hands,' she wrote to him on 5 August, 'but that speech of Gray's has besmirched everything.' Lawrence, however, was by now merely urging him 'to remember that no criticism will be listened to in this present crisis' (5 August 1914). Hobhouse too became more circumspect. He felt that their mistake in 1899 had been to keep up criticism during the early stages of the war. His feeling, like Scott's, was a mixture of a genuine conviction that the safety of the country was the overriding priority and a tactical judgment that this was an inexpedient moment to express dissent. He could therefore condone Lloyd George's decision to stay in the Government until the naval issue had been settled, but still told Emily Hobhouse that it was 'humbug for Ll. George to preach social reform & then go in for this policy, the ultimate meaning of wh. has been obvious all along' (5 August 1914).

Hobhouse was immediately convinced that the prospect was conscription and coalition. 'As to Liberalism it died last Monday', he wrote to Emily on 8 August, and on the same day grimly assured Wallas that political or social progress would become 'names without a meaning for our time'. To Hobhouse 'the world not only seemed different but became different on August 4th. . .It turned out in sober truth a different world from that which we knew, a world in which force had a greater part to play than we had allowed, a world in which the ultimate social securities were gone, in which we seemed to see of a sudden through a thin crust of civilisation the seething forces of barbaric lust for power and indifference to life' (*World in Conflict*, p. 6). His son Oliver later testified that the war was a shattering blow to him, striking at the whole foundation of his thought. He himself graphically expressed the taunt to which he was open: 'Do you mean that you, with your evolving ethics, wouldn't at any time have confidently maintained, on the basis of comparative sociology and psychology and ethnology, and at least five other elaborately-constructed sciences, that anything like the present war had become historically impossible?' (*CR*, cviii, 159)

The first revision of Hobhouse's opinions concerned his view of Germany. The weight of the German war machine was initially directed against Belgium. The guarantee of her frontiers had a special significance for many Liberals. In *Liberalism and the Empire* (p. 167) Hammond had quoted Gladstone: 'The same sacredness defends the narrow limits of Belgium as attaches to the extended frontiers of Germany or Russia or France.' This was the Gladstonian doctrine of international morality which, in its application to the Boers, had been a strong buttress to the Cobdenite doctrine of non-intervention. But Belgium was nearer home; and here Gladstone himself had explicitly revealed that for him the policy of non-intervention adopted in 1870 was a means not an end. 'If we had gone to war,' he growled ten years later, 'we should have gone to war for freedom, we should have gone to war for public right, we should have gone to war to save human happiness from being invaded by tyrannous and lawless power.'[3] In 1914 the two doctrines could no longer be squared. The Belgian issue separated Cobdenites like Morley, Hirst and Hobson from those of their pro-Boer allies whose latent Gladstonianism swept aside all lesser claims; and for Hobhouse, Hammond, Massingham, Murray, Trevelyan and Gardiner it facilitated the transition from principled support of neutrality to principled support of the war. 'Nearly all those who sympathised with the Boers as a small nation struggling for freedom now sympathise with the Belgians struggling for freedom', Hobhouse maintained to his sister (24 December 1914).

Initially, it must be said, he himself restricted his commitment as narrowly as possible. He remained unpersuaded that Grey had been proved right all along. The Government's White Paper left him cold. He told Emily that he wanted to be 'quite free to argue the whole merits of the case if ever a favourable opportunity arises, wh. can only be if the Allies succeed in holding out' (26 August 1914). The Government had done a wrong to its own country by committing it to war without exhausting the possibilities of avoiding it, but Britain was not doing wrong to any other country by fighting.

To other Radicals, however, Grey seemed, in the light of events, a worthier upholder of the Gladstonian standard than they had allowed. 'You spoke up for Grey on the White Paper,' Hammond told Ponsonby on 7 August, 'and the impatience of people over the rest will not matter when the time really comes to discuss all this inquest business.' To Hammond the White Paper was 'an immense relief'; it meant that they were 'men fighting in an honourable cause'. Barbara, too, apparently a more reluctant convert, did not see, after reading it, 'how we cld have stood out, unless we had played an inconceivably base part'.[4] While Hobhouse remonstrated with Massingham for committing the *Nation* to Grey's defence, therefore, the Hammonds merely acknowledged that he had been too violent in his reaction.

The Hammonds had two sets of close friends, the Murrays and the Ponsonbys. Gilbert Murray shared their view. Arthur Ponsonby continued to oppose the war and became one of the founders of the Union of Democratic Control (U.D.C.), along with MacDonald, C. P. Trevelyan, Angell

[3] A. J. P. Taylor, *The Troublemakers* (Panther edn 1969), p. 67.

[4] Lawrence Hammond (18 August 1914) and Barbara Hammond (19 August 1914) to Murray, MP 23a and 23b.

and E. D. Morel. Brailsford and Russell emerged as the most effective publicists for the U.D.C.'s condemnation of Grey. Hammond assured Ponsonby that he was not influenced by any weakness for the Liberal party as such in taking a more indulgent view, and he further maintained that the divergence now, unlike that in the Boer War, was only over the past. But the consequent difference of view in the present was considerable. With the German armies advancing upon Paris in September 1914, the Hammonds for a time found it painful even to argue. Barbara told Ponsonby that 'to say that you "can't support the Govt" in this present world seems like saying when the plague is devastating the land that you can't help the authorities because you don't think they took sufficient precautions beforehand'. She commended the 'sound rule of the R.C. Church that the wickedness of the priest doesn't invalidate the goodness of the sacrament'. A thinly veiled illustration made the point: 'e.g. ABC's attitude towards Belgium is right, towards Persia wrong' – and for e.g. she might as well have put E.G. So the right course was to 'make him extend his feeling abt Belgium to Persia, dont tell him that because he was wrong about Persia, therefore he has got to be wrong about Belgium too' (22 October 1914). Those Radicals who supported a war for Belgium were prepared to rejoice over Grey as a sinner come to repentance. 'The anti-war people like Mr Brailsford & Mr Bertrand Russell seem so absorbed by their hypocrisy hunt, that they see nothing else', Barbara Hammond expostulated to Murray. 'If you are ready to die for your hypocrisy & to let those you love best die for it, a good deal ought to be forgiven you – but they dont see that at all & picture the whole nation as comfortable Pecksniffs' (24 November 1914).

The Hammonds therefore had mixed feelings about the U.D.C. 'With their objects as expressions of pious opinions hardly anyone cld quarrel,' wrote Barbara, 'but I do wish that they wldnt mix it all up with what seems personal animus against Sir Edward Grey' (ibid.). Wallas stood aside for similar reasons. All three nonetheless helped Ponsonby with the draft of U.D.C. pamphlet No. 5 *Parliament and Foreign Policy* (1915). 'The argument is very sound', Hammond assured him (9 December 1914). But Murray wrote his study of *The Foreign Policy of Sir Edward Grey* – which Hammond helped him to revise – explicitly to counter U.D.C. pamphlets Nos. 3 and 4 by Russell and Brailsford. Whatever their views on the democratic control of foreign policy, the Hammonds were quite clear on the morality of Grey's support for Belgium. They were quite unmoved by the more cynical argument that Belgium could hardly have been a ground for war since German intentions here were widely known. Russell challenged Hammond as to whether he was ignorant of this. Hammond admitted that he was. 'If you say that you think the *Nation* has not allowed enough for the warlike forces in Germany in the past I agree', he continued. 'I think that has been the mistake of all the Peace people' (*Autobiog.*, ii, 46–7).

This mistake only made their bouleversement by the evidence of the White Paper more complete. As Murray put it in his tract: 'The statesman whom I had suspected as over-imperialist was doing everything humanly possible to preserve peace; the Power whose good faith I had always championed was in part playing a game of the most unscrupulous bluff, in part meant murder from the beginning' (pp. 10–11). To the end of his life Hammond maintained that Grey had been acting on a true intuition and 'was really doing for Britain what Franklin Roosevelt was to do later for the United States, breaking down a tradition of isolation that had become a dangerous weakness' (*L*, 13 February 1947). In the end Hobhouse's conviction that Germany had been hopelessly wrong from the beginning led him along the same path. 'You must remember', he told Emily, 'that the whole doctrine of force which has taken possession of Europe, & formed it into a camp, is Prussian in origin' (8 October 1914). The doctrine of force, as proclaimed by Treitschke, had been dominant since 1870 and it was 'the theory on wh Germany justifies the invasion of Belgium & in fact the whole plan of the war' (24 December 1914). Hobhouse's old suspicion of Idealism inevitably resurfaced. Kant was the last German thinker whom he recognised as in the humanitarian tradition of western civilisation, and thereafter a distinctive outlook had set Germany apart. 'Hegel's divine State, Treitschke's power, Nietzsche's contempt of restraint are fused together in the faith which animates the governing classes of Germany, political, military and academic', he alleged in *The World in Conflict* (p. 56). By the spring of 1915 he had come to the conclusion that 'in a far deeper sense than any of us supposed a year ago, we are to conceive her as standing in determined opposition to the ideals which, however imperfectly, the civilised nations of the modern world have been endeavouring to hammer out into practical shape' (pp. 101–2). This led him to the further admission 'that Grey was, perhaps inarticulately, aware of the kind of being that he was up against in his dealings with German statesmanship. We did not know it in the same way, and to that extent we misjudged him' (*CR*, cviii, 161).

For Hobson the war was 'the first of a series of shocks to my belief that the world was inhabited by a reasonable animal' (*Conf.*, p. 104). He came to think that his pre-war assumption that civilised man was 80 per cent rational was an illusion. The percentage would have to be halved. After the collapse of their neutrality committee, he and Wallas remained in association with Lowes Dickinson. Dickinson reacted as they did. With only 40 per cent to play with, the need to spread enlightenment was an even more pressing task. 'That is our war – those of us who believe in reason – our eternal and holy war', Dickinson proclaimed (*N*, 8 August 1914). He therefore immediately began to draw together likeminded men to organise for peace. They became known as the Bryce Group, taking the name of their eminent patron, the former Ambassador to Washington, and they transferred their meetings to Bryce's house from the end of October 1914. Dickinson was, by general agreement, the dominant influence. Hobson worked closely with Richard Cross, the Rowntrees' solicitor, whom he knew as business manager of the *Nation*. He also recalled Hobhouse as active in the Group, but this is not confirmed elsewhere. Although it included such a fierce critic as Ponsonby, the Group took no distinctive position on the origins of the war, which suited Wallas exactly.

Hobson, however, also joined the U.D.C. and was co-opted on to its Executive Committee in November 1914. He found his combative instincts fully roused by the fight against militarism. An emotional commitment for or against the war produced a strain on personal relations not entirely overcome by a demarcation of areas of intellectual agreement. Hobson and Brailsford bore the brunt of attacks from supporters of the war at the *Nation* lunches. Nevinson's record of one exchange with Morrison on 12 January 1915 – 'Hobson white with rage said "That's a lie"' – captures the style of argument. On 23 March 1915 Hobhouse and Hammond joined Morrison in attacking Brailsford as pro-German. This is the last occasion on which Nevinson records Hobhouse's presence. The constant disputes about the origins of the war were too much for him. Perhaps he sensed that an open conflict with Hobson could not be avoided except by his withdrawal. The Liberal supporters of the war were treading a narrow path here. When Murray had finished his defence of Grey, he told Hammond that 'though I differ greatly from Morel Brailsford & Co, I find all my real anger goes out towards the Jingoes' (18 June 1915). His fastidious approach succeeded in distancing his position from that of vulgar patriotism. As Shaw acknowledged, in an otherwise critical review, 'Murray was never fool enough to be a Jingo' (*NS*, 17 July 1915).

There was one unimpeachable test of sincerity in this situation. C. E. Montague had written in the *Manchester Guardian* on 24 August 1914: 'Europe must either smash Prussian Junkerdom or be smashed by it.' Exactly two months later he wrote to Scott: 'I have felt for some time, and especially since I have been writing leaders urging people to enlist, a strong wish to do the same myself.'[5] Scott was puzzled by his son-in-law's behaviour. Montague was, after all, forty-seven and, until he dyed his hair, he had great difficulty in finding a regiment. Madie Montague tried explaining to her father: 'He wants to kill a German.' Scott could still hardly grasp what was involved. 'Isn't it rum?' he confided to Hobhouse (20 December 1914). But Hobhouse did not find it rum at all. His first thought, on the outbreak of war, had been that his own son would be needed. Oliver Hobhouse, whose lack of application to work had previously troubled his father, had a commission and was training in Burma before the year was out. 'The generation which even their fathers thought too

[5] Oliver Elton, *C. E. Montague* (1929), p. 104.

much set upon amusement,' Hobhouse wrote feelingly, 'showed that the moment they were convinced of necessity they could give it up and go to drill' (*World in Conflict*, p. 23). Not only did Hobhouse approve of Montague's action: at Christmas 1914 he was evidently appraising his own grey hairs and provoking Emily's impatient refusal to believe that 'even if you were 2 years younger you would feel a bit happier with a Commission, because it surely would not be *you*' (28 December 1914). In March 1915, moreover, Ted Scott, Hobson's son-in-law, also enlisted, leaving the *Guardian* with a vacancy which Scott vainly tried to persuade Hammond to fill.

Scott and Hobhouse felt an acute personal stake in the fortunes of the war and exhibited an increasingly urgent desire to win. One reason for Hobhouse's withdrawal from the *Nation* was that he differed from Massingham in taking a more favourable view of Lloyd George. In this he was undoubtedly influenced by Scott, whose lengthy memoranda of interviews with Lloyd George and other ministers were destined in the first instance for Hobhouse's eyes. At the beginning of the war, of course, Lloyd George had been the champion of the new Liberalism as both a Radical and a progressive. 'I have no intention,' Hammond had claimed to Ponsonby, 'of reading a line of Asquith's rhetoric about small nations &c &c &c: Lloyd George of course is in a very different position' (20 September 1914). Hammond had been less ready than Hobhouse to concede that the war implied a halt to social progress. Immersed in his work on the *Town Labourer*, he drew more positive implications. The Napoleonic wars had admittedly been fought at a countless cost to the working class, but the present war involved different principles. The Prussian system, he maintained, 'represents all that the working-man is trying to modify and alter in his own society, developed and elaborated and armed into the most thorough system in the world' (N, 5 September 1914). In overthrowing a reactionary power, it was the moral task of a democratic society to save its citizens from the destructive consequences of war. In April 1915, believing 'that our nation should throw the power of a democracy into this momentous struggle', he naturally welcomed Lloyd George's initiatives in bringing the trade unions into a fuller partnership in the armaments industry – indeed this sort of organisation for war ought to go further (N, 24 April 1915). But was this really what Lloyd George stood for?

By May 1915 Scott had become convinced that stern measures were needed to tackle 'this whole vast question of national organization and of the rousing and disciplining of the working class'. He envisaged a weighty but vague role for Hobhouse – 'travelling about, seeing important people, inspecting works & conferring with labour leaders'. Since Hobhouse was merely acting as secretary to a hospital in France at the time, this was a dazzling prospect of promotion. Scott now confided to him that 'something not unlike a Prussian organization for the period of the war' was required to avoid unnecessary loss of life (7 May 1915). This was a poignant appeal for men with sons at risk. Hobhouse accepted the need for 'a much more rigorous discipline if we are going to win', which might 'even involve a kind of conscription in which every man will be available for the Government for some work, soldiering or industrial, which will assist the prosecution of the war' (*Memoir*, p. 51).

Hobhouse and Scott were relatively unmoved, therefore, by the end of the Liberal Government in May 1915. They took comfort from Lloyd George's enhanced power as Minister of Munitions. Other Liberals were more sceptical that a war for law and freedom could be won by Prussian methods. As Murray saw it, one scurrilous intrigue after another had weakened the Government until a reconstruction had taken place 'at the bidding of the very scum of journalism'. At this rate Britain would become 'a nation, not devoted to law or freedom or any of the causes which we thought we were supporting, but a nation very like Germany without its discipline.' The higher ideal had gone under and the hope 'that, for once, war would not necessarily bring oppression and reaction' had been defeated. With much of this Hammond agreed. It had been 'a most humiliating business'.[6] As one who 'ceased to be a Liberal when the Govt took to presecuting workmen & broke faith with the women', he forecast that the new Government, 'daring to do what its predecessor wanted at every turn in the last 4 years, will make a real onslaught on the working classes'. This opened up for the first time the prospect of revolution, which might well be successful. 'So that on the whole my forecast is cheerful', he assured Ponsonby (24 May 1915), though admittedly disappointing for people like themselves who would be hung or shot in the process.

The fall of the Liberal Government brought conscription palpably nearer and gave the issue of compulsion a new fierceness. Asquith remained prime minister but it was Lloyd George who was ascendant. At the *Nation* lunch on 1 June Nevinson observed 'violent opposition growing to conscription; violent distrust of Ll. George & of his Coalition.' To Hirst, who had followed Morley in opposition to the war, it was piquant to see 'the organised hypocrisy of Liberal Imperialism based upon the unholy alliance of Jingoism with Socialism falling to pieces'. But he was most moved by 'the wickedness, & folly, & shame' of compulsory service which, he told Scott, 'with Protection, the Censorship, & a military bureaucracy would make England no place for people like me' (21 May 1915). Scott's own more favourable view of the Coalition involved endorsing the ideal of 'a nation marshalled & regimented for service'[7] – language which may have caused Hobhouse some unease and was certainly unfit for Hirst's ears. So Scott made a

[6] Murray to Hammond, 20 May 1915, HP 30; Hammond to Murray, 29 May 1914, MP 23a.
[7] Scott to Hobhouse, 23 May 1915, MGP.

shuffling response to Hirst's challenge, asseverating the need to raise a large army but claiming that there was 'no reason to doubt that it can be done effectively without compulsion' (Wilson, p. 125).

Scott's realisation that compulsion was a dirty word may have been hastened by a memorandum from Hobhouse outlining the objections to compulsory service which would, he claimed, undoubtedly alienate a good deal of Liberal and Labour opinion. All the overtones of conscription were wrong. Murray reported to Hammond a remark of Milner's: 'I don't believe in this voluntary system, and I am not going to put myself out to make it a success' (20 May 1915). With Milner against it, the Liberals knew that there must be virtue in the voluntary system. 'If patriotism means love of our national characteristics and institutions and of individual liberty surely we ought to fight stoutly against Milnerism', Hirst pleaded with Scott (28 May 1915). Hobhouse remained more ambivalent about the paradox that the effort of defeating Germany might involve a surrender to the methods of German militarism. 'We accept these consequences lest a worse fate befall us', he claimed in March. 'If we do not fight our best, German militarism will sweep us away, and peace, Liberalism, and international freedom are abolished in Europe' (*AM*, cxv, 546). The strong possibility remained that by winning in the flesh they might be beaten in the spirit. It was a dilemma for which he could suggest no convincing solution.

(II) LIBERALISM BEATEN TO ITS CORNER

'I feel, increasingly of late, that I am not doing "my bit" in the world crisis', Wallas confessed to Murray (22 June 1915). His neighbour Hobhouse, 'vegetating here fiddling with a little hospital work & some journalism',[8] felt much the same. Both of them were over fifty. Like Lowes Dickinson and Gardiner, all they could do was regret that their age debarred them from active service. Tawney, at thirty-four, had been in the army for several months. By August 1915 it had become intolerable to Hammond, so he told Ponsonby, 'to see all the youth of the nation being swept into the trenches while I who have no children & have had 42 years of life am sitting here' (2 August 1915). After much debate he and Barbara had decided that he should accept the offer of a commission in the Lowland Territorial Artillery. 'The business of war is absolutely repulsive to me,' he admitted, 'but then so it is to thousands of others & I dont see why I should be exempted from its horrors because I have delicate feelings' (ibid.). His likeminded friends warmly commended his decision. 'I envy you', Hobhouse told him: 'The only thing to be done, worth doing, is to go oneself' (30 September 1915). Murray too started wishing he were a bit fitter

[8] Hobhouse to Hammond, 30 September 1915, HP 17.

physically: 'No one can be really at peace in his own mind now until he has in some way offered his life to his Country' (17 November 1915).

Hammond's first sacrifice was his beard, which had to be shaved off. Next was his dignity, when he was taught to ride a horse. The Hammonds also suffered financially, especially since at the same juncture Lawrence's mother, who had been mentally ill for ten years, was sent into a nursing home, where she stayed, at an heroic cost to the whole family, until her death the following year. But half of Oatfield was let to an officer and his wife, which also made it less lonely for Barbara. Hammond spent the autumn of 1915 training in Scotland. He found drill tedious but was attached to the horses and managed to get a few windows opened. He was impressed by the physical difficulty – and the moral fortitude – with which recruits from working-class occupations stood the rigours of army life. He and Tawney could now compare notes on army life which acted as a further reinforcement of their common experience and outlook. Lawrence was keen that Barbara should not lose interest in the *Town Labourer*, telling her that he regarded it as 'a spiritual bond between us if I am killed' (8 December 1915). But it was an anxious time for her and her feelings about the war became more intense. She told him her opinion that 'any man who hasnt offered to serve wld have a weight round his neck for the rest of his life' (4 December 1915).

For Wallas and Hobhouse too, the second year of war brought an untroubled confidence in the justice of the Allied cause and a single-minded desire for victory. To Wallas English soldiers were in a real sense 'facing death for Liberty' (*N*, 2 October 1915). He offered the personal confession for American readers 'that I believe that the war was mainly the result of German and Austrian aggression, that I intensely desire victory for the Allies, and that a decisive victory for the German governing caste in their present temper would be, in my view, a disaster to all that I most value in civilization' (*Men & Ideas*, p. 97). With all this Hobhouse agreed. 'I have always been a Gladstonian in foreign policies,' he argued to the pacifist Emily, '& in most wars have thought one party in the right. This time I think it is ourselves' (14 September 1915).

When Barbara Hammond met Hobhouse at the Courtneys in October she found him 'very gloomy (as always)', this time about Zeppelin raids, which illustrated the Government's incompetence. The Courtneys, old and dejected, were certainly not the people to cheer him up. Barbara found herself in profound disagreement with their proposals for peace negotiations. 'Pacifists *can't* face facts', she wrote to Lawrence.[9] In the House of Lords two weeks later Courtney publicly stated his view that the deadlock in the war was threatening the civilisation of Europe. 'Freedom of speech,

[9] Barbara to Lawrence Hammond, 19 October 1915 and fragment n.d., HP 6, ff.216–17, 221–6.

freedom of writing, almost freedom of thought have been struck at' (5 *Hansard*, xx, 196). At first sight it seems odd that this utterance should have greatly impressed supporters of the war like the Wallases, who, according to Ada, found it 'so sane & clear, & so "just"' (diary, 9 November 1915). Yet in directing attention to the domestic impact of the war, Courtney was raising issues which, with a Coalition Government in power, were now bringing Liberals closer together again. Moreover, even the U.D.C. was at pains to deny that its policy was 'Stop the War'. Hobson, like Courtney, was airing the possibilities of escaping from 'the grinding horrors of a military deadlock' at this time (N, 16 October 1915); and Florence Hobson was proclaiming with shrill insistence that a transcendant act of will by women, the saner sex, could end the war and usher in a new era of morality. Yet when Scott went to stay with them in November he could not find anything in Hobson's general view with which he disagreed. 'Germany must be beaten and must not be allowed to profit by her aggressions' (Wilson, p. 156).

The contentious issue of compulsion demoralised Liberals. The tactics by which it was handled were a source of discord. But the principles at stake tended to narrow rather than widen divisions between Liberal supporters and Liberal opponents of the war. By the autumn of 1915 Scott and Hobhouse had taken up an attitude towards organisation which involved a greater wariness of Lloyd George's proposals. 'I must tell you that my view of Ll. G. has been in some degree modified in your direction', Hobhouse admitted to Hammond (30 September 1915). He had indeed warned Scott that there could be no question of imposing further discipline upon labour without the *quid pro quo* of nationalisation. At the Trades Union Congress, Beatrice Webb told Wallas, there was considerable feeling among the delegates 'that the governing class is using the opportunity of the war to alter the institutions of the country so that any kind of resistance against industrial oppression can be put down' (13 September 1915). Opposition to compulsion united Labour with the upholders of unflinching Liberal principles. This was the *Guardian*'s natural constituency. It therefore adopted a pragmatic stance. As Scott put it, 'like most Liberals and the great body of organised labour, I regard compulsory military service as in itself a great evil, but I would unhesitatingly accept it, as I believe would most of its opponents if it could be shown to be necessary for the purpose of winning the war'.[10] When Hobhouse went to see McKenna, Lloyd George's bitter opponent, he was given a detailed statement of the case against conscription in terms of the unavailability of further industrial resources. This impressed Hobhouse and for the time being he accepted it.

The advocates of a more thoroughgoing prosecution of the war, however,

[10] Scott to Lansdowne, 17 September 1915 (copy), Balfour Papers, BL Add. MSS. 49864, ff.112–15.

held the initiative. Liberals were fighting a rearguard action which could only be successful if the fortunes of the war took a decisive turn. At the *Nation* lunch on 12 October Nevinson found a 'general sense of disaster & despair about Near East: also about home politics & the set agst Grey & Asquith'. Asquith, however, did little to rally Liberal support. His daughter's opulent wedding, for instance, jarred with his appeals for sacrifice from trade unions. Scott and Hobhouse had laid great stress upon exhausting every resource of the voluntary system before there was any resort to conscription. This was the rationale of the 'Derby scheme' adopted in October 1915. They acknowledged that a point might be reached when the voluntary principle had self-evidently failed; but until then they supposed it safe. This neat design, however, was undermined by one inconspicuous condition: Asquith's pledge that no married volunteers would be called up until all eligible single men had been taken. By the end of 1915 this condition had become paramount. So opponents of conscription were denied a clear issue upon which to fight. When Hobhouse saw McKenna again in December, he found that the compulsion of single men was taken as settled. 'They stole a march on us by dividing the interests of the married and single', he confessed to Scott. Asquith's 'nasty trick' had betrayed the cause of which he might have become champion (Wilson, pp. 165–6). Scott and Hobhouse had no doubt of the bad effect of the new Military Service measure in extending compulsion, directly or indirectly, to the whole work force. It was, wrote Hobhouse, 'a Bill which will not, as we think, contribute to the victory of British arms over Germany, but establishes beyond doubt the victory of German ideas over England' (*MG*, 8 January 1916).

'The self-contained, disciplined, military State is the political entity of the coming future', Hobhouse declared in January 1916.[11] It hinged upon compulsion, which had just been accepted, and protection, for which there was a vociferous demand. The new protectionism, as Hobson pointed out, sought to impose the existing war map upon future world trade. If Hobhouse slipped his Liberal moorings here, as Hobson later suggested, there is no evidence that he slipped very far. For though he acknowledged that 'there may be circumstances at the end of the war which will compel us to modify the Free Trade principle' (*Memoir*, p. 51), the thrust of his argument, like that of Scott's, was to put up as good a fight as possible against such proposals. It was not just the doctrine of Free Trade but the future of Europe that was at stake. Hobson therefore mounted his onslaught on *The New Protectionism* (1916) as not only 'a complicated form of folly': it was also 'a crime – I had almost written *the* crime – against civilization' (p. 113).

Hobson had implicitly revealed himself as a Cobdenite in 1914; he was,

[11] *Questions of War and Peace* (1916), p. 188.

as he confessed in 1920, 'steeped in the principles of Cobden',[12] and, appropriately enough, it was on the issue of Free Trade that he made one of the crucial political decisions of his life. Believing that the Liberal ministers had abandoned Free Trade in 1916, he resigned from the party. In this war, like the last, Hobson continually refreshed himself by returning to the wisdom of Cobden. Free trade, he reiterated, was indeed the true guarantee of peace. But what Cobden had failed to perceive was the special interests of powerful groups in a system of privilege and protection. Protection, imperialism and war were all remediable by a redistribution of wealth at home and a policy of the open door abroad. 'The only radical cure,' he concluded, 'is the progress of democratic control within each nation.'[13]

This diagnosis was not new to Hobson's friends. They had all accepted it before the war. They agreed with what he said in his U.D.C. pamphlet, *A League of Nations* (1915), that dangerous foreign policies had 'nearly all been the product of such group-pulls upon the instruments of national government' (p. 16). Where they parted company was on the question of whether Grey too had been 'usurping the name and pretext of the Commonwealth' in committing Britain to the war. Within the Bryce Group both schools of thought had been represented. 'I don't join the "Union of Democratic Control",' Wallas explained to Murray, 'because I dont hate Grey', and because when a peace settlement came to be debated, 'I may be fighting more or less on Grey's side' (22 June 1915). The ideas of the Bryce Group turned upon creating a League of Nations. By the end of February 1915 a firm draft proposal had taken shape and was printed for private circulation in England and America. The League idea began to gain general currency in Liberal circles, not least because of its ambiguity.

Wallas's approach was characteristic of him. He wanted to build upon existing practices and to turn the expertise of the professionals to better account. Better international organisation was certainly needed, but he was happy to leave its operation in the hands of the diplomats. He was, as he put it, a minimiser. Capturing the sympathy of men like Grey was therefore crucial. But Wallas's approach also led to a certain detachment from the Group since he was, as Dickinson later wrote, 'more concerned to press for international cooperation in general than our particular and definite plan for preventing war'.[14] Ponsonby was close to this position and he seems to have lost interest in the Group's work at a fairly early stage. Hobson stood at the other extreme. He was a maximiser. For him a League of Nations was the first step towards a world federation, which would

[12] *The Morals of Economic Internationalism* (New York 1920), p. 29.

[13] 'The Open Door', in C. R. Buxton (ed.), *Towards a Lasting Settlement* (1915), p. 101.

[14] *The Autobiography of G. Lowes Dickinson*, ed. Dennis Proctor (1973), p. 190.

alone wield enough power to guarantee peace. Dickinson considered this impracticable and also tactically inept; those like Hobson and Brailsford who took this line would not get what they wanted but they might 'easily help to prevent our getting what we ask for'.[15] The various drafts circulated in 1915 therefore represented a search for compromise. They centred on the creation of an international council to which all political – as opposed to justiciable – disputes would be referred. The aim was to give the public opinion of the world an effective organ through which to act. *Proposals for the Prevention of Future Wars* (1917) was the end result. 'Without pretending that public opinion is always and everywhere pacific,' Dickinson noted, 'we believe that, when it is properly instructed, and when time is given for passions to cool, it is more likely to favour peace than do the secret operations of diplomacy' (p. 23). He adopted the emphasis of Hobson not Wallas here. While the functions of the council would be similar to those of traditional diplomacy, it was 'intended that the composition of the Council should enable its members to take a more impartial, comprehensive, and international view than diplomatists have hitherto shown themselves inclined to take, and to suggest a radical settlement rather than a mere temporary compromise' (p. 19). Hobson was quite clear that if the Council were composed of foreign ministers 'international government would perish at its birth', since every Foreign Office was prey to narrow and obsolete notions (*A League of Nations*, p. 15). While no hard-and-fast method of selecting members was prescribed, therefore, the claims of the disinterested thinker, with his wide humanitarian sympathies, did not go by default.

In the summer of 1915 the work of the Bryce Group was brought together with the parallel Fabian effort to formulate proposals on international government, which was largely in the hands of Leonard Woolf. Hobson, Wallas, Cross and Dickinson were all present at an amicable conference – 'combining [as Beatrice Webb put it] the wisdom of the Fabians with that of the *Nation* group of writers' (diary, 5 June 1915). Woolf, Dickinson, Brailsford and Hobson were all active in founding the League of Nations Society. The writings of Woolf and Hobson during 1915 depicted the League as a move towards international government, including all Powers. The proposal, sponsored by the Bryce Group, that all member states should be required to delay war for twelve months pending a settlement, also found general favour. Whereas Woolf envisaged sanctions short of war as sufficient to enforce this, Hobson was readier to concede that armed force would be needed in the last resort.

These disagreements over the form of a League of Nations did not always correspond with attitudes towards the war. True, Hobson found general support for his ideals from Brailsford, but Ponsonby was unalterably opposed

[15] Dickinson to Ponsonby, 2 April 1915, in E. M. Forster, *Goldsworthy Lowes Dickinson* (1934), p. 165.

to armed sanctions. Support for the League and support for the war were not inconsistent. Indeed, Liberal supporters of the war needed a just peace to vindicate their position. The complementary ideas of a war to end war and a League to enforce peace gave a much-needed reassurance. Hobhouse accepted that a League of Nations would be required after the war. When he said in January 1916, 'I should agree with my friend, Mr Hobson, that there is no final guarantee of a permanent peace except in the formation of an international State' (*Q. of War & Peace*, pp. 198–9), he may admittedly have meant that they could agree on little else. For Hobhouse had radically revised his view of the value of an alliance that had now been cemented with blood, and thought that the most promising plan was to develop it after war. Germany would thus be excluded in the first instance – a plan all too like Hobson's fear that it would become a League of Conquerors.

'I agree with all you say about the future', Russell assured Murray at the end of 1915. 'I have no wish to quarrel with those who stand for liberal ideas, however I may disagree about the war' (*Autobiog.*, ii, 49–50). Instead of a sharp polarisation between Liberals who supported or opposed the Government over the merits of the war, there was now a growing alienation between the Government and a wide spectrum of Liberal opinion. Liberalism was on the defensive. Even Scott, who was a specialist in seeing the good side of Lloyd George, admitted to Hobhouse that if the Tories came in, as he now thought likely, it would be 'in alliance with the reactionary Liberals headed by Lloyd George' (20 January 1916). This was the alliance which had succeeded in imposing a full measure of conscription by May 1916. As Massingham put it in the *Nation*, 'The new coalition is Tory, with Liberalism beaten to its corner' (6 May 1916). Asquith's conduct had been inglorious and gave ground for the charge that he had clung more firmly to his place than to his principles. But there was also room for a more favourable view: that Asquith was exercising tact and restraint so that national unity might be preserved with as little violence as possible to Liberal ideas. Gardiner lent weight to this interpretation in a widely-read open letter in the *Daily News* on 22 April. Some of Lloyd George's pre-war supporters were emerging as Asquithians. Indeed the influential concept of an Asquithian Liberal may be said to date from 1916. Even in U.D.C. circles it was recognised that Asquith was a force for moderation – albeit not much of a force. In 1914 Russell had felt 'that if I should happen to meet Asquith or Grey I should be unable to refrain from murder' (*Autobiog.*, ii, 17). But by 1916, when Russell emerged naked from a swim in the pond at Garsington to find the prime minister on the bank, the encounter was far from homicidal. After a lecture tour by Russell that summer was banned, Keynes reported to Duncan Grant that Asquithian feeling ran 'amazingly high in favour of Bertie, all the more because it is put down to the hated Ll.G.' (10 September 1916).

Keynes was another frequent guest of Lady Ottoline Morrell at Garsington – indeed it was there that, according to a famous story, he and Asquith were introduced by the maid as 'Mr Keynes and another gentleman'. Keynes did not take the extreme anti-war position of friends like Lytton Strachey and Duncan Grant; his attitude was more like that of Leonard Woolf, that Germany had to be resisted and the effort redeemed by a just peace. Keynes's work at the Treasury made him a junior colleague of McKenna and Asquith, whose antipathy to conscription he more than matched. It also gave him exemption from military service. He was therefore able to evade an awkward decision in his own case while giving full support to those of his friends who became conscientious objectors. Asquith appeared to Strachey as 'a glutinous lecherous cynical old fellow'.[16] The nest of pacifists at Garsington was in turn a striking setting for the social life of a man leading his country in a deadly war. Keynes was a pivotal figure here, sympathetic to both Asquithian and U.D.C. attitudes.

During 1916 the Liberal dilemma became sharper. Liberal methods could only be vindicated by military victory; yet victory seemed unattainable without abandoning Liberal methods. It sometimes seemed as though Asquith's Liberal credentials were only being confirmed by his apparent readiness to lose the war. To Hobhouse the outlook seemed grim. 'This govt. will stand in History like Lord North's', he told Ada Wallas (diary, 31 January 1916). Hobson also recoiled from the prospect of a long war which, even if successful, would leave 'a semi-military tyranny lingering in the workshops and poverty in the home'.[17] Both Hammond and Murray took steps to protect the position of conscientious objectors when the Military Service Act came into operation; Hobhouse and Wallas took up Russell's case later. Hobhouse remained unconvinced of the measure's necessity. 'It isnt a question of shirkers,' he explained to Oliver, 'but of married men of 35 & 40 with families who will be utterly ruined' (29 May 1916). The list of British liberties which were being sacrificed grew longer: 'Free Speech, Free Press, Habeas Corpus, Voluntary Service, Free Trade – let them all go in this war for liberty!' (N, 26 February 1916).

This was Hobson's favourite theme. To him conscription was the kernel of the system of Prussianism which was being established. In the last year of peace Hobson had been eager to embrace a doctrine of the general will in order to urge the extension of state responsibilities. By 1916 he was insisting that only the Prussian conception of the state imposed itself as a superpersonality upon the individual citizen, whereas in the British conception 'the individual citizen figures as an end, with indefeasible rights attaching to his own personality'. He admitted that 'modern Socialism and the doctrines of the general or collective will have modified or confused this

[16] Michael Holroyd, *Lytton Strachey* (Penguin edn. 1971), p. 652.
[17] *Labour and the Costs of War*, U.D.C. pamphlet No. 16 (1916), p. 16.

simpler individualism', but modestly refrained from mentioning his own contribution. The war had raised real issues of political liberty which drove advanced thinkers like Hobson back upon the old Liberal tradition. He denied that war gave the state an absolute right to coerce the individual. He sought to undercut the case for conscription by proclaiming, as against the Prussian approach, 'that there is a net economy of political strength and progress in encouraging the free play of personal views and sentiments, even when they impede the smooth activity of some particular State function' (*N*, 10 June 1916). This resolved the Liberal dilemma by insisting that liberty and efficiency were not in conflict.

This complacent attitude was difficult to maintain. Lloyd George justified his own position as a radical to Scott by saying that the Liberal party had, so far as the war was concerned, become the Conservative party. Hobhouse was anxious about the *Guardian*'s support for Lloyd George, but remained intensely pessimistic about the outlook. Thoughts of a negotiated settlement were encouraged by President Wilson's offer at the end of May 1916 to participate in future arrangements to keep the peace. Dickinson was one who thought that this indicated a way out. 'Our own liberties are disappearing every day the war continues', he wrote to Scott, 'and in particular we have reverted to persecution of conscience' (10 June 1916). Wallas was in agreement; walking with Dickinson a fortnight previously he found himself, so Ada Wallas recorded, 'more in sympathy with him about the war than with anyone' (21 May 1916).

When Wallas stayed with the Webbs in July he struck Beatrice as 'an eminently good & also a remarkably successful man, with a fully satisfied conscience and even a certain self congratulation & self complacency'. She found him more resilient than herself in the face of events – 'The war is a world catastrophe, but not a catastrophe beyond the control of his philosophy' (6 July 1916). Unlike her, he still felt that he had things to say. This chimes in with his wife's reflections on his qualities a few months later: 'The kindness, the patience, the very slow maturing of his own position, the thing that makes G. more advanced & younger, more inspiriting I think as he nears 60 than he was at 40' (11 December 1916). The war had deepened his scepticism about socialism which had had 'no more influence than Christianity on either its origin or its course'. Its inadequacy as a *Weltanschauung* seemed clearer than ever and he thought it likely that 'the word socialism may go the way of "natural rights" and the "greatest happiness principle" and in our new need we may find a new name for our hopes' (*Men & Ideas*, p. 107). Wallas consequently had no use for the Fabian Society, the Labour Party or the Trade Union movement, of whose power he was suspicious. Not that there was any alternative of compelling attractiveness. On 5 August 1916 the *Nation* was inveighing against Asquith and Samuel for letting down Liberalism over Ireland, Free

Trade, Free Service and the Right of Asylum. 'I wonder whether they see clearly', Ada Wallas commented. 'For if these people went should we get better or worse' (1 August 1916). Wallas tackled Samuel directly two months later. He contended that the Coalition Cabinet leant wholly on the Right, and, invoking his usual political litmus test, maintained that 'an ordinary intelligent Radical working man would find it extraordinarily difficult to point out anything said or done by the Government on war-policy, on fiscal policy, on Irish policy, during the last year and a half which shows that liberal ideas and feelings have had any weight with them' (8 October 1916). Samuel's response, that things might otherwise have been worse, was hardly inspiriting.

In March 1916 the Government had set up a Reconstruction Committee with Asquith as chairman. Vaughan Nash became secretary to it and almost at once attempted to recruit Hammond to its secretariat at Dean's Yard, Westminster. 'The idea is,' he explained, 'to get things thought out & arranged for by the time peace comes' (28 March 1916). Nash knew that Hammond, much to his disappointment, had been pronounced medically unfit for service abroad. In view of this, he was released from the army and agreed to begin work for the Reconstruction Committee at the end of July 1916 for a salary initially settled as £300 a year. One result was that the Hammonds could resume work on the *Town Labourer*, which they discussed with friends, especially George Unwin, Wallas and Tawney. Tawney's career in the army was also over. He had been wounded in France in July 1916. Convalescing in England that autumn, he found that a chasm had opened up between his experience and that of civilians at home. He told the Hobhouses that he had never met a cheerful soldier; but his feeling was 'that we must fight until Germany feels herself beaten'.[18] Of the real life of the soldier, Tawney wrote in the *Nation*, 'the sensation of taking a profitless part in a game played by monkeys and organised by lunatics, you realise, I think, nothing'. He then added in a postscript that a reading of Wells's *Mr Britling Sees It Through* showed 'that some people at home do realize it' (21 October 1916). For the Wallases and the Hammonds, as for Tawney, this was the novel that captured their feelings in late 1916. 'We have got to set this world on a different footing', Mr Britling had exhorted, revising the atlas of Europe in red ink. 'We have got to set up the world at last – on justice and reason' (Bk. 3, ch. i).

In the summer of 1916 Emily Hobhouse set off for Germany as a self-styled messenger of peace and goodwill. She returned convinced that the German people wanted peace. Her efforts clearly embarrassed Leonard – 'you go your side of the street & I go mine', he told her (25 June 1916) – but he was unwilling to rule out the idea of a negotiated peace. On 29 September 1916 the famous interview with Lloyd George was published

[18] Ada Wallas diary, 12 November 1916, WP 49.

in which he asserted: 'The fight must be to a finish – to a knock-out.' Wallas was very much disturbed by this 'foolish & distressing speech', a reaction shared not only by Hobson, whom he telephoned, but also Hobhouse, who promptly composed a leader (Wallas diary, 30 September 1916). Such language, wrote Hobhouse, did not help the British case in America; it did not do justice to 'the fact that we stood for freedom and democracy against militarism'; and as a statement of war aims it usurped the functions of the Prime Minister and the Foreign Secretary (*MG*, 30 September 1916). Wallas found it sinister that the military immediately took the statement as official policy and that those who desired 'a comparatively inconclusive peace based on a conception of the general good of mankind' were being denied a proper hearing. 'At present ninety nine Englishmen out of a hundred intensely desire success for the British army and believe that a German victory would be a world-disaster', he told Samuel. 'But as the winter goes on I expect to find that nearly all of them who are liberals by principle, who would, for instance, have voted liberal at the election of 1900, will be driven into opposition to the combination which will effectively control the government' (8 October 1916). Wallas therefore remained convinced that the way to peace lay in organising opposition against the fight-to-a-finish policy and in looking to America for a lead.

Scott, on the other hand, told Hobhouse of his 'growing conviction that with the present men we shall *not* win the war and that the utmost we can hope for is a draw on bad terms' (28 November 1916). The inevitable alternative was a Lloyd George Government. Hobhouse could not accept this, for the same reasons as Wallas. He admitted that Lloyd George had 'explosive merits', but his pronouncements had sabotaged the sort of moderate peace that could otherwise have been negotiated. 'I infer that we want a moderate like Grey at the head of affairs', Hobhouse wrote to Scott (29 November 1916) – an ironic conclusion to twenty years of Radical criticism of British foreign policy. As the political crisis mounted at the beginning of December, therefore, Hobhouse found himself trying to keep Scott clear of entanglement with Lloyd George by pleading the merits of Grey. 'The difficulty I admit is to defend Asquith', he wrote on 2 December. But in categorising Lloyd George as 'a byword for neglect and inefficiency' and insisting that McKenna was the capable man ('whom they won't have because he knows too much of our real condition to push conscription hard') Hobhouse was taking up a virtually Asquithian position.

On 5 December 1916 Asquith resigned. On 7 December the *Manchester Guardian* welcomed Lloyd George's accession as head of what it termed a non-party government of national defence and urged him 'to preserve for the future of Liberalism all the treasure of his soul'. To Wallas it seemed the end of historic Liberalism. Ada Wallas noted that Hobhouse was troubled at the *Guardian*'s support for Lloyd George: 'He says he knows the things Ll. G. has been telling Scott for the last two years – none of them true' (11 December 1916). But he admitted that it was impossible to defend Asquith. Like Barbara Hammond, Hobhouse evidently thought 'that the Asquith regime means certain & moderate disaster; the Ll. G. either absolute disaster or success'.[19] Asquith inspired her with a kind of hopelessness. She did not accuse him of neglect or slackness, but his decency and decorum stood in painful contrast to the wanton sacrifice which was taking place.

Whatever the impact of the new Government on the conduct of the war, its bent in domestic policy was from the first put under a highly unfavourable construction. 'No *democratic* scheme of George's has ever come off', Hobhouse warned Scott. 'We shall probably have a series of them talked about, pushed to a certain point, then either dropped or turned into something reactionary.' The personal aspect of the changes reinforced this suspicion. The appointment of Milner, Hobhouse declared, 'doubles and trebles all my apprehensions' (9 December 1916). Wallas reacted with similar dread. And Murray, a more straightforward Asquithian, confessed to Hammond that the one pain and humiliation which he had hoped to be spared was that England should in her greatest crisis 'be governed by her worst men, such as Milner, Carson and Northcliffe' (12 December 1916).

Fortunately, in America better men appeared to be better placed. The change of government in England made Liberals readier to drink to the king over the water. Supporters of a League of Nations had hailed Grey's publicly expressed conversion – he apparently told Gilbert Murray more than once 'that he had been brought up in the other school, practised it and found it would not work'.[20] But with Grey now out of office, only President Wilson was left to carry their hopes. Wilson's speech of 27 May 1916, offering to participate in future arrangements to keep the peace, had found warm support from Liberals who feared Lloyd George. The American Note of 18 December 1916, inviting statements of terms as a basis for negotiation, came at an even more welcome moment, though its observation that the stated war aims of both sides were identical had a provocative effect. A German peace note had just been published which, despite its unacceptable tone, seemed to Hobhouse to bring the end of the war six months nearer. He was therefore exercised that the British reply should be conciliatory and, contributing the leader to the *Manchester Guardian*, sought to put the best gloss upon Wilson's initiative while repudiating any implication that the Allied cause was no better than the German. 'The interest of Americans in international justice and world peace,' he maintained, 'is a very genuine interest, and appeals to all the elements of political idealism in the great commonwealth' (22 December 1916). There

[19] Barbara to Lawrence Hammond, 7 December 1916, HP 8.
[20] Murray to Hammond, 21 March 1941, HP 30.

was some reason to suppose that Lloyd George could be talked out of his readiness to regard the whole matter as a pro-German plot. Eventually the British reply on 10 January 1917 stated Allied war aims with notable emphasis on the principle of nationality (muted when it came to Poland in deference to Russian wishes). Ada Wallas found Hobhouse 'rather pleased with our answer to America in its politeness' (17 January 1917). Within days Wilson made a speech to the Senate calling for 'peace without victory', which British Radicals once more welcomed as a statement of their view. It encouraged prospects for working up a liberal opposition against Lloyd George's cabinet and for bringing the better mind of England into accord with that of America. On 3 February 1917 Wilson broke off diplomatic relations with Germany as a result of the commitment to unrestricted submarine warfare. In Highgate this brought to the Wallases and Hobhouses new hope of success in the war and of justice in the settlement. 'I went in the morning', recorded Ada Wallas (8 February 1917), 'to watch the skaters. Lovely sun. L.T.H. pleased. His article in the M.G. on the reception of Wilson's note stands out now as the sanest the press produced.'

(III) RECONSTRUCTION

The more the Allied cause was construed as a Gladstonian crusade for public right and a Wilsonian crusade for democracy the happier the Radicals became – except when they thought about Russia. For twenty-five years or more Hobhouse had been involved in organisations supporting Russian freedom. In the February Revolution 'the finest of all causes' took a step forward which he had hardly hoped to see in his lifetime. He told Oliver that he 'felt happy for the first time since the battle of the Marne ended...It redeems the whole war for me' (25 March 1917). He could not entirely break the disposition of a lifetime – 'one has been so many times disappointed that one looks for fresh disappointments'[21] – but even he had to admit that the revolution had begun well. With no end in sight to the war, with food shortages becoming apparent, with a bitterly cold winter dragging on, there were few enough indications of better days to come. 'One needs the Russian revn. to keep ones spirits up', Barbara Hammond confessed to Lawrence (23 March 1917).

With the change of Government the Reconstruction Committee became more prominent and its membership was reinforced, notably by the recruitment of Beatrice Webb, Seebohm Rowntree and Thomas Jones. Hammond was one of the few to stay on at Dean's Yard but his position was not entirely satisfactory. He regarded his salary of £300 as a provisional arrangement – he had, after all, earned three times as much in his previous civil service post. When it became clear in April 1917 that others of comparable

[21] Hobhouse to Scott, 18 March 1917, SP, BL Add. MSS. 50909, ff.79–80.

seniority were to be paid more, he felt slighted, and the fact that his status was also arbitrarily changed to take him away from office work did not remove this grievance. In the event, however, he was almost certainly better suited to his role of independent investigator, and in this capacity he was able to travel extensively and observe experiments in wartime controls at first hand. His chief contribution to the plans for Reconstruction, therefore, lay in his wide-ranging reports which took advantage of the unusual measure of latitude which he was allowed. In a general statement on Reconstruction he claimed that the great problems of education, capital and labour, and agriculture were more amenable to solution because the war had abolished the word impossible. It seemed necessary to him to understand how the conditions had changed since the last great European war. 'The note of 1815 was a note of despair,' he wrote; 'the note of 1917 is a note of hope.'[22]

Work on the *Town Labourer* was not, then, a way of taking Hammond's mind off his work: it was his work. A draft of the book had been practically completed in the eighteen months before the outbreak of war. As with the *Village Labourer*, what was originally envisaged as one book was ultimately published as two. The *Skilled Labourer* (1919), the last volume of the trilogy, therefore included some material dating from well before the war, for example Barbara's chapter on the Yorkshire Luddites which had been finished in November 1913. The difficulty, of course, was length, especially in the chapters on industrial history, which were mainly Barbara's responsibility. Her uncompleted draft on cotton would alone, it was calculated, take up a quarter of the book. Lawrence was meanwhile concentrating upon religion and finding Murray's *Four Stages of Greek Religion* a fruitful source of inspiration. George Unwin told Hammond that he considered this section 'one of the very best (if not *the* best) in the book' (16 August 1914).

Unwin was a mutual friend of Hammond and Tawney and the acknowledged expert on the Industrial Revolution in Lancashire. He went through the whole manuscript in the early weeks of the war. The Hammonds had, he told them, 'done a piece of work I have often wanted to see done, and cast an entirely new light upon a dark period from sources hitherto unexplored'. His chief criticism was one of emphasis. 'I have always consoled myself for the tragedy of the agricultural labourer at this time,' he explained, 'with a conception of certain creative activities whereby the main body of the English proletariat was laying the foundation of its present better condition.' The Hammonds offered him insufficient consolation. 'I should like a glimpse of morrow in midnight', he told them (1 September 1914). The bitter and tragic note of the *Village Labourer* had

[22] Memorandum, n.d. but 1917, quoted in P. B. Johnson, *Land Fit for Heroes* (1968), pp. 57–8.

fitted its subject. 'But the *town* labourer *did* emerge', claimed Unwin. 'By 1830 this was not yet quite accomplished but it would be easy to forecast it.'[23]

The war postponed plans for publication. When Lawrence enlisted the problems of revision had not been solved. Barbara sent the typescript to Wallas at the end of October 1915, admitting that it would need cuts. At the beginning of December he wrote to tell her how highly he thought of the book. 'You *must* get the book out so as to influence the social discussion that will follow the making of peace', he insisted (4 December 1915). Moreover he made the crucial suggestion that the book should be divided rather than shortened. The Hammonds followed the substance of his suggestion for holding over all the chapters on industrial history, and to these they eventually added 'Oliver the Spy' which Wallas envisaged as the centrepiece of the *Town Labourer*. This, then, was the reshaped manuscript to which the Hammonds returned in earnest in the autumn of 1916.

It had now become a matter of urgent importance to them that their book should come before as wide a public as possible, the sort of people whom the Workers' Educational Association (W.E.A.) might reach. Longmans agreed to publish it at 12s 6d. The Hammonds fought hard to bring the price down to 10s 6d which entailed further cuts. Lawrence was haunted by the idea that the book would appear at an inopportune moment and pressed Longmans to bring it out in June 1917. The proofs were read by Wallas and Tawney. Tawney thought the book '*tremendously* good' and told the Hammonds that he envied them their 'power of shooting a philosophy dead in a phrase' (26 February 1917). Wallas, too, found that the book moved him profoundly. It would, he thought, 'have a real and important effect on the temper of the governing classes after the War. When the average Oxford don thinks of scores of W.E.A. classes reading your book he won't find it possible to be perfectly self complacent' (4 March 1917). He later commended it to research students as 'a piece of research so important and masterly that it will be used in the universities of the world for generations to come'.[24]

The preface to the *Town Labourer* (1917) related the Hammonds' purpose concisely and explicitly to the demands of the hour. Their premise was that the mistakes and troubles of an age derived above all from a false spirit, a tendency to accept uncritically the phenomena of the time. Thus the social system produced by the industrial revolution reflected a spirit of complacent pessimism, a socially divisive theory which regarded men and women as expendable servants of economic power. 'In its extreme form,' they claimed, 'this theory made the mass of the nation the cannon-fodder of industry.' But the war had shaken all this apart. The iron laws had been

[23] Unwin to Hammond, 1 October 1914 (bound as 1912), HP 16 ff.279–80.
[24] 'Social research', TS for *New Republic* (8 September 1917), WP 13.

discredited. 'For as the world sees what kind of life Europe would lead under the shadow of a gospel that makes a god of military power, so it comes to understand what humanity must lose if it makes a god of industrial power' (p. x). The paradigms of military and industrial society evidently had more in common than Herbert Spencer had ever dreamt. A new world was there to be made in the spring of 1917 and the autocratic spirit was under sentence. Murray, indeed, tried to persuade the Hammonds that the preface should mention the Russian Revolution directly. 'It seems to me to have altered the whole aspect of the world and given hope to liberal causes again' (29 March 1917). The Hammonds prudently rejected this suggestion, fearing that the Revolution might turn sour before publication.

The *Town Labourer* is the classic study of the social and economic conditions of working people during the industrial revolution. It takes a pessimistic view of the standard of living in this period. It considers that in a time of expansion the workers were shut out from a share of the surplus profits. It contains detailed surveys of working conditions, and the two moving chapters on child employment are among the most memorable parts of the book. But it is important to note what a very large share of the space is devoted to such subjects as the mind of the rich, the conscience of the rich, the spirit of union and the spirit of religion among the poor, the mind of the poor, the ambitions of the poor. These are the themes of the concluding six chapters. The constructive force of the book derives from its analysis of the ideologies of the age. The Hammonds wrote of 'the great process described in this volume, the exploitation, that is, of the mass of a race by the classes holding economic and political power' (p. 226). But they did not maintain that this was a consciously chosen policy. Most people, they suggested, took what they had in an unreflecting way. They had not made the world and they took it as they found it. The Bible had accustomed them to think that the poor would always be with them; and so it seemed. 'But if the established order is its own justification to many minds,' the Hammonds continued, 'it remains true that the turn which social history takes in any age results in part from the ideas and opinions that are ascendant' (p. 195). Hence their sustained attention to the way a prevalent outlook was created from the ideologically convenient parts of religions and economic doctrines. The way that the costs of industrialisation were distributed was consequently accepted by all classes as immutable, but in retrospect it was clear enough who had benefited from this amalgam of fatalistic maxims. Tawney wrote to the Hammonds that their achievement lay 'in destroying the historical assumptions on which our modern slavery is based, unknown both to the slaves & the masters' (24 June 1917).

The book was as subversive of ideas about capitalism as its predecessor had been of ideas about landed property. This was the way that the new Liberal argument ran. But when the seventy-nine-year-old Morley and the eighty-five-year-old Courtney were presented with copies of the *Town Labourer* they inevitably found difficulties in accepting its message. 'It comes at the right moment – that at least is quite clear', wrote Morley (8 July 1917), skirting round aspects that were perhaps less clear. Courtney, equally benign in tone, was obviously unwilling to accept this account of the political economy of his youth as the whole truth. 'In minor matters we may have to correct our "personal equations" ', he admitted, anxiously and obscurely (19 July 1917).

In fact, though the *Town Labourer* more easily bears a socialist construction than the *Village Labourer*, it is just as much a document in the moral reformist tradition. Barbara Hammond found it predictable that one of its few bad notices should be in the *Fabian News*. 'What a good fellow Graham Wallas is', she commented to Lawrence. 'He has none of that spirit' (7 June 1917). Tawney, on the other hand, was wholly in tune with the Hammonds' approach, as he made clear in an important review in the *Times Literary Supplement* (19 June 1917). The English lack of dexterity with ideas, he claimed, meant that working-class history 'presented a constant series of contradictions between the innate conservatism of the most conservative class in this conservative island and the revolutionary Continental theories, Jacobin, Socialist, Syndicalist, or Communist, in which from time to time it seemed to catch a reflection of its own moral and social ideals'. Hence the working-class mind was the great puzzle, with the exhibition of ready patriotism in 1914 seeming to contrast oddly with the creation of industrial difficulties in 1917. But this could be explained most easily, not by reference to agitators, but by understanding what the experience of industrialisation had branded upon workmen's minds. There was, Tawney concluded, no easy way out. 'The process of industrial "liberation", if such a term may be borrowed from the arsenal of Socialism, is the process of changing not a system (for the analysis of the older economists still largely holds the field), but the spirit and motives of those engaged in it.' Current economic problems, then, were at bottom psychological. He conceived industrial conflict not as an expression of inherent contradictions but as taking place 'between the two partners in the business on which, as they know when both sides stop to think, the future of the country depends'.

This line of thought owed much to Wallas. He was often told how well his *Great Society* read in the changed conditions of wartime. When Hammond published a series of articles on reconstruction as *Past and Future* (1918) he sought Wallas's permission to dedicate the volume to him 'as a slight acknowledgment of my debt to your guidance and inspiration' (14 October 1917). The leading idea of his book, Hammond explained in the preface, was 'the necessity of accommodating the industrial system to the needs of human nature and the demands of the human will' (p. viii).

He followed Wallas in thinking that state socialism was no longer a promising solution to the problem of poverty. He was not grudging in his references to the Fabians, but he held that collectivism was only one of two strains in the socialist movement of the 1880s; it was one which constituted a protest against poverty rather than slavery and demanded order rather than freedom. The other strain, originating with Morris, was more relevant now. 'Morris was impatient of the machine itself, not merely anxious to see the machine controlled by public spirit, and directed with greater efficiency' (p. 108).

Hammond found himself in substantial agreement with Cole here. Cole, of course, always attributed his conversion to socialism to the influence of Morris, and his wartime writings, especially *Self-Government in Industry* (1917), sought to develop this conception in the form of Guild Socialism. Hammond had become a wholehearted enthusiast for trade unionism as the most effective of the defences of the poor. In the *Town Labourer* (p. 258) he eulogised the early-nineteenth-century trade union as 'a school of heroism and public spirit'. The present war for democracy, which could not have been waged without the trade unions, hammered home the lesson; where there had been failure, the cause had been a reluctance to take them into full partnership and a tendency to rely upon the methods of bureaucracy rather than democracy. The important conclusion seemed to him to be 'that the support of the Trade Unions had been essential to the prosecution of the war, and that the Trade Union is as integral a part of our national life as the House of Commons' (*Past & Future*, p. 99). Hammond went far here towards subscribing to the Guild ideal as stated by Cole, but in the end he pulled back. Wallas wrote to him of the esprit de corps of powerful vocational organisations 'as involving a really terrific social strain' (7 April 1918). The problem of reconciling these sectional conflicts had not been resolved to Hammond's satisfaction. He was actively collaborating with Cole on reconstruction problems in 1917–18. With other Labour sympathisers like Tawney, Thomas Jones and J. J. Mallon, they were members of the Romney Street Group which held a lunch weekly in Dean's Yard. But Cole remained dissatisfied with Hammond's approach, thinking him too ready to endorse the Whitley Councils as an expression of the reforms needed.

The Whitley Report, appearing in March 1917, had recommended that joint industrial councils should be set up at all levels of industry. Cole himself had initially welcomed the proposals, before going smartly into reverse in face of Guild hostility; and Hammond continued to fight this battle, trying to make Reconstruction favourable to Labour and Labour favourable to Reconstruction. The Whitley Committee, he felt, carried special weight: first as embodying its own principle of equal representation for employers and trade unionists, and secondly in the quality of its outside experts, among whom were Mallon and Hobson. Hobson, like Hammond, was primarily identified with Labour by 1917. The *Town Labourer* had been dedicated to him. 'It is the most completely satisfactory book I have read for many years,' he wrote to Barbara Hammond, 'and I feel confident that it will have a great influence in evoking energy for the tasks which immediately confront our so called "democracy"' (5 July 1917).

Hobson's scepticism about the current provenance of this term was, of course, a means of arguing that what was needed was more democracy. In *Democracy After the War* (1917) he announced that he was 'compelled to to accept as substantially correct the general Socialist analysis, presenting, as the main cause of what is wrong in politics and industry, the direction of human industry by capitalists in the pursuit of private profit' (p. 7). But this conversion to socialism, apparently implying a repudiation of his liberal past, turns out, on closer inspection, to involve a surprisingly familiar line of analysis. To Hobson the enemy was militarism, which he saw as a manifestation of a will to power. Like the Hammonds, he regarded the development of capitalism as analogous to this since power was increasingly realised through property. Hobson did not, of course, condemn property as such. He drew upon the distinction between property for use, which was good, and property for power, which was bad, and should really be regarded as 'improperty' (the unproductive surplus under a new name).

Improperty lay at the centre of the circle of reaction, succouring imperialism, protection, militarism, bureaucracy and authoritarianism. Cutting the taproot remained as important as ever, but Hobson insisted that socialists underestimated the difficulties which this operation involved. The forces of reaction were powerful and united; they were defended by pervasive ideological influences in society at large. To Hobson the way out lay in making the onslaught more general – 'if social democracy is to deserve its title and to realize its meaning, it must broaden its outlook and its policy' (p. 155). He reaffirmed, in short, the need for a union of all progressive forces in order to carry the day.

In essentials the problem came down to the need for a better psychological approach. 'It is necessary to sap the intellectual and moral defences of the enemy', Hobson claimed (p. 139). What was most needed was to awaken 'the sense of sin' in the upholders of the existing system. It was a vulgar error to suppose that the propertied classes and their intellectual henchmen were united in a conscious plan to combat democracy; their unconscious servitude was the real difficulty. Hobson proposed, therefore, 'to sow the dissension among the enemy which self-knowledge would bring' by exposing the secret biases in current intellectual systems (p. 140). 'I do not mean,' he conceded, 'that this new Appeal to Reason among the allies and auxiliaries of reaction can at all dispense with the organisation of democratic forces among the subject classes, or even with the necessity of a bitter struggle which may take the form and substance of a class war' (p. 141). But the battle of ideas was the crucial theatre, and Hobson approvingly quoted Bertrand Russell: 'Men fear thought as they fear nothing else on earth.' As Hobson saw it, there were two major reactionary ideologies which needed rooting out. The supposed 'laws' of classical political economy were one; hence his pleasure in the *Town Labourer*. The other was the Idealist theory of the absolute state, on which, across the Heath, in a cool Highgate garden, Hobhouse was also brooding.

Hobhouse was more than usually gloomy in the late spring and early summer of 1917. The situation seemed bad at home, in Russia, and at the front. Scott went so far as to reject an article he had written for the *Manchester Guardian* at the end of May because of its unduly pessimistic view of the Allies' position. On 13 June there was an air raid over Highgate which Ada Wallas watched with Nora Hobhouse. From their gardens they heard aeroplanes close overhead. This was a telling microcosm of the war for Hobhouse – Oliver was serving in the Air Force now – and in the dedication of the *Metaphysical Theory of the State* (1918) he declared that he 'had just witnessed the visible and tangible outcome of a false and wicked doctrine', which had its origin with Hegel.

This was, of course, no sudden revelation. When alluding to German philosophers two years previously, he had recommended 'reading their theories day by day to the refrain of the war news' as the best way of penetrating their obscurities (Q. *of War & Peace*, p. 26). The war purged Hobhouse and Hobson of their pre-war ambivalence towards Idealist philosophy and identified them clearly among its liberal critics. When, in April 1915, S. K. Ratcliffe appealed to Wallas to weigh in at the Sociological Society against 'the new Super State doctrine now being developed by the Round Table fellows & others', he explained: 'Hobson, as you know, is ill, & Hobhouse is away' (19 April 1915). The leading Idealist philosophers, notably Bosanquet and Muirhead, were equally resolute in their defence of the Hegelian doctrine despite its current taint of Prussianism. They leant heavily upon Green's formula that will, not force, was the basis of the State. With Hegel glossed in this manner by Green, Bosanquet faced the war (in a phrase to which Muirhead attached special significance) 'fairly well fitted out in a philosophical point of view'.[25] In their view the perversion of German philosophy had taken place after Hegel; in Hobhouse's view the Idealist theory of the state had inherent flaws, as William Clarke had presciently indicated shortly before his death.

The *Metaphysical Theory of the State* is therefore a rigorous critique of the doctrine stated by Bosanquet in *The Philosophical Theory of the State* (1899). This doctrine, Hobhouse suggested, rested upon a fatal ambiguity. Bosanquet defined the State, in an Idealist sense, as the expression of the

[25] *Bernard Bosanquet and his Friends*, ed. J. H. Muirhead (1935), p. 165.

moral life of a community; but he also frequently slipped into the common usage of the term State for an organisation exercising power. On the first definition, the state represented all that was best in human life; this purely formal claim could then be passed off as a comprehensive justification for whatever the everyday state of the second definition claimed it must do. Hobhouse conceded that while it would be 'true to maintain that the best life can only be realized in society, it would be untrue to identify that best life with the state. Underlying Bosanquet's account, in fact, there is a serious confusion between the state and society' (pp. 75–6). Hobhouse was evidently disposed to regard the two notable achievements perfected by the Bosanquet family at the turn of the century – the theory of the state and the googly – as curiously similar; and after twenty years of reading Bosanquet's spin he could spot when the ball came out of the back of his hand.

Hobhouse returned to the charge he had made in *Democracy and Reaction*, that Idealism was fundamentally conservative. By talking of the 'real' will of the state as being always right, it attributed to actual conditions a rationality which only the ideal will manifested. The ends which a man chose might well turn out to be misconceived, Hobhouse admitted, but 'so far as he really chooses them that choice is for the time being his real will, in the true sense of real as that which is not merely supposed to be but is' (p. 45). The term mind of society, he now insisted, was only a metaphor; it implied no pretension to a higher wisdom as the real will of society as a whole. It is noteworthy that in *Democracy After the War* Hobson restated the essentials of his pre-war theory, with one exception: no mention of the general will. Hobhouse was likewise concerned to uphold the judgment of the individual citizen as against the all too fallible state. Both Hobhouse and Bosanquet spoke out for the right of conscientious objection to compulsory service; but Hobhouse could not square this with Bosanquet's general doctrine. He himself found the old empiricist notions a better safeguard. In a hostile world the English liberal tradition, which he has often criticised as narrow and class-bound in its conceptions, appeared in a favourable light. As he grumbled to Scott (26 March 1917), 'this country or rather its governing class doesnt *really* love liberty. It was the Puritans & following them the nonconformist manufacturers who won liberty for us.'

(IV) DEBAMBOOZLED

Until 1914 almost all those who signed the British Neutrality Committee's letter were warm partisans of Lloyd George; by the time he had become Prime Minister not one of them was his supporter. In April 1917 Hobhouse was declaring that if it were a choice of 'Georges', he was for the monarch.

Some Liberals, like Murray, Gardiner and G. M. Trevelyan, were able to translate this antipathy into an admiration for Asquith. A number of U.D.C. figures were drifting steadily away from the Liberal party and towards Labour – Hobson, Ponsonby, Dickinson, Morel, C. P. Trevelyan, Charles Buxton – though none of them formally transferred his allegiance before 1918. But Labour's appeal to the intellectuals was not restricted to this element. Arnold Toynbee, married to Murray's daughter, and J. J. Mallon, soon to marry a daughter of Gardiner's, were supporters of the war, as were Tawney, Hammond and his Oxford friend J. L. Stocks. Asquith's supersession, so grievous to the fathers-in-law, was generally accepted as inevitable by these men – indeed Tawney and Mallon had helped Tom Jones in December 1916 with a memorandum for Lloyd George stating the democratic case for a government of national emergency. Only Scott stood out as a prominent progressive ally of Lloyd George. Many of these divisions stemmed ostensibly from questions of foreign policy. Yet on the shape of the international settlement after the war there was a wide measure of agreement between the Asquithians, the U.D.C., and the Labour supporters of the war, not to mention the disinherited progressives who were now leaderless.

This pattern has its confusing aspects. It becomes most comprehensible, however, once it is recalled that all these groups had been united in the pre-war period by the ideology of progressivism. In this outlook they remained united, though the tactical pressures of the party system worked now to divide them politically. The new Liberalism, because of its insistence on the substantive compatibility of the aims of Liberalism and Labour, saved the Liberal party from a lingering death: before 1914 by giving it hope of continued life, after 1914 by making its death sudden. If the choice between the Liberal party and the Labour party was only tactical, this had the effect of recruiting Liberal support from socialists before 1914 and Labour support from liberals afterwards. The social democratic case for the Liberal party had been seen at its most cogent in 1910, and it was not disappointment with the Liberal record in this respect that produced disaffection. Where the Liberal party let down its intellectuals thereafter was on a range of issues where its competence ought to have been guaranteed by its own historic tradition: woman suffrage, Ireland, civil rights, conscription, Free Trade. Many progressive intellectuals turned hopefully to Labour because they thought the struggle for social democracy could be better conducted in a party whose liberalism was not tainted.

In many ways this development represented the triumph of Ramsay MacDonald, whose consistent argument it was that Labour was the true representative of progressivism. He was deservedly the central figure in the 1917 Club, which Hobson and Nevinson took the lead in founding to bring together Liberal and Labour people who shared a similar outlook on the war. Molly Hamilton, the Woolfs and Brailsford were among its active members. Its dubious premises in Gerrard Street were uncomfortable and draughty, the stairs were cramped and smelly, and the street outside was patrolled by an embarrassing number of prostitutes. The club was long recalled as having 'all the squalor and dinginess associated in the popular imagination with a conspiratorial den of Bolsheviks and thieves'.[26] The sentiment of the members was in favour of a negotiated peace.

This was the line which the *Nation* adopted in the early months of 1917, and it led to a ban by the Government on its overseas distribution. The entry of America into the war in April deprived it of the consolation of outside support. Wilson's wholehearted commitment to the Allied cause seemed to make peace more distant than ever. A letter from Hobson in the *Nation* on 23 June was headed, 'An American Victory in 1920?'. The Hammonds could not share these sentiments. Barbara told Lawrence that 'the *Nation* clique' had become soured by the war: 'They have always enjoyed thinking themselves a small highminded minority ready to make sacrifices for ideals in a world of self seekers, & now here are the self seekers calmly throwing away their lives not to mention their fortunes for their country & the highminded minority dont like it, specially as they happen to be making no sacrifices on this occasion' (28 March 1917). Even the ban which the Government imposed on its overseas distribution left her unmoved. 'I am sick of intellectuals', she commented (21 April 1917). When Smuts visited the Hobhouses at this time, he found Leonard similarly resistant to Emily's advocacy of peace.

Tawney too was unrepentant in his support for the war and told Wallas: 'I have thought all I can, but I cannot see that we could have kept out of it' (Ada Wallas diary, 31 May 1917). But Lloyd George was dissipating such support as he might have had from Labour sympathisers. When Henderson was virtually dismissed from the Government in August 1917 because of his insistence on participating in an international socialist conference in Stockholm, Barbara Hammond found Lloyd George's defence of the action most sinister. The Wallases too were firmly on Henderson's side. 'The threat of a Gen. Election is execrable,' Barbara Hammond wrote to Lawrence (16 August 1917), 'but I think if they do have it there will be a surprise for them. It will be rather a shame for old Asquith.'

Henderson's withdrawal from the Coalition was a crucial moment in the creation of the modern Labour party. In the course of the next twelve months most of the ambiguities about the party's role were resolved. It emerged as a fully independent contender for power in the new situation created by the war, the disruption of Liberalism, and the Russian Revolution. Henderson's visit to Russia in the early summer of 1917 had caused him to revise his previous hostility to the Stockholm conference. He came

[26] Douglas Goldring, *The Nineteen Twenties* (1945), p. 145.

to see it as a means of rallying European social democracy in face of what he regarded as the Bolshevik threat. In this he saw eye to eye with progressive intellectuals who had welcomed the February Revolution but who found Bolshevism crude and repellent. For example, Litvinov's conception of socialism struck Hobhouse, who met him in January 1918, as 'the sort of schoolboy stuff which one has been denying for 30 years to be anything but a caricature' (Wilson, p. 331). Henderson's hopes of sustaining a leftist alternative to Bolshevism in Russia were disappointed; but in Britain he emerged as the master-builder. The Labour party was moulded into the sort of instrument which could undercut revolutionism by a more thoroughgoing reformism. In this sense the policy was counter-revolutionary. But seen as a moral reformist movement responding to a mechanical revolutionist challenge, it was a stand also for liberal and democratic values against the Bolshevik conception of vanguard leadership.

This is even true to some extent of the Webbs, whom the war dislodged from their mechanical reformist bunker. Beatrice's affirmation of 'our persistent adherence to the Democratic movement, despite all discouragements' (diary, 6 July 1916) would, perhaps, have been timelessly true in her own mind; but it was also objectively true by mid-1916. 'Sidney seems impervious to depression,' she told Wallas some time later, '& is just now enjoying himself helping Henderson to reorganise the Labour party.'[27] When Scott talked with Henderson in December 1917 he found him unreceptive to ideas about a progressive alliance of Radicals and Labour; instead his policy was to enlarge the bounds of the Labour party to bring in the intellectuals. Haldane and Webb, acting with Henderson in an advisory role, told Scott the same story: 'It had been already decided to run 350 candidates of whom 200 should be drawn from the trades unionists and 150 from the intellectuals' (Wilson, p. 320). Once Labour had its own middle-class brains, the progressive argument for the Liberal party was fundamentally vitiated – unless, of course, they were the wrong middle-class brains.

By 1918 Cole was determined to work with Labour if he could; indeed Beatrice Webb frequently suspected him of seeking to supplant Sidney as Henderson's chief adviser. Cole, of course, was more radical than either, and he was pro-Bolshevik until at least 1919. He projected his moral revolutionist hopes on to Russia and looked for a Guild Socialist outcome to the upheaval. At the same time he sought to contribute some intellectual stiffening to the earthbound Labour party. The well-known rhyme by his friend Maurice Reckitt is genuinely witty and perceptive:

Mr G. D. H. Cole
Is a bit of a puzzle;
A curious role

[27] B. Webb to Wallas n.d. (late 1917?), WP 9.

That of G. D. H. Cole,
With a Bolshevik Soul
In a Fabian muzzle...

But it is misleading if it suggests that Cole never knew whether he was Lenin or Webb. In fact he never knew whether he was Morris or Hobson. His vacillations were on the moral not the mechanical axis.

Hobson became chairman and Cole secretary of the Labour Party Advisory Committee on Trade Policy and Finance – the beginning of Cole's warm espousal of Hobson's economic views. Tawney, Mallon, Brailsford, Ponsonby, Toynbee, Woolf and Hammond were among others who served on these bodies, notably the committee on International Questions, which came under a strong though by no means exclusive U.D.C. influence. When Scott pondered to Hobhouse on the identity of 'the men who in effect are going to guide the newly risen and rather blind giant', his general hopes for their future influence did not entirely overlay his selective misgivings about their past record. 'If it were men like Toynbee and Tawney one would feel pretty safe,' he commented, 'but I imagine the Webbs are at present chiefly pulling the strings' (30 January 1918).

The voice of Liberalism was muted. Asquith offered uneasy support for the Coalition, unwilling to strike when the war was going badly and unable when it was going well. Hobhouse was one of those who felt in the autumn of 1917 that it was time for Grey to speak with a view to influencing German attitudes in favour of an acceptable peace. The prolonged, bloody and fruitless Flanders offensive had exacted a terrible price by November 1917. Hobhouse drew the conclusion that negotiations were hardly likely to be worthwhile until the Allies were once more back upon equal terms.

To Hobson, such talk was a revelation of the Never-Endian mentality. He was at this time preparing his *Richard Cobden, the international man* (1918) which largely consisted of Cobden's letters upon international questions. Hobson argued that to Cobden the Crimean War was 'the crucial experiment which proved the validity of his principle of non-intervention' (p. 389). He quoted passages from a speech of 1855 (pp. 117–19) to show that the contemporary claims that it was a war for liberty against despotism were rejected by Cobden as sham idealism which obscured the actual motives at work. For Hobson the application to 1917 could hardly have been clearer. In a satirical dialogue, he imagined himself pressing this charge against an author of statements on war aims, and getting the reply: 'The people are quite satisfied with what you call our rhetorical stunts about the liberation of small peoples, the rescue of the world from German domination, making the world safe for democracy, and so forth. They bite their teeth into these glorious phrases and so keep their noses out of the real business of the war.'[28] War propaganda seemed to Hobson to foreclose the possibility of

[28] Lucian, 1920, *Dips into the Near Future* (1918), p. 79.

defining intelligible – and negotiable – aims. Meanwhile the material and ideological demands of a war that might last until 1920 were reinforcing a totalitarian system which would be difficult to dismantle.

Would no one speak for peace, sanity and liberty? The policy of a negotiated peace in many respects lay in the logic of the Asquithian position. It was, however, the Tory Lord Lansdowne who was left to make this case in his public letter of 29 November 1917. Ada Wallas, to whom Graham read it aloud, thought that it was 'a fine courageous statesmanlike letter,' and she noted that it was approved by all of the Liberal press including a *Manchester Guardian* leader by Hobhouse, and denounced freely by the Tories (2 December 1917). The Letter went down well, of course, at the 1917 Club. An Address of Thanks to Lansdowne, which Courtney, Noel Buxton and Hobson all signed, was organised by Hirst. The Labour statement on war aims followed up close behind. Liberal views on peace, it seemed, were represented in England by the improbable combination of Lansdowne and Labour, with, of course, the ultimate hope that Wilson would exercise a decisive influence. Wilson's Fourteen Points for a peace settlement, declared in January 1918, confirmed his position as the surrogate leader of British Liberalism.

In the early months of 1918 Germany mounted an effective onslaught which made this period more anxious than any other. Massingham was deeply shaken by the success of the German armies. Barbara Hammond offered Lawrence the mordant consolation 'that even the *Nation* realises now that Germany is not a little baa lamb bleating for peace from allied lions' (26 February 1918). The stress upon Hobhouse was increased by the news on 6 January that Oliver was wounded, followed by a fortnight of suspense before it was confirmed that all was well with him. During this interval Hobhouse suffered acutely from what contemporaries called neurasthenia. He wrote a letter contradicting Emily Hobhouse's opinion that the war would soon be over (6 January 1918). Yet when he met Hobson at tea Ada Wallas recorded that he also contradicted Hobson's view that Lloyd George had given up hope of an early victory and was pinning his hopes on 1919 (diary, 14 January 1918). Hobhouse remained ill and sleepless for many weeks, his rationally-grounded optimism unable to quell his deepseated depression. 'Surely you are *much* too gloomy', Scott wrote to him reprovingly on 28 March. Only a week later his own son Ted was listed as missing, but, equally characteristically, Scott's iron fortitude was resiliently maintained until he was found at the end of April.

Since October 1917 a Writers' Group had been dining together each month at the Reform Club, including Wallas, Hobson, Hobhouse, Murray, Dickinson, Webb, Massingham, Gardiner, J. A. Spender and Arnold Bennett. At the Group's meeting in February 1918, attended by Grey, Henderson and McKenna, Wallas was surprised at the radicalism of the

Asquithian McKenna whose hopes for peace seemed to turn largely upon international Labour. The members were agreed that the Lloyd George Government should be overthrown and when they dined with Asquith in March they amicably discussed with him the need for the conscription of wealth in a post-war Budget. Indeed at this time the degree of unanimity between the Asquithians and Labour struck the American observer Ray Stannard Baker very strongly. Henderson, he reiterated in his confidential reports back to America, represented the views of liberal elements – 'liberal with a small l' – in England, a position which he equated with that of Wilson.[29] The measure of agreement here could be summarised as a sweeping programme of democratic reforms at home and a League of Nations to control foreign affairs. The small l, however, was the real hallmark of 1918. It stamped the difference between pre-war progressivism and a new situation where Henderson not Asquith held the initiative.

In April 1918 the *Nation* was calling for an Asquith–Grey–Lansdowne–Henderson Government. For men who had believed for four years that Liberalism was being betrayed over Ireland, and for three years that it was being betrayed over conscription, Lloyd George's introduction of a measure for Irish conscription was an agonising twist of the knife. Even so, for good or bad reasons the Lloyd George Coalition remained safe. Scott's ambivalent comment to Hobhouse (12 April 1918) – 'Asquith will never fight for a principle' – was one side of the story; Murray's appraisal of the Asquithian dilemma another. Hobhouse made a plea to Smuts on behalf of Ireland – 'an imperial matter, not without its analogies to the case of the Transvaal nineteen years ago' – and justified the breach of protocol by announcing that there was 'no Leader of the Opposition in England' (*Smuts*, iii, doc. 827). The Maurice Debate, early in May 1918, was Asquith's only challenge to the Government; when he muffed this opportunity Lloyd George emerged stronger than before. Faced with this collapse of the Liberal opposition, the Writers' Group found itself divided at its meeting on 15 May. For Spender the reconstitution of a progressive alliance was the remedy. Wallas, however, supported by Bennett, argued that Labour would not accept this. His own suggestion for a peace manifesto to be circulated among the belligerents was for the moment adopted. But when he proposed to drop the very word 'liberal' in favour of 'humanitarian' he found himself at odds with Murray and the rest, for whom this was sacred ground. Four days later Wallas went walking with Hobson and, as Ada Wallas recorded, they 'discussed joining the Labour party, on the whole H. wants to keep free but will probably' (20 May 1918). At the Writers' Group in June Murray produced his liberal manifesto. The Group found it too simply a defence of Asquith and Grey and it was withdrawn for revision. Wallas thought that he would in any case be unable to sign it and produced a

[29] Baker–Polk transcripts, Letter 3, 25 March 1918.

draft of his own at the next meeting. But by the time it was ready in October it had been overtaken by events.

The Allies remained on the defensive well into the summer of 1918. On 12 June Ada Wallas noted that three days previously Hobhouse had thought it 'better we should fight until annihilated than give in, very hopeless, and the news since is worse'. The psychological pressures of the war were therefore maintained almost to the end. Not until the last days of September did people suddenly realise that Germany was beaten – and the relief was correspondingly great. 'The successes seem almost more than one can grasp', Barbara Hammond wrote to Lawrence (30 September 1918). The armistice was accepted in mid-October but within days there were disturbing signs that the press and public opinion was out for vengeance rather than a just and humane peace. Barbara Hammond found the successive speeches by Lloyd George and Wilson in mid-November a painful contrast, and took comfort from the prospect that Wilson would have the main say in making the peace. 'I always said I'd sooner win the war under a cad than lose it under a gentleman,' she told Lawrence (13 November 1918), 'but one does wish that the cad cld become a gent. for a day or two at the end.'

There was little joy for Liberals in Lloyd George's strong political position. Even Scott now saw the Coalition as merely 'a reactionary movement of large possibilities' (Wilson, p. 362). What with woman suffrage and the university franchise, Barbara Hammond could congratulate herself that she had two votes to cast against Lloyd George. In Hemel Hempstead she unavailingly worked for the Labour candidate, who polled less than a quarter of the total poll; and in the Oxford University election she presumably voted for the Labour candidates and for Gilbert Murray who stood as a Liberal. Hobson stood as an independent with Labour backing for the new Combined Universities seat and polled very creditably in a hopeless contest. Other prominent figures in the U.D.C. were roundly defeated, but then so were Asquith and Henderson. 'We are greatly distressed by your fate in this vile election', Hammond told Ponsonby (8 January 1919) who finished at the bottom of the poll in Dunfermline Burghs. Labour did less well overall than many had expected earlier in the year and the independent Liberals met with catastrophe. They were all tarred with the same brush.

'The one outstanding virtue of the Labour Party', reflected Beatrice Webb, 'a virtue which is its very own, not imposed upon it by its intellectuals, is its high sense of international morality' (12 December 1918). The Labour party had more convincing credentials here than any other party after the war. Noel Buxton, who had been defeated as a Liberal in 1918, was arguing a year later 'that those who belong to the school of Campbell Bannerman are indebted to the Labour Party for urging views, both about the Peace Settlement and about Social Reform, which he would have expressed but which the Liberal leaders of to-day have left to the Radical section of the Liberal Party'.[30] Keynes was publicly to bemoan the fact that in this immoral election the Liberal leaders did not go down with their flags flying very gloriously – a point which Barbara Hammond put more violently in private to Lawrence (10 April 1919): 'What a moral position Asquith & Co cld have secured if they'd taken the right line abt indemnities instead of trying to go one more Jingo.'

Most of those who looked to Labour in this situation did not doubt the Asquithians' convictions so much as their courage; but it was a heavy charge against them that they lacked the courage of their convictions. Could they be trusted to stand up and be counted when it came to peace-making? Asquithians, like Gilbert Murray and J. A. Spender, were more prominent in the League of Free Nations Association, formed during the spring of 1918, than in the League of Nations Society, with its U.D.C. connexions. There were initial differences over policy here – whether and when Germany should be admitted – and mutual suspicions which had to be cleared away before the League of Nations Union could be constituted, under Grey's patronage, in October 1918. Hobson for one was initially sceptical about the value of these respectable colleagues.

In November 1918 Hammond was invited to go to the Peace Conference as the correspondent of the *Manchester Guardian*. In December he was joined by Barbara and by Rosalind Toynbee, who was able to be with her husband by acting for three months as Hammond's secretary. In the hotel suite which they used for a time the pretentious Louis Quinze decor and the execrable service stood in ironic apposition. Barbara used to have 'a vision of our all 3 sinking to decay & death in that vast ornate room & the last survivor ringing & ringing at the bell & ordering 3 coffins from the stolid impassive waiter'.[31] Such quarters were appropriate to their mounting disillusionment. The intense hopes generated by the sudden ending of the war had already been jolted. Hobhouse had predicted in 1915 that a successful settlement would require a combination of barely compatible circumstances. One condition was the success of the Allies, with the consequent strengthening of Jingoism. But there must then supervene 'an exercise of wisdom and self-control for which the intensity of passion provides no very favorable conditions' while the complex problems of harmonising diverse interests were tackled (AM, cxv, 549). The Coupon Election had already illustrated the fragility of such assumptions and the frailty of democratic control. President Wilson was left in splendid isolation as the last, best hope of liberalism.

For the struggling small nations making their case in Paris it was, like

[30] Quoted by H. N. Fieldhouse in Martin Gilbert (ed.), *A Century of Conflict* (1966), p. 178.
[31] 'Recollections of Peace Conference 1918–19', unfinished, HP 126.

the old faction fights in the Liberal party, war to the knife and fork. Hammond ruefully remarked that one dinner which he attended on the Champs-Elysées must have put a penny in the pound on the Estonian income tax. Keynes was the Treasury representative at Versailles. He and Hammond observed at first hand what liberals at home grasped more belatedly – not least through their writings. Wilson was incapable of enforcing the kind of peace that would enshrine the Fourteen Points. By the middle of May, Keynes had privately written him off as a fraud, and on 7 June 1919 he resigned from his post. On the same day the *Nation* published Hammond's article on 'The Catastrophe of Paris'. 'The Peace Conference is a failure,' he alleged, 'because all the Governments alike are using the victories won by the democracies of the world for the old selfish ends, because each of them still believes in the old ideas of national prestige and pursues the old schemes of national ambition.'

The general thrust of liberal criticism was inevitably against the French. When Barbara Hammond had cycled over to see G. M. Trevelyan in March she had found him deep in gloom over the treatment of the Saar Valley. His conclusion was 'that there is only one decent race on the earth – the Anglo-Saxon: & the worst is that because they are good the bad members of them use their goodness as an excuse for doing bad things'.[32] If Germany was guilty of making the War, then France must be guilty of making the Peace. But Keynes sought to spread the blame more widely and Hammond, with his unshaken Francophilia, went further in ascribing the responsibility to the Americans. On this reading, the real failure was Wilson's. Ten years later Murray was still confidently assuring Hammond that 'Mr G in 1918 would have made the nations rise to a sense of their duty or died in the attempt' (14 December 1928). Keynes persuasively explained Wilson's role in terms of self-deception: he had been bamboozled by Lloyd George into supposing that the actual victors' terms fell within the words of the idealistic pronouncements by which he was bound. Both Keynes and Hammond agreed that Lloyd George, sensing the enormity of what was being done, later intervened on the side of moderation and good sense; but he too had bound himself by his words; and it was by then impossible to debamboozle the old Presbyterian.

To opponents of the war the Peace terms were in a way a more predictable disappointment than to men who had justified the war by the purity of its aims. Hammond wrote that, 'The soldiers had believed that if they gave their rulers victory, that victory would be used to establish a new spirit in the world and to make war impossible' (N, 7 June 1919). Self-determination and a League of Nations had been complementary ideals. Once the Peace undermined the first, the desirability of the second came into question, especially if Germany were not to be admitted. 'The breath

[32] Barbara to Lawrence Hammond, 10 March 1919, HP 11.

of democracy is nowhere to be found', Hobson commented on the Draft Covenant.[33] 'It is much too like the Holy Alliance,' Hobhouse wrote to Scott a few weeks later, 'just a formal bond pledging us all to maintain a thing wh. is intrinsically unjustifiable' (20 May 1919). Yet in the end the League seemed by far the most promising aspect of the whole settlement and Hobson, like Keynes, consistently argued that it should be accepted with a view to its future reform rather than be rejected out of hand.

The Writers' Group was still in being and in June it decided to support its criticism of the Peace terms by commissioning a substantial pamphlet. 'We thought we cd get Keynes to do the financial part,' Hobhouse wrote to Hammond, 'but it was unanimously felt that the best man to draft the whole wd be you if you wd undertake it' (13 June 1919). Keynes, however, was soon at work on independent lines meeting this felt need. *The Economic Consequences of the Peace* (1919) at a stroke established itself as the classical indictment of Versailles. It was not, of course, the book that Hammond would have written, but from beginning to end it was based upon assumptions to which he subscribed. The opening sentence – 'The power to become habituated to his surroundings is a marked characteristic of mankind' (p. 1) – located the problem as one with which the *Town Labourer* had grappled. The closing sentence, dedicating the book 'to the formation of the general opinion of the future' (p. 189), indicated the only hope of remedy.

In the autumn of 1919, 'at the dead season of our fortunes' (p. 188), some such consolation was much needed. 'Did ever [a] set of men do such evil in the world as those who met at Paris', Dickinson demanded of Scott (27 January 1920). 'Literally they have destroyed Europe and the whole heritage of civilisation.' For Hammond, nearing his fiftieth birthday, the very activity of writing was presenting unaccustomed difficulties. 'I *think* it is the strain of Paris & the haunting horror of our general collapse; I hope it is not premature old age', he confided to Murray (24 March 1920). Hobhouse, as ever, was not to be outdone in such matters. The new year of 1920, he conceded to his sister, could hardly be worse than 1919. But he now proclaimed his conviction that 'my anticipations pessimistic as [they] are, are always wrong by being not pessimistic enough' (4 January 1920).

[33] Quoted in Keith Robbins, *The Abolition of War* (1976), p. 188.

7

Hobson's choice

(I) PROBLEMS OF A NEW WORLD

It had become grimly apparent to Graham Wallas that 'the nations of the earth, confused and embittered by the events of 1914–20', might soon be compelled to witness 'another and more destructive stage in the suicide of civilisation'.[1] The world had to be looked at in a new way. Problems had become more intractable. In 1904, to be sure, 'the absorbing domestic crisis hanging over us' had already worried Barbara Hammond. Her servant had given notice and, so she told Mary Murray, she faced the prospect of having to 'try a series of life's failures, for I will not have the responsibility of a young girl, &, except for special reasons, a high class servant will no more go on as a "general" than a Professor wld teach in a preparatory school' (1 January 1904). One or two servants living in at wages which reached £30 to £40 a year by the war years were an indispensable support to the lives of busy middle-class intellectuals. (It would be interesting to know which was greater: the number of books which Hobson wrote during his life or the number of days he devoted to domestic chores.) The wartime shortage of domestic servants did not prove as permanent as it seemed at the time – the slump saw to that; but living in was never again the norm, and expectations were permanently disrupted. After the war Barbara Hammond told Mary Murray that they now 'managed by getting in extra daily help & doing a lot ourselves – wh. is not conducive to work but that can't be helped' (10 August 1921). It was in the summer of 1916 that the new order had hit the Wallases. After ten years Emma and Letty bade them a tearful farewell. When Ada Wallas looked for replacements she found that there were none. 'Perhaps one ought to be glad,' she wrote in her diary (17 June 1916), 'its been no life for a woman – but its convenient for us.'

The Hammonds had never been robust and in the 1920s they were hampered by a series of medical problems. In particular, in 1924 Barbara faced a serious operation on her feet since, as she explained to Mary Murray (22 December 1924), 'the only alternative is to become an obese old woman, snarling on a sofa'. They were, however, much better off financially than ever before, chiefly because Barbara had, in the course of 1919, accumulated

[1] *Our Social Heritage* (1921), p. 25.

family legacies totalling ten thousand pounds, yielding an income of £400–500 per annum. At Oatfield they were able to maintain as comfortable an existence as they wished – not very comfortable by ordinary standards, but luxurious by the standards of frequent visitors like the Tawneys who, so Arnold Toynbee put it, 'could have shaken down easily among the Desert Fathers'. But, as he acknowledged, the Hammonds' austerity differed from that of the Tawneys by not being imposed upon their guests. Instead, the Hammonds 'gave their human guests most-favoured-bird-and-beast treatment'.[2] Earth closets were accordingly replaced with water closets and two bathrooms were built. After the war horse-riding became a favourite recreation. But the Hammonds' intense devotion to all forms of creation was most characteristically seen in Barbara's vigilance as gamekeeper when the young larks were being hatched. She made it her task to ward off the attention of the cats and gave her charges names which reflected her tolerant dismay at their insouciance and precocity. 'Stopes, Keynes & Russell left their summer school by 5.30 yest. heaven be praised', she reported to Lawrence (6 August 1924). 'The cats are free today.'

Lawrence was, so he once told Gilbert Murray (4 February 1933), 'sufficiently outside the Bloomsbury set to think the Forsyte Saga an immense achievement'. The manner of attack on Victorian cultural values which was typified by Lytton Strachey struck a jarring note, though the satirical thrust was often of a kind which older liberal intellectuals had anticipated; and James Strachey recalled to Hammond 'how excited my brother himself was when he first got hold of your and Mrs Hammond's books' (7 February 1934). Barbara Hammond regarded Radclyffe Hall's *The Well of Loneliness* as 'a disgustingly erotic book & Lord, how dull'. She was evidently incensed by its message 'that perverts or inverts ought to be at liberty to satisfy their physical cravings on as many objects as they like'.[3] Likewise, when Beatrice Webb spent some time with the Wallases she noted that they were 'shocked at the gradual disappearance among many of their own circle of young relations & friends of all belief in sexual self control. "Contraception", one niece had said, "renders chastity quite unnecessary" & she was apparently acting on this axiom' (diary, 27 September 1925).

Another old friend, Sydney Olivier, however, adopted the alternative style of condescension towards the free thinking attitudes of the young. Aldous Huxley, he maintained, was merely taking up notions which were already old hat when Rupert Brooke had naïvely delighted in their originality twenty years previously. 'You discovered and introduced me to Samuel Butler nearly 50 years ago', he told Wallas (19 December 1926).

[2] *Acquaintances* (1967), pp. 88, 101.
[3] Barbara to Lawrence Hammond, 27, 29 August 1926, HP 14.

'We were really Butler's contemporaries. We take all that for granted: recognised it and went ahead.' There were certainly ample biographical grounds for adopting this attitude – a world-weary refusal to become unduly exercised about foibles of conduct whose power to shock had long since been exhausted. Hobhouse hit it off perfectly on one occasion at a dinner at the L.S.E. He offered some port to a new member of staff who was a fervent Baptist. 'I would sooner commit adultery' said the Baptist. 'So would we all', retorted Hobhouse (H–L Letters, pp. 1098–9).

It was tempting, however, to interpret the questioning of traditional standards in a much more sinister light. Liberals who believed that a general assault upon civilised values had begun in 1914 were inclined to see everything around them as symptoms of decline, and a more conservative perspective was the natural corollary. Lawrence Hammond found clear evidence that 'G.M.T. has been moving to the right' in Trevelyan's *British History in the Nineteenth Century* (1922). 'Is it the war that has changed him?' he pondered to Barbara. 'I suppose so' (19 June 1922). Even Hobson in *Problems of a New World* (1921) pointed to a process of social disintegration which he maintained had begun in the pre-war years. The authority of fathers and husbands, schoolmasters and employers, had been challenged; there was a 'freer vent for selfishness and a lack of restraint in all matters of the appetite' (p. 41). This was manifested in the arts. 'The ruthless audacities of post-impressionism, futurism, cubism, symbolism were the announcement of a world breaking away from all settled laws of life and plunging into chaos' (p. 43). It was equally manifest in the sciences, where Freudian psycho-analysis came 'to complete the demolition of the claim of man to be a reasoning animal' (p. 44). Barbara Hammond – 'Lord, how I do loathe the psych. ans.' – was even more emphatic, asking Lawrence: 'Can disgustingness or folly go further or be more far-fetched?' (10 October 1918).

It should be said that Wallas's reception of the new insights was expressed in more temperate and reflective terms, though it is true to say that his formal psychology remained essentially pre-Freudian. And if Hobson really believed the denunciations which he voiced, his fortitude in braving the company at the 1917 Club commands an awed respect. In fact, when Virginia Woolf made a New Year's enumeration of her friends in 1919, she included Margaret Llewelyn Davies and Hobson in 'the set that runs parallel but does not mix, distinguished by their social & political character'.[4] Conversely, when Hobson gave his essay *Notes on Law and Order* (1926) to be published by the Woolfs' Hogarth Press, he revealed his view of Samuel Butler and Havelock Ellis as 'the most stimulating general thinkers of their age in Britain' (p. 13) and entered a general plea for 'a free margin of disorder around the order of our lives so as not to take ourselves too exactly' (p. 15).

[4] Bell (ed.), *The Diary of Virginia Woolf* (1977), p. 234; cf. p. 326.

The prominent theme of the decline of religion provoked an ambivalent response. The conduct of the churches during the war had certainly not won them any credit. 'The greatest crisis in history has found them without counsel or policy or guidance, merely re-echoing the passions of the worst crowd', wrote Dickinson in 1916.[5] To Nevinson the clergy's 'wriggling contortions in attempting to reconcile patriotic imprecations with belief in the Christian verities amused rather than edified', and reinforced his sceptical relativism.[6] It was likewise Wallas's assessment, as he told his wife (13 November 1919), that 'the feeling of pity and love for one's fellow men, as affecting national policy, varied in inverse ratio with Christianity'. He remained firmly anti-clerical and, for example, joined a deputation to the Home Secretary against the blasphemy laws in 1929. Indeed one of the few chapters of *Our Social Heritage* (1921) with a real cutting edge is that on the Church. What struck him most – and most unfavourably – about ecclesiastical pronouncements was 'the absence either of clear conviction or serious intellectual effort' (p. 261). The attitude to religion based on 'good form' and 'good sense', prevalent in England and America, prevented people from deciding whether they really accepted Christian dogma and had 'a real tendency to sterilize the intellectual life of our nations' (p. 281). He was quite unimpressed by recent sophisticated defences of the Eucharist which drew upon fashionable anthropological insights about the 'eating with the God', or 'eating the God', as fulfilling an age-old craving for a sacramental religion. To a Victorian rationalist like Wallas, eating God was wrong.

Yet when Wallas was confronted with the erosion of traditional *mores*, Beatrice Webb gleefully detected in him a 'change of front towards religion & its sanctions – not for himself but for the world at large' (diary, 27 September 1925). Hobson, too, attributed the weakening of moral obligations to the attenuated state of religion. Murray was now 'inclined to think that it is true, what we thought was parsonic rubbish when people said it to us twenty years ago, that this age has gone to the Devil, or rather near him, by laying all the emphasis of its beliefs and emotions on material and mechanical things, circumstantial selection, and the economic interpretation of history &c &c.' What was in danger of being forgotten was 'the importance of will and spiritual effort and duty'. It seemed clear to him in the light of events that 'if you take phenomena like Lloyd George, or the average daily paper in England or America, one thing that is clearly wrong with them is their godlessness'.[7] Yet Murray, like Hobson and Wallas – all three of them pillars of the Rationalist Press Association – remained deeply uneasy. They conceded that religious sanctions might have been useful but

[5] E. M. Forster, *Goldsworthy Lowes Dickinson* (1934), p. 160.
[6] *Last Changes, Last Chances* (1928), p. 12.
[7] Murray to Shaw, 13 November 1920, SP 50542, ff.49–50.

they were unpersuaded that Christianity was true. When Murray confided to Hammond that before the war he 'used to feel the world comparatively friendly or at least hopeful, whereas I now feel it utterly alien and hostile', Superstition took its place with Protection, Corruption, War and Vulgarity among the threats he perceived (19 July 1924). As a matter of intellectual integrity, it was as important as ever to keep up the good fight against it.

In a bleak and unfriendly world, however, the personal consolations of faith made a more potent appeal. 'As I get older,' Hammond confessed, 'I feel myself moving more and more from the negative and critical line about religion and more and more inclined to think that the radical reaction against religion made the mistake of the radical reaction against the social life of the middle ages.' Russell's taunts now seemed to him 'like the crudities of the bold rebel in the Victorian nursery'.[8] Hobhouse found himself under even greater stress. His intellectual system, of course, rested on a firm conviction that cosmic forces ultimately made for progress. Oliver Elton, who had overlapped at Corpus with both Hobhouse and Wallas, and who remained, as he told Wallas (10 May 1930), 'a high & dry old Victorian agnostic', seized on this as the vulnerable aspect of Hobhouse's thought. There seemed to Elton to be a dubious implication that the effort of human will and intelligence, which Hobhouse postulated, would work out under the guidance of an ill-defined but beneficent force or principle – 'but, really,' he demanded, 'isn't it Old Provvy over again, depersonalised?' The death of his wife in 1925 pushed Hobhouse along a path which was already signposted in his published work. He told the Hammonds that 'it made me believe in what most people wd call God – I will say a spiritual element fundamental in Reality' (19 October 1925). He refused to accept 'that a being like Nora came about by the random collocation of "genes" in the ramifications of physical heredity'; he remained unclear about an after life; and he feared deceiving himself into an unworthy kind of intellectual dishonesty. 'I can only be sure,' he explained, 'that that same great spiritual effort wh made her & made all that is good & beautiful will do its best for its children whose fate is often so tragic' (ibid.).

Hobhouse was in his late fifties at the end of the war, though he often seemed – and felt – older than Wallas and Hobson who were five years his senior. After the war the Hobhouses moved house from Highgate back to Wimbledon, and the Wallases left for Chelsea shortly afterwards. The London School of Economics remained as a meeting ground, though Wallas was much more closely integrated into its institutional life than Hobhouse, whose range of outside activities was in no way diminished. The expanded role of Trade Boards made further calls on his time and he became chairman of several new ones established during the wave of Whitleyism in 1919

[8] Hammond to Murray, n.d. but perhaps 1924, MP.

and 1920. At the same juncture the Martin White chair was made into a full-time appointment. The result was that he could no longer write for the *Manchester Guardian* with the frequency which had been usual since 1916 – he and Scott had been writing nearly half the leaders between them in the later part of the war. Scott, however, prevailed upon Hobhouse to keep his directorship, telling him: 'The only thing that, from my point of view, matters is that you retain an effective connection with the paper and that I see you regularly' (10 January 1921). This condition was fulfilled by Hobhouse's flying visits to Manchester every month, but a gap remained which Scott was at a loss to fill.

Until 1918 Hammond barely knew Scott, though there had already been efforts to engage him for the editorial staff of the *Manchester Guardian*. But after he had represented the paper at Versailles, and a further attempt to secure his full-time services had failed, Hammond was asked to go to Manchester to give the sort of summer relief on the editorial corridor which Hobhouse had previously supplied. 'Hammond's visit was a great pleasure', Scott told Hobhouse (2 August 1920). 'He is such a nice chap &, as you say, he did some first-class work.' Staying at The Firs, with its awesome regime of cold baths, fresh air and raw fruit, had no terrors for Hammond. Scott, for whom the main drawback of his frequent train journeys to London was 'the wicked persistence of most people to keep windows closed',[9] found that the Hammonds were people after his own heart. Barbara Hammond – 'My idea of hell is a closed Austin 7: of Purgatory a closed Austin 12'[10] – was a sympathetic hostess at Oatfield, especially after she gave up meat-eating as unhealthy. 'I have come to the conclusion,' Scott told her a few months before his eightieth birthday, 'that one ought to sleep in the open air in order to be at home with nature. I shd like to try it' (29 June 1926). His notorious meanness towards his staff was breached, as it had been for Hobhouse a generation earlier, by uncharacteristic avowals that the paper should increase its remuneration. Lawrence Hammond was treated almost like a son by the old man – his own son Laurence had died in 1907 – and, whereas for thirty years it had been 'Dear Hobhouse', by the end of the 1920s Scott was diffidently using the name Lawrence in his letters to Barbara. It was at this time that he told his son Ted that Hammond really knew him better than anyone else.

Hobhouse, however, was not displaced and after a year or two of more tenuous contact exercised his reversionary rights. In the hot summer of 1922, therefore, Hammond and Hobhouse were both at The Firs since Hobhouse had lost some of his Trade Board work and proposed to give his free time to journalism instead. Barbara Hammond, who was a connoisseur of Hobhousiana, relished accounts from Lawrence of Hobhouse's re-

[9] Scott to Hobhouse, 9 January 1917, MGP.
[10] Barbara to Lawrence Hammond, 26 August 1928, HP 14.

discovered enthusiasm for Manchester, where the air was cool and refreshing, unlike that of Wimbledon. 'We both did our best,' Lawrence reported (3 June 1922), 'to live up to his famous aphorism that the only mistake the pessimists make is in not being pessimistic enough.' But when the temperature dropped overnight, Hobhouse's first comment was, 'The infernal cold weather makes me bilious.'

Hammond had good reason for resentment since his own scope as a part-time journalist was restricted by Hobhouse's return. A full-time post was not what he wanted. Hammond was in a cleft stick here since the inquiries he was also making of friends in the universities, like Toynbee and Stocks, suggested that there was little hope of finding the kind of opening that appealed to him. The launching of 'Modern Greats' at Oxford had seemed to offer an opportunity for Lawrence to win the academic recognition that he coveted. But the only invitation that Stocks could drum up was neither financially nor intellectually worthwhile. Barbara made it clear to Lawrence that 'from the point of view of getting the Ford lectures or anything of the kind' he would only prejudice his chances by such an arrangement (10 June 1922). In any case her impression of 'the carping critical atmosphere of Oxford' (ibid.), 'the arid and cavilling atmosphere of Oxford' (13 June 1922), was less indulgent than his.

Hammond therefore continued to supplement his income by a few weeks of journalism in Manchester each summer. Hobhouse, however, found his capacities in this respect increasingly curtailed by ill health, and in 1924 he was laid low with phlebitis at The Firs while they were both there. 'A specialist had come in when he was thought to be in great danger,' Hammond recalled, 'and had told him that he was going to get over that attack. Hobhouse's relief was ecstatic.'[11] But his convalescence seems to have marked a perceptible turning point in his relations with his host. Hobhouse's complete obliviousness of the feelings of the nurse, and his failure even to say good-bye to her when he left, came to Scott (so Lawrence told Barbara) as 'a revelation of the extent of his selfishness' (14 August 1924). Barbara's reply (15 August 1924) showed her better inured to the ways of the great democrat. 'The Hob. gives one the same sort of satisfactory feeling that a complete work of art does; there are no incongruities, it is all nicely finished & complete & harmonious.' And she concluded: 'I think I partly blame Nora Hobhouse, but perhaps he was impossible to alter.' But Leonard Hobhouse's continual illness thereafter, combined with Nora's death in 1925 and Emily's the following year, made him a tragic figure to whom the Hammonds extended a heartfelt compassion.

Scott never gave up the idea of installing Hammond permanently on the *Manchester Guardian* – perhaps even as his successor. In 1919 the offer had been £1000 a year, a motor car and a new house in the country with a

[11] Hammond to Murray, 7 March 1937, MP.

first-class shelter. In 1925 further permutations were tried: £1500 a year, work at the London office, special taxis to meet trains, a motor car and a house outside Manchester, a motor car and a chauffeur. Barbara Hammond maintained a disconsolate insistence that it was for Lawrence to decide what he wanted to do. 'Life,' she told him, 'is not agreeable to me now, but I daresay it would be no more disagreeable in the country near Manchester than here, and when, if ever, it becomes agreeable again, I expect I could be quite as happy there as here' (19 June 1925). In the end it was Montague's retirement which prompted a formal proposal to Hammond. 'I keep thinking of the new pillar which is needed to keep the M.G. safe', Scott told him (29 July 1925). At Christmas 1925, therefore, Hammond began his most sustained spell of work as a journalist since he had left the *Daily News* nearly twenty years previously, and, despite some illness, he put in five nights a week at Manchester for much of the year. Scott was overjoyed. 'Nobody has quite your touch', he told Hammond (21 September 1926). From this time on Hammond, though less closely committed himself, acted as confidant to both C.P. and Ted Scott – not always compatible roles – and advised them on the continually nagging issue of recruitment to the corridor at Cross Street.

(II) RATIONALISM BEATEN TO ITS CORNER

It bemused many of Scott's friends that, in an otherwise honourable old age, he should devote so much effort to saving Lloyd George's soul. Lloyd George, it must be said, always played up well in this drama. 'Come and see me sometimes and correct my faults', he would plead, adding, with what Scott took to be partial sincerity, 'Or help my best self' (Wilson, p. 384). So Scott persisted in his appointed role. 'The foxiness of Ll.G. was repellant to many upright radicals,' Keynes later observed to Hammond (23 March 1933), 'but caught, I think, some sort of echo in C.P.S.; he was never so much shocked as some people were by Ll.G.'s methods.' And in 1918, after all, Lloyd George had been swept to power, at the head of his hard-faced followers, with all the right phrases about liberty and justice on his lips. 'What fun if the vested interests have to unvest themselves by their own votes', Barbara Hammond exclaimed to Lawrence (12 February 1919), reflecting on one aspect of a piquant situation. She speedily acknowledged that with such a House of Commons it hardly looked as though the Government meant business, which only led her to the equally piquant reflection that 'after all its the wkg classes who returned the vested interests to power' (22 February 1919). To Hobson, who regarded Lloyd George as non-principled rather than unprincipled, it seemed that 'the bright images of a land fit for heroes and a world living in amity, touched his sympathy and stirred his imagination as he painted them, but they carried neither intellectual nor moral conviction and no lasting will towards their fulfilment'.[12] Wallas considered that the whole process had 'left in the minds of tens of thousands of British working men and women a conviction that, as many of them now complain, they were "had"', and was a sobering illustration of the manipulation of public opinion.[13] 'Mr George's success,' commented Brailsford, 'reduces the rational element in politics to the lowest and most negligible level which English experience has ever known' (N, 22 January 1921). The Lloyd George Coalition was not devoid of constructive achievements, but its characteristic stamp of reactionary opportunism damned it in liberal eyes. Even Tom Jones considered that by 1921 only the *Manchester Guardian* stood between the Prime Minister and depravity.[14]

It was once more the Gladstonian issues of nationality, freedom and public right which provided the crucial test. If Poland had been released under the peace settlement as a result of the principle of self-determination, why was Ireland held in bondage? The Irish situation rapidly worsened in 1920, as the Government prepared to suppress the nationalist movement. In the minds of old pro-Boers it all fitted an obvious paradigm. 'We are moving to war as surely as we were in the summer of 1899', Hammond told Murray (21 June 1920), and by September was asking him whether there was 'any chance of getting up a protest from men of letters against the Govts bloody policy in Ireland?' (2 September 1920) A Peace with Ireland Committee began to take shape, instigated by Basil Williams, Tawney, Hobhouse and Hammond. Murray felt just as keenly and confessed to Barbara Hammond that he had been 'lying awake and worrying over this Irish business, as no doubt you have for some time' (2 January 1921). The activities of the Black and Tans seemed to amount to Government by Murder. In a widely-read Irish Supplement to the *Nation* Hammond claimed that the ruling error was unmistakeable: 'England treats Ireland not like a sister nation but as a subject race' (N, 8 January 1921). When he went to Ireland in the spring of 1921 to investigate personally for the *Nation* he found that the whole process of the law gave a higher priority to protecting the good name of the Royal Irish Constabulary than the lives of ordinary Irish workmen. His passionate exposure of British policy, of course, had already laid him open to the charge of 'condoning crimes of the utmost deliberation and atrocity',[15] but his second *Nation* supplement in April showed him unrepentant. Coercion, he maintained, was being used not against murderers but against a popular and national movement; and murder, though regrettable in itself and unhelpful to the Irish cause in England, was not the root problem, which was being evaded by a resort to terror. 'Revolution,' he concluded, 'is a more terrible weapon

[12] *Problems of a New World* (1921), p. 121. [13] *Our Social Heritage* (1921), p. 103.
[14] Thomas Jones, *Whitehall Diary* (1969), i, 180–1.
[15] Hilton Young to Hammond, 2 December 1920, HP 18.

in the hands of a Government than it is in the hands of a people. Lenin has shown that in Russia; Mr Lloyd George has shown it in Ireland' (*N*, 30 April 1921).

It was, above all, Ireland that put Lloyd George out of court for many Liberals. In the *Manchester Guardian* Scott took so unmistakable a line of outrage that even Lloyd George was forced to recognise that they had been 'hopelessly at variance of late' and that there was no point in meeting (Wilson, p. 394). Scott was admittedly once more in the offing (summoned to London by Hammond) when Lloyd George concluded the negotiations for the Irish Treaty in December 1921; but though this too could be construed as a hopeful sign that Lloyd George was seeking redemption, for other Liberals Lloyd George was by now a lost soul. Indeed, for many of them, like Massingham, politics came to revolve around finding an alternative to Lloyd George. But since he had apparently persuaded the country 'to live without parties and without principles', public opinion seemed unhappily ready to accept 'Lloyd-Georgeism, knowing it to be bad, in fear lest a worst thing befall it' (N, 14 May 1921). Was it to be Lloyd George for ever and ever? It was as a composite 'anti-Lloyd George' that the high-minded (but high Tory) Lord Robert Cecil gained some credence with Liberals. 'Neither Asquith nor Cecil nor the Labour people nor Grey give the country the impression that they mean business', Hammond complained to Murray (16 May 1921). In April 1922, however, Murray's enthusiasm for Cecil – 'I feel in some queer way that R.C. has kept himself clean from the general filthiness of the war'[16] – led him to canvass support for a manifesto urging his claims. Neither Hammond nor Wallas were impressed by this strategy. 'That kind of thing had real effect in Victorian politics,' Hammond told him, 'but the electorate is now such a vast mob and the real power depends on getting press and caucus' (15 April 1922).

The Liberal party, so its old chief whip Herbert Gladstone wrote in 1922, 'depends altogether on principles & the solution of current needs by the application of those principles'.[17] But after 1918 this vision of politics seemed mocked by the ascendancy of the Lloyd George regime. When Scott commented to Hobhouse after Courtney's death on his 'unshakeable stand for principle, for which in these days hardly anyone seems resolutely to stand', he was irresistibly led to add: 'could any contrast be greater than that between his whole mentality and that of Lloyd George, which seems to have infected our whole politics?' (31 October 1919) In 1923 the Hammonds finished their not always congenial task of producing a Life of Lord Shaftesbury. 'Sheer uprightness & character – I often wonder how far it has really lost its power in this far more ironical age', Galsworthy wrote in thanks for his copy (18 August 1923). This was the last book which the

[16] Murray to Hammond, 13 April 1922, HP 30.
[17] Memorandum (?July 1922), HGP 46110, ff.181, 183.

Hammonds were able to present to Morley, whose death that autumn had a perceptible resonance for English Liberalism. 'Morley was the last of the great, the true, Liberals', wrote Massingham (*H.W.M.*, p. 23). To Hirst, who had remained perhaps his closest disciple, it seemed obvious that the interment of a man who had been 'a Lucretian to the end' should be marked by a brief address from Hobson; but the possibility of 'a Hobsonian funeral and a service at Westminster Abbey' had been foreclosed by the adoption of more conventional observances. 'It is the end of a chapter,' he wrote feelingly to Hammond, 'and of a life which has consoled me more than anything else for the horrors, cruelties, and perversities of this hateful age with its false prophets and professional impostors, its office seekers, profiteers, wirepullers – all obsequious worshippers of Force, Popularity, and Pelf' (27 September 1923).

In such a wicked world the *Nation* itself could hardly stay afloat. When Leonard Woolf took Brailsford's place as a colleague of Massingham, Tomlinson, Hobson, Hammond and Nevinson, he regarded them as 'so high-minded – the particular brand of high-mindedness seemed to be peculiar in those days to Liberals who lived in Hampstead and Golders Green – that I always felt myself to be a bit of a fraud in their company'.[18] The *Nation* had, of course, always depended on subsidies from the Rowntrees and by 1921 they were no longer prepared to cover the sort of losses that were piling up. Here lay the makings of the final crisis. It was precipitated by political differences in the wake of Lloyd George's fall from power at the end of 1922. Massingham devoted nine out of ten *Nation* lunches to tirades against Lloyd George, often coupled with the name of Scott, the evergreen apostle of Liberal reunion. Resuming communion with Lloyd George seemed to Massingham to give honest Liberals the choice of withdrawal or ranging themselves with Labour as the only party with 'a scrap of principle left' (*H.W.M.*, p. 101). Massingham's letter of resignation in December 1922 added his own malaise and the divisive effect of his personality upon the proprietors as reasons for ending his editorship. It is also clear that he could not raise sufficient funds himself to take over the paper; and here the group led by Keynes and Ramsay Muir, with whom the Rowntrees were also in touch, had a telling advantage since they could afford to relaunch the *Nation* as the organ for the views of the Liberal Summer School movement. In many ways this was a highly appropriate transfer of control. Keynes and Hubert Henderson, the new editor, gave the paper a new lease of life. But Massingham's departure took place amid secrecy, confusion and bitterness which left behind a squalid impression.

'The *Nation* was his creation,' Tomlinson explained, 'but he had to leave it as though it were a grocer's shop and he was the retiring manager' (*H.W.M.*, p. 125). This was the received version among Massingham's

[18] Leonard Woolf, *Downhill All The Way* (1967), p. 93.

staff who, partly as a result of his disingenuous representations, loyally took his part. Hammond arranged with Hobson, Tomlinson, Nevinson, Laski, and initially Woolf, that they should all resign with Massingham. The fact that the paper had been sold over his head was how they kept explaining to each other their indignation against the Rowntrees. 'It's all very well for you to talk against cocoa,' Hammond's friend Arthur Clutton-Brock ribbed him, 'but remember how you swilled it down at Cadbury's, well knowing that it had been got by slave labour' (25 January 1923). Hammond, Hobson and Nevinson all made their strong feelings about the way Massingham had been treated known to the Rowntrees; and although Hammond was on cordial terms with Henderson he initially offered firm resistance to the proposal that he should continue to write for the *Nation*, which was what Keynes would have liked. Hammond considered that Keynes had behaved 'curiously' – though admittedly not 'infamously' like the Rowntrees – and felt that he could not honourably remain a contributor.[19]

The more he discovered about the whole affair, however, the more his doubts grew as to whether he had put the blame on the right shoulders. The Rowntrees set out their side of the case to Hobson, and Hammond himself heard of the Summer School's role from Ernest Simon, whose 'queer tale' he reported back to Barbara. 'I am beginning to feel very angry with H.W.M.', she responded. 'It is one thing playing ducks and drakes with your own fortunes & another thing playing it with your friends finances' (8 May 1923). Like Virginia Woolf, she felt that her husband had suffered a loss of morale and of money because his interests had been subordinated to the whims of the famous editor; though in Woolf's case there was admittedly the consolation of the literary editorship under the Keynesian regime. Hammond, with his concern to spare the feelings of a man who had suffered enough, seems to have kept his real view of Massingham to himself. He refused to write his biography. It was twenty years later that he described him to Murray as 'a lightweight whose judgment was beneath contempt' (3 May 1944).

So Massingham left the *Nation*, and most of his staff with him. The *Nation* lunch came to an end, despite Laski's attempts to revive it. 'It was too great a fellowship to be allowed to scatter', he told Hammond (5 September 1924). The new *Nation* was submitted to the scrutiny of the old guard in May 1923 – 'Lytton Strachey & Keynes are of course star turns,' Barbara Hammond admitted to Lawrence, 'ditto I suppose Mrs Woolf tho' I never care much for her' (6 May 1923).

In the post-war period of reaction and political upheaval liberal democracy was on the defensive. In the new edition of *Human Nature in Politics* (1920), Wallas acknowledged in the preface that there was no longer any

[19] Hammond to Murray, 2 April 1923, MP.

danger of exaggerating human rationality. Indeed, Brailsford, in commenting on the book, considered that Wallas's persistent confidence in the 'young thinkers of our time' was undermined by the force of his critical analysis, as seen in the light of events. The implication was that Wallas merely threw up his hands in horror when confronted with the implications of his own prescient work. When Laski wrote what he deliberately intended as a kind review of *Our Social Heritage* he said: 'If one were to assess the progress of political theory in the last ten or fifteen years, I think no small part of what it has gained would have to be traced to Mr Wallas' (*N*, 9 April 1921). Laski had real affection for Wallas, who had been largely responsible for his return from America to a post at the L.S.E. in 1920. Within a year or two, however, the fulsome appreciation which he had poured into Wallas's ear while his appointment hung in the balance had been overlaid by a more sceptical appraisal: a change which it would be unfair to explain entirely in terms of self-serving.

Laski regarded Wallas as the quintessential English mind. He was 'full of real insights' but could never sustain an abstract discussion without resort to concrete illustrations; he was 'rarely logical and about eight times out of ten patently in the right' (*H–L Letters*, p. 303). When Laski succeeded Wallas as Professor of Political Science, after his unexpectedly early retirement in 1923, he claimed that the revered expert on administration had left the affairs of the department in a shambles; but there is no suggestion that Wallas had merely lost his grip. His teaching retained its inspiring character. His work in progress still made a fruitful basis for Socratic discussions in his seminar where, so his student Lionel Robbins recalled, 'one almost felt that the future of the human race depended upon the substance and the candour of the answer'.[20] His characteristic approach, however, with its abundance of shrewd *aperçus*, its avowed preference for the vernacular in academic study, and its ready recourse to anecdote, was less vulnerable in lectures and classes than in books, where its lack of constructive force stood more nakedly exposed.

In *Our Social Heritage* Wallas was asserting 'the necessity of conscious purpose as against half conscious drift in human affairs.'[21] The book seemed to Laski sadly inadequate to the prospectus. 'Wallas attacks everyone else and then tells you that he believes in liberty, equality, and the free play of reason, which is like telling a man to wash himself in a parched desert' (*H–L Letters*, p. 329). But the conviction grew upon Wallas that social salvation depended upon solving the problems of inventing political machinery and harnessing the forces of the intellect. The validity of Bentham's aims survived the supersession of his methods. *The Art of Thought* (1926) was the result of Wallas's quest. 'I shall argue,' he had

[20] Lord Robbins, *Autobiography of an Economist* (1971), p. 88.
[21] Wallas to Shaw, n.d. (?March 1921), Shaw Papers, B.L. Add. MSS. 50553, ff.7–11.

explained to the Hammonds, 'that severe impartial thought can be driven by feeling without diminishing the intensity of the feeling, if the thinker knows what he is doing' (26 August 1923). Wallas had decided that ultimately his social thought was to be about thought itself. If only he could solve this problem, everything else would fall into place. Hence his image, in Robbins's eyes, as 'a Captain Shotover of the Social Sciences' (Robbins, p. 87).

The real charge that was brought against Wallas's political thought (and also that of Hobhouse, who could have understudied Shotover) was that it was utopian. It took insufficient account of prevailing social realities; it therefore lacked a strategy of change and in effect sustained the status quo. Laski commented on the draft of *The Art of Thought*, 'I conclude after four hundred pages that Wallas wants a world in which men are happy and work together in a kindly and pacific spirit – who in God's name ever wanted any other kind of world?' (*H–L Letters*, p. 589). Kingsley Martin responded in the same way after hearing Wallas give a course of lectures in Cambridge, writing: 'The great difficulty I feel is that however keen, able and clear-headed your group of thinkers is, the world in general just uses those bits of their work that seems convenient; your own example of the utilitarians shows what I mean fairly clearly – people were delighted with "laisser faire" economics when it meant high profits, but no one thought of applying what he [*sc.* Bentham?] or Adam Smith said about good wages or social reform' (11 March 1921). Likewise, Brailsford maintained that the 'young thinkers', to whom Wallas wished to appeal, were inclined to bypass his psychological criticism in favour of a more definitely economic analysis. Trotsky was currently mounting 'a case against democracy as an elaborate *camouflage* for the "dictatorship of the bourgeoisie"', and the grounds for this were easy to see (N, 22 January 1921).

The most constructive alternative in sight was some form of functional representation. In *The Acquisitive Society* (1921) Tawney presented a seductive vision of the radical resolution of current difficulties. Harmony could only be achieved, he suggested, in a Functional Society organised upon a professional basis around the discharge of services which had a value for the whole community; whereas the existing Acquisitive Society had a rationale of individual gain which exacerbated conflict. Wallas found much to admire here; but, in acknowledging that Tawney's 'social sympathy is as authentic as that of William Morris', he revealed also why he was not convinced. In the true moral revolutionary tradition Tawney had exaggerated the unselfishness of both vocational organisations and individual workers in a future dispensation where the common good would be the only economic motive. The danger was that when the forces which the moral revolutionist invoked had proved abortive the mechanical revolutionist would come to the front. 'Tolstoy helped to produce Trotsky,' Wallas concluded, 'and the Tolstoy–Morris side of Mr Tawney may encourage the Trotsky habit of mind in England' (*N*, 11 June 1921). Wallas had, of course, a deep suspicion of vocational organisations on the grounds that they were conservative and inward-looking. Cole's claim that they provided a superior alternative to the state struck him as absurd. All that would happen, as Hobhouse put it, would be that existing and undesirable forms of sectionalism 'would be crystallised and consecrated by the Guild system'.[22] Hobson's attitude to functional representation was less overtly hostile. In *Problems of a New World* (1921) he characterised Guild Socialism as the 'most definite form which the demand for industrial democracy has taken in this country' (p. 173), and as such worth exploring as one solution to the industrial problem, along with Whitley Councils, Trade Boards and Nationalisation. But of course this falls some way short of an endorsement of Cole's *Weltanschauung*.

Hobson was also prepared to extend this line of extenuation to include Bolshevism, on the grounds that it too rested upon a common case for an economic view of politics, an insistence on proletarian control of government, and a substitution of functional for regional representation. He explained the noisy anti-Soviet clamour of 1920 as 'directed by a just perception that if once the notion of industrial unionism caught on as an electoral idea, capitalist democracy was doomed' (p. 165). Hobson was ready, therefore, at this time, to assert two propositions: that the existing government of Britain did not give real power to the workers and that the Soviet experiment in Russia did. He did not, however, draw the conclusion that Britain needed a Bolshevik revolution. Instead he considered it 'reasonably possible that a people like the British, escaping the destructive experience of a class-war, might attain a form of moderate socialist-communism compatible not merely with a high measure of personal freedom but with private enterprise in many fields of economic activity' (p. 202). His doubts about the power of unconstitutional action remained as strong as ever, though he now admitted that some alloy of force was always necessary in political action. His claim was that 'a British revolution can only be made good by an appeal to reason and justice' (p. 204). This could, perhaps, be called a compromise, but since 'no better term exists to connote the provisional harmony which alone is possible in an ever-changing world' (p. 256), he was ready to accept the description with equanimity.

Wallas's rejection of Bolshevism was more clear-cut. The 'scientifically conscientious ruthlessness' of Lenin and Trotsky[23] had been licensed by the combination of a determinist dogma with a 'mechanist' conception of the subservience of reason to instinct. Through this combination, he wrote in *The Art of Thought*, they were able 'to convince themselves that such a

[22] *The Elements of Social Justice* (1922), p. 180.
[23] *Our Social Heritage*, p. 249.

"bourgeois" intellectual process as unbiased reflection before one acts in obedience to one's simplest animal instincts, is at the same time biologically impossible, and also biologically possible but politically and economically inadmissible' (p. 34). In fact, Hobson, with his disdain for the pathetic naivety of scientific socialism, shared this theoretical position, but it must be admitted that in Wallas's case it fed upon more vivid fears. Even in 1918 Ada Wallas had noted that: 'We, G. & I, dread the power of the soldiers & the formation of so-called workmen's councils really in the hands of soldiers' (diary, 2 November 1918). Hammond, too, consumed with the iniquities of the terror in Ireland, clearly took the view that liberty was indivisible. 'Kerensky was speaking at a meeting in London about the Bolsheviks,' he wrote by way of illustration, 'and somebody said they were democrats. "If it is democracy", he answered, "to banish your opponents, to suppress all meetings and newspapers, and to lock up people who disagree with you without trial, by what signs do you ask me to recognise tyranny?"' (N, 30 April 1921)

Wallas persistently, and sometimes provocatively, pointed to the frailty of democratic institutions. Thus he teased Beatrice Webb, with her no-nonsense approach, by arguing: 'No reason to believe in a particular institution because there seems to be no better alternative institution' (*BWD*, iv, 74). But he voiced his scepticism in the spirit of a protective parent saying, 'My child is not strong and should not be taxed too far (but may yet, with luck, surprise you all)'. Hobhouse was similarly committed to a system of whose defects he could hardly be unaware. In *The Elements of Social Justice* (1922) he restated his view of the necessity for popular control, while admitting that 'the power of conscious democracy is practically limited to certain critical decisions, and largely to a veto on the proposals of the bureaucrat' (p. 188). The difficulty was not to guard against a bad or selfish will but to find any will at all. Hobson, too, who had once more helped Hobhouse with his draft here, was ready to admit that 'friends and enemies of Democracy alike know that it is a failure'.[24] As might be expected, however, such an admission was only a spur for efforts to redeem the failure.

Reason and democracy therefore still constituted the terms of the problem and the means of its solution. Hammond remembered a conversation with Wallas and Halévy about the way Germany had been defeated by the liberal nations – 'they took great confort in this reflection' (L., 13 February 1947). Wallas continued to pin his faith upon the reality and efficacy of intellectual freedom. 'The whole world,' he declared to his daughter May, 'now seems to be full of organisations, parties, nations, churches, classes etc. which all preach that for tactical reasons one ought not to say what one really thinks; and that way intellectual sterility and social reaction lie'

[24] *Problems of a New World*, p. 237.

(20 June 1922). His reading of events was therefore totally different from that of Shaw, whose prescription for socialism now comprised an enforced equality of incomes – 'Direct unhesitating compulsion should be a matter of course', he told Wallas (5 June 1928). This was obviously an injunction with undisguised affinity for dictatorial methods. 'A Bolshevik as far as I can tell is nothing but a socialist who wants to do something about it', Shaw confessed in 1919. 'To the best of my knowledge I am a Bolshevik myself.'[25] This shift from the mechanical reformist to the mechanical revolutionist position was perhaps to be expected of (in Lenin's famous phrase) a good man fallen among Fabians. But even the most indulgent of Shaw's old friends were shocked a few years later by his extenuation of Italian Fascism in a widely-read interview. 'Imagine the hot indignation and withering wit with which the meagrely-fed Irish journalist of the eighties, writing in his dark lodging, would have chastised the rich world-famous dramatist of 1927 defending the pitiless cruelties and bombastic militancy of the melodramatic Mussolini', commented Beatrice Webb (*BWD*, iv, 156). Wallas was unmoved by Shaw's defence that it was as futilely pious to resist Mussolini as Lenin. 'Young Fascists,' he remonstrated with Shaw, 'don't step, strong and silent, out of the cradle; they are made, or prevented from being made by discussion' (13 February 1927). Shaw's advocacy of bomb-throwing as the only effective response to the threat of force therefore missed the point; or, rather, conceded it with a Shavian *Schadenfreude* calculated to affront earnest Liberals.

There is clearly considerable force in the sort of criticism which Wallas (b. 1858) and Hobhouse (b. 1864) met from Laski (b. 1893), Tawney (b. 1880), Martin (b. 1897) and Brailsford (b. 1873). Put in this way the contrast seems clear. Both Wallas and Hobhouse were undoubtedly open to the charge that their defence of rationalism depended on arguing at a level of abstraction which was either unhelpful or woolly-minded. It is tempting to see in this a telling reason for the decline of Liberalism as economic evolution rendered its cherished procedures inapplicable. The critics were all committed to the Labour party. But so, of course, were Hobson (b. 1858) and Hammond (b. 1872) who would be much less easy to categorise. The political division was probably relevant, but was not, in their minds, a crucial division. 'I don't know whether you are a member of the party – probably not', Tawney wrote to Wallas when seeking advice (14 June 1921).

The supposed confrontation – of generation, of party, or of belief – is in fact less stark than it appears at first sight. In *The Acquisitive Society* Tawney offered a scornful justification for making a class analysis: 'To deplore "ill feeling", or to advocate "harmony", between "labour" and "capital" is as rational as to lament the bitterness between carpenters and

[25] David Caute, *The Fellow-Travellers* (1973), pp. 113–14.

hammers or to promote a mission for restoring amity between mankind and its boots' (p. 113). Yet Tawney's fundamental assumption was that it was 'the creed which affirms the absolute rights of property' which provoked 'a counter-affirmation of the absolute rights of labour, less anti-social, indeed, and inhuman, but almost as dogmatic, almost as intolerant and thoughtless as itself' (p. 31). Again it was a disinterested appeal to principles rather than the class struggle which suggested a solution. The conditions of harmony would have to be created by structural reform. Hobson is to be found making exactly the same point: 'It is idle to trust to "common sense" or "a sound heart" in order to obtain "a square deal" when the cards are packed against you.'[26] In his case he was reiterating the arguments of thirty years and more. It was also common ground that where men's treasure was, there would their hearts be also. 'The Great War,' wrote Hobson, 'has demonstrated how much easier it is to effect a levy upon life than a levy upon property.'[27] Barbara Hammond agreed exactly, telling Mary Murray that 'the older one grows the more one learns that many will sacrifice their lives but not their property' (5 September 1921).

Laski found the Hammonds agreeable and stimulating company; he regarded their great trilogy as a splendidly sustained historical achievement. Indeed he bracketed *The Town Labourer* with Wallas's *Francis Place* as books which destroyed 'the hypothesis of a spirit for good in what, for want of a better phrase – one calls the master-class' (*H–L Letters*, p. 206). But was not the hypothesis which the books destroyed essential to their authors' belief in the avoidability of the class war? Hobson offered a crucially different reading here. To him *The Town Labourer* and *Lord Shaftesbury* demonstrated 'the most remarkable of modern advances in social ethics'. The glow of moral indignation over the treatment of labour had won a wide acceptance for the idea of standard minimum conditions. 'It is, indeed, a comforting reflection,' he wrote, 'that this, the most important achievement of "practical socialism", has been at least as much the fruit of social compunction among the well-to-do classes as of the organised working-class force.'[28]

In *Free-Thought in the Social Sciences* (1926) Hobson offered the fullest statement of his view on the relation of social thought to social action: a treatment which was not only hailed by Laski as admirable, but which elicited the author's acknowledgment to 'my friends Professor L. T. Hobhouse and Mr R. H. Tawney' of 'the formative influence which their writings have had upon the tenor of my argument' (p. 7). Hobson wanted to show why the social sciences made such slow progress by examining the obstacles to disinterested thought within them; he also wanted to vindicate free-thought as both the goal and agent of social amelioration. In this he

[26] *The Conditions of Industrial Peace* (1927), p. 117.
[27] *Free-Thought in the Social Sciences* (1926), p. 239.
[28] Ibid., p. 249.

returned to problems which had long fascinated him, as shown by *The Social Problem* (1901), *Imperialism* (1902), *Work and Wealth* (1914) and *Problems of a New World* (1921). The central section of the book is on the development of economic theory, which Hobson considered much more susceptible of an economic interpretation than history in general. His view of orthodox economics as a conservative defence of existing property arrangements was, of course, long established. Adam Smith's great contribution to knowledge had, he thought, been open to later abuse. 'It was a "baggy" system, in that you could pick it up at various points, and it would fall into quite different shapes' (p. 70). It was the perfect illustration of a general difficulty in the social sciences, that the material was 'softer, more plastic, and more complex', while the interests at stake were more intense than in other fields (p. 16).

Not that pressure was usually applied crudely or directly. Hobson did not challenge the integrity of the thinkers who actually built the system. The quack with his conscious desire to deceive was no object for ridicule; but he found comedy in the unconscious servitude of the scholar who believed himself immune from outside pressures. Hobson's theory of knowledge easily explained how this kind of self-delusion could arise. 'Curiosity', he maintained, 'directed to the unsorted mass of phenomena, shouts specific questions at them, selecting, rejecting, and arranging them in order to extract answers to these questions' (p. 61). Value judgments of some kind were always there. So the builders of orthodox economics were 'hardly, if at all, conscious of the biases, personal or class, that were continually operative in their choice of intellectual starting-points, terminology, and formulas, the adoption of working hypotheses, and above all in the valuation of evidence' (p. 88). Men had a redoubtable capacity to invest their self-interested beliefs with disinterested motives. 'Psychology has almost wiped out hypocrisy' (p. 45).

If orthodox economic theory was Hobson's chief target, his analysis was hardly less subversive of Marxian economics as an equally transparent ideology. Indeed he relished 'the accuracy with which each party detects the pragmatic or interested reasoning of the other, while it seems compelled by the very nature of this mental process to ignore the corresponding bias in itself' (pp. 162–3). He did not deny that the Marxist analysis contained a nucleus of truth; but the reasons for its widespread adoption were much more sociological and psychological than scientific. Drawing upon Sorel, he depicted Marxism as a myth which enlisted the instincts of self-assertion behind a *Weltanschauung* which explained the present and promised the future. And, rather like Pareto, he explained its special appeal for intellectuals by pointing to the 'blend of intellectual and aesthetic satisfaction' evoked by the revelation of 'some simple, large generalisation, claiming to bring harmony into a world of apparent conflict and disorder' (p. 156).

Such a myth justified itself by its power to challenge entrenched interests, sheltering behind their own more insidious ideologies of conservatism. 'The positive tactics of assault demand bolder, simpler, and more inflammatory myths than the more passive tactics of defence' (p. 148). This led to an interesting conclusion for Hobson, whose own allegiance to the forces of radicalism rather than conservatism was never in doubt: 'While, therefore, it may well be true that a disinterested science and art of economic welfare would lean more to socialism than to capitalism, the fact that socialism is the aggressor, alike in the intellectual and the practical fields of conflict, will lead us to expect in it larger elements of fallacy and fiction' (p. 159). In order to be ideologically effective, therefore, the side with the better case was putting forward scientifically more dubious propaganda. Hobson seems to be claiming that the disinterested thinker will have to bring in his verdict against the evidence actually being marshalled because of his own privileged access to the real facts of the case.

In terms of this argument, however, are the credentials of the disinterested thinker himself any longer secure? Hobson did not seek to exempt himself from the implications of his own analysis, and sometimes his sardonic reflections suggested that complete relativism could not be resisted. Thus he wrote elsewhere that 'the desire to discover some hidden truth and to present it in an interesting and elaborate design drives the scholar and the scientist to the most intricate modes of self-deceit in the selection, rejection, and appraisal of evidence and the processes of reasoning they employ, all conducted, they easily persuade themselves, in the dry light of disinterested science'. The insights of psychology thus turned the light of comedy upon 'the pretence of Reason to be Master – or even Freeman – in the human household'.[29] But in *Free-Thought in the Social Sciences* he went beyond this in arguing that, precisely because psychology gave self-knowledge, it therefore also gave the morally scrupulous inquirer the means of guarding against his own biases if he would only make the effort to observe himself. In this connexion Hobson was confident that where there's a way there's a will. 'Intellectual craftsmanship,' he explained, 'with the personal pride or satisfaction in good work which it evokes, is so alluring and dominating a force in most of its regular practitioners that, though they may sometimes weakly yield to narrower pragmatic or emotional biases, they will normally return to the more disinterested course, helping to get out truths irrespective of their immediate utility or popularity' (p. 271). If the sociological or psychological reasons for wanting to believe something could be disentangled, the question of whether it was true would be better perceived; and the perpetual advantage of truth would then tell. 'A good argument is more pleasing than a bad argument' (p. 279). More broadly, Hobson believed that shallow and irrational

[29] *Notes on Law and Order* (1926), p. 14.

impulses made a quicker response but that, once rationalism had time to mobilise, the fact that it represented deeper and more permanent purposes gave it the advantage.

Hobson's argument escaped most of the objections urged against Wallas and Hobhouse. He was stating what they wanted to believe, but stating it in more persuasive terms. To analyse the theory in terms of the theory, one might say that his argument fulfilled the same ideological function but that its formal content was simply superior. Moreover, when the case for rationalism was put in this way it appealed to basic assumptions about human nature and the world which were by no means restricted to one generation of Victorian liberals. Scott viewed Massingham's displacement as 'a real loss of journalism & to the Liberal spirit' and viewed the remodelled *Nation* with foreboding. 'To pass from that to the arid intellectualism of Keynes will be a change indeed', he told Hammond (1 March 1923). Bloomsbury and Cross Street were more than a train journey apart. Yet Keynes, no less than Massingham, took the ultimate rationality of the world for granted and the amenability of human nature to rational persuasion as his political premise. When he wrote 'My Early Beliefs' (1938) he acknowledged that 'I behave as if there really existed some authority or standard to which I can successfully appeal if I shout loud enough – perhaps it is some hereditary vestige of a belief in the efficacy of prayer' (*JMK*, x, 448). Hobhouse touched on the same delicate area in writing of the impression made upon himself and Emily as children by their father's iron rectitude, 'which we took as of course as a part of the natural framework of things, so much so that it was only with surprise and lingering incredulity that we came to discover that such a standard is not universal'.[30]

With a battered but unbroken confidence in rationality went a rueful but unquenched belief in the efficacy of ideas. Keynes's famous dictum, that 'Practical men, who believe themselves to be quite exempt from any intellectual influences, are usually the slaves of some defunct economist' (*JMK*, viii, 383), represented what oft was thought but ne'er so well expressed. Laski was enthusiastic about the dinner he had with Massingham, Hammond and Nevinson in October 1923 where they all agreed that 'the only real difference between a theorist and a practical man is that the latter does not even know he is acting upon assumption' and that 'in the long run the theorist is more influential' (*H–L Letters*, p. 550). To Hobson, too, despite all discouragements, the world continued to provide evidence that the moral and intellectual appeals of personal liberty, equality, justice, and humanity were gaining more and more ground. 'There is after all some satisfaction in feeling that one has gone pegging on at what seems to be the truth', wrote Murray; for, he told Hammond, 'though one has at

[30] Ruth Fry, *Emily Hobhouse* (1929), p. 38.

present an impression of general defeat, we have had much more success than failure. The intelligent young Tory is, on such subjects as Peace, Womans Rights, Education & many social & industrial questions as advanced as an average radical was thirty years ago. And the Spaniards are ceasing to use horses in Bullfights!' (12 March 1926).

(III) HOBSONIAN AND KEYNESIAN ECONOMICS

When Hobson broached his familiar diagnosis of 'chronic under-consumption' in *Incentives in the New Industrial Order* (1922), he found himself suddenly in an unprecedentedly strong position to refute the reply that general over-production and unemployment were impossible. 'They are *seen* to be due to the inability of large populations, with the desire to consume the goods that are produced, to buy and consume them because of the lack of incomes or purchasing power', he could write (p. 50). A few months later *The Economics of Unemployment* (1922) systematically reinforced this appeal to the object lesson of the contemporary industrial scene. His first chapter was largely confined to citing widespread testimony to 'a belief in a limited market, incapable of such expansion as to take off all we can produce' (p. 14). Unemployment had become a dominant problem in post-war politics; there were now pressing reasons for Hobson to promote underconsumption to a central role in his economic analysis; and he found that his views could less easily be dismissed in current debate.

The war itself had opened new economic perspectives. During it Hobson had been extremely reluctant to believe that increased government spending had brought any generally diffused gain to the community. He had insisted that labour was bearing most of the costs of the war and that, though it took a larger share of the national product, its real income was less than before the war. By 1922, however, he had changed his tune. 'Under the stimulus of high consumption,' he acknowledged, 'the system showed hitherto undisclosed powers of productivity' (*Econ. of Unemp.*, p. 7). The implication was that the waste of cyclical depressions could be avoided by simulating the economic equivalent of war. For, though the flotation of large war loans had increased the lien of the rentiers upon the wealth of the community, during the war 'the working classes, or at least four-fifths of the population, lived in a definitely higher standard of material comfort than ever before' (*Incentives*, pp. 53–4). The prescription was two-fold. First, to restore effective demand to something like the level of the war years. Second, to remove the deadweight of debt by some form of capital levy. In *Taxation in the New State* (1919) Hobson defended the levy by discovering a further lesson from the war. 'The policy and ethics of the proceedings,' he explained, 'are closely analogous to those of military conscription, in which the urgent need of the State is held to override the private rights which each competent citizen has in the vital resources of his personality' (p. 193). Hobson's enthusiasm for the principle of conscription had hitherto been a well-kept secret.

Hobson's thesis remained what it had always been: that underconsumption was due to over-saving which in turn arose from a maldistribution of income. He sought to be emollient in stating his case, hastening 'to explain that the over-saving of which I speak refers solely to the proportion of saving to spending, and does not imply any fixed limit to the amount that can be serviceably saved' (*Econ. of Unemp.*, p. 37). After thirty-five years of experience in controversy he was clearly not going to repeat the sallies against thrift of *The Physiology of Industry*. Yet saving remained the target of his criticism and he saw any tendency to exalt its economic usefulness as an extenuation of the position of the rich, who happened to be good at it. In a notable comment on the psychology of nineteenth-century society, Keynes wrote that 'it was precisely the *inequality* of the distribution of wealth which made possible those vast accumulations of fixed wealth and capital improvements which distinguished that age from all others' (*JMK*. ii, 11). Hobson indignantly quoted this passage in every major work on economics which he published during the 1920s, to show how economists condoned inequitable distribution in deference to a supposed invisible hand which promoted economic progress.

On one level, of course, this was simply misrepresenting Keynes's (historical) point. 'The forces of the nineteenth century have run their course and are exhausted', he had claimed. 'The economic motives and ideals of that generation no longer satisfy us: we must find a new way and must suffer again the *malaise*, and finally the pangs, of a new industrial birth' (ibid., p. 161). Only in *Rationalisation and Unemployment* (1930), with its perceptibly more conciliatory approach towards Keynes, did Hobson cease to use him as an Aunt Sally and, indeed, now conceded his substantive point that the expansion of British trade in the nineteenth century 'enabled us to apply to the increased productive plant an unrestricted share of our national income' (p. 61). At a deeper level Hobson disagreed with Keynes because he thought the economic benefits of spending were as important as those of saving.

To Hobson saving and investment were two words for the same activity. Even in 1930 he was writing that all incomes had to be 'employed either in buying consumables (spending) or in buying capital goods (saving)' (ibid., p. 34). Likewise he would write of someone wanting 'to pay persons to put up more mills and machines and fill them with more raw materials, i.e., he may wish to save instead of spending' (*Incentives*, p. 50). So underconsumption implied actual over-investment. Hobson insisted that 'the vital distinction between spending and saving, so often obscured by dwelling upon the merely monetary aspect' lay in the fact that saving consisted 'in paying producers to make more non-consumable goods for use as capital, instead of paying them to make more consumable goods and consuming them' (*Econ. of Unemp.*, p. 34). It was on this point that Keynes (and D. H. Robertson) diverged, so that by the time of the *Treatise on Money* (1930) Keynes was able to make a clear distinction between, on the one hand, the saving of the consumer – 'the negative act of refraining from spending the whole of his current income on consumption' – and, on the other, the investment of the entrepreneur – 'the positive act of starting or maintaining some process of production or of withholding liquid goods' (*JMK*, v, 155).

The distinction between saving and investment was thus crucial to Keynes's analysis. The effect of saving as such was merely to reduce consumption, and hence all prices and all incomes. So far Hobson was in agreement. But whereas it followed for him that the savings constituted excess investments, for Keynes equilibrium would be restored if investment to the same value also took place. For an orthodox economist, who believed that the interest rate established a natural equilibrium price for money which entrepreneurs could afford and savers would accept, there was no difficulty in thinking of saving and investment as identical. For Hobson, however, who wanted to insist that the natural check of a falling rate of interest was inoperative, it would have been extremely helpful to distinguish two separate – and hence potentially discordant – activities. On his explanation, a lower interest rate might not indeed affect savings which were virtually automatic. But a lower interest rate ought also to have made hitherto unprofitable projects into paying propositions. Did Hobson believe that entrepreneurs were unresponsive to the new opportunities for profitable investment? When he wrote that declining trade 'removes those tempting opportunities for highly profitable investment, which, far more than any consideration of average rate of interest, prompt the saving of ambitious, greedy, and speculative persons' (*Econ. of Unemp.*, p. 53), he was not addressing this point at all. Instead 'investment' was regarded from the psychology of the saver once more.

There was no theoretical reason why Hobson should not have followed – or indeed anticipated – Keynes's alternative analysis, as even the sort of terminology which Keynes adopted is lurking in Hobson's work. When Keynes dealt with the case where investment exceeded saving he argued that 'consumers' expenditure will be increased relatively to producers' output of available goods, with the result that the prices of consumption goods will rise; and the new investment in excess of the volume of saving will be made possible, not by voluntary abstention from consumption by refraining from spending money income, but by involuntary abstention as the result of money incomes being worth less' (ibid., p. 157). In his U.D.C. pamphlet *Labour and the Costs of War* (1916) Hobson had for once been concerned with just this position, since he was indignant at the profligate expansion of the government borrowing requirement in excess of 'real' saving. 'For,' he argued, 'if you add to the quantity of money that the Government can spend without adding to the supply of goods that are for sale, the necessary result is to put up prices.' This inflation, he maintained, represented no one's savings – 'But when it is spent, by its effect in raising prices, it forces some people to perform real acts of abstinence' (p. 15). If Hobson could see, when he wanted to, that the act of investment worked through the price level to require corresponding saving, why could he not see, as the 1920s unfolded, that there might conversely be an attempt to save beyond the current willingness to invest? (Such saving would, in the language which Keynes adopted from Robertson, be abortive.)

There are several sorts of answer. Personally, Keynes and Hobson were in a quite different position. Keynes was forty at the time when he began seriously rethinking the problem of economic disequilibrium. He admitted that there was a good deal in the *Treatise* 'which represents the process of getting rid of the ideas which I used to have and of finding my way to those which I now have' (*JMK*, v, xvii). Hobson had not seen forty in the twentieth century. The authoritative exposition of his famous theory of underconsumption lay in four pre-war books, three of them published by 1896. 'It is undeniable,' he reflected later, 'that a heresy becomes an intellectual property which rouses in its owner a sense of scarcity value and of personal attachment that are liable to lead him into methods of defence which carry stormy emotional bias and may cause him to transgress the bounds of sweet reasonableness' (*Conf.*, p. 91). Keynes was continually testing his ideas upon formidable critics like Robertson and R. G. Hawtrey, schooled like himself in the Marshallian tradition; Hobson was a heretic, sitting in his house in Hampstead, meeting the deadline for his latest book.

Moreover, just as Keynes never lost sight of the crucial role of investment, so Hobson kept his eye firmly upon consumption. He simply did not see that his analysis of the wartime experience might be put in terms of government investment. 'This full employment and high pace of production,' he explained, 'were directly attributable to the pressure put on to the industrial machines at the consumptive end' (*Incentives*, p. 54). Consumption was always the crux of the problem, and, apart from the anomalous situation of the war, underconsumption was, in the twentieth as in the nineteenth century, an endemic condition. Insofar as there was any disparity between saving and investment, Hobson always explained it by reference to the transitional phenomenon of idle balances lying in the banks. 'The ordinary workings of our property system,' he wrote in 1933, 'place in the hands of the possessing classes incomes which normally exceed their desired expenditure and so naturally and necessarily form a fund for over-investment or, later on, for idle deposits' (*Ec*, iv, 461). It would be hard to find a better exposition of Hobsonian economics in one sentence.

Both in theory and in practice the form of Keynes's analysis suggested that a slump could be cured by stimulating investment. Admittedly, there was some ambiguity over how this might be done. His new departure in the early 1920s began with a commitment to an active monetary policy which would influence businessmen's expectations through the interest rate. This was the message of the *Tract on Monetary Reform* (1923). Indeed, in the early drafts of the *Treatise*, on which Keynes was working in 1924, this policy appeared as the exclusive remedy since 'expenditure, on the production of *fixed* capital, of public money which has been raised by borrowing, can do nothing in itself to improve matters', and might do actual harm (*JMK*, xiii, 23). In public, however, Keynes had put the matter very differently. 'Does Unemployment Need a Drastic Remedy?' he asked, only to answer that the Treasury should institute a capital expenditure programme of, say, £100 million a year. 'There is no place or time here for *laisser-faire*', he concluded. 'Furthermore, we must look for succour to the principle that *prosperity is cumulative*' (N, 24 May 1924). There was thus a disjunction in Keynes's approach. In his study he felt the weight of Hawtrey's advocacy of what became known as the Treasury View: that if public works were expanded they did not add to employment unless bank credit were also expanded, in which case they were unnecessary. But in the world of active controversy he responded to more urgent pressures. In confronting the problem of stimulating domestic investment, he claimed, 'we are brought to my heresy – if it is a heresy. I bring in the State; I abandon *laissez-faire* – not enthusiastically, not from contempt of that good old doctrine, but because, whether we like it or not, the conditions for its success have disappeared' (N, 7 June 1924). The ideological and psychological needs which a public works policy fulfilled are obvious; what remained was the task of establishing a rigorous scientific justification for it.

For Keynes, then, the problem was how to correct over-saving by increasing investment; for Hobson it was how to correct over-saving by increasing spending. And he already knew the answer. The distribution of income was wrong – morally and economically. So, by a happy chance, a just redistribution would create the right ratio between saving and spending, and this would ensure the smoothest running of the system. Criteria of efficiency and justice could, of course, both be assimilated to Hobson's organic paradigm, and he made the interlocking charges against the prevailing system that it guaranteed waste, fostered conflict and undermined incentives. When he came to compile his last long survey of the problems of economic welfare, *Wealth and Life* (1929), he hinted that loyal readers might find his analysis of over-saving rather familiar. 'We get back, in other words,' he admitted, 'to our old source of economic evil, the unearned surplus, the *causa causans* of discord and of waste' (p. 293). As it stood, it was functionless wealth, and thus waste; whereas its true social function should be to provide proper incentives for useful activity. Thus in *The Conditions of Industrial Peace* (1927) Hobson could explicitly combine the ethical and economic arguments in the proposition 'that what people *ought* to have is what is necessary to sustain them in the efficient performance of any productive work they are able to do, and that what they *ought* not to have is anything in excess of this true subsistence fund' (p. 63).

The problem of incentives was in practice rather more complex. In Tawney's functional society it was to be brushed aside in favour of an appeal to honour and social service. Hobson, however, doubted the possibility of working such a transformation. He would write of the division of labour producing 'shredded man' through 'the dehumanising effects of specialised production' (*Wealth & Life*, p. xx). But he had only palliatives to offer. 'Most work is, and will continue to be, dull, tiring and otherwise undesirable in itself,' he acknowledged, 'though these disagreeabilities may be mitigated by shorter hours, change of work or other improved conditions' (*Cond. of Ind. Peace*, p. 55). A change to public ownership would plainly make little difference to the psychology of work. 'Social service, or the well-being of the community at large,' he judged, 'is not likely to have any considerable effect as a motive in the mind of men who continue to do the same work under the same technical conditions and even the same personal control as before' (*Incentives*, p. 114). In fact, since 'neither the politics nor the economics of any Western nations seems adaptable to ideal socialism or communism', it was not worth pondering over the ethics of utopian reconstruction (*Cond. of Ind. Peace*, p. 119). For himself, he disbelieved 'both in the need and the practicability of wholesale sudden transformations, either in human nature or the institutions it imposes' (*Econ. of Unemp.*, p. 118). Facile convictions that social psychology could be overturned in favour of the ideal of social service seemed to Hobson to miss the point. Indeed he repudiated 'the sharp antithesis of an acquisitive and functional society' (*Incentives*, p. 145).

In *The Elements of Social Justice* (1922), which Hobson had criticised in draft, Hobhouse had developed the same approach, maintaining 'that if we take human nature as it is – and it is really useless to take it as it is not – some measure of remuneration by achievement as distinct from effort does directly or indirectly promote achievement' (p. 142). It was no good saying that a man 'ought of his own free will to give his best to society without reward' since this begged the whole question of 'free will' (p. 143). The problem was the Benthamite one of enlisting the disposition of the individual as the agent of collective welfare. The problem of attaining the ends of socialism by liberal means turned on psychology and incentives. Before the war Hobhouse had spoken of founding a Liberal Socialism upon this principle of consent; he now called it 'the point of division between Socialism proper and the Social Liberalism which seeks the harmony of the communal and the individual' (ibid., p. 146). But to the end he insisted that the argument for incentives 'would be more plausible if there were no such thing as inheritance' (*Memoir*, p. 284). Hobson's current vision of 'not capitalism' was likewise a mixed policy of some nationalisation, some controls, some private enterprise – all linked by an equitable fiscal system. He warmly endorsed a remark by Keynes: 'The true socialism of the future will emerge, I think, from an endless variety of experiments directed towards discovering the respective appropriate spheres of the individual and of the social and the terms of fruitful alliances between these sister impulses' (N, 24 May 1924).

Hobson's resolution of the economic problem into one of costs and surplus suggested a double remedy for underconsumption. Costs should be seen to include proper provision for the worker's standard of life; and it followed that 'a normally full wage of efficiency in a competitive industry will tend to keep down profits also to a subsistence wage for capital', thus checking over-saving (*Econ. of Unemp.*, p. 74). The surplus, on the other hand, should be attacked through progressive taxation and here, as ever, Hobson had to admit that 'the assumption is adopted that surplus wealth with "ability to bear" varies directly with the size of the income or the estate' (*Taxation in the New State*, p. viii). This double policy had an obvious political bearing, and it became the basis for the I.L.P. document *The Living Wage* (1926), on which Hobson collaborated with H. N. Brailsford, A. Creech Jones and E. F. Wise. 'All of us realise,' it claimed, 'that the low purchasing power of so many millions of wage earners is among the most potent causes of the widespread unemployment which has cursed our country during the last six years' (p. 2). The attempt to give the ethical appeal for a living wage an economic justification was characteristically Hobsonian; and the analysis firmly asserted that too much of the national income had gone in investment, too little in wages. An elaborate scheme of fiscal redistribution, including family allowances, was one method of increasing the ratio of spending to saving. In sustaining the parallel case for raising wages, the pamphlet gave an attention to monetary policy hardly matched in Hobson's other work, arguing for credit expansion as part of an effort at stabilisation.

Hobson consistently suggested that more equal distribution 'would evoke a dynamic economy of consumption that would not merely furnish full employment to all existing powers of production, but bring about improvements in technique and organisation at an accelerating pace' (*Wealth & Life*, p. 449). The economy of high wages brought gains to the whole community; its dynamic aspect showed the way out of the impasse otherwise created by pressure for wage reductions in bad times. But two separate arguments were really being rolled up together here. One was an argument for higher wages as the precondition of the higher productivity that would pay for them. 'It is a matter of the reasonable application of incentives', Hobson would argue when on this tack (*Cond. of Ind. Peace*, p. 68). This was the organic line of reasoning. The other argument was strictly underconsumptionist. Hobson maintained that though the *proportion* of saving to spending would certainly be reduced by equalisation, the *amount* of saving would in fact increase because of the larger national income which higher consumption would generate.

The economics of growth provide the most promising way of reconciling the Hobsonian and Keynesian approaches, both of which were concerned with the way that effective demand could determine the size of the national income. This led Keynes in the *Treatise* to depose thrift from its honorific position – which has a Hobsonian ring – and to suggest that enterprise had instead been the motor of economic growth. 'If enterprise is afoot, wealth accumulates whatever may be happening to thrift; and if enterprise is asleep, wealth decays whatever thrift may be doing' (*JMK*, vi, 132). Keynes's intellectual revolution, it has been claimed, was to challenge the idea that a dog called *savings* wagged his tail labelled *investment* and to put in its place the idea that a dog called *investment* wagged his tail labelled *savings*. When the *Treatise* was nearly ready, Keynes told Hobson that he saw 'how very near it really comes to your own view'. Hobson replied that the views in *Rationalisation and Unemployment* 'you may find even closer to yours'.[31] It is true that in it he described cyclical unemployment as 'an attempt on the part of the industrial community to apply to the purchase of capital goods and the operation of the "Capitalist System" as a whole, a larger proportion of the current money-income than can find profitable or useful employment therein' (p. 36). This is consistent with Keynes, as are other references to 'the failure of would-be "savers" to effectuate their money savings by converting them into real savings' (p. 41).

What Hobson had in mind was the 'lag' of investment behind saving as idle balances accumulated. 'Money available for investment waits in bank reserves, or is utilised for short loans' (p. 133). This was a sort of subterranean distinction between saving and investment. Keynes now acknowledged that he ought to take account of underconsumptionist theories like Hobson's. 'At bottom these theories have, I think, some affinity to my own', he reasoned. 'But they are not so close as might be supposed at first sight.' He cited in support the fact that they supposed an actual over-investment, whereas, he insisted, 'on my theory, it is a large volume of saving which does *not* lead to a correspondingly large volume of investment

[31] Keynes to Hobson, 23 April 1930; Hobson to Keynes, 24 April 1930, quoted in Alan J. Lee, 'A study of the social and economic thought of J. A. Hobson' (London PhD 1970), p. 290.

(not one which *does*) which is the root of the trouble' (*JMK*, v, 160–1). For Hobson a dog called *over-savings* was still wagging a tail labelled *over-investment*. The theoretical difference was neatly summed up in 1932 by Lionel Robbins (who disagreed with both of them): 'In Mr Keynes's view the difficulty arises when the monetary savings are not turned into real investment, whereas in Mr Hobson's view it arises because that real investment is excessive in relation to real consumption. For Mr Keynes, one way out of the slump would be a revival of investment; for Mr Hobson, this would simply make matters worse' (*Ec*, xii, 420).

For Hobson, therefore, over-saving continued to mean under-spending; whereas for Keynes it meant under-investment. The two theories were alternatives. Thus when Robertson expressed his reservations about the *Treatise*, he told Keynes that 'I believe I get more and more Hobsonian, believing that investment can be "excessive" even if it doesn't outrun saving, and that the only way out of slumps is a drastic redistribution of leisure' (*JMK*, xiii, 202). Hobson, for his part, showed diminishing enthusiasm for public works, a policy he had endorsed in *The Economics of Unemployment* but subsequently ignored. It did not figure among *The Living Wage* proposals four years later. Moreover, credit expansion, which did, also fell out of favour with Hobson, so that by 1929 he was giving rein to his old suspicion of monetary palliatives. 'No juggling with credit can cure the maladjustment which periodically chokes the channels of industry and stops production', he warned (*Wealth & Life*, p. 289). A managed currency would not in itself affect the distribution of income, which was the paramount consideration. He mounted a withering attack on 'the crooked practices of governments' who had 'either fabricated money, or incited banks to do so', which was 'just common cheating due to cowardice' and had had the effect of 'enabling sharp greedy men to thrive on the misfortunes of their simpler fellow-men' (ibid., pp. 419–20). Having heaped up the coals of his wrath, he poured them upon the head of the unfortunate Robertson for making the case for a gently rising price level as a means of generating confidence. This was 'debasing the moral currency', Hobson snorted, and he asserted that 'to feed people on illusions, i.e. on misrepresentation of the facts, cannot nourish them for any serviceable activity' (p. 425). This was a different language from that which Keynes had been talking since the time of the *Tract*, in which he castigated conservative bankers for trying 'to shift public discussion of financial topics off the logical on to an alleged "moral" plane, which means a realm of thought where vested interest can be triumphant over the common good without further debate'. His conclusion was different: that when entering 'the realm of State action, *everything* is to be considered and weighed on its merits' (*JMK*, iv, 56–7).

(IV) THE TRUE DIVISION OF PARTIES

Before the war the Liberals had been a broad-based party of the left; after the war they were merely spread thin. There was any number of constituencies in which the Liberal party could poll creditably; there was only a handful which it could rely upon winning. The realities of post-war politics hit home in the 1922 General Election which Scott thought 'a disaster for the Liberal party worse if possible than that of 1918 because there was less excuse for it' (Wilson, p. 433). In some places, it is true, there was an obvious progressive cause; for example, Norman Angell, as Labour candidate for Rushcliffe, had the support of Arnold Bennett, Noel Buxton, Lady Courtney, Lowes Dickinson, Gooch, Hobson, Keynes, Massingham, Russell, Webb and Tawney. 'I wonder if it would be possible to constitute a Radical group standing in foreign policy for justice rather than British interests,' Murray asked Hammond, adding quickly, '(though I believe them to coincide)' (18 November 1922). This was wishful thinking at more than one level. To Hammond, who had supported J. J. Mallon as Labour candidate at Watford, the election signalled 'the end of Liberalism', but, he reassured Murray, 'the Labour Party will be immensely better in personnel than before' (17 November 1922).

Hammond was, as Murray knew, a closet Labour supporter. Although in 1925 Scott described him to Lloyd George as 'a member of the Labour Party' (Wilson, p. 481), it seems that neither of the Hammonds ever officially belonged to it. Hammond duly paid a subscription to the Fabian Society for several years – 'By the way, you might as well join the F.S.', was how Webb put it to him (8 February 1923). But that seems to be the extent of his institutional links with Labour; and he let his membership of the 1917 Club lapse in 1928. In 1923 the Hammonds voted for the Liberal at Hemel Hempstead, and in the absence of a Labour candidate he was triumphantly returned. 'I hope Labour won't fight it again', Barbara Hammond confided to Mary Murray (16 December 1923). For that notable ex-Fabian Wallas, matters were even less clear, though he probably belonged to the Liberal association in Hornsey. 'I believe that it is everybody's duty to take sides publicly in politics,' he told Murray, 'and yet for the moment I can't do it' (14 February 1922). He was left swinging between the Liberals and Labour and felt himself nearest the position of the *Manchester Guardian*. Scott himself, with his sharp distinction between 'bad Labour' and 'good Labour', still thought in terms of a progressive alliance, led by Lloyd George, to bring good Labour and Liberalism together. If there was one thing that united the two sections, however, it was a common mistrust of Lloyd George, not least among the ex-Liberals in the Labour party. It was when the Liberal party reunited for the election of December 1923 that Massingham announced his conversion to Labour; Masterman and Gardiner had evidently considered doing likewise. 'The tide has simply gone over Liberalism', Massingham maintained (H.W.M., p. 73). Russell admitted in 1930 that he did not like the Labour party, 'but an Englishman has to have a Party just as he has to have trousers, and of the three Parties I find them the least painful. My objection to the Tories is temperamental, and my objection to the Liberals is Lloyd George' (*Autobiog.*, ii, 195).

The Labour party was Hobson's choice. Now that politics had come down to brass tacks, it was clear that Labour alone had the capacity to represent working-class interests. This was where Hobson's sympathies lay but he had to admit that he 'never felt quite at home in a body governed by trade union members and their finance, and intellectually led by full-blooded Socialists' (*Conf.*, p. 126). His longstanding friendship with MacDonald gave him a certain position, and he was one of those consulted in December 1923 about whether Labour should try to form a minority government. He thought it should. Scott in turn played a large part in persuading the Liberal party, which now held the balance, to put Labour in office. The Liberals were, indeed, in an inescapable predicament. They were prisoners of their own ethic. Only a 'capitalist party' would conspire to keep Labour out of office; a party of goodwill would set aside party advantage in the interests of the community. So Scott argued; so events dictated. The experience of the first Labour Government made many Liberals turn Burke upon his head and conclude that magnanimity in politics is seldom the truest wisdom.

Scott had fair warning of the difficulties. When he saw MacDonald in January 1924 he found him emphatic that there must be no 'dependence' on the Liberals, a matter on which he showed 'a curious sensitiveness' and spoke 'as though this were a matter of deep importance' (Wilson, p. 453). The last thing the Labour party would tolerate was a tutelary relationship to the Liberals. The gap between the progressive ideal and current politics is pathetically illustrated by the interview which Scott and Hobson had with MacDonald in July 1924. 'We need a conciliator', MacDonald said as they rose to leave. 'Then you had better find seats, I suggested, for Hobson and me', Scott recorded (Wilson, p. 462). The *Manchester Guardian*, where Scott, Hammond and Hobhouse were working together for a time that summer, did its best to prevent the Government from foundering over the treaty it had made with Soviet Russia. But by the autumn the whole ramshackle arrangement had fallen apart. While the Labour party lost some seats in the ensuing General Election, it was the Liberal party which was routed.

'The real tragedy of post-war democratic politics was the failure of the first Labour Government', Hammond wrote later (*MG*, 29 April 1938). He had apparently been 'rather fond of saying that the Liberals in the House are supplying all the brains' and Barbara Hammond was ready to admit to Mary Murray that 'perhaps one's friends' failings seem more conspicuous in office' (10 June 1924). Hobhouse had naturally held lower expectations of the Labour party in the first place – 'I don't expect any improvement from them' he once told Emily (4 January 1920), judging that they were incompetent and would 'be entirely in the hands of the civil servants'. Recently bereaved, and prostrated by ill health in November 1924, he found prospects equally bleak. When Scott urged his familiar contention that the crucial question was the Liberals' relations with Labour, Hobhouse tried to explain that his difficulties with the Liberal party were more fundamental. He doubted if it any longer stood for anything distinctive. On the other hand, 'moderate Labour – Labour in office – has on the whole represented essential Liberalism, not without mistakes and defects, but *better* than the organised party since C.B.'s death' (7 November 1924). The Liberals in the 1924 parliament had failed to present a coherent third view. Hobhouse concluded from this 'that the distinction between that kind of Labour man who does not go the whole hog for nationalisation on the one side & the Liberal who wants sound progress on the other is obsolete'. So – 'if we divided parties by true principles' – the extremes of left and right would flank a real division between progressives and conservatives. It was clear that 'ordinary Labour' and 'Good Liberal' stood together. It was *party* that got in the way. Two days later Hobsouse added: 'Why not make it our object to maintain principles, define aims, advocate causes, & let party organisation adapt itself to these?' (9 November 1924). And in a further effort before he posted the letters:

> It seems to me that there is possible a distinctive kind of Socialism being one based not on the Trade Unions but on the community & social service. The constitution of the Labour party binds it tight to the Trade Unions & their sectional selfishness, a most serious defect. I have once or twice written in the *M.G.* that the Liberal party might teach true Socialism in the point of view of the community as a whole, but I don't think hitherto they have shown much enthusiasm for this role (15 November 1924).

The position Hobhouse was stating here was substantially that of all progressives, whether reluctantly Labour like Hammond – 'I am a Labour man so far as I am party' was how he put it to Mary Murray (17 September 1924) – or whether quizzically Liberal – 'Am I a Liberal?' – like Keynes. Gardiner had written of the need for 'a Radical revival which will liberate and give expression to the living forces of Liberalism and at the same time bring within its movement that body of advanced opinion which, while rejecting the Socialist theory in its universal application and finding in the Labor party a tendency to class politics, wants an instrument of policy unemcumbered by any homage to class interests in the other directions' (N, 14 May 1921). Massingham feared, even as he joined the Labour party, that it was 'beginning again to settle down to a class organisation i.e. to a mere wages and hours party, with an irreconcilable Communist wing'. Its downward slide could 'only be averted by attaching a much larger middle-class element than it now attracts'.[32]

Keynes admitted in 1926 that 'the progressive forces of the country are hopelessly divided between the Liberal Party and the Labour Party' (*JMK*, ix, 307). But, as against joining the Labour party, the Liberal at least had the advantage of being able to 'work out policies without having to do lip-service to trade-unionist tyrannies, to the beauties of the class war, or to doctrinaire State Socialism – in none of which he believes' (ibid., pp. 309–310). It was right and proper that those Liberals who wanted to die in the last ditch for capitalism – the Alfred Monds, the Winston Churchills – should desert to the Tories. The Liberals who remained 'should be not less progressive than Labour, not less open to new ideas', and should recognise that great changes could not come except with the aid of Labour in promoting the three political goals of economic efficiency, social justice and individual liberty (ibid., pp. 310–11). The real root of Keynes's objection to Labour, as he had revealed in 1923, was that, though there were sophisticated problems of economic policy to confront, 'I do not believe that the intellectual elements in the Labour Party will ever exercise adequate control' (ibid., p. 296).

The Tory party, now securely established in power, was as unappealing as ever. 'I am afraid we are in for real reaction and jingoism', Hammond wrote to Murray (18 December 1924). Yet no constructive alternative was in sight. 'I wish I tho't any good wd come of political changes,' Leonard confessed to Emily Hobhouse, 'but I really don't think Labour has much in the way of ideas' (17 May 1925). The Hobsonian proposals for a living wage, adopted by the I.L.P., were one attempt to remedy this deficiency. One difficulty here was a disparity between the political aims and the economic reasoning of the campaign. The *New Leader* under Brailsford's editorship helped to popularise Hobson's underconsumptionist views within the Labour movement, but Hobson himself was never a member of the I.L.P. *The Living Wage* (1926) argued a familiar case, based upon revitalising the economic system by correcting its (remediable) malady of underconsumption. This, it held, was 'the alternative and antithesis to a catastrophic strategy' (p. 54). But the claim for a living wage had by then become part of a policy, *Socialism in our Time*, which was advocated as the alternative to gradualism. The ideological force of the campaign came from socialists who disbelieved in the ability of the system to pay a living wage and rejected or ignored Hobson's scientific case. When MacDonald resisted the policy document, therefore, Hobson was in the curious position of half sympathising with him. 'I was asked as an economist, not as a politician,

[32] Massingham to S. K. Ratcliffe, 4 December (1923), copy kindly made available by Professor A. F. Havighurst.

to join the small Committee which drew it up,' he explained, 'and am not concerned with the use which may be made of it in the Labour Party or the Country.'[33] Hobson had, moreover, suffered a rebuff from the trade union elements in the party because of his insistence that the separate gains of individual strong bargainers were no part of socialism as he understood it.

The Liberal party, then, continued to hold attractions for the intellectuals. 'As the constituencies don't seem to appreciate the Liberals,' Barbara Hammond wrote to Mary Murray, 'its a pity their brains can't fertilise the Labour fields, which badly need them; perhaps that will come ultimately if L.G. succeeds to the leadership' (10 June 1924). The internal factionalism of the Liberal party made Lloyd George's emergence in this role peculiarly difficult. 'He is nothing if not a Radical,' Scott noted, 'yet circumstances have made him appear as the leader of the right wing of the party – of the "bad Liberals"' (Wilson, p. 472). Ever since the war the left-wing progressives in the party had been Asquithians, *faute de mieux*. It was Lloyd George's patronage of the Liberal Summer Schools which broke this impasse, even before he became leader of the party in 1926. The summer schools brought together the Manchester group under Ted Scott and E. D. Simon with the Cambridge-orientated *Nation* group under Keynes and Hubert Henderson. 'Until the Liberal Party is based again on "the intolerable disease" of life-long thought, it must continue to decay', Wallas declared (N, 6 March 1926). 'As an egalitarian radical who distrusts the basing of politics mainly on vocational organisation,' he told Samuel, 'I find it very difficult to call myself by any party name' (22 April 1926); but both he and Hobhouse were ready to go and talk to the summer school. 'The political summer school,' Hammond wrote, 'may in the long run prove almost as important a contribution to the politics and mechanism of representative government as the institution of Parliament' (*MG*, 20 August 1924).

The *Political Quarterly* was launched in the late 1920s as a sort of summer school for all seasons – winter, spring, summer and autumn would each see a new copy. William Robson and Kingsley Martin, both lecturers at the L.S.E., broached the idea in 1927. Among the thirty-two signatories to its initial appeal were Cole, Lowes Dickinson, Hobhouse, Hobson, Laski, Mallon, Martin, Olivier, Robson, Scott, Tawney, the Webbs and Leonard Woolf. Shaw gave a thousand pounds. Keynes joined the small steering committee. The original plan was for Hammond to become editor but he eventually decided that he was not the man for the job. How far he felt a political difficulty here is not clear. In his correspondence with Tawney and Woolf at the end of 1928 he seems to have spoken more as a Liberal than as a Labour supporter. Indeed Woolf urged on him that, since 'the

[33] Hobson to MacDonald, 7 October 1926, in David Marquand, *Ramsay MacDonald* (1977), p. 455.

Quarterly is to be progressive, i.e. it must include the general outlook of both "Liberals" and "Labour",' Hammond might consider becoming joint editor with Laski – 'the combination of the two colourations in a joint editorship would therefore have obvious advantages' (19 December 1928). In fact, failing Hammond, the editorship was shared, first by Robson and Martin, and later by Robson and Woolf. This latter-day *Progressive Review* started publication in 1930 and proved longer-lived.

The Liberal Industrial Inquiry grew out of the summer schools, including Walter Layton, E. D. Simon, Henderson, Rowntree and, of course, Keynes on its executive committee. Hobhouse served on one of its special committees, concerned with Trade Boards. 'I told them I was not a member of the Liberal Party', he made clear (*Memoir*, p. 67). He thought some members, like Layton, merely orthodox in their thinking. 'I find the Classical Economists too being upheld among the Liberals with whom I have been trying to work', he informed Barbara Hammond (25 May 1927). But he hoped that they might 'wake up the Labour Party, which seems to make no constructive effort', and of one member (Keynes himself?) he wrote that he was 'much more of a Socialist than MacDonald or Snowden (which is not saying very much)' (*Memoir*, p. 67). Hobson was similarly ambivalent about the Inquiry's report, the Liberal 'Yellow Book', which seemed to him to have evaded some difficulties in its desire 'to escape the taint of socialism' (*Wealth & Life*, p. 386n.). But in fact he made considerable use of its findings and was clearly drawn towards its approach.

The Yellow Book, *Britain's Industrial Future* (1928), elaborated a programme of national development with active state intervention and a much fuller use of public boards. In economic policy it followed up hunches which Keynes had mentioned four or five years previously. The Liberal party manifesto *We Can Conquer Unemployment* (1929) was derived from it. This sketched out a two-year programme of public works, financed by borrowing, for immediate implementation. It described the Treasury View as 'hoary with antiquity and clothed in the utmost respectability' but asserted that it was 'nevertheless completely fallacious' (pp. 53–4). The nature of the fallacy, however, was left largely unexplained beyond a reference to 'frozen savings'. Indeed, in seeking to prove that the money could be raised, the argument became practically circular. 'If capital is not available for absorption of the unemployed on a policy of national development, then it is not available for their absorption at all', was the triumphant conclusion (p. 56) – but one that could as easily point tragically towards fatalism. At bottom it was an appeal for boldness, in the hope that the injection of new demand would 'give just that stimulus which is wanted in the present condition of economic inertia to set industry moving vigorously again on the normal line of progress' (p. 9). *Labour's Reply to Lloyd George* (1929) was drafted by Cole, Hobson's colleague in the early years of the Advisory Committees. In making a nod towards underconsumption and in characterising unemployment as an organic disease, the document had a Hobsonian flavour. The proposals for expenditure which it listed were 'to be met, except when it is directly reproductive, out of taxation' (p. 18) – a hint of the role of redistribution. Presumably increased consumption would do the rest, but this was not made explicit. It was, however, the 'madcap finance' of Lloyd George's scheme which attracted most criticism. 'The essence of his plan is to spend borrowed money like water during the next year or two in the hope that, before the brief emergency period is over, something will turn up', it expostulated, showing no receptiveness to the Keynesian insight that investment might promote recovery.

Curiously enough, this kind of deprecation of the Liberal proposals did not enjoy the support of Hobson himself, who accorded them a sympathetic appraisal. He seized on the reference to 'frozen savings' (which was admittedly more consonant with his analysis than Keynes's) and sought to show how a road loan would put them to work. Moreover, through the wages paid, 'the general stimulus to industry afforded by the increased purchase of commodities would soon be represented by enlarged production throughout the economic system'. By transposing the argument into his own terms he had in fact brought out its dynamic character. 'The efficient cause of the employment of the idle labour, capital, and money savings', he concluded, 'is thus seen to be the increased demand for consumable goods from the expenditure of road-workers made possible by the road loan' (N, 30 March 1929). Read in this light, the Keynesian proposals found reinforcement from Hobsonian arguments. Indeed this aspect was given new attention in the pamphlet *Can Lloyd George Do It?* (1929) which Keynes and Henderson subsequently produced. There they pointed to the effect of new employment in giving 'an increase in effective purchasing power which would give a general stimulus to trade' since 'the forces of prosperity, like those of trade depression, work with a cumulative effect' (*JMK*, ix, 106). But, of course, the burden of the case still rested upon the positive effects of *investment* as against saving. 'It is not the miser who gets rich; but he who lays out his money in fruitful investment' (ibid., p. 123).

The Liberals faced the 1929 General Election in better heart than at any time since the war. Wallas explained in 1928 that 'the Liberals seem to have more intellectual stuff in them (largely owing to Keynes, Layton, H. D. Henderson etc. . .) than the Labour people. And it seems more possible for the Liberals than for the Labour Party to provide the machinery for a progressive block in the House of Commons.'[34] Hobson felt much the same, admitting privately that 'I wish I could find enough intelligence in labour

[34] Wallas to Lippmann, 8 March 1928, in Martin J. Wiener, *Between Two Worlds* (Oxford 1971), p. 193.

leadership to reassure one for the future.'[35] Ever optimistic, Scott confided to Hammond that 'The new policy on unemploymt. is, I fancy, going to do the Liberals a lot of good' (21 March 1929). And to Barbara he wrote with relish of the prospect of the Liberals holding the balance. 'Can't you imagine Ll.G. balancing?' he demanded. 'He will need some looking after' (23 May 1929). But in the event the Liberals' performance, in seats if not in votes, was an anti-climax. With 23 per cent of the vote, they had 59 M.P.s; whereas Labour, with 37 per cent, had 288. Still, the Conservatives had been beaten, and many progressives, like Hobhouse, did not care how so long as it had been done. 'As it is,' he told Margaret Llewelyn Davies, 'I am sorry the Liberals did not get more seats, as I think (I know it's blasphemy) they carry more brains to the square inch than Labour, most of whose men are merely dull and terribly afraid of their permanent officials' (*Memoir*, p. 67).

Hobhouse was writing from his hospital bed in France. Beset by gangrene and phlebitis for the past five years, he had never fully recovered from Nora's death. On his sister's deathbed he had said to her, 'Emily, you were always brave', and she had whispered back, 'Yes, too brave.' 'The dying out of one's generation in the sixties is terribly saddening', he admitted to Barbara Hammond (25 June 1926). The next year he was reminding her of 'all the old South African days when we all put up a good fight together' (25 March 1927). Each summer he went to France for medical treatment. There was no special cause for alarm when made his annual crossing in 1929. This time, however, he was suddenly taken ill and died on 21 June 1929. He was, wrote Hobson in an unwontedly fulsome tribute, 'one of the less known of the great men of our time' (*Memoir*, p. 72).

35 Hobson to Oswald Garrison Villard, 15 October 1927, Villard Papers (copy courtesy of Alan Lee).

8

The bleak age

(I) A SOCIALIST FANTASY?

The Hammonds' reputation as the most influential social historians of their generation rests on the half dozen volumes which deal with the consequences of the economic transition between the mid eighteenth and the mid nineteenth centuries. The shape of this *oeuvre* was determined early. What became the labourer trilogy was its foundation; and this was finally completed with the publication of *The Skilled Labourer* (1919). The least satisfactory of the three books as a work of art, it was, no doubt in consequence, the first to be accorded recognition in the pages of the *English Historical Review* as a work demanding academic notice. Its structure was determined by what had been left out of its predecessors, and it is chiefly notable for its rather uneasy treatment of the Luddite movement and for its mock-heroic account of the activities of the government spy, Oliver. The Hammonds had been committed since before the war to writing their *Lord Shaftesbury* (1923) for a series edited by their friend Basil Williams, prior to tackling a work on the Chartists, which was where their interest really lay. 'Do you remember,' Barbara asked Lawrence, 'the many hundred times you have said that none cld be interested in Shafter himself & that the only way to write a readable book about him was not to mention him?' (2 September 1923) On the whole, this is not a happy frame of mind in which to write a biography, and the Hammonds' imperfect sympathy with Shaftesbury's political and religious outlook led to some failures of historical imagination on which later writers justifiably seized.

G. D. H. Cole had planned a four-volume economic and social history of England for Methuen, of which the Coles would write the first and the Hammonds the third. Volume Two was the difficulty. 'I asked Tawney to do this, and could never get an answer', Cole told Hammond (24 February 1923). But, though the project then foundered, Methuens pressed Hammond to deliver his book on the Industrial Revolution nonetheless. The rather whimsical overtones of the provisional title, 'The Spell of Production', were banished as the work progressed and it appeared as *The Rise of Modern Industry* (1925). It was a work of synthesis which sought to portray the process of industrialisation in England against a long historical perspective. The Industrial Revolution had to be seen 'as a departure in which man passed definitely from one world to another, as an event bringing confusion that man is still seeking to compose, power that he is still seeking to subdue to noble purposes' (p. 240). Along with the contemporaneous French Revolution, it had 'changed the mind and outlook of mankind' (p. 241). The term revolution was well justified, then, to describe an age in which fundamental changes in the life of the mass of the people had taken place. That these changes had initially been for the worse was, of course, one of the Hammonds' firmest conclusions. The Hammonds believed that 'England would have been happier, stronger, freer, if industrial power had advanced with slower stride' (p. 250), but they did not suppose that economic growth was bad in itself. It was, rather, the failure to harness it to good social ends that turned it, for the space of two or three generations, into a catastrophe instead of a blessing for the bulk of the population.

The Hammonds were admittedly less interested in the causes than in the consequences of industrialisation. It is a fair criticism that they could have made more of their essentially Hobsonian view of the role of consumption. 'When capital was applied to production on a large scale,' they maintained, 'it gained its profits by producing in bulk; producing, that is, for mass consumption. Energy and brains were now devoted to satisfying, not the luxurious taste of the classes that were served by the commerce of medieval Europe, but the needs of the poor consumer' (p. 210). They summarised this view even more trenchantly in the preface. 'Mass production demands popular consumption' (p. viii). Yet the implications of this apparent growth of widespread purchasing power were not developed. The Hammonds concentrated on the inequity of the distribution of wealth and the evil effects – from child labour to the poor quality of town life – of ceding all power to the capitalist. It was only later that these ravages were checked and this neglect repaired. 'By the middle of the nineteenth century,' they concluded, 'it was possible to discern the chief contributions that England was to make to the task of creating a society out of this new chaos. Those contributions were Factory Law, the Civil Service, and Trade Unions' (p. 255).

The Rise of Modern Industry enjoyed a very solid success as a textbook. At the L.S.E. Tawney and Eileen Power recommended it along with the work of their colleague Lilian Knowles as introductory reading for the students. 'They chew the latter till they get thirsty,' Tawney told Hammond, 'and then intoxicate themselves with you' (23 January 1926). The Hammonds' view of the Industrial Revolution, however, was about to receive its sternest challenge. In the preface to his magisterial *Economic History of Modern Britain*, vol. 1 (1926), J. H. Clapham denounced 'the legend that everything was getting worse for the working man, down to some unspecified date between the drafting of the People's Charter and the Great Exhibition' – a memorable rebuke which was invariably taken as meant for the Hammonds. As part of his effort to bring quantitative evidence to bear wherever possible, Clapham tried to plot the course of real wages in the period 1785–1850. He concluded that on average agricultural labourers were slightly better off in 1824 than thirty years previously, and that by 1850 the mass of industrial workers had improved their earnings by perhaps 40 per cent in the previous sixty years.

All subsequent assessments of the Hammonds' work have been heavily influenced by the continuing controversy over the standard of living. They were the leading 'pessimists' in their generation, just as Clapham was the leading 'optimist'. In the *Town Labourer* there is a sentence, the first half of which is often quoted: 'For the revolution that had raised the standard of comfort for the rich had depressed the standard of life for the poor; it had given to the capitalist a new importance, while it had degraded the workpeople to be the mere muscles of industry' (p. 36). This is, rather surprisingly, virtually the only categorical statement by the Hammonds which would be vulnerable to Clapham's riposte. Part of the reason for this rests in their reluctance to quantify their statements. Barbara Hammond wrote as 'one whose ignorance of mathematics is profound' (*EcH*, i, 419), and this was undoubtedly more than polite self-depreciation. Some of the materials with which Clapham worked had been available when the Hammonds started writing, notably the researches of A. L. Bowley on wage rates published in the *Statistical Journal* from 1899. But this was his sort of arsenal not theirs. With their 'bows and arrows', they acknowledged that the ease with which the new practitioners 'bring their modern pieces into action might easily lead a superficial observer to suppose that it was not more difficult to practice their skill than to admire it' (QR, cclii, 291).

It is to the Hammonds' credit, however, that they did not seek to brush aside criticism that was, in every respect, inconvenient. They had, in the first edition of the *Town Labourer*, made assertions about the growth of population which laid them open to attack. They had suggested that the birth rate was stimulated by the increasing demand for child labour in the cotton industry, and had further maintained that 'it is well known that population increases with a decline in the standard of life' (p. 14). This interpretation became much less plausible in the 1920s with the publication of a number of works on demographic history, notably *Population Problems of the Age of Malthus* (1926) by the young Cambridge historian G. T. Griffith. The suggestion was that a falling death rate, associated with improvements in public health, was a likelier explanation; and at the time this view won general assent (although later work has in turn shown up its inadequacies). The Hammonds made two responses. In the first place, they revised the *Town Labourer* so as to take account of Griffith's findings and omitted their tendentious claim about the standard of life. Secondly, Barbara Hammond published in *Economic History* for 1928 a careful criticism of the statistics on which Griffith had based his conclusions – an article which is still recognised as an invaluable warning of the pitfalls here. Couched in generous terms, it elicited from him the acknowledgement that 'I think you have quite demonstrated that the figures are unsatisfactory and unreliable' (19 February 1928). The Hammonds, then, were prepared to submit their original conclusions to a critical re-examination in the light of new knowledge rather than to entrench themselves in a blinkered defence of their presuppositions.

It was in this spirit that they treated the standard-of-living debate. Where the statistics appeared to confute them, they conceded the point with a good grace. 'Statisticians smite & we offer the other cheek', Barbara Hammond commented wryly to Lawrence (8 August 1929). She probably found a stoical attitude more of an effort than he did. 'I think the *Village Labourer* is a very good book, so there', she wrote on another occasion. 'Clapham is like a badly cooked cake' (15 August 1928). Lawrence too would write privately of 'the new school which argues that if only one paid attention to statistics it wd become clear that everything went well at the Ind. Rev.',[1] which betrays his irritation at the ideological overtones of the new school of optimists. What the Hammonds sought to do was to put this sort of revisionism into perspective. The statisticians, they claimed with heavy banter in 1928, 'tell us that they have got the figures into order and that those figures show that there was no Industrial Revolution. Little happened affecting social life except that the poor became richer' (*QR*, cclii, 288). By the time that Lawrence Hammond presented his reply to Clapham in 1930 he had reached a conclusion at once more dispassionate and more discriminating. 'Let us take it that so far as statistics can measure material improvement there was improvement', he conceded (*EcHR*, ii, 219). This was where the Hammonds finally let the quantitative controversy rest. In *The Age of the Chartists* (1930) they restated their comment of two years earlier, but drained of its venom. 'Statisticians tell us that when they have put in order such data as they can find, they are satisfied that earnings increased and that most men and women were less poor when this discontent was loud and active than they were when the eighteenth century was beginning to grow old in a silence like that of autumn. The evidence of course is scanty, and its interpretation not too simple, but this general view is probably more or less correct' (p. 3).

The Hammonds' response to Clapham has been criticised as feeble, and it was left to another generation of historians, notably Ashton, Hobsbawm and Hartwell, to re-evaluate the statistical evidence. But it should be noted that in his article, 'The industrial revolution and discontent', Hammond dealt fairly effectively with the deficiencies of the figures on agricultural earnings, and he discovered that Clapham's average was in fact an average

[1] Hammond to Ponsonby, 2 January 1928, PP c.670, f.90.

of county averages, which concealed the fact that 60 per cent of labourers fell below it. It is ironical that the great exponent of quantitative history should have been detected in an elementary fallacy of method by a historian relying on 'bows and arrows'. Clapham conceded the point here, while insisting that in any average 50 per cent were likely to fall below. In a sense this reinforced Hammond's contention, since he thought Clapham in general too much impressed by the 50 per cent above each of his averages. Later research has shown that Clapham's claims for the growth of real wages in industry cannot be upheld. The new analytical tool here was the Silberling price index, which had not been available at the time the Hammonds wrote, and which, combined with the Bowley wage index, provided a strong indication of an upward movement. In fact, the reliability of the Silberling index was itself undermined in the late 1940s by the technical criticism of T. S. Ashton, who was himself a prominent optimist. The net result, once the implications had been thrashed out over the next twenty-five years, was to narrow the dispute between optimists and pessimists to whether there was a marginal rise or an actual fall in real wages in this period. As the debate progressed, in short, there turned out to be a better quantitative case for the Hammonds' position than they realised when they spoke their final word in 1930. But at the time the apparent weight of new evidence was against them, and it speaks well for their sense of objectivity as historians that they bowed to it.

'I have not heard that Clapham has resigned yet', Tawney wrote to Hammond (27 February 1930). In fact there was plenty of room for both approaches to co-exist since Clapham resolutely refused to be drawn from the quantitative ground whereas the real force of the Hammonds' argument was qualitative. This was widely recognised with the publication of *The Age of the Chartists* (1930) which, after a ruthless abridgment as *The Bleak Age* (1934), was largely reincarnated as the Pelican *Bleak Age* (1947), and as such because the Hammonds' best-known successor to the labourer trilogy. Here the problem was not that of marginal changes in real incomes, which, with the fruit of experience, Hobsbawm has dismissed as trivial,[2] but that of how economic change was experienced by the mass of working people. In this the Hammonds were foreshadowing the concerns of the most fruitful modern work in this area of social history, notably E. P. Thompson's *The Making of the English Working Class* (1963). Their emphasis also anticipated later interpretations which explained discontent in terms of relative deprivation. 'The greater the wealth of the time,' Lawrence Hammond argued, 'the more evident the power of man, the greater and more biting the sense of neglect and oppression in the classes which were excluded from any share in its enjoyment' (*EcHR*, ii, 226).

[2] See E. J. Hobsbawm, 'The standard of living debate', in Arthur J. Taylor (ed.), *The Standard of Living in Britain in the Industrial Revolution* (1975), pp. 180, 187.

In *The Age of the Chartists* the Hammonds developed several themes introduced earlier in their studies. In particular, the use of the classical world as a point of reference was made firm and explicit. Hammond had told Murray that the last two chapters of *The Rise of Modern Industry* 'put what I tried to say abt my views of the influence of the classics' (17 August 1927), and Murray was invited to criticise the draft of *Age of the Chartists* where the remedy of the ancient world was invoked to meet the discontent of the new. In Greece and Rome, 'The class struggle was veiled or softened by the moral influence of common possessions; the practice of social fellowship was stimulated by the spectacle of beautiful buildings, and the common enjoyment of the arts and culture of the time' (p. 8). In early nineteenth-century England, on the other hand, common enjoyment had almost no provision, beauty was allowed no scope, and in their place stood the personal satisfactions of acquisition and individual success. Religion offered little consolation. The Church of England, 'though freed from its worst abuses, still stood for resignation to the established order and consideration for the rich'.[3] Nonconformity was narrowly ascetic in its social puritanism. 'The Methodists did with the English Sunday what they did with the English theatre' (p. 258). The life of the working class was reduced to eating, drinking, working and sleeping. 'Manchester before the Ten Hours,' Hammond wrote to Murray, 'without park, library, gallery or theatre (except for a short expensive season) and without popular music, was really an epitome of that life' (19 February 1930).

Against all this, the Chartist movement stood out as a heroic movement of protest – 'imagination in action' (p. 276). It was part of the process of 'forming a new social mind, disturbed by changes that had destroyed the basis of custom in their lives' (p. 29). The Hammonds pointed to Chartism and trade unionism as the constructive working-class contribution to the taming of industrialism. Their argument was 'that our immunity from violence is largely due to the growth and success of our trade unions', which acted as 'a school of discussion where men learnt to talk out their differences' (*L*, 18 April 1934). The curbs and restraints of collective organisation were not unwelcome. 'The men are working very hard,' Barbara once reported to Lawrence Hammond when Oatfield was being repainted, 'too hard for my taste, and I wish that a Trade Union could produce a little less zeal in them' (5 August 1926). They wished, on the whole, to sacrifice zeal to amenity, and accordingly invested their hopes in the imputed public spirit of the working-class movement. Their approval was conditional. It is a just criticism of their historical work that it refused proper acknowledgement of the violence of much early trade-union organisation; and conversely that it persistently discounted the reports of government spies as evidence of paranoia rather than as indicating the possibilities

[3] *The Bleak Age* (Pelican edn, 1947), p. 119 (not in *Age of the Chartists*).

of a real insurrection. Although the Hammonds welcomed the advent of Chartism, and recognised that it represented a class struggle, it was the fact that conflict was averted which finally dispelled the bleakness of the age.

The reason for this, they suggested, lay in the emergence of two political agitations which cut across class lines, those for Free Trade and for Factory Acts. Unlike Chartism, these did not frighten off religious support but rather made a distinct appeal to sectarian rivalries. 'The Nonconformist clergy befriended the poor against the landowner; the Church clergy befriended the poor against the manufacturer' (p. 289). Suddenly, instead of a clear class conflict, 'the worst that could be said of the rich by the poor was being said by the rich of one another' (p. 287). The two quarrels of the poor – against rich landowners and rich industrialists – were pursued to victory through a fundamental breach in the class solidarity of the rich. The process of civilising town life could now begin. 'The Ten Hours Bill was in this sense the most important event of the first half of the century' (p. 350). In his Hobhouse Memorial Lecture, *The Growth of Common Enjoyment* (1933), Hammond pointed to the move towards a different view of social values which had subsequently taken place, gradually at first, quickly between 1900 and 1914, and even faster since the war. 'Modern England is as compared with that England a leisured society', he concluded. 'This is really a fundamental revolution' (p. 12). He repeatedly affirmed that there had been substantial progress towards building up 'a civilisation in which the want of money shall not cut people off from all the interests of a civilised society' (*L*, 11 November 1936).

In this perspective the Hammonds themselves emerged as optimists of a kind, or at least as convinced reformists. 'The optimist, then, stepping from the last century to this,' Hammond concluded, 'will find much to comfort his hopes of human happiness, but the pessimist will answer that it looks as if it is much easier for man to blame the past than to avoid its errors' (*Spec.*, 30 April 1937). Their assumptions have, indeed, met recent challenges from Marxist historians like Thompson – understandably enough, though marred by some imprecision when the Hammonds are identified as Fabians. Calling them socialists in fact obscures the fact that they attributed the social evils of the early nineteenth century not to capitalism but to unrestrained capitalism. They were really socialists only in the sense in which all democratic collectivists were called socialists in the 1890s. Hirst was doubtless not misunderstood when he challenged Hammond in these terms: 'Are you sure that you do not make a poetry of State Socialism, and underestimate the need for individual enterprise, self-education, and the development of higher ideas of pleasure through the competition of good with bad forms of entertainment?' (18 September 1933) More widely, however, the Hammonds were construed as socialists only with some violence to their essential meaning. 'Hammond himself was not a Communist,' read one obituary, 'but he contributed to that treason in almost every line he wrote. He was an enemy of the civilisation that made his life work possible.'[4] It may be, of course, that the ideological purchase which their books obtained was different from what the Hammonds would have wished. Be that as it may, it is clearly true that the Hammonds' work has always met criticism from those who impute its defects to political bias. As Tawney posed the question, was not 'the Hammonds' magic mirror too often a distorting glass?' (*PBA*, xlvi, 281)

In January 1929 the *Quarterly Review* published an article by A. A. W. Ramsay entitled 'A socialist fantasy'. It was a categorical attack upon the Hammonds for devoting themselves 'largely to the interpretation of British economic history in the interests of one particular section of political opinion' (*QR*, cclii, 32). They had, it was alleged, misused Home Office documents so as to produce a misleading account of child labour, trade unionism, the truck system and other matters in which the authorities could be portrayed in a poor light. They had dealt unfairly with contemporary philanthropists – 'Hannah More thought fit to begin by teaching the poor the principles of Christianity, whereas she ought, according to Mr and Mrs Hammond, to have taught them the principles of Socialism' (p. 61). An inflammatory presentation of biased evidence had built up a wholly distorted picture. 'A hundred passages throughout *The Town Labourer* show us that the arousing of this class prejudice is one of the objects of these writers themselves' (p. 63). Anna Ramsay later averred to Barbara Hammond that she 'had no intention of insinuating that there was any intentional suppression of the truth on your part, but only that I thought you had been misled by partisan feeling' (23 April 1929). If so, her article was a failure; it could only be read as an accusation that the Hammonds were producing propaganda not history. All their historical friends – Trevelyan, Basil Williams, Reginald Lennard, Eileen Power, Tawney, Gooch – responded fiercely to it because of this clear suggestion of bad faith. The Hammonds were deeply shaken. They were both ill with flu when the *Quarterly* arrived and lay on sofas in different rooms consoling themselves with Greek literature. 'For 24 hours after hearing of this article,' Hammond told Murray, 'we went about slinking like whipped dogs grateful for a nod from anyone in the street and thinking we shd have to recall the *TL* from the market' (5 February 1929).

The charges levelled were, to be sure, dauntingly specific in character. 'However obvious the malevolence, and foolish the tone,' Barbara Hammond admitted to Arthur Ponsonby, 'it is difficult to believe that she has got all her facts wrong' (4 April 1929). It was, after all, fourteen years since the research for the book had been completed, and the Hammonds were clearly apprehensive that serious errors might have been uncovered,

[4] Peter Barry, *Truth*, 6 May 1949 (in HP 149).

thus lending support to their indictment for misrepresentation. They already knew that there was one misquotation from a letter written by Peel in 1830. 'This slip,' they acknowledged, 'was the result of a misunderstanding between the person who copied and the person who read the copy' (*QR*, cclii, 283). This embarrassing admission arose from the fact that, owing to illness, Barbara Hammond had only read the Home Office papers herself as far as 1826. 'I never knew Barbara caught out', Lawrence claimed to Murray (7 February 1929); and none of her own research was shown to be deficient. The 'misunderstanding', however, was over the work done by Molly Hamilton, whose methods – 'She has rushed & dashed at the papers' – had disquieted Barbara Hammond at the time.[5] Her own solicitousness over detail shows up from several comments to Lawrence over the years as she sought to track down errors in the standard works on the period. 'It shows how careful you have to be to look up originals' (20 February 1917). 'How difficult it is to find anything out except from original authorities' (23 August 1927).

What is striking about the Ramsay–Hammond exchanges is that, with these minor exceptions, the accuracy of the *Town Labourer* was vindicated in almost every particular. Barbara Hammond returned to the Public Record Office to check references and the *Quarterly* was persuaded to give space for a reply long enough to permit a detailed rebuttal on a few leading test cases. As it happens, one of these concerned an episode which has subsequently received independent historical investigation, apparently without any reference to this historiographical controversy.[6] This was the seamen's strike of 1815 in north-east England, the account of which in the *Town Labourer* (pp. 28–30) Anna Ramsay spent four pages in assaulting. Legitimate differences of emphasis will remain, here as elsewhere, but a close comparison of the different versions suggests that the Hammonds had no reason to modify their account, which summarised the affair ruthlessly but fairly, whereas Anna Ramsay's counter-charges rested upon one major blunder and a number of tendentious readings. It is important to observe the difference between these exchanges and the Hammonds' debate with the Cambridge school of economic historians, like Clapham and Griffith. 'I aspire to play jackal to Prof. Clapham's lion', Anna Ramsay had claimed (p. 33). 'Historians at Cambridge,' Trevelyan assured Hammond (with idiosyncratic spelling), 'all think you have bold out the lady middle stump' (9 May 1929).

For those who followed the controversy, the result was a triumphant endorsement of the Hammonds' credentials as historians. Even so, it is easier to raise than to lay doubts, and a vague feeling that there was no

[5] Barbara to Lawrence Hammond, 20 June 1914, HP 6.

[6] See Norman McCord, 'The seamen's strike of 1815 in north-east England', *EcHR*, 2nd ser., xxi (1968), 127–43.

smoke without a fire may have persisted among those who did not examine the Hammonds' reply. As Cole put it: 'A *Quarterly* article is a sort of living burial, is it not?'[7] The Hammonds could, however, rest secure in the knowledge that their work was accepted as a genuine contribution to knowledge by other specialists working in the field, whether or not they held the same views. Of the leading optimists, Clapham remained on cordial and Griffith on respectful terms. George Unwin, before his death in 1925, had been one of their most constructive critics. T. S. Ashton wrote of his disgust at the Ramsay attack, which he regarded as an outrage. 'I imagine Clapham can't feel very happy about it,' he added; 'but if there is to be a change as to the way in which economic history ought to be written – if we have to divide ourselves into camps (which Heaven forbid) – I have no hesitation about my allegiance.'[8] The Hammonds' standing can also be inferred from other signs: the invitation to Lawrence to become a candidate for a chair at Manchester in 1930 and MacDonald's offer of a knighthood the following year; the honorary doctorates for both of them at Oxford in 1933; Lawrence's election to the British Academy in 1942; and the offer (like the knighthood, refused) of a Companionship of Honour.

None of this is to suggest that the Hammonds were other than deeply committed political figures, nor that what they wrote on social history is beyond revision and challenge. But though their history had its ideological uses it was executed as part of a scientific enterprise. Only they could have written it; only they would have posed the problems they did in quite that way; but the rules of evidence and method to which they adhered were part of an effort at objectivity which gave their work its scholarly value. They were used to controversy; but when their history was treated as mere propaganda they felt wounded by an unwarranted slight upon their intellectual integrity. 'The Labourer books must be judged for what they are,' they claimed: 'studies of a period inspired by a particular outlook on the past, and prompted by the belief that a mass of painful and terrible truth, of great importance in the life and imagination of the English people, was receiving less attention than it deserved' (QR, cclii, 290).

(II) REFORMISM BEATEN TO ITS CORNER

Wallas's younger colleagues at the L.S.E., like Harold Laski and Kingsley Martin, agreed that in his later years he became increasingly self-absorbed and that Ada Wallas played a much-needed role in delicately puncturing his pomposity. In April 1928, if Laski is to be believed, he was insisting in conversation that no-one had 'put psychology in its proper perspective between Aristotle and my *Human Nature in Politics*' (*H–L Letters*, p.

[7] Cole to Hammond, Friday (February 1929), HP 22, f.43.
[8] Ashton to Hammond, fragment, n.d. but probably July 1929, HP 22, f.225.

1050). And on his seventieth birthday he made a speech, invoking the influence of Plato and Aristotle, of which the keynote was: 'have I, G.W., too kept the faith?' (ibid., p. 1064) His unfinished last project, *Social Judgment* (1935), which he described to Hammond as 'a book about constructive social imagination under a shorter title' (7 October 1930), was concerned with the problems of decision-making in society. Like much of his later work the analysis was at once at an unhelpful level of abstraction and in an anecdotal form which laid it open to the charge of banality. Yet Wallas was, of course, in deadly earnest. 'The practical affairs of life,' he explained to Shaw, 'seem to me to be more and more dependent on the way we think and feel about the universe. The question how much the ordinary man will have to eat twenty years hence will depend very largely on the fate of the philosophies of Lenin and Eddington and Mussolini and Jesus Christ' (21 February 1929). Nearer home, this tallied, of course, with his belief that hard thinking was the indispensable condition of political effectiveness. 'The only chance for Liberalism,' he wrote to Elie Halévy, 'is that the middle voters may come to think of them as doing genuinely disinterested thought, as I am sure that E. D. Simon, Layton, H. D. Henderson (of the *Nation*) etc. are doing.' He added, somewhat ungratefully of a politician who always hailed him as the master-builder of ideas: 'Samuel is entirely disinterested but not very clever.'[9]

'Many of my friends call me a "liberal"', Martin told Wallas in 1927. 'I doubt if there is any difference of substance between my views and those of Keynes, for instance' (24 January 1927). Later that year Hammond introduced Martin to the *Manchester Guardian*, and Scott at first took to him with unusual enthusiasm. Martin's Nonconformist background, and his Cambridge connexions with Lowes Dickinson and Keynes, alike spoke well for him. He looked like 'good Labour'. The problem was that of strengthening the editorial corridor in preparation for the editor's retirement. But would Scott ever retire? 'C.P. is not "steam mill mad" like the contemporaries of Watt and Boulton but oatmeal mad', Lawrence Hammond wrote to Barbara. 'He licks up his raw oatmeal with tremendous zest every morning. I think he will see us all out' (7 August 1924). Hammond seems to have known from an early date that Ted Scott was the designated successor. Montague was formally offered the editorship, but he knew that it was only a gesture and retired gracefully. C. P. Scott, now over eighty, remained. When Hammond worked on the paper in the summer of 1927 he found him dilatory and with little grasp on overall policy. Montague's death in 1928 aged him. By 1929 the pretence about his authority was fairly open, and either Ted Scott or W. P. Crozier was always at the office. When Martin suddenly fell out of favour with C. P. Scott, therefore, Hammond considered that he was being badly treated and sympathised with his

[9] Wallas to Halévy, 8 October 1929, WP 10.

difficulties. There was some clash of political outlook here and the presence of Crozier as editorial janissary seemed to impugn the paper's radical credentials.

With the Labour Government in office, Martin's line was that the Liberals should not use their parliamentary leverage to bargain for electoral reform but instead, as he told Hammond, 'cooperate in regard to the unemployment plan & all the other progressive things they have talked so big about recently' (4 June 1929). The editor himself was pulled both ways. He still had the interests of the Liberal party at heart. But, then, what was the Liberal party if not the appointed agent of a progressive policy? In July 1929 the great C. P. Scott retired. The fact that he kept his old room and continued to attend at the office every night did not, of course, help Ted Scott to establish his authority. The obituaries which he and Hammond had been furtively preparing since 1928 remained unprinted; but if he would not die at least he was fading away. Hammond continued to play an important part in the paper's affairs. He was far from confident that the *Manchester Guardian*'s policy would prove sufficiently warm towards Labour, and reported incredulously to Barbara that Arthur Ransome had 'found Ted quite ready to support liberal cooperation with the Tories!' (8 August 1929) Ransome's politics were of a similar obscurity to those of Hammond – 'Ransome by the way is Liberal not Labour' (ibid., 11 August 1929) – and he strongly favoured the attempt to enlist Ransome as a leader writer.

Arthur Ransome, however, eventually decided to go off and write *Swallows and Amazons* (1930), and instead the Scotts appointed Malcolm Muggeridge. Muggeridge's father had been a well-known Fabian, one of the leading opponents of Shaw's policy over the Boer War, and was now a Labour M.P. His son had an impeccably progressive upbringing. The Fabian visitors he recalled 'were, in my father's sense, cultured; had been to the university, mostly Oxford or Cambridge; had contributed to the review columns of the *New Statesman* and the *Nation* (then still separate), and maybe written books; called Lytton Strachey "Lytton", and Keynes "Maynard", and Shaw "G.B.S."'.[10] The father's values and ambitions were fostered upon the son. He went to Cambridge and strengthened his links with the left-wing establishment by marrying a niece of Beatrice Webb. In short, he was tailor-made for the *Manchester Guardian* – or almost so. 'He married a niece of Lord Courtney', Ted Scott assured Hammond (6 March 1930), which was to put the Potter connexion in a rather more sympathetic light. Muggeridge and Ted Scott hit it off well from the start, and this appointment made it easy to dispense with Martin who, when his contract ended in 1930, moved on to become editor of the *New Statesman* – a post for which Hammond had earlier refused to become a

[10] Malcolm Muggeridge, *Chronicles of Wasted Time* (1972–3), i, 50.

candidate. Muggeridge, Ted Scott explained to Hammond, was 'as completely devoid of party or other political prejudices as anyone intensely interested in politics could be. And a pretty writer. Altogether a swan' (n.d. but November 1930). C. P. Scott benignly concurred, though his good opinion of Muggeridge was hardly reciprocated.

In 1929 all three political parties had accepted that unemployment was the crucial issue. There were no easy solutions here, either in theory or in practice. The theoretical rigour of the Treasury View remained unbreached. The practical difficulties of mounting a public works programme could not be wished away. There was, moreover, no guarantee that an expansionary programme would indeed have pulled Britain out of recession without structural changes of a kind that few were ready to contemplate. Whether the obstacles were chiefly economic or chiefly political, the fact remained that the whole reformist analysis of the problem was on trial. The Labour party's vaguely Hobsonian commitment led nowhere; the Keynesian proposals of the Liberal party were pushed aside; the underconsumptionist current in the I.L.P., which Oswald Mosley sought to channel behind his own proposals for national development, also ran into the sand. The setting-up of the Economic Advisory Committee fell far short of Hobson's idea of a National Industrial Council. The MacDonald Government clung to orthodox solutions in the belief that – failing socialist reconstruction – it was best to sit out the crisis without resort to mere tinkering. The advocacy of protective measures by Keynes and E. D. Simon in 1930 disconcerted many Liberals who believed that at least Free Trade must be kept pure. Hammond shared this feeling.

So the Government's increasingly precarious hold had to be justified by appeals to other issues. 'I am very unhappy abt the Govt,' Hammond told Ponsonby, 'for it seems absolutely essential that it shd stay in for disarmament and India and it looks to an outsider rather rocky' (18 March 1931). But even where Liberals and Labour could agree, it turned out to be a mixed blessing. In the spring of 1931 the proposed land tax revealed unexpected snags in the inducement it would give to the spoliation of the countryside through ribbon development. Keynes joined with G. M. Trevlyan in a protest that was backed by Hobson and the Hammonds. 'Apparently,' Trevelyan commiserated with Hammond, 'the Liberal and Labour Alliance – an excellent thing in itself – is to be cemented at the expense of what is left of the amenities of the country' (5 May 1931). Not only, then, did the Liberals thirst in vain after electoral reform; their thirst remained unquenched by a progressive response on unemployment either; and when the long-promised land tax appeared, the cup was unexpectedly bitter.

The Labour Government staggered towards its collapse in the financial crisis of August 1931 and was replaced by a National Government under

MacDonald. The bulk of the Labour party stood sullenly aside, refusing to countenance any cuts in unemployment benefit. To Hammond it seemed that the crisis had been badly handled all round and Labour hardly given a fair chance to act. 'But,' he told Murray, 'if the alternative was a sudden collapse of sterling with the pound going like the mark, of course anything is better than that' (26 August 1931). He was inclined to spread the blame more widely than Murray, but they were broadly of the same view. Hammond believed that if Arthur Henderson had replaced Snowden, things might have been different; but the cowardly action of the Labour Government in letting things slide was to him undeniable. 'As a result,' he told Murray, 'we have naked class war and the prospect of another credit collapse' (31 August 1931). To some extent this echoed the sentiments of a letter which he had just received from Ted Scott – 'The general drift of politics seems to me terribly bad. I doubt if we shall ever get away again from the war of the classes' (30 August 1931). And yet, though the class war might be bad, who was responsible for it?

On this question there had been acute differences of opinion on the *Manchester Guardian*. Ted Scott was away when the National Government was formed. He returned to find that Crozier had given it warm approval in his leaders. To Muggeridge, on the other hand, it was a great betrayal. 'I wonder on which side of the barricade these clever young men will ultimately find themselves', Ted Scott commented (ibid.). But in fact he found himself drawn into opposing the Government and exposing its pretensions to be considered National. For a start, if the talk of saving the pound were to be taken seriously, he thought a capital levy worth consideration. The factitious nature of the crisis, and its patent exploitation by the forces of conservatism, made an increasingly unfavourable impression upon him, so that by the time of the General Election at the end of October 1931 he had swung the paper into outright opposition to the National Government. In this it is possible that his father-in-law may have played some part. Hobson complained that the policy of balancing the budget had not considered 'the reactions of those measures upon the two deeper economic troubles, an adverse external trade account and the great and growing waste of unemployed resources of production' (*PQ*, ii, 464). And in his satirical dialogue *The Recording Angel* (1932), he maintained that 'The ruling classes in politics and business were determined to enforce their verdict and their will upon the electorate', and had directed a misleading propaganda barrage to that end (p. 26).

Hammond remained more troubled and uncertain. 'I am in despair about this election', he wrote to Murray. 'It seems to me that we are really heading now for a class struggle' (16 October 1931). The Labour party seemed to him irresponsible and the danger of an irreconcilable Left alienated from the political system could not be discounted. He regarded those

Liberals who, under his old college friend John Simon, had clearly thrown in their lot with the Tories as quite mistaken, and it was Lloyd George whom he applauded for 'pointing to the danger of this concentration against Labour and the use of the word National' (ibid.). In Hemel Hempstead the sitting Conservative was opposed by a Labour candidate and by a Liberal who was not a Simonite. The Hammonds decided to vote Liberal.

Men like Murray and Hammond lacked the economic tools to tackle the job in any other way. Murray's argument was 'that a collectivist state has to balance its Budget and has to pay for its foreign food quite as much as any other state'.[11] As it stands, of course, there is a *non sequitur* between the balancing of the Budget and the balance of payments, which can perhaps be bridged by invoking the need to restore confidence in the pound by government economies. Keynes was able to mount a sustained criticism of the economy programme in the *New Statesman and Nation* (now published jointly) by appealing to its effect upon demand for labour. Britain's decision to leave the Gold Standard in September 1931 was only a vindication of an approach for which his rational arguments were of long standing. 'I can give you a slogan for the next election', he said to Arthur Henderson. 'Hitherto, the pound has been looking the dollar in the face, now it's kicking it in the arse.'[12]

But to those who had looked at the crisis through the spectacles of orthodox economics, drastic economies to save the pound lay in the logic of the policy to which the Labour Government itself had been committed. This was MacDonald's own position, and he made his unpalatable political choices accordingly. The Hammonds sent a letter supporting his candidature at Seaham in the election. The initial assumption was that MacDonald's would prove the stern path of duty while the rest of the Labour party would enjoy the luxury of opposing measures which were necessary but unpopular. As Hammond told Murray, 'it looks as if the next election will be fought on the dole and the next Labour Govt elected to deal with it' (26 August 1931). But by the time the election came, it was clear that the appeal for a Doctor's Mandate would carry all before it. Toynbee took the same line as Hammond, and pointed out to him that they were 'in the same dilemma as during the War, when one couldn't afford not to defeat the Germans and yet could do nothing to moderate the victory' (26 October 1931). They entered and left the Labour party with similar sentiments. 'If Labour had been able to carry the T.U.C. with them in making the cuts, they would have established themselves, I think, as the true heirs of the Liberals, and we should have got back to the two-party system' (ibid.). As it was, it was a choice of evils. In the elections, as they by now foresaw, the

[11] Murray to Hammond, 27 August 1931, copy, MP 23a.
[12] Kingsley Martin, *Editor* (Penguin edn, 1969), p. 60.

Conservatives triumphed overwhelmingly. Labour was reduced to a remnant of fifty M.P.s; independent Liberalism was annihilated. The National Government pleased the Hammonds no more than the Treaty of Versailles.

The crisis had been the making of Ted Scott as editor. He had set his stamp upon the *Manchester Guardian*. But being on the wrong side of the class war had its problems for a paper with an AB readership. He told Hammond that 'it seems to me broadly that politics are getting into an ugly shape and that we shall be driven more and more to take an anti-property line. And that is fatal to a 2d. paper. I myself feel that I am getting much more of a socialistic way of thinking (or rather feeling), but the more I look at the socialist party the less I like it' (16 November 1931). He knew that Hammond had not followed him so far, and he agreed with him that the Opposition in the new parliament was feeble. But as to the Liberals, there was only the incorrigible Lloyd George, who would ruin any party, while 'most of the rest seem to me the sort that will come down on the wrong side of the fence whenever the pinch comes – as now' (ibid.). When the Liberals moved right, only Labour was left. 'If we couldn't even keep the Liberal party alive when it had leaders, money and traditions', he demanded of Hammond, 'what hope is there of starting a new party? I'm afraid there is nothing for it but the political education of the trade unions. But there may be a smash first' (22 November 1931).

'I am afraid I am but a feeble help to my dear Ted in these days,' C. P. Scott wrote to Hammond, 'but I think we pretty well agree about things' (22 December 1931). Recent events had in fact largely passed him by. In January 1932 he died, aged eighty-five. Hammond was asked to write his biography and was given full access to the voluminous papers which had been kept. *C. P. Scott* (1934) was actually a joint production since Barbara Hammond did most of the reasearch and wrote the sections on woman suffrage and the Taylor will. Published so soon after Scott's death, the book is somewhat indulgent to him; certain stories were suppressed; and not all that the Hammonds uncovered increased their admiration. Even so, the picture it gives is, so far as it goes, a fair one; and more can be read between the lines. 'It is a fine piece of biography and psychology', was Hirst's justifiable comment to Hammond. 'Indeed the fact that it leaves my mind still a little doubtful about Scott's real character and especially as to how far and how often he lost his hold on principle under the influence of L.G. is probably a proof of your art and veracity!' (11 July 1934) C. P. Scott was lucky in the hour of his death; only three months later Ted was drowned in the Lake District. This real tragedy hit all his friends with numbing effect. Hobson said simply that Ted's death could not be 'condoned'.

In the winter of 1932–3 unemployment was to reach its peak of nearly three millions. The fortunes of the Liberal party had plummeted with those of the economic system which it had offered to resuscitate. Politically and economically, reformist solutions lay discredited. To a young man like Muggeridge the failure of the MacDonald Government marked 'the end of any notion that the Labour Party, or any Social Democratic party similarly constituted, can be an effective instrument of fundamental social change' (Muggeridge, i, 196). To an old man like Wallas the prospects also seemed bleak. In February 1932 Beatrice Webb noted with some satisfaction that he had 'dropped his liberalism as a possible creed: he thinks that American capitalism will fail to give a decent and continuous livelihood to its people; and that Soviet Russia will succeed in doing it'. Perhaps she misread Wallas's scepticism here, as so often before, and projected her own solutions upon him. But a sense of defeat and despair was palpably present. 'Poor liberalism!' she remarked. 'Even aged Liberals are reconsidering their faith out of sheer disgust at the ways of profit-making capitalists, more especially in U.S.A.' (*BWD*, iv, 299–300) Wallas's quest remained uncompleted. He died in August 1932, rather suddenly, after being active to the end. Laski was probably right to conclude that 'two of his books did a big job' (*H–L Letters*, p. 1401). *Francis Place* was a pioneer work in social history and *Human Nature in Politics* inaugurated a new approach to political science. Beyond that, he was remembered as a teacher who made a great contribution to the L.S.E. in its formative years; and his personal influence made a lasting impression on a wide range of those who knew him. 'Taken all in all,' Webb summed up, 'I feel I have learned more, and gained more intellectually from Graham Wallas than from any other friend' (*Ec*, xii, 404).

(III) STALIN, GOD AND KEYNES

Virginia Woolf's nephew, Julian Bell, who had thought of himself as a Labour supporter since adolescence, recorded with some dramatic overemphasis that in the Cambridge he first knew in 1929 and 1930 'we hardly ever talked or thought about politics. For one thing, we almost all of us had implicit confidence in Maynard Keynes's rosy prophecies of continually increasing capitalist prosperity' (*NS*, 9 December 1933). But with the collapse of capitalism, the prospects of reforming it receded too and more drastic alternatives urged themselves forward. The collapse of the 1917 Club is a fitting symbol; in 1931 Hobson, withdrawing from a meeting in protest against the confusion of the accounts, fell heavily downstairs. Just as 1914 saw the initial hammer blow to hopes of progress, first in the international order and then in economics, so 1931 saw further nails knocked into the coffin – only this time the economic problem was in the forefront, with international repercussions to follow. And just as Hobhouse used to recommend reading Hegel to the accompaniment of the war news, so Marx's writings suddenly acquired a compelling resonance. John Strachey had been a Labour M.P. since 1929 and one of the leading proponents of the radical economic policies of his friend Oswald Mosley, whom he briefly followed into the New Party. But by the end of 1931 he had broken with Mosley and was systematically studying *Capital*, which he found 'a tremendous experience, especially at the moment, when one sees so many of Marx's predictions being uncannily fulfilled'.[13] Although never an actual member of the Communist party, his book *The Coming Struggle for Power* (1931) became the most influential Marxist publication of the decade. It exposed the structural instabilities of capitalism and pointed to the inexorable necessity of building a new and stable civilisation, as Russia was doing.

Stephen Spender was the son of Harold Spender and consequently had been brought up, of course, with a strong belief in progress. 'History,' he recalled, 'seemed to have been fulfilled and finished by the static respectability, idealism and material prosperity of the end of the nineteenth century. This highly satisfactory, if banal, conclusion was largely due to the Liberal Party having found the correct answer to most of the problems which troubled our ancestors.'[14] This was all very well until 1931, when Spender turned twenty-two. Events then rudely intruded. If reformist tinkering had failed, perhaps it showed that the system itself was incapable of being reformed. But did that mean that there was no correct answer? When Spender threw over moral reformism, he was able to salvage his belief in progress by finding the correct answer instead in moral revolutionism. 'I was constantly preoccupied with the idea of judgment', he reflected percipiently; 'for on a certain level of my mind it seemed impossible not to believe that everything we do is judged, and that life is a kind of sum which has meaning because good is related to bad, and there is an answer' (Spender, p. 209). In many ways these underlying assumptions would have been common to a moral regenerationist like Bosanquet as well as to a moral reformist like his father. In *Forward from Liberalism* (1937) he followed Laski in quarrelling with liberalism because of its blindness to 'the fact that liberal justice, liberal freedom, liberal individualism, rest on the institution of property and the interests of a certain class' (p. 83). But Marxism could sweep away this fundamental confusion by establishing justice and equality upon the abolition of property. The ends of liberalism and the promise of progress could be realised by these means. 'I am a communist,' declared Spender, 'because I am a liberal' (p. 202).

In a world that was polarising between the challenging doctrines of fascism and communism, straight-line theories of progress suggested that, as Shaw put it, there was 'no apparent way out except Marxian Communism' (*PQ*, ii, 462). At Cambridge, Communism was attracting many of the most able and prominent young men in the early 1930s. Donald

[13] Hugh Thomas, *John Strachey* (1973), p. 114.

[14] Stephen Spender, *World Within World* (1951), pp. 1–2.

Maclean, whose father, Sir Donald, had actually led the Asquithian opposition in the 1918 Parliament, was writing in 1933 of the capitalist society 'which is doomed to disappear' and of 'the rising tide of opinion which is going to sweep away the whole crack-brained criminal mess'.[15] John Cornford was the son of the impeccably liberal Francis and Frances Cornford. By 1932 he had forsaken his youthful enthusiasm first for Lloyd George radicalism and then the New Party to become a Communist, and was trying to complete his parents' education on similar lines. Their principled tolerance and bewildered scepticism may be considered a paradigm of parental liberalism. A few years later, Gilbert Murray had to undergo trials on a less heroic level, admitting to Hammond that he had not seen the *Daily Worker* until his son Stephen 'introduced it into the house some weeks ago. "Golly, what a paper!"' (4 January 1940) Julian Bell clearly recognised the psychological needs which a Marxist commitment fulfilled. 'But this is only one side of the picture', he argued. 'If Communism makes many of its converts among the "emotionals", it appeals almost as strongly to minds a great deal harder. It is not so much that we are all Socialists now as that we are all Marxists now' (*NS*, 9 December 1933). In fact this gives a misleadingly clear-cut impression of Bell's position – 'I *can't, can't* get clear about politics', he wrote in a private letter in 1934.[16] But it draws attention to the ambivalent way that ideas of progress were both rejected and not rejected by those who, to rephrase Spender, were communists because their fathers were liberals.

Using the language of William Morris, the moral revolutionists looked to the abolition of property to resolve their dilemmas; but in practice it was the Russia of Stalin which had to bear their hopes. As a mechanical reformist Shaw found no difficulties in adapting his views to the new situation. 'From henceforward,' he declared in November 1931, 'owing to what has happened in Russia, you are either a Communist, or what MacDonald and Snowden are, whatever that may be.' Fabianism was *passé*. But it had in fact triumphed all the same, because the process of making Russian Communism a success had been 'a process of turning what used to be called Communism gradually and under pressure of experience into Fabianism'. The Bolsheviks had admittedly been tinctured with old-fashioned notions of liberty at the time of the revolution; but that, along with other anarchistic irrelevances, had been squeezed out by the pressure of events. What had happened, then, to the democracy in social democracy? Lenin's purges of his opponents had shown how 'to cure the shortcomings of democracy'. And now Stalin stood in his place, an opportunist with the overriding object of establishing the Soviet state as a perfect state. 'That is

[15] Bruce Page, David Leitch and Philip Knightley, *Philby. The spy who betrayed a generation* (Penguin edn, 1969), p. 75.

[16] Peter Stansky and William Abrahams, *Journey to the Frontier* (1966), p. 111.

his object,' Shaw concluded, 'but he does not care how he gets there; he will take every method.'[17]

The old cynic could hardly have given a more candid exposition of the mechanical revolutionist case. His joke was that, over Lenin's tomb, there should be inscribed the motto 'The inevitability of gradualism'. When the Webbs went to Russia in 1932 they found that many a truth is spoken in jest. Their mechanical reformism had inoculated them against any sympathy for the Russian experiment in the 1920s; but what with the consolidation of Stalin's power and the collapse of the second Labour government, they were by now in a more receptive frame of mind. They found little revolutionary ferment in Russia. Instead there was a centralised bureaucratic system in which the plans of the experts replaced the wastefulness of capitalism. Their painstaking exposition of its formal beauties appearel in *Soviet Communism: a new civilisation?* (1935). The famous question-mark in the title of the second edition of 1937 bears comparison with the curious incident of the dog in the night-time in *Silver Blaze*: there was no question-mark. The Webbs – and indeed Shaw – were in their late seventies at the time, but to hint at senility does them an injustice. They had always regarded socialism as a *Weltanschauung*: in the sense that particular changes in property relations had to be accomplished by one means or another. With these somewhat attenuated criteria to apply, the Webbs had no difficulty in affirming that the Russia of 1936–7 was a new civilisation. 'We see no sign in the USSR of any weakening on the stern prohibition of private profit-making', they wrote in justification; 'meaning by this either the buying of commodities with the object of selling them at a higher price (termed speculation), or the hiring of workers for the purpose of making pecuniary gain out of their product (termed exploitation)' (2nd edn, p. 1214). They vindicated their consistent commitment to socialism and showed, in their old age, that they remained true to the convictions of forty years. 'Now we have a suspicion, which we trust may be unfounded,' Hobhouse had once written, rather coyly, 'that Mr Webb and his friends do not really believe in "the will of the people" as the true source of governmental power: if it is for them a force at all, it is only as so much fuel to be utilised by the superior wills of a virtually self-appointed aristocracy of talent' (N, 13 June 1908). It is hard to believe that he would have been surprised at the Webbs' last crusade.

In 1927 Laski had described the Bolsheviks as a 'doctrinal aristocracy', all too easily corrupted by the seizure of power. 'The leaders who seize power for one end,' he wrote, 'may choose to maintain power for quite different ends.'[18] The claim of the National Government, however, to be

[17] 'What Indeed?', TS lecture report, 26 November 1931, Shaw Papers, BL Add. MSS 50557, ff.279–93.
[18] David Caute, *The Fellow-Travellers* (1973), p. 160.

the only means of maintaining confidence in the pound seemed to him 'tantamount to an insistence that if socialists wish to secure a state built upon the principles of their faith, they can only do so by revolutionary means' (*PQ*, ii, 468). He became a leading advocate of collaboration with the Communist party, which he now defended against the charge that it was committed to dictatorial methods. His friend Kingsley Martin trod an even more wary path, refusing to open the *New Statesman and Nation* to criticism of Stalinist Russia for fear of helping Hitlerian Germany. Martin's capacity for extenuating Russian behaviour, indeed, showed him flexible to the point of contortion. It was a choice of evils. In his Hobhouse Memorial Lecture *The Decline of Liberalism* (1940) Laski argued that contemporary economic developments had created a situation in which events were determined by force and fear. 'At such a point,' he concluded, 'the basic procedures of liberalism, free inquiry, acceptance of democratic decisions, the preservation of individual freedom, are not likely to be highly regarded. A social order whose way of life is challenged will not easily accept the methods of a debating society' (p. 17). Without a means of reformulating the economic agenda, liberal democracy stood condemned.

The position of the fellow-traveller was in many respects a tortured one; yet in one obvious respect it was comfortable since he could project his hopes of regeneration on to Russia while himself remaining at a safe distance. Muggeridge followed a purer quest for perfection, and in the autumn of 1932 he left for Russia, intending to make it his home. His disillusionment was swift, his scorn Swiftian. It was as though William Morris had seen the future and it did *not* work. Moreover, he found that the supposedly liberal press at home did not want to know what was going on. Within six months he was equating the *Manchester Guardian*, which had cut his despatches, with 'the Kingsley-Martin–Bernard-Shaw–Sidney-and-Beatrice-Webb slop that frothed round that dark tyranny'.[19] As many examples would show, when moral revolutionists came to face the fact that Stalinism did not embody their vision, they had the option of falling back upon the less strenuous expectations of reformism. Not for Muggeridge, however, the mere scaling-down of utopia; he faced 'the total reversal, in the light of what I had seen and understood in the USSR, of everything I had hitherto hoped for and believed' (Muggeridge, i, 274).

When he returned to England in 1933, he came to the conclusion that it was not just that the revolutionary prospectus had proved over-ambitious. Instead he questioned 'the assumption on which I had lived from my earliest years, that such and such changes, brought about peacefully through the ballot-box, or drastically through some sort of revolutionary process, would transform human life; making it brotherly, prosperous and just, instead of, as it always had been, and still was for most people, full of

[19] David Ayerst, *Guardian* (1971), p. 512 (3 April 1933).

poverty, exploitation and conflict. I no longer believed this, nor ever would again' (ibid., ii, 17). The whole notion of progressive human nature was thus fallacious. Experience was to show Muggeridge 'that the world of time is irretrievably imperfect, whereas delight is only in perfection'[20] – and so, failing to discover the kingdom of heaven on earth, he looked elsewhere. The ultimate rationality of the universe was still assumed, and a need to believe was therefore construed as evidence for the desired belief. 'To accept this world as a destination rather than a staging-post,' he later dclared, 'and the experience of living in it as expressing life's full significance, would seem to me to reduce life to something too banal and trivial to be taken seriously or held in esteem' (ibid., i, 18). His friend Hugh Kingsmill gave him the concept of Dawnism to characterise all efforts to solve the troubles of the individual by collective action, which were necessarily vain. With a yearning for belief as ardent as that of Robert Elsmere, Muggeridge combined a conviction of original sin as stern as that of Mr Gladstone. After Russia he settled down to writing a hostile study of Samuel Butler. Full circle.

For Hobson, of course, it was an argument of comforting familiarity that 'the vicious circle as it first appeared is no closed circle, but an ascending spiral' (*Crisis of Liberalism*, p. 183). Stalin and God were not alternatives which had any appeal for him. In *God and Mammon* (1931) he called Christianity 'this futile endeavour to fit an oriental, ascetic pacifism on to the Western temperament and valuation' (p. 55). His own analysis of the social functions of religion, which owed much to Weber and Tawney, led him to plead for a true rationalist religion which would allow everyone to 'keep body and soul together' (p. 58). The Comtean overtones here were also brought out in *Rationalism and Humanism* (1933) with its 'earnest invitation to Rationalists to count themselves as Humanists, and to regard Ethics as the mediating principle' (p. 11). He regarded Bolshevism, moreover, as essentially similar in its appeal, though with an inversion of the attempt to subdue economic ends to spiritual. Now there was an economic Bible; Marx and Lenin were worshipped as the saints of a new social order; the millennial vision, after a few years of trial and fasting, was a further religious device; and a God-State was exalted, based upon repression and persecution. 'Whether regarded as a political or an economic religion,' Hobson commented, 'it is as abhorrent to Rationalism as any of the preposterous theologies it seeks to displace' (*God & Mammon*, p. 58).

He recognised that in the 1930s it was 'not the logic of Marxism or of any theoretic socialism that is the main motive in a radical movement, but the plain exhibition of the failure of capitalism to serve the interests of the people.'[21] But he found both positive and negative reasons for upholding a

[20] Quoted in Richard Ingrams, *God's Apology* (1977), p. 115.
[21] *Property and Improperty* (1937), p. 137.

reformist analysis. His longstanding conviction that it showed a record of success remained unshaken. He retained a faith in the effectiveness of redistribution through taxation – a movement which he wanted to take further but which had already created better conditions. When he gave the first Hobhouse Memorial Lecture, *Towards Social Equality* (1931), he detected 'a most important movement towards social equality' in the erosion of rigid conventions of social status (p. 19). Instead, more flexible disparities based on patterns of consumption had appeared – not, indeed, the promised land, but an encouragement to believe that further egalitarian moves were possible. This was currently a favourite theme. In his broadcast talks, *The Modern State* (1931), he cited the great increase in progressive taxation, along with the extensions of state intervention in industry, documented in the *Yellow Book*, and the improved social services, as the great changes which had, since the turn of the century, made politics so real for everyone. In a later broadcast on underconsumption, he stressed 'the increased taxation of higher incomes and of inheritances by which the increased public services are maintained', and concluded: 'This policy is actually the most revolutionary movement of our time, for it is a confiscation of the income and property of the rich for the direct benefit of the poor, who are the chief beneficiaries of nearly all the expenditure on public services' (*L*, 31 October 1934). Listening to this broadcast, Frances Stevenson recorded that Lloyd George, 'looking at me significantly, pointed his finger to his own breast, meaning: I did it'.[22]

Conversely, the Russian experiment, although Hobson wanted it to have a fair trial, held less and less attraction for him. 'There is a world of difference between assent and consent', he argued. 'The former implies a submission, the latter an expression of personality. A morally sound communism, indeed any securely practicable communism, implies a conscious and continuous desire for the good of the community far stronger than appears to exist in any civilized people' (*Wealth & Life*, p. 222). Leninist revolution had therefore necessarily been mechanical in character, and Hobson continued to rely upon Laski's exegesis here even after Laski himself denied its dictatorial drift. Hobson dismissed the contention that 'The bad education and traditions of the past have moulded a "human nature" which, as regards its social feelings and attitudes, is unfitted for immediate and whole-hearted and clear-minded acceptance of the new order' (ibid., p. 223). This was, he felt, to beg too many questions and to create a closed system insulated from inconvenient truths. He warned that when 'we are told that the folly of democracy has been exposed, and that groups of skilled self-appointed rulers who understand what the people ought to want (what is really good for them) are destined to take the place of popularly chosen

[22] A. J. P. Taylor (ed.), *Lloyd George. A diary by Frances Stevenson* (1971), p. 285 (29 October 1934).

rulers, we should be slow to accept such arrogant assertions' (*Rationalism & Humanism*, p. 26).

Hobson developed this view at length in *Democracy and a Changing Civilisation* (1934). He blamed the Hegelian penetration of Marxism for the emergence of this doctrine of the real will as distinct from what people would actually choose. 'So the Communist Party, or rather its leaders, represent what the proletariat *would* will if their will were "free", in the sense of knowing all the relevant facts and framing policies in accordance with their true interests' (p. 64). He did not, of course, accuse Lenin and the Bolsheviks of a mere thirst for domination; but their passionate commitment to the welfare of the people had reinforced their will to power. He now made the further assertion that 'this dictatorship, like those of Italy and Germany,' was endeavouring 'so to dominate by cooked history and biased propaganda the minds of the young as to mould them into a common standard of belief, emotion, aspiration and conduct' (p. 70). By 1938 he was pointing to 'the convergence of Fascism and Communism in their "real" operation, both political and economic' and maintaining that 'this evolution of Sovietism signifies a repudiation of economic equality and liberty not widely distinguishable from the Government of Germany and Italy in its essential features' (*PQ*, ix, 50–1).

If it was a choice between dictatorship and democracy, then, Hobson was absolutely unequivocal in his choice. He found grounds for faith in democracy even in the darkest hour – because it was just before the dawn. 'Man has in reserve some powers which he only uses when he is "put to it" in some peril that menaces his very life', he suggested (*Recording Angel*, p. 108). These turned out to be 'the natural advantages enjoyed by Truth over Falsehood, Cooperation over Conflict, Justice over Injustice, Economy over Waste' (ibid., p. 124). Equity was socially functional and reason the path to it. He found in the common sense of the people a natural wisdom, mainly conservative, but capable of expressing creative urges. Common sense, he admitted, 'regarded on its intellectual side, is opportunist and compromising. On its moral side, it refuses to be swept away by passion: it eschews fanaticism and grievance-hugging' (*Democracy*, pp. 81–2). There was, too, the hope that education and experience could raise it 'to the higher level of "reasonableness"' (p. 156). The nature of these claims, however, did not suggest that expectations ought to be pitched too high.

This was fully recognised in the essentially modest nature of Hobson's policy proposals. He concluded that 'the logic of events is bringing into clearer vision the choice between social democracy and the authoritative State operating as a safeguard for capitalism' (ibid., p. 42). Economic equality and planning should therefore have a wide appeal to all who wanted democracy to survive. In the early 1930s, when 'rationalisation' in industry was the vogue, he sought to argue that true rationalisation would involve using state planning to aim at maximum production through better distribution. In *From Capitalism to Socialism* (1932) he made it clear that his own proposals to absorb the irrational surplus by true rationalisation did not involve complete public ownership (although routine, standardised industries ought certainly to be taken over). Indeed he regarded the possible paralysis of creative and innovative activities as 'a final argument for a limited as against a complete socialism' (p. 36). It is not wholly surprising, therefore, that he supported the proposals outlined in *The Next Five Years. An essay in political agreement* (1935). This plea for planning and a more radical approach to the economy than that of the National Government had the active support of left-wing Conservatives like Harold Macmillan as well as many disinherited progressives. Among those who signed it were Norman Angell, A. G. Gardiner, G. P. Gooch, Hammond, Hobson, J. J. Mallon, J. H. Muirhead, Gilbert and Mary Murray, and H. W. Nevinson. Hobson reflected that, with proportional representation, a powerful Liberal party could have been created on this platform. 'For,' he explained, 'this progressive Liberal policy is nearer to the average electoral mind than any full-blown Socialism' (*Conf.*, p. 125).

When he argued for 'A British Socialism' in 1936, therefore, it was one with a conciliatory approach to 'middle opinion' in both its economics and its politics. Planning was the word. A limited programme of public ownership was linked to it, but hardly such as to disturb industry fundamentally. 'Suppose that the banks, the railways, the coal mines, and other key industries were nationalised,' Hobson suggested, 'would it not be to the obvious interest of the public to leave the actual operation of these industries in the hands of their present experienced managers?' (*NS*, 1 February 1936). His political argument rested on 'the failure of Socialism to make a sufficiently intelligible and equitable impress upon the minds of the mass of the wage-earners on the one hand, and of the salaried, professional and public employees upon the other' (*NS*, 25 January 1936). There was thus a need to broaden its appeal by reinstating the liberal arguments for measures generally advocated as socialism.

In *Property and Improperty* (1937) Hobson sought to do this by showing that socialism ought to have no quarrel with 'property' as such but only with 'improperty' – a term which he revived after twenty years to cover what had at various earlier stages been called property for power, or irrational gains, or the surplus. Hence Hobson tried, not for the first time, 'to reconcile two lines of progressive policy commonly held to be divergent, viz. the equality of opportunity that forms the basis of enlightened "liberalism" and the growing demand for public ownership, operation and control that forms a practicable socialism. As we see it, these policies not merely are not opposed, they are organically united' (pp. 179–80). A familiar argument. Furthermore, in one of his last political articles, Hobson identified the 'middle course, irregular and opportunist in its concrete application', which would 'continue to be our path of progress', as 'a new Liberalism which differs from the old in that it incorporates economic equality of opportunities in its full sense' (*PQ*, ix, 54–5).

Hobson was clear that, as things stood, economic democracy had to come 'through what I would call the rationalization of the Labour Party', meaning its adoption of his kind of progressive policy (*Conf.*, p. 181). Keynes had been faced with the plea in the late 1920s that 'what Liberals need is the imagination to convince Labour that there is a way out for it from the prison disclosed to them by Karl Marx, Lenin and others'.[23] That the process of convincing Labour had not gone very far by 1931 was all too clear. 'The basic cause of the collapse of the second Labour Government,' Hobson affirmed, 'was the failure of most of its leaders and followers to realize the dangers of a financial situation which lay outside their understanding of politics and economics' (*Conf.*, p. 121). Keynes concurred in this view. The trouble was, as he saw it, that Labour held orthodox views as to what was economically sound, though was often ready – and even eager – to do what it believed economically unsound. But the Labour leaders had been 'totally out of sympathy with those who have had new notions of what is economically sound, whether the innovator has been right or wrong' (*PQ*, iii, 157). Furthermore, he believed that the necessary process of intellectual emancipation would not involve Labour in abandoning its ultimate goals. Keynes, unlike Hobson, did not believe that equity was always economically functional: this had been a point of friction between them. But he was now ready to argue, in almost Hobsonian terms, 'that those things which are urgently called for on practical grounds, such as the central control of investment and the distribution of income in such a way as to provide purchasing power for the enormous potential output of modern productive technique, will also tend to produce a better kind of society on ideal grounds' (ibid., p. 159).

A. L. Rowse, who was a sympathetic Labour student of Keynes's ideas, responded that the proper deduction to be drawn was that Labour – minus MacDonald *et al.* – now offered a hopeful field for Keynes's views; but that he in turn 'should reflect, that the only way of embodying them in our policy is via a political movement' (ibid., p. 415). Rowse argued that Keynes attached too much importance to appeals to intelligence, whereas in politics it was less important to hold right views than 'to place yourself in touch with the group interest which will make your views, when right, effective' (*NC*, cxii, 328). There is indeed evidence in Keynes's activities in the 1930s of an attempt to do this. The Liberal party was no longer an available instrument. The merging of the *Nation* with the *New Statesman*, with

[23] Philip Kerr to Keynes, 25 August 1927, in Michael Bentley, *The Liberal Mind 1914–1929* (Cambridge 1977), p. 149.

Keynes as proprietor, gave him a progressive audience. But Keynes did not, after the experience of 1929, project his views in the arena of mass politics. Instead, the *General Theory* was, as he declared in the preface, 'chiefly addressed to my fellow economists'.

If, however, Keynesian economics had an ideological deficiency in isolation from Labour, the deficiency of Hobsonian economics, on the other hand, was scientific. This is abundantly illustrated by the fact that the leading academic critic of underconsumption at this time was Evan Durbin. Durbin was at the L.S.E., where general equilibrium theories found their warmest advocates, and worked closely with his colleague Lionel Robbins, one of Keynes's most persistent critics. But Durbin was also a member of the Labour party and, along with his friend Hugh Gaitskell, one of its most prominent younger economists. 'I was brought up,' he told Hammond, 'in the Nonconformist cum Liberal tradition, and as a child I was seriously confused about the distinction between God and Mr Gladstone' (27 March 1940). If the Hobsonian analysis of underconsumption could not impress Durbin, it was plainly not because he did not want to believe in it; indeed, without it he was in a quandary as to what economic advice to offer Labour; and he made an unavailing effort to synthesise what Keynes had said in the *Treatise* within an orthodox framework, which suggests his openness to persuasion. But the views of Hobson, rather to his chagrin, were lumped together by Durbin with the cruder fallacies of other heretics. In his book *Purchasing Power and Trade Depression* (1933) Durbin acknowledged that the theory of underconsumption had been 'preached with consuming passion' to the Labour movement as 'a golden cure for poverty and distress, for unemployment and insecurity'; but this was a hope he could not share, believing 'with reluctance that this theory does not tell us the truth about the processes of monetary circulation or describe the real alternatives that are before us' (2nd edn, p. 190).

According to Durbin, the real problem was the top-heavy growth of the capital goods industries, which therefore claimed an unduly large share of such voluntary savings as were available. In controversy with him, Hobson pointed to the barrenness of the only two alternative courses available to reverse this: either wage cuts to redistribute income towards the saving classes, or a wastage of resources in the capital goods industries. 'I still believe that they are the only alternatives within a system of private enterprise', Durbin replied. 'If, however, we assume a central authority capable of co-ordinating credit and taxation policies a third possibility becomes available' (*Ec*, xiii, 424). Planning was his refuge – a way of producing savings not by increased inequalities in income distribution but by increased taxation. Hobson's underconsumptionist argument for broadly the same policy left him as unpersuaded as ever. It is important to note that the vogue for planning, especially in Labour circles, had no essential connexion with the policy of demand management towards which Keynes's ideas were pointing; though, to be sure, in Hobson's formulation there was a more obvious compatibility. From the time that G. D. H. Cole opted for reformism in the late 1920s, his emphasis was much more strongly upon the institutional changes associated with planning than upon considerations of aggregate demand and growth.

In the 1930s Keynes and Hobson drew closer together personally and ideologically: but not, despite efforts on both sides, scientifically. They were agreed in pointing to over-saving as the root difficulty. But for Hobson over-saving manifested itself as excess real capital or, equally, was 'testified by the amount of idle capital on deposit' (*Ec*, xiii, 410). In private correspondence in 1931 Keynes referred Hobson to the Banana Parable in the *Treatise* to indicate how excess saving entailed a transfer of wealth from producers to savers; and argued that this in turn caused production to be cut back, resulting in unemployment and lower incomes all round. At the new, lower level of national income the excess savings were indeed absorbed – they did not lie idle in banks; but neither did they create new capital, merely made good the losses that had been incurred. Hobson sent Keynes some 'Notes on Oversaving' in August 1931 which avoided speaking of idle balances and pointed to the failure of consumption to keep pace with production. Keynes replied that 'this exposition of your point of view brings us much nearer together' but insisted that Hobson was only outlining one case. 'You are pointing to the exit of diminished savings as a remedy for the situation you are contemplating', he noted. 'But I suggest to you that there is also another way out besides the way of increased consumption, namely through a fall in the rate of interest' (*JMK*, xiii, 332–3). For a lower interest rate would make investment profitable, absorbing the extra savings in that way.

In the *Treatise* a lower interest rate was Keynes's theoretical prescription for increasing investment; but of course in *Can Lloyd George Do It?* the emphasis had been upon public works. The issue could be resolved by stating that public works were a special case for a country unable, for exchange rate reasons, to reduce interest rates sufficiently; and after Britain went off the Gold Standard in 1931 Keynes accordingly ceased for the time being to advocate public works. By this time, however, his mind was turning in a new direction, partly under the stimulus of the 'circus' of younger economists at Cambridge with whom he was arguing out his theory. Richard Kahn, his most constructive critic here, had published his seminal article on the effect of public works upon secondary employment in 1931. This took up the hints about the cumulative nature of economic recovery in *Can Lloyd George Do It?* and made them into an analytical tool with a real cutting edge. In Keynes's hands this became 'The Multiplier', the title he gave to an article in the *New Statesman* for 1 April 1933.

He was by now thinking of aggregate effective demand as the determinant of the level of economic activity. Insights which he had previously expressed in terms of monetary theory were now refomulated as applying to levels of output. In particular, he came to recognise that a money economy behaved in a different way from a barter economy, and that attitudes towards the choice between holding money or other assets were crucial to investment. The interest rate in fact measured liquidity preference; it was the price of money; and thus it would not continue to fall until it reached zero, because at a certain level savers would prefer the liquidity of money to low-yield assets. But it could not be assumed, even at this level of interest, that investment would prove sufficiently attractive to employ all unused resources, including labour. The important conclusion followed that the economy might be in equilibrium at less than full employment.

This system of ideas, at which Keynes had arrived by 1933, gave a full theoretical rejoinder to the Treasury View. Output and employment were now at the centre of the picture, and their management required a state responsibility for investment which went far beyond a cheap money policy or the 'special case' argument for public works in 1929. *The General Theory of Employment, Interest and Money* (1936), however, was more than a neat theoretical modification of the prevailing orthodoxy. It challenged the finality of existing theories by insisting upon uncertainty as the subject-matter of economics. It was 'the existence of *uncertainty* as to the future of the rate of interest' which accounted for liquidity preference (p. 168). Instead of the abstraction of economic man, with clear motives and perfect foresight, there stood the social psychology of a particular society moving through time and forming expectations from necessarily insufficient data.

In the *Treatise* Keynes had defined saving and investment in such a way as to show that they might not be equal. This was a useful polemical point. It led, however, to the sort of misunderstanding of which Hobson was guilty: that idle balances were the trouble. Moreover, it created suspicion among economists that Keynes's argument depended upon a peculiar definition. In the *General Theory* Keynes therefore held to a book-keeping identity of savings and investment. But in a disequilibrium situation some 'investment' would be in the form of unwanted stocks or other losses. If the propensity to save remained constant, then in order to produce an equilibrium situation the national income would fall – and at the new, reduced level actual and desired savings would indeed be equal in volume, though absolutely smaller. (This equilibrium situation would hardly be one of full employment.) This situation could be remedied either by increased consumption or by increased investment. Keynes, of course, preferred investment as a means of increasing the national income, through the multiplier, in a dynamic way.

In the *General Theory* Keynes identified 'the root of Hobson's mistake' in his supposition that excessive saving caused the actual overproduction of capital (p. 367); whereas he should instead have explained 'that a relatively weak propensity to consume helps to cause unemployment by requiring and *not* receiving the accompaniment of a compensating volume of new investment' (p. 370). In short, if the community was not willing to invest the amount that people desired to save, their attempted over-saving would prove self-defeating; and the community would become impoverished until the amounts it desired to save and was willing to invest were commensurate. Savings could not 'lie uninvested', as Hobson was still maintaining in 1937 (*Property & Impropery*, p. 48). In his autobiography Hobson reiterated that some savings 'lie idle in banks', in order to explain the imbalance (*Conf.*, p. 193n.). 'Mr J. M. Keynes, though not in full agreement with my analysis, has paid a handsome tribute to my early form of the over-saving heresy', he commented (*Conf.*, p. 194). The *General Theory* had indeed rescued the analysis of *The Physiology of Industry* from oblivion and hailed its publication as 'an epoch in economic thought' (p. 365). Its insight that consumption limited production and not production consumption was singled out as putting 'one half of the matter, as it seems to me, with absolute precision' (p. 368).

Much of Hobson's subsequent fame derived from this tribute. If Keynes himself admitted so much, did it not seem plausible that Hobson's famous heresy was the real beginnings of the subsequent revolution in economic thought? Stanley Unwin, for example, in writing of Hobson, was at pains 'to point out that he anticipated Keynes, who in the great depression of the nineteen-thirties arrived at similar views'.[24] Now it is a wholesome thing to have the loyalty of one's publisher; but a wider doubt is raised as to the source of this distortion. In fact, in Unwin's case as in others, this opinion was pretty clearly accepted on the authority of Cole. Cole's warm welcome of the *General Theory* was spiced with the reflection that it 'pushes at one blow off their pedestals all the classical deities from Ricardo to Wicksell, and all their attendant self-canonised sprites from Vienna and the London School, and puts in their vacant places not indeed Marx, but Mr J. A. Hobson and the late Silvio Gesell' (*NS*, 15 February 1936). Two years later Cole was – justifiably enough – pointing to the fact that, after Hobson had been cold-shouldered for years, 'of late Mr Keynes and some others have recognised that there is a large element of truth in his specifically economic doctrines, as well as in his general humanistic approach' (*PQ*, ix, 439). On Hobson's death Cole wrote a highly sympathetic appraisal of him in the *Economic Journal* itself, again indicating that the *General Theory* 'paid belated tribute to his work' on underconsumption (*EcJ*, l, 353). It was, however, on the centenary of Hobson's birth that Cole advanced the full claim. 'Hobson, in effect, anticipated Keynes by more than forty years in

[24] *The Truth about a Publisher* (1960), p. 187.

stating the essentials of the doctrine of full employment', he wrote (*NS*, 5 July 1958). The extent of this had allegedly not been apparent at the time of the *General Theory*. 'For me at any rate,' Cole concluded, 'what is commonly known as the Keynesian was much more the Hobsonian revolution in economic and social thought' (ibid.).

Cole had many good reasons to admire Hobson, whose outlook he largely shared. Precisely because of this, however, he failed to appreciate the full novelty of Keynes's approach, as is seen in his response to the Lloyd George programme in 1929 and his insistence that planning was the real alternative in the 1930s. If Cole's claims were exaggerated, therefore, why did Keynes himself give them so much leverage? It was Keynes, after all, as editor of the *Economic Journal*, who commissioned Hobson's obituary notice and suggested its tone. He had, in fact, approached Hammond first, admitting that 'The *Journal* in past days, and I myself personally I am afraid, did so little justice to J.A.'s work that I am anxious to have a really good notice now' (9 April 1940). Yet now that the full story of the composition of the *General Theory* is in print, it is clearly apparent that the theoretical discussions of Keynes and his most helpful critics – Kahn, Roy Harrod, Joan Robinson – owed nothing to Hobson. His name, indeed, was chiefly invoked as a code-word for fallacious objections to marginalist analysis – 'he is being Hobson about spades', Joan Robinson wrote on one occasion (*JMK*, xiv, 613). The chapter in the *General Theory* dealing with Hobson (and other underconsumptionists) was only added at a late stage, and met Harrod's objection as 'a tendentious attempt to glorify imbeciles' (ibid., p. 650). Admittedly, Harrod was later kinder in his references to Hobson, and was in any case overruled by Joan Robinson, whose influence generally gave the work a more left-wing tone. But it is still curious that the one work of Hobson's singled out for commendation was by now nearly fifty years old and had been written in collaboration.

The explanation is surely not that Keynes in fact derived any appreciable help from Hobsonian theory, which was on a different tack, but that by 1935 he felt a warm sympathy for an old man whose ideological position was so close to his own. 'Thanks very much for taking so much trouble about the Mummery', he wrote to Kahn. 'Hobson never fully understood him and went off on a side-track after his death. But the book Hobson helped him to write, *The Physiology of Industry*, is a wonderful work. I am giving a full account of it but old Hobson has had so much injustice done to him that I shan't say what I think about M's contribution to it being, probably, outstanding' (*JMK*, xiv, 634).

Once the *General Theory* had been published, it validated Hobson's approach. Its argument led 'towards the conclusion that in contemporary conditions the growth of wealth, so far from being dependent on the abstinence of the rich, as is commonly supposed, is more likely to be impeded by it' (p. 373). The Keynesian implication was that investment should be stimulated, either privately or publicly. But the Hobsonian implication that inequality should be eroded through redistributive taxation found ample support. The reception of Keynesian economics by the Labour party was very much a question of using new arguments to support policies which had always had an obvious appeal. It was Keynes with a Hobsonian twist. This version had a verisimilitude which remedied the scientific deficiencies of Hobson's analysis and the ideological deficiencies of Keynes's. In *The Socialist Case* (1937) Douglas Jay cited Keynes's authority for the inference 'that there is a strong general presumption in favour of maintaining effective demand by increasing consumption rather than investment'. And he concluded that 'the central contention of Mr J. A. Hobson, vaguely expressed but consistently felt by most socialists to be correct, has a substantial measure of truth' (p. 208). Jay, like Durbin and Gaitskell, who helped him with the book, put the emphasis upon planning; and it was through this door that Durbin came to accept from Keynes an economic outlook which he had mocked as a golden cure for poverty when offered by Hobson. In *The Politics of Democratic Socialism* (1940) he made Keynesian 'prosperity measures' part of his four-fold path of reform.

To Keynes himself, it seemed that the leaders of the Labour party were blinkered by dogma in not seeing that they might mobilise wide support for their practicable programme. 'Why cannot they face the fact that they are not sectaries of an outworn creed mumbling moss-grown demi-semi Fabian Marxism, but the heirs of eternal liberalism?' he demanded in a dialogue with Kingsley Martin (*NS*, 28 January 1939). The question was one of moving 'out of the nineteenth-century *laisser faire* state into an era of liberal socialism', of which, on his expansive definition, there were by now many potential champions, including Winston Churchill and Herbert Morrison. Indeed, Keynes found 'no one in politics to-day worth sixpence outside the ranks of liberals except the post-war generation of intellectual Communists under thirty-five' – a suggestive exception since he affirmed that 'with them in their ultimate maturity lies the future' (ibid.). It was both fitting and significant, therefore, that Keynesian economics should offer a path back to reformism for disillusioned young Marxists. John Strachey's *A Programme for Progress* (1940) was the fruit of his reading of Keynes plus the impact of the Nazi–Soviet pact in 1939. It was reviewed in the *New Statesman* under the patronising title 'A Social Democrat'. In a letter to Gaitskell in 1954, Strachey recalled that after 1931 he had come to believe that democratic socialist governments were doomed to impotence: 'Keynes and your own group – Douglas [Jay], Evan Durbin and yourself, and the experience of the New Deal, had converted me by 1940 to the view, which I put forward in a book called *Programme for Progress*, that a way through did exist' (Thomas, p. 273).

Hobson remained resilient and sardonic to the end. He was hopeful that the advance of fascism in Europe would clarify the atmosphere so as to unify a popular front against it. At meetings of the U.D.C. he would survey the accounts and conclude that the organisation was likely to be poor enough to survive until the next war. He was much moved by the testimonial which the U.D.C. presented him on his eightieth birthday. 'Twenty years have taught us practically nothing in the base art of politics', he blandly told Ponsonby (26 September 1938). But he could now get around very little. Hammond did not see him again after the outbreak of war in September 1939, and that winter he became too feeble to go to the Reform Club. He died in April 1940. 'I was relieved to see Hobson's death,' Hammond wrote to Murray, 'for though he had kept his mental vigour in a wonderful way, he was beginning to fail I think' (2 April 1940). His life had hung by a thread for fifty years but he had outlived nearly all his more robust contemporaries, and outwritten them too, as his astonishing list of published books testifies. By the time the author of *Imperialism* died, the outbreak of the South African war was half a long lifetime away; and, in a pleasing paradox, his heretical views were beginning to find acceptance as the new conventional wisdom of another generation. When Smuts heard the news about Hobson – 'there was a good man for you' – he reflected: 'Our circle is rapidly contracting, and soon the rest will be gone too' (*Smuts*, vi, doc. 492).

Epilogue

Sans everything

Gilbert Murray emerged from the First World War an Asquithian Liberal, and such he remained; but, more important, his outlook was now governed by an overriding commitment to the League of Nations as the means of preventing war. He wrote later that he and Hammond 'were in two senses "deviationists" from the true Morley–Hirst tradition': meaning that while Hammond's active concern for welfare challenged Cobdenite Liberalism at home, his own constructive pursuit of peace challenged it abroad.[1] In this, of course, he was asserting instead the Gladstonian standard. Hammond made this claim specific. If the Treaty of Versailles had inflicted injustices upon Germany, as all progressives believed, then the situation must be redressed. Appeasement, in this sense, was a policy of magnanimity to be carried out from a position of strength, and involved finding a means of redressing Germany's legitimate grievances. This did not involve siding with Germany against France. Hammond's favourite proposal in the early 1930s was to transfer one of the colonial mandates to Germany on the ground that this would remove an obvious cause of war. 'The whole position seems so gloomy,' he told Murray, 'that I feel it is especially the moment for a Gladstonian gesture' (26 August 1931). Murray, it must be said, remained unpersuaded that this was the right Gladstonian gesture.

The National Government, however, failed to match this sort of mood altogether, and its supposedly Liberal members seemed particularly culpable. Sir John Simon had once been a fellow contributor to *Essays in Liberalism*, but Hammond now agreed with Toynbee that he was 'the worst Foreign Minister we have had',[2] and in the 1935 General Election sent a letter of support to his Labour opponent in the Spen Valley division. Hammond was still toying with the idea of a colonial concession in Africa, though by this time he was ready to accept Brailsford's suggestion that, instead of transferring mandates, all non-governing peoples should be put directly under the League of Nations. Murray clearly thought that this was taking internationalism rather too far, or at least too fast, and cautioned him 'to remember that a League civil service will have to have its due proportion of Roumanians, South Americans, etc., who will not be very good material' (24 September 1935). Taking up with the League evidently did not entail

[1] F. W. *Hirst*, by his friends (1958), p. 3.
[2] Hammond to Mary Murray, 22 February 1933, MP 23a.

laying down the white man's burden. And with things as they stood, the League's function of resisting aggression would in fact protect the already satisfied colonial powers: a reflection which made it easier to respond to the moral appeal for collective resistance against Mussolini's Abyssinian campaign. As Toynbee wrote to Hammond, 'isn't it curious to see the internationalists saving the British Empire while the Imperialists are on the run?' (1 September 1935).

In 1932 Hammond agreed with the Gladstone family to undertake a major historical study for which he was to be given £1000 and free access to all papers in their possession. Hammond's work on Gladstone progressed while the international situation worsened throughout the 1930s. As his contribution to *Essays in Honour of Gilbert Murray* (1936) he presented an interim report on 'Gladstone and the League of Nations Mind'. This was Hammond's term for Gladstone's fundamentally European outlook upon international politics – a European sense, he maintained, which was rooted in his view of classical antiquity. Gladstone's fruitful misunderstanding of Homer had led him to fuse a Greek conception of politics with Christian theology; the result was a conception of Europe as a moral community with a heart and mind and conscience. Hammond argued that 'if to-day the wise men of our age could summon to Geneva one giant from the Dead, will any doubt that the world would hear again that noble thunder echoing down the Christian ages from the windswept Plain of Troy?' (p. 118)

Failing Gladstone's reappearance at Geneva, the League of Nations revealed its mortal frailty. Hammond later wrote ruefully that 'most of us thought of it as a self-acting mechanism, forgetting that its efficiency depended on the power behind it' (*L*, 13 February 1947). But the hazy ideal of a foreign policy based upon international morality and collective security continued to set progressives against the National Government. With the rise of fascism and the growing strength of Germany, the word appeasement exchanged its Gladstonian overtones for those of cynicism, *realpolitik* and dishonour. Opposition to the foreign policy of the Chamberlain Government produced a sort of shadow popular front in which liberal intellectuals like Hammond found a natural place. He supported the critical line taken by the *Manchester Guardian*. He welcomed Churchill's warnings about the 'non-God religions' of communism and fascism, and he argued that there was no hope of Great Britain standing aside by taking a purely self-regarding line. 'This is a policy of despair, and of stupid despair', he commented. 'There is no reason to expect that the ruin of Europe will leave us intact' (*MG*, 10 December 1936). He insisted that foreign policy could not be conducted on short-sighted and insular considerations. Hitler and Mussolini, he suggested, would rule Europe by putting its mind into a prison, and he concluded that 'the life of the English mind is not a separate thing quite apart from the life of the mind of Europe; it lives and develops in the medium of this larger world' (*MG*, 21 March 1938). Looking at the present state of British politics, he therefore bemoaned 'an unnatural and arbitrary distribution of political strength, the result partly of the organisation and perpetuation of the National Government, partly of a false condition of politics of which the National Government was itself a consequence' (*MG*, 29 April 1938).

By 1933, the year Hitler came to power, both the Hammonds were sixty. Lawrence wrote to Mary Murray that 'if public events go so wrong, men and women passing into old age have no consolation for the sorrows that are inevitable. What makes old age so grey I think is that friend after friend goes and the whole background of life is saddened. At present I feel that sensitive people suffer from the success of man in prolonging life. After 60, or in some cases before for most people there is more unhappiness than happiness in life' (4 February 1933). He had only just suffered the blow of Galsworthy's death, following closely on that of another old friend, Vaughan Nash. Moreover, the mental instability of his brother Nicholas had for a long time cast a dark cloud over the Hammonds' lives; and his suicide in May 1933 was a further setback. Barbara Hammond's health was no longer a problem but Lawrence's now became critical. Sciatica in 1935 was followed by an alarming breakdown the next year. This may have been misleadingly diagnosed at the time; at any rate, early in 1937 he had a serious heart attack which caused his whole way of life to be modified. He had to spend a good part of every day on the sofa and there were spells when he could not work at all. With his family's history of debilitating decline, he confided to Murray his feeling that death was 'much less to be dreaded than the perils of old age' (7 March 1937).

Under these conditions Hammond restricted all outside activities; he even refused to write the preface for Wallas's posthumously collected essays; and with Barbara's help he set himself the single task of finishing his book on Gladstone. *Gladstone and the Irish Nation* (1938) was intended as Hammond's masterpiece. A long and thorough treatment, it drew upon years of research and a lifetime's interest. It was, of course, a vindication of Gladstone. It cited a mass of unpublished evidence, including Gladstone's diary, to acquit him of the cruder charges of self-serving, which had been current in Unionist circles since the 1880s and to which Lady Gwendolen Cecil's Life of her father had recently lent colour. Hammond had little difficulty in showing that Gladstone did not put forward Home Rule as a ploy to capture the Irish vote. 'It is safe to say,' he concluded, 'that if everything Gladstone wrote between July and December 1885 on the Irish Question had been published at the time, no suspicion could have fallen on his motives or his conduct' (p. 426). Now it may well be that in establishing his point here Hammond exaggerated with hindsight the consistency of

Gladstone's views upon Ireland, and likewise that he failed to do justice to the tactical considerations in which the problem was necessarily enmeshed. Recent historical work has seized upon these neglected possibilities, and, read in conjunction with Hammond's account, this undoubtedly adds a further analytical dimension to the story. Even in 750 pages, Gladstone's full complexity and ambiguity defied Hammond's attempt at a definitive assessment.

Gladstone and the Irish Nation, however, stands unsurpassed as the basis for a historical understanding of his career. The most fruitful subsequent studies of Victorian Liberalism have developed insights originally offered by Hammond. He had for years been fascinated by the paradox that the pressing social problems of the nineteenth century, on which he himself had written with so much knowledge and passion, had been regarded by contemporaries with a mixture of ignorance and unconcern; whereas Victorian politics reached fever pitch over issues remote from the interests of the ordinary citizen. 'In the England of the fifties,' he suggested, 'parliamentary politics supplied excitement for the imagination to a people ill supplied with theatres, music, amenities, or amusements' (*PQ*, ii, 239). In the years of Gladstone's prime, politics were conducted as a public spectacle, enlisting the combative or generous instincts of the working-class voters who had recently been admitted to the system. Gladstone found that his peculiar views forged a direct link between his outlook and that of the poor, bypassing the habits of mind of the educated and upper classes. It was 'Christianity as a spiritual power, a bond between men and nations, a great principle to which all reasons of empire and state must give way, in other words, Christianity in all those espects for which it hardly existed in the politics of the upper classes', which gave Gladstone, with his incomprehensible theology, nonetheless a common ground with 'the Miners' Leaders, who were trade union secretaries in the week and local preachers on the Sunday' (pp. 549–50). Gladstone flattered their self-esteem by asking them to contribute to the moral judgment of the world on great events; he in turn concluded 'that the common people had a sense of justice which wealth and power had corrupted in the governing classes' (p. 728). Finding his power as a great orator, he drew up strength from the people, who gazed upon him as upon a god, and he accepted with equanimity his isolation among his own class. 'Gladstone,' Hammond wrote, 'became the greatest popular leader of his age, though he never mastered or seriously studied great social problems on which their comfort largely depended, because he offered the working classes something that satisfied their self-respect' (p. 706). Tawney told Hammond that it was only after reading his book that he realised 'how great Gladstone was' and felt that he 'understood the adoration accorded him' (1 April 1943).

In the Home Rule crisis Gladstone found his spirit of European sympathy resisted by the narrow spirit of national pride, represented in the ruling class by Salisbury, and in the new business class by Chamberlain. In pitching his appeal instead to the working class, he united British democratic sentiment with Irish popular feeling (and even went some way towards promoting labour issues on the analogy with Irish coercion). Home Rule had in fact shown that only democratic forces could be relied upon to press home the fundamental issue. 'For Gladstone saw in the world on one side power, force, and violence, all the influences that divided mankind. He saw on the other the movement towards the moral unity of the world, based on mutual respect between peoples' (p. 541). Thus in the last twenty years of his life 'politics took more and more the character of a struggle between the spirit of empire and the spirit of justice' (p. 739). Chamberlain personified one; Gladstone the other.

The publication of *Gladstone and the Irish Nation* coincided almost exactly with the Munich agreement in the autumn of 1938. The appeals which had left Joseph Chamberlain cold in the 1880s had evidently not moved Neville Chamberlain either. Munich seemed to Hammond 'the greatest surrender any British Government had made for a century and a half' (*MG*, 16 May 1939). The betrayal of the Czechs gave him lasting pain. He told Murray that it was 'the insensibility of N.C. that fills one with despair' (4 March 1939). To be sure, it might be one thing to accept Munich as a disagreeable necessity. But five months later, when Prague lay open to German invasion, Chamberlain was still defending the merits of the agreement. Murray publicly alleged that 'when a large part, and perhaps the most thoughtful part, of the nation is daily and hourly harassed by thoughts of the hideous suffering inflicted on millions of innocent human beings, and the monstrous crimes against humanity which are daily being perpetrated with success, the Prime Minister somehow leaves the impression – no doubt an unjustified impression – of being entirely indifferent to such issues' (*Times*, 4 March 1939). Hammond agreed wholeheartedly. 'It must have been a shock to some who praised him for having the courage to do the dirty work of the world, under pressure of a dreadful alternative, to find that he did not know it was dirty', he commented to Murray. 'I remember Herbert Paul saying at a very foul moment in the Boer War "I wd rather be a Hottentot than an Englishman at this moment". N.C. is driving all decent minded people to feel like that' (4 March 1939). Had he known of the Prime Minister's own opinion at this moment, that he 'ought to be good for at least one more Parliament after this to exasperate and infuriate the *Gilbert Murrays* of this world',[3] it would hardly have cheered him. Moreover, Munich must have played some part in overshadowing the publication of his book, which proved a bitter disappointment. Fewer than five hundred copies were sold before the war broke out. This was roughly

[3] Quoted in Maurice Cowling, *The Impact of Hitler* (Cambridge 1975), p. 294.

what the publishers had expected, and they had priced it accordingly at 36 shillings; but to the author, of course, it looked as though the price had killed the book. It took until 1946 to sell the edition of a thousand (apart from about 80 copies which perished in the blitz).

In little more than twelve months, from the spring of 1939 on, the power of the National Government crumbled and then collapsed; and instead the motley crew of anti-appeasers established its ascendancy. Churchill had written to his son as early as November 1936: 'All the left wing intelligentsia are coming to look to me for protection, and I will give it whole heartedly in return for their aid in the rearmament of Britain.'[4] By the summer of 1939 there was a flood of calls for his return to power as an earnest of the Government's determination to resist aggression: a view which united dissident Conservatives with the bulk of Liberal and Labour opinion. With war perceptibly near in August 1939, Hammond wrote to Crozier volunteering his services to the *Manchester Guardian*, and his offer was swiftly accepted. Despite their age and infirmities the Hammonds moved to Manchester for the duration of the war. It was an unpalatable existence; they missed Oatfield; they found the gloom of Manchester depressing; but the remarkable thing was how well their health stood up to these strenuous conditions. Lawrence Hammond felt happy that he was able to play a full part as a leader writer. The issues he had to face touched his deepest commitments and many of his articles were reprinted in the volume *Faith in France* (1946).

When the Churchill Coalition was formed in May 1940 it gave progressivism a central political role which it had lacked since 1914. Hammond wrote of 'a summons...such as no man living can remember to our spirit, our courage, our tenacity, our self-discipline and self-sacrifice' (*Faith in France*, p. 18). The people's war brought a people's government in which ordinary Labour and good Liberals were the ascendant elements. Churchill evoked nostalgic memories of the Edwardian period by obligingly shedding his inter-war role as class warrior and coming forward instead as a populist orator of Gladstonian proportions. Anti-appeasement was the dominant myth; it helped displace the Guilty Men of Munich; and it prepared the ground for the overthrow of the Chamberlain consensus in domestic policy too. Keynes suddenly moved to a pivotal position inside the Treasury. Labour's patriotic response to the common cause was symbolised by the massive presence of Ernest Bevin as Minister of Labour.

War socialism has been aptly defined by A. J. P. Taylor as socialism with the difficulties left out. It was just the sort of socialism which progressive intellectuals had always favoured. The change of heart manifested by the Dunkirk spirit sanctioned far-reaching but conflictless social change. The *Manchester Guardian*, in Hammond's unmistakeable tones, declared

[4] Martin Gilbert, *Winston S. Churchill*, v (1976), p. 800.

that 'in opposing Hitler we must call upon the feeling for liberty and human right all over the world and make ourselves its champion as much as France made herself the champion of equality in 1792'. There could be no going back to 1939 but instead 'make up our minds for great changes in our own society' (*MG*, 3 October 1940). Left-wing aspirations for the social revolution may have proved too high-flown. George Orwell acknowledged in April 1941 that 'I see how my political predictions have been falsified, and yet, as it were, the revolutionary changes that I expected *are* happening, but in slow motion.'[5] But the social revolution in slow motion had more to commend it to elderly liberals – it was the sort of revolution in which they could play a dignified role. Lady Mary Murray, at rising eighty, would resolutely refuse to be put forward in the queue at the Oxford Co-op. Everyone could do their bit.

There were, of course, limits beyond which egalitarianism could hardly be pushed. Some Liberals looked back regretfully at the world they had lost. When Harold Nicolson had dinner in Trinity College, Cambridge, in January 1941 he sat next to the Master, G. M. Trevelyan. He recorded looking round 'upon the mahogany and silver; upon the Madeira and the port, upon the old butler with his stately efficiency. "It is much the same", I say to him. "Civilisation", he replies, "is always recognisable".'[6] Beatrice Webb, looking forward at eighty-three to a new civilisation, also found material compensations in the present. She confided to the Hammonds that she was 'very exhausted from having written the 36-page Introduction to the 3rd edition of our *Soviet Communism* on the thesis that Stalin is not a Dictator and that the U.S.S.R. is a Political and Industrial Democracy' (10 July 1941). But there was also the consideration, as she told Shaw, that the reissure of this prophetic text would 'bring in quite a nice little sum of money and enable us to go on living here in comfort for the duration of the war' (19 March 1942).

Russia played a decisive role in the alliance against Germany. Hammond acknowledged to Murray that Stalin had 'created an Army that has saved us all' (22 February 1943), and he was ready to concede it full honour, not least as a means of winning Russian confidence for the peace settlement. His deepseated mistrust of Germany was usually expressed in Francophile terms. 'If mistakes or misfortunes should estrange Britain and France,' he wrote in 1944, 'history will repeat itself, Germany will recover her power for mischief, post-war Europe will be fatally weakened, and a third war will be almost certain' (*Faith in France*, p. 211). But this took him a long way towards understanding Russia. Although he wrote of a France 'ready to take her part in the defence of the West' (ibid., p. 195), he envisaged

[5] Diary, 13 April 1941, *The Collected Essays, Journalism and Letters of George Orwell*, ed. Sonia Orwell and Ian Angus (1968; Penguin 1970), ii, item 57.
[6] Harold Nicolson, *Diaries and Letters 1939–45*, ed. Nigel Nicolson (1967), p. 140.

Germany as the abiding threat. He told Murray that he was terrified 'that we shall let Germany revive as a Power from fear of Russia', rather as fear of France had misguidedly permitted Germany's resurgence after Versailles (3 May 1944). The German temper was the real danger, as it had been in 1914; attempts to extenuate it struck him as misconceived. He summed up ominously to Murray: 'You and we have survived into a queer England' (3 May 1944).

Yet they ought not to have found it so queer. By the time the war in Europe ended in 1945, the views which they had spent a lifetime propagating had found an unprecedentedly widespread acceptance. The spirit of justice had apparently triumphed over the spirit of empire, and international relations were in future to be based upon the United Nations Organisation. The war had brought higher living standards for the working class, and full employment was to be maintained by abandoning the mechanism of the free market in favour of Keynesian techniques for managing the economy. Moreover a Hobsonian process of redistribution was at work. The war had seen the imposition of direct taxation with a steeply progressive rake – the liberal version of from each according to his abilities. And social welfare was to be guaranteed through comprehensive social insurance as outlined by the Beveridge Report – the liberal version of to each according to his needs. The new consensus was stamped with popular approval when Labour won a general election outright for the first time in July 1945. Social democracy had arrived under liberal auspices. It has often been remarked that the work of the Attlee Government turned the hopeful proposals of men like Hobson, Hobhouse and Wallas into concrete achievements. But they were dead by then. It was the Hammonds and the Murrays who were privileged to survive into the new world. As *The Times* obituary of Hammond put it: 'Like other late Victorian Liberals, he lived to see many of his ideals realized' (9 April 1949).

The Hammonds returned to Oatfield from their Manchester exile during the three-week interval after polling day in 1945 while the votes were being counted. They voted Liberal in Manchester, and for Cole as Labour candidate for Oxford University. Everyone on the *Manchester Guardian* apparently expected a repeat of the 1935 result, or even another 1931. The landslide victory of the Labour party, and the virtual elimination of the Liberals, came as a stunning shock. A two-party result of this sort, Murray argued to Hammond, showed 'that the present division is quite a wrong one. Socialist v. anti-Socialist is unreal; working class v. middle and upper is disastrous' (27 July 1945). This led him to think that 'there will be more re-shuffling before we settle down. The Left Wing of Labour is practically totalitarian, and that may produce new splits' (31 July 1945). In reply, Hammond conceded that this was an interesting point – 'I suppose Cripps and Laski are both totalitarian *au fond*' – and revealed his anxiety that 'the pressure on the Govt to reduce armaments and drop conscription and let down the New L. of N. will be very strong' (1 August 1945). Hammond's interest, in fact, largely centred on foreign affairs in the post-war years. He remained deeply hostile to Germany, warmly sympathetic to France, warily sympathetic to America, and watchful of Russia.

The Murrays found it rather a strain as octogenarians in an age of austerity. 'The sufferings of the world weigh upon us less than the absence of servants', Gilbert wrote to Barbara Hammond (19 June 1946). He strongly approved of Hammond's project for a short life of Gladstone, whose current low standing he attributed partly to the Labour wish to denigrate Liberalism. Hammond wanted to compensate for the disappointment of his *magnum opus* and to bring the Gladstonian message home in a final effort. In the centenary volume *C. P. Scott* (1946) Hammond had argued that it was 'too soon to assert that the Liberal Party has dropped out of the race as an independent party and that the "Progressive movement" of the future has to be sought either in Labour with a faint Liberal fringe or in a liberalised Conservatism' (p. 239). Later in the year, however, he confessed to Murray: 'I hope that Liberal ideas will grow in influence but I dont think the Liberal party will' (18 December 1946). 'What is wanted,' he explained, 'is a Labour leader who can do in this crisis with the Labour public what Winston did so successfully with the ordinary man in the war' (11 February 1947). But Bevin, the chief contender as a plebeian Gladstone, was too immersed in foreign affairs. 'We have to prove to the world that we can provide full employment and a decent standard of life while keeping our liberties', Hammond maintained. As part of the necessary readjustment of ideas, the workers would 'have to get rid of the fears and inhibitions bred in the days when they were exploited, and adjust themselves to the responsibilities of power' in order to raise production (*L*, 6 March 1947).

Hammond confided to Murray that with his low vitality, he was 'at heart defeatist' (24 August 1947). 'There are very few people now to whom the Jameson Raid means anything', he recorded sadly (12 January 1948). When the Hammonds sent Trevelyan the new edition of *The Bleak Age*, he wrote back that 'an age that has no culture except American films and Football pools is in some respects bleaker than the one you tell of. The advent of real democracy coinciding in time with 2 World Wars has done the business – cooked the goose of civilization' (5 November 1947). Murray likewise admitted to them that 'I find myself growing "conservative", in the sense that I am terribly anxious to preserve civilization and Liberality' (10 January 1948). Pondering the fundamental conservatism of Gladstone, which he discussed with Hammond, reinforced Murray in this conviction. 'Indeed,' he wrote, 'I should say now that our main purpose ought to be conservative – i.e. the preservation of civilisation. Odd that the cons. Party does not emphasize it' (16 March 1949). To the end Hammond put the problem in a more progressive light. The challenge to the western peoples, he maintained, consisted in matching the Communist lessons about common culture and social equality without falling into the political tyranny and degraded view of human rights prevalent in Russia. Here lay the abiding task of liberalism. 'Even in the western societies,' he noted, 'there are some who accept the Russian philosophy and condone or approve, in the name of Communism, methods and ideas that would have been revolting to Jaurès in France and to William Morris' (*L*, 30 September 1948). He emphatically reaffirmed the values of empiricism, tolerance and forbearance.

Hammond was by now old and frail, forced by his angina to go to bed at 8.30 p.m. The very slow work on his book, eventually published as *Gladstone and Liberalism* (1952), drove him to despair. 'I doubt whether I shall ever finish it', he told Murray (23 July 1948), adding some months later that while he had been 'quite happy writing on his Irish policy', where Gladstone had 'a superb record', there now appeared 'a great many buts when one follows his career closely' (13 March 1949). Hammond left the book barely more than half written when he died in April 1949, aged seventy-six. 'In his generation,' Brailsford wrote in tribute, 'liberal humanism inspired a notable group of men, as disinterested as they were able. Though Nevinson and John A. Hobson were among them, there was none who surpassed Hammond in courage, humanity and creative skill' (*NS*, 16 April 1949). The *Daily Worker* obituary commented that it was 'remarkable and regrettable' that he never became a socialist (11 April 1949). Hamilton Fyfe contributed an article, 'Almost the Last', to *Tribune*: 'They are nearly all gone, that band of brothers-in-arms who, some fifty years ago, joined in a crusade against cruelty, stupidity, individual intolerance and national complacency. Henry Nevinson, J. A. Hobson, H. W. Massingham, A. G. Gardiner, E. D. Morel, Graham Wallas – what do these names mean to the generation of to-day?' (6 May 1949)

The Webbs were also dead by now but their memory was better protected by the dominant Fabian hagiography over which the still spritely Shaw presided. When *Our Partnership* was published in 1948 Hobhouse was identified in the biographical index as: 'A cousin of Henry Hobhouse and therefore a friend and helper of the Webbs.' It was axiomatic that the Webbs had been the architects of the welfare state. Hirst took a sardonic satisfaction in seeing his warnings against collectivism amply fulfilled by the Labour Government – 'I wonder what the ruffians have done today' (*F. W. Hirst*, p. 38). But Barbara Hammond was now a lonely old woman, reluctant to say 'I told you so' in either a Fabian or a Liberal tone of voice. She drew closer to Gilbert Murray, especially since Mary Murray was now increasingly incapacitated by hardening of the arteries, and the surviving correspondence between them amply conveys the anxieties of their old age.

When 'My Early Beliefs' was posthumously published in 1949, Gilbert Murray wrote that Keynes's 'comment about the thinness of civilisation and the immense degree to which it depends on convention and tradition is one of the things one gradually learns in life. It is one side of the fact that old people turn Conservative; the other side is that their minds get more sluggish and they cannot understand new things' (1 June 1949). His own philosophical conservatism was now finding practical sustenance in the conditions of his life. 'A complaint from the cook makes one tremble, like the threat of a Third World War', he admitted (19 August 1949). A bureaucratic confusion over Barbara Hammond's income tax suddenly took on sinister significance. 'I wonder if this lack of coordination has always gone on,' he mused, 'or whether it is part of the results of the Socialist state' (26 August 1949). Three months later his last pair of servants left. 'Why can't we simply import Chinese or negroes?' asked the great internationalist and erstwhile opponent of Chinese labour in the Transvaal (25 November 1949). With the General Election of 1950 approaching, Murray revealed that he would vote Conservative. 'The Socialists seem to talk such complete mythology, with almost no relation to facts', he explained. 'The Conservatives are decent, but not persuasive, and the poor Liberals are apparently enthusiastic but few in number' (9 February 1950). Both he and Barbara Hammond found the election depressing, with its result a virtual deadheat between Labour and Conservatives, and the Liberals nowhere. Barbara Hammond would 'try & partly succeed in feeling that it is a good situation for reducing the hubris of both other parties' (26 February 1950), but by the end of the year she had lost her equanimity. 'What a nightmare of a world, & how I long for Churchill to be at our head' (1 December 1950).

With the crisis of the Korean War, it seemed to Murray that only a statesman of genius would do. Though president of the United Nations Association, he was forced to admit that 'the preaching of goodwill does not cut much ice' (15 September 1950). Moreover, there hardly seemed to be 'much of a case for an entirely independent Liberal Party; its characteristic policy is to be Peace, Lower cost of living, and U.N. Who will differ?' (26 July 1951) In the 1951 General Election he publicly spoke for the Conservatives, admittedly in a constituency where there was no Liberal candidate. It seemed to him 'that the world is now divided into a Socialist–Revolutionary part and a Conservative–Liberal part', and his only regret was that when Churchill returned to power his first speech suggested 'the jingo side of him rather than the liberal' (27 October 1951). But on reflection he was still sure that 'Winston has given the real lead to Liberal thought in the last few years' (16 December 1951).

The 1951 election was the turning point for Barbara Hammond, who now made up her mind to vote Conservative. She admitted to Gilbert

Murray that a sudden attack of flu had physically prevented her from doing so, but she felt no mental qualms. 'Mary Stocks said to me some days ago, "What ever wld our husbands say if they knew we were going to vote Tory?" I answered that I felt quite certain that Lawrence wld be voting Tory too' (2 November 1951). She felt glumly that an offer to provide an armchair for everyone could have turned the election either way and that Churchill was faced with impossible odds in explaining the realities of the situation. 'After all, Labour has the enormous advantage of having during their term of office put down the mighty from their seats & exalted the humble & meek & redistributed wealth, only unfortunately the humble & meek have turned very nasty in the process & are so much enjoying the sight of the rich being turned empty away that they don't realise that they too may soon be empty, & instead of sitting in armchairs (which I am sure the Communists will gladly offer) will be sent off to Labour Camps' (2 November 1951). In 1952 she felt as much irritation at the mindless acceptance of Labour platitudes by her daily help at Oatfield as she had once felt at the lack of trade-union consciousness in the men who painted it in 1926.

When George VI died, Gilbert Murray reflected on 'what a hold the monarchy now has, and how it keeps the empire together', adding: 'Yet I suppose we were all republicans once as a matter of course' (6 February 1952). He was firmly convinced of 'the fact that our Western or Christian civilization is better than that of Asia or Africa. It is not merely that we prefer it' (29 December 1952). His Easter Day revelation in 1953 was: 'I do think that the poor old British Empire was a mighty fine thing!' The current experiment in self-government in British Guiana rubbed the point home. 'What can you expert if you tell these negroid–Indian–South Americans that they are everybody's equals' (14 October 1953). Considering Toynbee's charge that Western Civilisation had been responsible for the slave trade and the extermination of the Jews, Murray insisted that 'we did repent of the slave trade as the weaker civns. did not, and we did react in horror against the Nazi genocide, whereas the coloured peoples would hardly have bothered about it' (29 November 1954). The dissemination of the hydrogen bomb introduced a further worry. 'If only the Russians and Chinese had a glimmer of what they call "bourgeois morality", or even bourgeois common sense – but that is just what they reject' (23 February 1955).

Things were no better at home than abroad. 'I hate these strikes', Murray declared. 'If only people would spend a few hundred million less on tobacco, drink, gambling and amusements we should lower the cost of living and perhaps save the country from a crash!' (27 December 1953) A holiday in Cyprus, he discovered, meant an air fare of '£100, which puts it beyond the reach of non-unionists' (13 March 1953), and even a hotel in

Dorset now charged 'two guineas a day, only suitable for leading trade-unionists' (22 February 1954). But he and Barbara Hammond did manage to share several companionable summer holidays together. She told him, 'I miss having people to talk to whose ideas on politics are not limited to the question of their own share of the national income' (4 July 1954). With her feeling that 'the poor middle class has been fairly battered about' (11 January 1955), she accepted his opinion that 'the Trade Unions which were an admirable weapon in a class war are a terribly bad instrument for governing a country' (13 January 1955). He was repeatedly 'rather horrified by the strikes. The Trades Unions are really governing the country, and the left elements in the T.U.s governing the rest' (25 April 1955). Where would it stop? 'In order to satisfy the Welfare State must we provide television *plus* a dog & a garden, and if so, what is to happen to any new form of amusement that may be invented?. . .I may be quite senile and stupid, but I can't help thinking that the country, or at least the working classes have got into a sort of trades-union state of mind, and most classes are trained to think only of their own comfort and interest' (29 September 1955).

'In 1950 as in 1914,' Hobhouse once predicted, 'there will be those who lament that the old breed has died out, that the hardy virtues of the fathers have perished, that the poor are coddled, and the sick cured, and the feeble kept alive, while the strong have to bear the burden' (*World in Conflict*, p. 26). But it is hardly likely that he foresaw this lament as arising from his old friends. This is indeed a curious ending to the story of a group of liberals who were, it is argued, also social democrats. Two points, however, need to be made. The first is in extenuation of liberalism. The despairing cries of Gilbert Murray (who was never in fact a social democrat), and the less strident pleas of Barbara Hammond (who was less of one than Lawrence), represent the final position of liberals who had moved appreciably to the right over the years. 'Our mood,' wrote Bertrand Russell of himself and Murray, 'was like that of St Jerome and St Augustine watching the fall of the Roman Empire and the crumbling of a civilization which had seemed as indestructible as granite.'[7] To those who grew up confident in the power of rationalism the world had turned out for forty years to be a disconcerting place. 'Ever since 1914, at almost every crucial moment, the wrong thing has been done', Russell wrote when he reached ninety (*Autobiog.*, iii, 134). This leads to the second point, which is in extenuation of these particular liberals. Murray was ninety in 1955, with a totally invalid wife of the same age. Barbara Hammond was well on in her eighties, living alone and suffering from arthritis. Members of the Victorian bourgeoisie, they had in their prime actively abetted the destruction of its privileges. But this did not make them personally better prepared to face

[7] Gilbert Murray, *An Unfinished Autobiography* (1960), p. 209.

the vicissitudes of the new order, and their infirmities by this time made them vulnerable to its rigours. Gilbert Murray admitted that 'it is an unspeakable comfort to have some little unearned income left' (15 January 1956).

At the end of 1954 he broached the suggestion that Barbara Hammond might at some point wish to join him as his companion. He thought her domestic troubles at Oatfield were 'intolerable, and I don't see how you can bear the expense of having the new couple *plus* somebody to teach them to do their work' (9 March 1955). At home he was comparatively well placed with two daily cooks, though even these were apt to vanish suddenly. 'It really is rather dreadful that a condition of full employment should have such effects', he remarked (13 August 1955). Little wonder that he did 'not really understand the economic and financial problems, now that Keynes has made them so much harder' (1 September 1955) – not least for ninety-year-old professors seeking domestic help. 'I am afraid the truth is that old people have and give a great deal of trouble', he admitted. 'The trouble that hits you most is having to get servants to look after your house' (26 July 1956). He recognised how much better off he was than Barbara Hammond. 'It almost looks as if you ought to move to a more populous place where life is easier (though uglier) and day women more plentiful', he told her. 'How painful it is to be living in the middle of a social revolution!' (3 April 1956)

During Murray's adult life, there was never a period of twenty years without a searing and divisive national crisis in which the Gladstonian principles of international morality, law and public right were put to the test. 1886, 1899, 1914, 1938 could be seen as stepping stones to 1956, when the Conservative government made its ill-fated attempt to defy the United Nations and seize the Suez Canal. 'It seems to me,' Hammond had once told Murray, 'that a politician who talks of the Canal as if it were the Thames had abt as much respect for the L of N and as much capacity for understanding its ideas as Beaverbrook' (13 June 1935). But to the aged president of the United Nations Association the invasion appeared as a 'daring attempt to stop the "anti-West" conspiracy of Nasser's usurpation' (*Sunday Times*, 16 December 1956). The United Nations, he explained, had fallen into the hands of the comparatively uncivilised nations of Asia and Africa, and 'if we continue moving blindly in the same equalitarian direction that is now fashionable, there is a real danger that not merely the British Empire but the whole "Western" or "Christian" civilisation will become of less and less account' (ibid.). The liberal outcry at home, which united all shades of centre and left-wing opinion, did not move him. After Munich he had written scathingly that Neville Chamberlain 'seems to ignore completely that moral idealism which lies near the root of the British character, he pours contempt upon the League of Nations, and when people passionately protest in the streets against this attitude, he imagines – apparently he really does imagine – that they are Communists' (*Times*, 4 March 1939). But after Suez Murray himself wrote: 'The enemies of what we Europeans call "civilisation" have always got a common cry of "Communism" and an extremely powerful leader in Russia' (*S. Times*, 16 December 1956).

The past seemed a better place than the present, let alone the future. Like all pro-Boers at the end of their lives, Murray took to reminiscing about the old South African days. He was trying to write an essay in memory of Hirst. But old men forget. 'Can you remember who the six Liberals were, and was it *Liberalism and the Empire* that we wrote?' (9 November 1955) Murray died in 1957. A couple of years previously Barbara Hammond had told him of her 'curious feeling of taking it for granted that Lawrence is going to turn up soon without any idea about why or when or wherefore' (12 December 1954). As long as she remained at Oatfield she felt that the birds which they had fed together were a bond between herself and Lawrence, whose loss she grieved so keenly. Perhaps it is why she refused to leave. But by 1957 her memory had clouded over, and though she lived on until 1961, she was now oblivious of an alien world in which she no longer wanted any part.

Bibliographical notes

Prologue Original Sin and the Modern State

For my understanding of Marx I am much indebted to Loyd D. Easton and Kurt M. Guddat, *Writings of the Young Marx on Philosophy and Society* (New York 1967); Shlomo Avineri, *The Social and Political Thought of Karl Marx* (Cambridge 1968); George Lichtheim, *Marxism. An historical and critical study* (2nd edn 1964); and Anthony Giddens, *Capitalism and Modern Social Theory* (Cambridge 1971). There is much reference to social control in recent writings on welfare reform. As will be seen, my way of putting it in the text owes much to the concise formulation in a review essay by Keith Nield: 'That much quoted phrase "the growth of collectivist sentiment" is but a poor metaphor for the political *will*, and the economic and ideological *necessity* to reorganise the State, to strengthen its central functions and to manipulate its potential for social control – not least through education and shrewd measures of social reform. However much radicals were seen to press for it, such reform was essentially a conservative measure, the *sine qua non* of new ideologies of industrial management and ultimately of the quest for "national efficiency"', *Bulletin of the Society for the Study of Labour History*, 30 (Spring 1975), p. 67. For examples of Liberals who turn out to be Liberal Unionists see Robert Graves *Goodbye to All That* (1929) and the interesting book by Katharine Chorley, *Manchester Made Them* (1950); most other examples can be illustrated from the present work.

In clearly perceiving the importance of intentions historians owe much to the writings of Quentin Skinner, esp. 'Meaning and understanding in the history of ideas', *History and Theory*, viii (1969), 3–53. The recent history of sociology by Geoffrey Hawthorn, *Enlightenment and Despair* (Cambridge 1976) has a lucid short introduction dealing with these problems. He poses the dilemma: 'If beliefs are externally caused, it seems impossible to see how they can be rational. And if they are rational, it seems impossible to see how they can be externally caused' (p. 6). This seems to me to confuse explaining the belief with explaining who held it, and I hope that my formulation may have escaped this difficulty. I recognise that there may be a further problem in explaining which beliefs were themselves available. In working towards a concept of ideology I am conscious of developing insights which I find helpfully put by Hobson, esp. in *Free-Thought in the Social Sciences* (1926), which is analysed historically in ch. 7, ii, below. There are also some germane reflections in his *Conf.*, e.g. on what I call radical bourgeois false consciousness: 'When

George Bernard Shaw argues in favour of an absolute equalization of income, as he does in his *Intelligent Woman's Guide to Socialism*, he leaves himself open to the retort that he must know quite well that such a condition precludes any effective interference with his own large body of wealth' (p. 73).

On nineteenth-century Liberalism D. A. Hamer, *John Morley. Liberal intellectual in politics* (Oxford 1968) has much to offer; and I owe to it the reference to John Morley, 'Young England and the political future', *FR*, i (n.s.) (1867), 491–6, from which I quote. See also Hamer's *Liberal Politics in the Age of Gladstone and Rosebery* (Oxford 1972) esp. pp. 141–3. My understanding of electoral realities is sketched in my article, 'Electoral sociology of modern Britain', *History*, lvii (1972), esp. p. 35 for the views of the Liberal intellectuals as represented by *Essays on Reform* (1867). This subject has now been fully analysed in the perceptive study by Christopher Harvie, *The Lights of Liberalism* (1976), esp. p. 173 on the academic Liberals as victims of their own logic. The work of David Cresap Moore is of fundamental importance in assessing the other face of early Victorian Reform and is now available as *The Politics of Deference* (Hassocks 1976). R. T. Shannon, *Gladstone and the Bulgarian Agitation 1876* (1963) is a masterly analysis of Gladstonian methods in operation. For other works on Gladstonian Liberalism, esp. those of Hammond and Vincent, see notes to epilogue. Original sin reappears in ch. 1, ii, below, with full references. In 1917, as an old man, Bryce wrote to Dicey of the youth of that day that 'their zeal for the end – viz. the bettering of the condition of the mass, seems to make them ignore the difficulties which the means present. They seem to think human nature perfectible, just as the men of 1789 did. Perhaps it is well that mankind should never shake itself free from this illusion' (Harvie, p. 241).

Ch. 1 The Passion for Improving Mankind

(I)

I have relied a good deal upon the biographical material in the Wallas Papers, chiefly in WP 48. Ada Wallas left some fragmentary notes, dated 9 Aug. 1934, which contains a few vividly recalled anecdotes, of which I quote one in the text. There is a much fuller set of biographical notes by May Wallas (daughter) – clearly a draft for a published work, possibly the projected introduction to *Men and Ideas* (1940). This account is useful in that it draws upon family tradition but I have tried not to rely upon it in the absence of corroborative evidence, which often exists elsewhere in WP or in Wallas's publications. *Ec*, xii (1932), 395–412 contains addresses given at the L.S.E. after Wallas's death; that by Sidney Webb is the most vivid; that by Harold Laski (reprinted from the *New Statesman*) is complemented by his 'Lowes Dickinson and Graham Wallas', *PQ*, iii (1932), 461–6. The *DNB* notice (short and sympathetic) is by Alfred Zimmern who knew Wallas well in his middle years. There is an excellent modern study by

Martin J. Wiener, *Between Two Worlds. The political thought of Graham Wallas* (Oxford 1971), which offers a systematic treatment of Wallas's thought and draws upon his papers. Since Wiener wrote, the death of May Wallas has led to the opening of further ('private') Wallas papers to research, notably the family letters in WP 42–7 and Ada Wallas's diary in WP 49. These contain some interesting retrospective comments on which I have drawn to try to build up a fuller personal picture of Wallas than Wiener was able to convey. Wallas's writings were often anecdotal, and chance reminiscences of his early life are often to be found, e.g. *Art of Thought* (1926) p. 111 on his education and the citations in the text to *The Great Society* (1914). H. W. Nevinson, *Changes and Chances* (1923) is a full and generally reliable autobiographical account, paralleling Wallas's career at Shrewsbury and Oxford; his *Running Accompaniments* (1936) is a series of uneven but often revealing essays. Wallas's impression of his father is given in a presidential speech to the Rationalist Press Association, 7 June 1926, in WP 12; and his recollections as recorded by Gilbert Slater, sent to Ada Wallas 15 Jan. 1933, WP 32.

I have not seen any Hobhouse papers which bear directly upon his early life; but good use of family letters is made in Stefan Collini, 'Liberalism and Sociology'. The memoir by J. A. Hobson and Morris Ginsberg, *L. T. Hobhouse: his life and work* (1931) contains much valuable material within a short compass and I have followed it closely in this chapter. The *DNB* article by A. Shadwell is not particularly useful. The address by Wallas at the Hobhouse memorial service, 27 June 1929, in *Ec*, ix (1929), 247–50, is deeply revealing about both men, and the notes on which it is based are also in WP 17. Ernest Barker, 'Leonard Trelawny Hobsouse', *PBA*, xv (1929), is an intelligent appraisal of Hobhouse's career. I have also drawn heavily in this section upon Ruth Fry, *Emily Hobhouse, a memoir* (1929), to which Leonard contributed childhood recollections, esp. an appendix – virtually a dissenting report – to ch. i, pp. 36–9.

From 1880 on there are frequent references to Wallas in the letters published in Margaret Olivier, *Sydney Olivier* (1948), which also includes a fragment of autobiography. Norman and Jeanne Mackenzie, *The First Fabians* (1977) offers a highly readable account which also uses further Olivier manuscripts, as quoted in n. 8. The definitive work on T. H. Green is *The Politics of Conscience* by Melvin Richter (1964), to which my treatment is much indebted, esp. to pp. 102–4 on Green's theological ambitions. Richter, and also Wiener, make more of the explicitly Evangelical heritage here than my account which is to some extent written against them; and for a related criticism on this point see the sharp note of dissent by Stefan Collini in his review of Wiener, *Historical Journal*, xv (1972), 827–30. I do not wish to belittle the seminal ch. 3 of Noel Annan, *Leslie Stephen* (1951), esp. p. 110: 'The intellectual heritage of Evangelicalism has been too readily forgotten.' But by now it has perhaps been too indiscriminately recalled.

(II)

In citing Green's writings I follow Richter in referring to his *Works* in three volumes, ed. R. L. Nettleship (1885–8), except the *Lectures on the Principles of Political Obligation,* often reprinted separately, to which the references are by paragraph number. These lectures, though published posthumously, were first delivered from October 1879 on (see Richter, p. 192n.), and I have taken the liberty of supplying this as the publication date in the text. I am conscious that the way in which I describe Green's relation to Hegel owes much to John Plamenatz, *Man and Society*, ii (1963), pp. 217–22. The notion that Green pioneered the idea of a welfare state is still to be found in the textbooks but should have been scotched by a careful reading of Richter, esp. p. 293. On the crucial question of temperance, Brian Harrison, *Drink and the Victorians* (1971), pp. 208–9 is brief but percipient.

William S. Peterson, *Victorian Heretic. Mrs. Humphry Ward's 'Robert Elsmere'* (Leicester 1976) now provides a scholarly study with a full bibliography. This supersedes Enid Huws Jones, *Mrs. Humphry Ward* (1973), which is often rather thin. Janet Penrose Trevelyan, *The Life of Mrs. Humphry Ward* (1923), by her daughter, is still indispensable, though some matters are skirted over, e.g. the Acland connexion is ignored. Mrs Ward's own *A Writer's Recollections* (1918) is badly organised but good on Oxford in the 1870s and on *Robert Elsmere*. Some of it draws upon her introduction to the Westmoreland edn of *Robert Elsmere,* 2 vols. (1911), i, pp. xiii–xliv. John Morley, *Life of Gladstone,* 2 vol. edn (1906), ii, 597–601 prints Gladstone's letters to Acton of April and May 1888 on *Robert Elsmere*; W. E. Gladstone, '"Robert Elsmere" and the battle of belief', *NC*, xxiii (1888), 766–88 followed in May. There is a rather slight review of the reviews in Basil Willey, 'How *Robert Elsmere* struck some contemporaries', *Essays & Studies,* x (1957), 53–68. Mrs Ward's notes of her interviews with Gladstone are printed in Trevelyan, pp. 56–60, which also publishes some of her important letters to Gladstone; see esp. 12 & 15 April 1888, Gladstone Papers, B.L. Add. MSS. 44503 ff.152–4, 170–5. *In Memoriam. Mrs. Humphry Ward and the Passmore Edwards Settlement* (1921) is useful for its contribution from Wicksteed; and L. P. Jacks, *Life and Letters of Stopford Brooke,* 2 vols. (1917) has some useful material on his work in Bloomsbury. See also Peter d'A Jones, *The Christian Socialist Revival, 1877–1914* (Princeton 1968), esp. pp. 394–403.

In using works of fiction in this chapter I am fully conscious of the pitfalls that await me. We have Mrs Ward's own authority for identifying Grey closely with Green. She wrote to Gladstone that she felt 'a sort of responsibility laid upon me with regard to Mr Green, whom you may possibly mention in your article..."The parting with the Christian mythology is the rending asunder of bones & marrow" – words which I have put into Grey's mouth [ch. xxvii], were words of Mr Green's to me (though this is for yourself alone)' (17 April 1888, Add. MSS. 44503 ff.184–6). A comment by Gilbert Murray is also pertinent in this connexion. 'It is rather curious: when Mrs Ward puts people in books, she somehow hurts them, with all decency and gentility. Whereas Shaw, with all his "cheek", does not hurt at all' (Murray to J. L. Hammond, 5 Dec. 1905, HP 30 f.24). Since *Major Barbara*, as Shaw put it in an introductory note, 'stands indebted to him in more ways than one', Murray was well placed to judge.

Helen Bosanquet, *Bernard Bosanquet* (1924) is a serviceable concise account of his life. J. H. Muirhead, *Reflections by a Journeyman in Philosophy* (1942) is particularly good on Balliol in the 1870s (ch. 3) and on life in Bloomsbury in the Ethical–Unitarian–Fabian milieu. Muirhead also edited *Bernard Bosanquet and his Friends* (1935) which contains many revealing letters. My account of Bosanquet's thought rests primarily on *The Civilisation of Christendom* (1892), esp. 'Individualism and socialism' and 'Liberty and legislation', pp. 304–83; and Bernard Bosanquet (ed.), *Aspects of the Social Problem* (1895), which contains the paper by C. S. Loch, 'Pauperism and old-age pensions', pp. 126–66, originally delivered in May 1892. A. J. M. Milne, *The Social Philosophy of English Idealism* (1962) contains fairly adequate summaries of the work of Green and Bosanquet but lacks the kind of historical dimension which so distinguishes Stefan Collini, 'Hobhouse, Bosanquet and the State', *Past & Present*, 72 (1976), 86–111. The approach of the C.O.S. is ably delineated in Charles Loch Mowat, *The Charity Organisation Society, 1869–1913* (1961), esp. pp. 68–73; and this is both amplified and qualified in Gareth Stedman Jones, *Outcast London* (1971), pp. 256–9, 265–7, and in José Harris, *Unemployment and Politics* (Oxford 1972), pp. 105–10.

(III)

This section makes considerable use of the letters to Wallas in the private section of his papers, notably from Nellie Wallas, n.d. 'Monday' (1885), Mary Talbot Wallas (Mollie, later Mrs Muirhead), 10 May 1885, and the Rev. Gilbert Innes Wallas, 24 July 1885, WP 42. Information on Shobrooke is from personal inspection, *Walford's County Families* (1860 and 1918), and Wallas's MS paper on 'Tithe', read at Kelmscott House in the spring of 1886, WP 16. In suggesting some analogies between the position of Wallas and that of Elsmere, it may be thought that I am obscuring an important difference, viz. that Elsmere's case turned upon the historical evidence for Christianity whereas Wallas seems to have felt the scientific objections to be crucial. These, however, overlaid earlier doubts which had a historical basis, according to Wallas in 'The future of Cowper–Templeism', N, 24 July 1909, p. 597. Moreover, the salient aspect of the conflict in both cases was between the claims of intellect and those of faith. Furthermore, the psychological similarities seem to me strong enough to justify my treatment.

(IV)

The Hobhouse *Memoir* is again useful for Oxford in the 1880s. R. R. Marett, A *Jerseyman at Oxford* (1941), chs. 5 and 6 is a good account by a friend of Hobhouse. For Margaret Llewelyn Davies see the entry by Joyce

Bellamy, H. F. Bing and John Saville in *DLB*, i, 96–9. Charles Roberts, *The Radical Countess* (Carlisle 1962) is an affectionate biography of Lady Carlisle, written late in life; alas, he denies (p. 54) that she once said in a meeting: 'Rise up my middle-class sons-in-law.' *Rosalind Howard, Countess of Carlisle*, by Dorothy Henley (1958) is a memoir by her daughter with a useful appendix by Gilbert Murray (pp. 145–8). Mrs Howard became Lady Carlisle in 1889; I have used the more familiar later style throughout. Gilbert Murray, *An Unfinished Autobiography* (1960) is a posthumously published fragment, some of its best parts concerning Lady Carlisle's circle. *The Autobiography of Bertrand Russell*, 3 vols. (1967–71) covers his early years with wit and perception, and prints many letters of considerable interest.

Michael Sadleir, *Michael Ernest Sadler* (1949), pp. 68–9 has information on Acland and the Inner Ring; see also Roger Davidson, 'Llewellyn Smith, the Labour Department and government growth, 1886–1909', in Gillian Sutherland (ed.), *Studies in the Growth of Nineteenth-century Government* (1972), pp. 227–62, for a very good study of one of Hobhouse's contemporaries. There is a relevant letter from Llewellyn Smith to Wallas, 25 June 1929, WP 8. The thorough and well-researched study by Gillian Sutherland, *Policy-making in Elementary Education, 1870–95* (Oxford 1973), is good on Acland, esp. pp. 314–19. The entry on John Burnett by Norman McCord and John Saville in *DLB*, ii, 71–6, prints the conclusion of the lecture on 'Trade unions as a means of improving the conditions of labour' which he prepared in the summer of 1886. I quote this in the text as being almost certainly the substance of his remarks at Oxford. The parliamentary activities of Acland's group are mentioned in Asquith's *Memories and Reflections*, 2 vols. (1928), i, 156–60; and John Morley, *Recollections*, 2 vols. (1918), pp. 323–4. See also Michael Barker, *Gladstone and Radicalism* (Brighton 1975), pp. 175ff. for a fuller treatment, lending rather more credence than mine to the extent to which Morley was influenced. L. A. Atherley-Jones, *Looking Back* (1925) was written when he was gravely ill and has no material of value. His article 'The New Liberalism', *NC*, xxvi (1889), 186–93, was followed by G. W. E. Russell, 'The New Liberalism: a response', ibid., 492–9, and J. Guinness Rogers, 'The middle class and the New Liberalism', ibid., 710–20.

Hobhouse's sketches of intellectual autobiography are to be found in the preface to *Development and Purpose* (1913) and in the note prefacing 'The philosophy of development' (1924), reprinted in L. T. Hobhouse, *Sociology and Philosophy* (1966), p. 296. His laboratory work was recalled in a letter to F. S. Marvin, 19 Aug. 1906, Bodleian MS Eng. lett. d. 257, ff.159–60. Spencer's *The Man versus the State* was first published in the *Contemporary Review* between February and July of 1884; I have used the Pelican edn, ed. and intro. Donald Macrae (1969). J. D. Y. Peel, *Herbert Spencer, the evolution of a sociologist* (1971) is an important modern study of which space forbids me making fuller use here. David G. Ritchie, *The Principles of State Interference* (1891) comprises essays originally published several years previously; the first three are a riposte to Spencer, the fourth an exposition of Green. E. P. Hennock, 'Poverty and social theory in England', *Social History*, i (1976–7), 67–91, provides a timely demonstration that there was an appreciable time lag between the social concern manifested in the 1880s and the adoption of innovative remedies.

Ch. 2 Good Men Fallen Among Fabians

(I)

My aim here has been to retrace the familiar Fabian story *from Wallas's point of view*. Both Shaw and Wallas left copious reminiscences of early days. I have drawn on several impressions recorded in Ada Wallas's biog. notes (9 Aug. 1934), WP 48; Gilbert Slater's reminiscences, WP 32; and lectures given late in life by Wallas: 'Ends and means', 30 Oct. 1930, MS draft, WP 12; 'Social purpose in education', *M. Post*, 1 Jan. 1923; and 'Conditions of organised purpose', to the Institute of Public Administration, 9 Nov. 1922, file copy from shorthand notes, WP 13. Webb's address on Wallas's death (*Ec*, xii (1932), 403–4) describes their first encounter. The published version of Shaw's letters is invaluable and prints the important letters to his early biographer Archibald Henderson, esp. 3 Jan. 1905, Laurence, ii, 479–506. This letter is the source for many recollections of the 1880s, esp. pp. 490–1 on the Three Musketeers; when Shaw published a version of this in *Sixteen Self Sketches* (1949) this passage was redrafted (pp. 67–8) to include Bland in the 'Politbureau'. I have preferred the earlier account on all disputed points. Shaw's first attempt at Fabian history was *Tract* 41, 'The Fabian Society: what it has done and how it has done it' (1892), which I quote from his *Essays in Fabian Socialism* (1932). Shaw's claims have been subjected to extensive historical revision, notably in A. M. McBriar, *Fabian Socialism and English Politics* 1884–1918 (Cambridge 1962), whose methodical account is of great value; and in Paul Thompson, *Socialists, Liberals and Labour* (1967) which is an admirable study of London politics 1885–1914.

For Shaw and Wicksteed on the value theory, see McBriar, pp. 31–5. On the Land Reform Union etc., E. Eldon Barry, *Nationalisation in British Politics* (1965), pp. 60ff. is useful. Webb drafted *A Plea for the Taxation of Ground Rents* (1887) for the United Committee for advocating the Taxation of Ground Rents and Values, of which Lord Hobhouse was president. ('Lord Hobhouse and his unimpeachably respectable committee', according to Shaw, *Fabian Essays*, p. 189.) I take the point about the line from Pope's *Epistle to Burlington* from Raymond William's unfailingly illuminating study *The Country and the City* (Paladin edn 1975), p. 77. On the Comtean influence on Webb in particular, see Willard Wolfe, *From Radicalism to Socialism. Men and ideas in the formation of Fabian socialist doctrines* 1881–9 (1975), esp. pp. 194–7, 267–9; this careful study has much to contribute in enlarging our understanding of the ethical influences at work among the early Fabians; cf. ch. 2 on Mill. The account of the economic circle at Beeton's house in Archibald Henderson, *George Bernard Shaw: man of the century* (New York 1956), pp. 274–5, and 'The Society's Jubilee', *EcJ*, l (1940), 401–9, must be qualified by A. W. Coats, 'The origins and early development of the Royal Economic Society', *EcJ*, lxxviii (1968), esp. pp. 354–5. T. W. Hutchison, *A Review of Economic Doctrines 1870–1929* (Oxford, 1953) is useful for Wicksteed, esp. p. 97 on his view of socialism. The Hampstead Historic Society is alluded to in Shaw, *Tract* 41, p. 144; and E. R. Pease, *The History of the Fabian Society* (1916) redated its account in the 2nd edn (1925), p. 64 as a result of Wallas's correspondence with Pease in 1916. *N.B.* Pease was not in London 1886–90, i.e. during the heyday of the Three Musketeers and the H.H.S., and his account for these years therefore lacks the intimate knowledge of the Society's affairs which sustains other sections. Wallas's letters to Pease of 10 Jan. 1916 and 4 Feb. 1916 are in WP 10 and chiefly concern this period; his review of Pease is in *Men & Ideas*, pp. 103–7 as 'Socialism and the Fabian Society'; and another MS version (part of which May Wallas inserted at p. 105n.) is in WP 12.

On versions of Marxism current in the late nineteenth century, I have followed George Lichtheim, *Marxism* (1961), esp. Pt. 5, ch. iv. See also Stanley Pierson, *Marxism and the Origins of British Socialism* (1973), esp. ch. iv. E. P. Thompson, *William Morris. Romantic to Revolutionary* (1955) was a flawed masterpiece which the author revised in the 2nd edn (1977) by removing the flaws. I find its account of Morris wholly persuasive and I have relied upon it implicitly. It will be seen that my comments are virtually a paraphrase of pp. 773, 801, 721 and 790–1. On the Fabians' understanding of Marx, Wolfe, pp. 206ff., esp. p. 208 on Webb and Marx, is perceptive and Wallas's comments on Pease are full and indicative. J. W. Hulse, *Revolutionists in London* (Oxford 1970) contains some interesting judgments on the 'unorthodoxy' of socialists like Shaw, Morris and Bernstein, which could perhaps usefully be integrated into my analytical framework. See also Kirk Willis, 'The introduction and critical reception of Marxist thought in Britain, 1850–1900', *Historical Journal*, xx (1977), 417–59.

The most important of Wallas's MS drafts of the 1880s are 'Education', probably his first lecture, given at Kelmscott House in 1886, WP 15; 'Tithe', also at Kelmscott House, probably in the spring of 1886, WP 16; 'The Morals of Interest', n.d., WP 16; and 'Notes' for Wallas's debate with Stopford Brooke at the Bedford Debating Society, n.d. but 1888 from internal evidence, WP 16. This is a full technical treatment of 'rent', clearly following Sidney Webb, 'The rate of interest and the laws of distribution', *QJE*, ii (1887–8), 188–208. For further analysis see McBriar, pp. 37ff. and David M. Ricci, 'Fabian Socialism: a theory of rent as exploitation', *Journal of British Studies*, ix (1969–70), esp. pp. 106–9.

In writing of the Fabians as part of the *nouvelle couche sociale* (a favourite term of Webb's) I am conscious of the large debt all scholars owe to 'The Fabians Reconsidered' in E. J. Hobsbawm, *Labouring Men* (1964), esp. pp. 257–9, 266–8. The anecdote about Shaw and his watch is from 'The money-power at war', N, 11 Dec. 1909, p. 454, and there is another version in Ada Wallas's notes; likewise the Colonial Office reminiscence is given (less fully) in *Men & Ideas*, p. 124. The origin of the *Fabian Essays* is dealt with clearly in Norman and Jeanne Mackenzie, *The First Fabians* (1977), pp. 93, 109–10. The memorandum of May 1888 in WP 10 includes comments from Wallas, Webb, Olivier and Shaw and is a document of high interest.

The Practical Socialist was 'a monthly review of evolutionary or non-revolutionary socialism'. Edith Simcox, 'Socialism and political liberty', i (1886), pp. 34–7, 53–5, and Wallas 'Personal duty under the present system', pp. 118–20, 124–5, were both papers which had been read to the Fabian Society. In arguing that Wallas did not adopt socialism as a new religion I am writing against Wolfe, pp. 229–30, with whose account mine should be compared since we use the same range of sources – 'Tithe', 'The Morals of Interest' and 'Personal duty'.

(II)

J. H. Muirhead, *Reflections by a Journeyman in Philosophy* (1942), esp. pp. 86–8, 91–7, has many valuable points on the ethical movement and on Clarke and Wallas. There is some information on the South Place and other societies in Warren Sylvester Smith, *The London Heretics* (1967), pp. 104–30. William Clarke, 'The limits of collectivism', *CR*, lxiii (1893), 263–78, showed some change in his views, of which there were signs as early as 1890. This is one of the articles reprinted in *William Clarke, a selection of his writings* (1908), ed. Herbert Burrows and J. A. Hobson, which contains a biographical sketch, pp. xi–xxix. See also Peter Weiler, 'William Clarke: the making and unmaking of a Fabian Socialist', *Journal of British Studies*, xiv (1974–5), esp. pp. 96–7. Muirhead married Mary Talbot Wallas: 'Who taught me to feel what Green taught me to think' – dedication of his *The Service of the State* (1908). There are some germane reflections in Muirhead's letters, esp. to May Wallas, 20 Sep. 1936, WP 41; see also the letter from Sidney G. Green, 18 Sep. 1937, ibid., for Wallas's connexion with the South Place Ethical Society. Correspondence over the C.O.S. and Wallas's extension lectures in the early 1890s is in WP 1 and WP 10. Most of Shaw's letters to Wallas have been published; but Laurence, i, 275–7 (16 Dec. 1890 to Olivier) is a bit of a puzzle since there is a copy of this letter (also 16 Dec. 1890) to Wallas in WP 1.

The diary of Beatrice Potter (Webb) is a document of unique standing. It is the basis for *My Apprenticeship* (1926; 2nd edn 1946). When the Wallases saw her draft she found them 'quite unexpectedly enthusiastic – "a work of art" Graham calls it' (diary, 27 Sep. 1925). *Our Partnership*, ed. Barbara Drake and Margaret I Cole (1948) prints more extensive extracts, 1892–1911. I have quoted from the published version wherever possible. There are, however, discrepancies between this and the typed transcript in the Passfield Papers, and also between the typescript and the original MS in Beatrice's (admittedly difficult) handwriting, though it seems to me that previous researchers have not adequately appreciated this. My references to the 'diary' are therefore always to Beatrice's own MS. The new edition of *Our Partnership* (Cambridge 1975) has a useful introduction by George Feaver, pp. ix–xlvii. Margaret Cole, *Beatrice Webb*

(1945) benefited from personal knowledge but is rather spare. Kitty Muggeridge and Ruth Adam, *Beatrice Webb. A life, 1858–1943* (1967) is a readable account showing considerable familiarity with the typescript version of the diary; ch. vi on Chamberlain can be supplemented by Peter Fraser, *Joseph Chamberlain. Radicalism and empire, 1868–1914* (1966), ch. v, and the appendix to *Beatrice Webb's Diaries 1924–1932* (1956), ed. Margaret Cole, pp. 311–16. The entry of 14 Feb. 1890, on Sidney, must read 'London cad' not 'card' as in Muggeridge and Adam, p. 119; the version in *MA*, p. 349 is, of course, understandably tactful; and *MA*, p. 353, embarrassed at so much 'human nature' in the entry for 10 Oct. 1891, prints it as 'a few brief intervals of confidential talk'. There are some light-hearted anecdotes to be found in Anne Fremantle, *This Little Band of Prophets. The British Fabians* (New York, Mentor Books 1960), e.g. p. 48 for Alys Pearsall Smith (later Mrs Russell) redecorating Wallas's rooms.

Alfred F. Havighurst, *Radical Journalist: H. W. Massingham* (Cambridge 1974) is a solidly researched study; see ch. iii for the Fabian period. *H.W.M.* (1925), ed. H. J. Massingham, contains a selection from his writings; see also Shaw's contribution, pp. 209–16. See Mackenzie, esp. pp. 148–50 for the efforts of Webb and Wallas to contain Fabian enthusiasm. The gist of 'To Your Tents, O Israel', from the *Fortnightly Review* (Nov. 1893), is printed in *OP*, pp. 110–14; in my interpretation I am expanding upon the shrewd treatment in Henry Pelling, *The Origins of the Labour Party 1880–1900* (2nd edn, Oxford 1965), p. 147.

Sidney Ball. Memories and impressions of 'an ideal don', arranged by Oona Howard Ball (Oxford 1923) contains some useful material but its inadequacies distressed his friends. 'What a production about poor old Ball. I hate to think of the impression people who did not know him would get from it' (Hammond to Murray, 17 June 1923, MP 23a). See also 'Modern Oxford – from a progressive point of view', *PR*, i (1896), esp. pp. 212–14; Joseph Clayton, *The Rise and Decline of Socialism in Great Britain 1884–1924* (1926), esp. pp. 31, 50–1, 93–4; the Hobhouse *Memoir*, esp. pp. 28, 30; and Ball to Wallas, 18 Sep. (1887), WP 1. The Samuel Papers in the House of Lords Record Office contain an interesting series of cards for the Russell Club and the Society for the Study of Social Ethics, 1890–5, A3, 1–9; there is also correspondence from Webb and Wallas; and see Viscount Samuel, *Memoirs* (1945), esp. pp. 13–14. *The Autobiography of Bertrand Russell*, i (1967), pp. 76–80 is a percipient account of the Webbs at this time. There are some Webb letters in the Haldane Papers in the National Library of Scotland, but nothing from Hobhouse; and I have been unable to discover any reference to him in Haldane's daily letters to his mother for 1893 (NLS MS 5950).

(III)

Hobson left virtually no personal papers, though there is a small collection of material now in the University of Hull Library. His autobiography, *Confessions of an Economic Heretic* (1938) was a work of reflection not documentation, but is indispensable; it has been reprinted with an introduction by Michael Freeden (Brighton 1976). There is a good entry in the *DNB* by R. H. Tawney. G. D. H. Cole, 'J. A. Hobson (1858–1940)', *Ec*, l (1940), 351–9 is a noble atonement for years of professional neglect. H. N. Brailsford, *The Life-Work of J. A. Hobson*, L. T. Hobhouse Memorial Trust Lecture, No. 17 (Oxford 1948) is a sympathetic account by a close friend of later years. The best biographical source is the entry by Alan Lee in *DLB*, i (1972), 176–81, which includes a bibliography; and this draws upon the author's excellent unpublished thesis 'A study of the social and economic thought of J. A. Hobson', London Ph.D. 1970. My own treatment here draws on material from my introduction to Hobson's *The Crisis of Liberalism* (1909; new edn, Brighton 1974), pp. ix–xliv.

There is an interesting comment by Smuts on the Hobsons in *Smuts*, ii, doc. 324 (28 Nov. 1906). On Hobson in relation to economic tradition, see Hutchison, A *Review of Economic Doctrines*, pp. 118–29. I am unable to accept D. J. Coppock, 'A reconsideration of Hobson's theory of unemployment', *Manchester School*, xxi (1953), 1–21, which advances Hobson's claims in a Keynesian context. There is an interesting short statement of Hobson's own view of underconsumption in the minutes of the Rainbow Circle for 2 Feb. 1898 (written by MacDonald, with corrections in Hobson's hand). Erwin Esser Nemmers, *Hobson and Underconsumption* (Amsterdam 1956), is a detailed study by an economist, but again the way in which the problematic is specified is not, I think, historically valid. There are some interesting points about the professionalisation of the economic profession in A. W. Coats, 'The role of authority in the development of British economics', *Journal of Law and Economics*, vii (1964), 85–106. There are two revealing letters from Hobson to Richard T. Ely 27 Dec. 1889 and n.d. (Mar. 1890) in the Ely Papers, State Historical Society of Wisconsin; copies of these were made available to me by Melvyn Stokes. See also bib. note to ch. 5, i.

For the influence of Charles Booth, as seen in *Problems of Poverty* (1891), see John Brown, 'Charles Booth and labour colonies, 1889–1905', *EcHR*, 2nd ser., xxi (1968), 349–60, and his debate with Trevor Lummis, ibid., xxiv (1971), 100–13; also the interesting treatment by Gareth Stedman Jones, *Outcast London* (Oxford 1971), pp. 303–8. Hobson, like Wallas, acknowledged a great debt to Ruskin, and his study *John Ruskin, Social Reformer* (1898) is his major work of this period other than those cited in the text; see p. 104 for the deduction from Ruskin of the organic law, 'From each...' etc. On the origin of this slogan I follow Shlomo Avineri, *The Social and Political Thought of Karl Marx* (Cambridge 1968), p. 234. For Hobson's deeply rooted hostility to marginalist analysis see his 'Neo-classical economics in Britain', *PSQ*, xl (1925), esp. pp. 350–5. The organic paradigm in Hobson's thought is strongly emphasised in Michael Freeden, 'Biological and evolutionary roots of the new Liberalism in England', *Political Theory*, iv (1976), 471–90. Hobson's critique of Bosanquet was developed in 'The social philosophy of charity organisation', *CR*, lxx (1896), 710–27; it is reprinted in *The Crisis of Liberalism*, pp. 192–217, and the cross references are identified in my notes to the new edn. (1974), pp. xl–xli.

(IV)

Beatrice Webb's diary, esp. 25 Sep. 1895, is invaluable on Wallas's growing unease; and there is an important retrospective account, 27 Sep. 1925, partly printed in *BWD*, iii, pp. 73–4. For the reasons explained in the text I am more sceptical than Wiener of Beatrice Webb as an authority on democracy and do not follow his account, pp. 31–47, though there is much of value here on the effect of Wallas's School Board activities. See also below ch. 7, ii. The crucial section of *Tract 70* is reprinted and commended in Pease, pp. 251–2. Wallas's review of Pease is a key document, reprinted as 'Socialism and the Fabian Society', *Men & Ideas*, pp. 103–7; there are earlier drafts in WP. The most important of Shaw's letters are 24 & 31 Aug. 1895 to Janet Achurch (esp. Laurence, i, 549, 555); and (on Clarke) to Olivier/Wallas, 16 Dec. 1890 (i, 275–7) and to Henderson, 3 Jan. 1905 (esp. ii, 495–6). Clarke's role in the Rainbow Circle is well covered in Bernard Porter, *Critics of Empire, 1895–1914* (1968), pp. 165–7, drawing on his correspondence with MacDonald, also used in David Marquand, *Ramsay MacDonald* (1977), pp. 55–7; cf. p. 48 for the close relations between Hobson and MacDonald at this time. There is a useful folder on the Circle and the *Progressive Review* in the Samuel Papers, A 10/1–23; see also Samuel, *Memoirs*, p. 24 and *Conf.*, pp. 51–5, 94–6. The chief unexplored source, however, lies in the surviving minute books of the Rainbow Circle, 4 vols., 1894–1924, in the possession of Mr S. S. Wilson. These minutes are very full and reliable; they form the basis of my account of the aims and membership of the Circle and they throw further light on the early days of the *Review*. For retrospective comments see also the minutes for 9 June 1920, after Stapley's death, and 5 March 1924, entertaining MacDonald, Olivier, Noel Buxton and Trevelyan as Labour cabinet ministers. Hobson's treatment of Manchesterism in *The Social Problem* (1901), esp. pp. 20–30, clearly derives from his paper of 5 Dec. 1894; likewise Clarke's paper of 9 Jan. 1895 forms the basis of 'Political defects of the old radicalism', *PSQ*, xiv (1899), 69–86. The delay in publication may be accounted for by the abortive project for a volume of essays (postponed 8 June 1898). The *Review* articles upon which I have chiefly drawn are: (Clarke), 'Introductory', *PR*, i (1896–7), 1–9; Haldane, 'The New Liberalism', and comment by Robert Wallace, ibid., 133–47; J. Keir Hardie and Samuel, 'The Independent Labour Party', ibid., 247–59; James Oliphant and Henry S. Salt, 'Can the social residuum be stamped out', ibid., 451–62; 'What is the land question?', ibid., 481–92; 'Is democracy a reality', *PR*, ii (1897), 20–9; 'Industrial legislation and liberty', ibid., 119–26. The line of argument which Samuel was developing through the Rainbow Circle culminated in his *Liberalism* (1902); see e.g. p. 149 for his critique of socialism – 'The State should be the sole capitalist' etc., and pp. 338–9 on imperialism and social reform. For an able treatment of the development of the Liberal Imperialist analysis of politics see H. C. G. Matthew, *The Liberal Imperialists* (Oxford 1973), esp. pp. 125–40; and see pp. 14, 148–50 for a warning against seeing their 'imperialism' as intrinsic. There is now a biography of *C. P. Trevelyan* by A. J. A. Morris (Belfast 1977) which draws fully upon his papers.

Ch. 3 Imperialism

(I)

The centenary memoir, *C. P. Scott 1846–1932* (1946) contains much useful material including the obituaries by Hammond, Montague and Hobhouse; it is clear from HP 35 that Hobhouse's was written at the end of 1928; these writings usefully supplement J. L. Hammond, *C. P. Scott* (1934). The paper's own centenary volume, *The Manchester Guardian* by William Haslam Mills (1921) is a fine personal sketch but has otherwise been superseded by the admirable work by David Ayerst, *Guardian* (1971), of which I make considerable use. Equally useful on general points is Alan J. Lee, *The Origins of the Popular Press in England 1855–1914* (1976). Mrs Humphry Ward and C. E. Montague, *William Thomas Arnold* (Manchester 1907) assists, esp. the middle section by Montague. There is some tension in interpretation between the authors; see Hobhouse's scornful comment on Mrs Ward's section, 'A great journalist', *N*, 8 June1907, p. 572. Oliver Elton, *C. E. Montague* (1929) is a good memoir. For a more astringent view of Scott see Spenser Wilkinson, *Thirty-Five Years* (1933); W. P. Crozier commented privately to Hammond (20 Dec. 1933, HP 24) that 'in one or two of the stories there is nothing out of character, although S.W. dots the "i"s emphatically'. Neville Cardus, *Autobiography* (1947) has some shrewd impressions of the later Scott. The correspondence between Hobhouse and Scott in MGP begins in 1896 and is the fullest series of Hobhouse's correspondence to survive. I have drawn on other letters in the Scott–Taylor and general series of MGP of which I made fuller use in *Lancashire and the New Liberalism* (Cambridge 1971), esp. ch. 7. The papers of the Transvaal Committee are divided between MGP and the Hobhouse papers in the possession of Mrs J. Balme.

For Hobhouse's opinions in this period see 'The ethical basis of collectivism', *IJE*, viii (1898), 137–56; 'The foreign policy of collectivism', *EcR*, ix (1899), 197–220; leaders (attrib. chiefly on internal evidence) esp. *MG*, 23, 24, 25, 28 Feb. 1899; 8, 9, 14, 16, 25 March 1899; 4, 7 July 1899; 1, 22 Aug. 1899; 4 Sep. 1899. His retrospective comment on Fabianism is in 'The career of Fabianism', *N*, 30 March 1907, pp. 182–3; and see bib, notes to ch. 4, iii. In my edition of *Democracy and Reaction* (Brighton 1972) I trace its origin and transformation from the original articles, *S*, 14 Dec. 1901 – 8 Feb. 1902, at p. xv and in the notes. For Morley's critique of its thesis see 'Democracy and reaction', *NC*, lvii (1905), 361–72, 529–49; reprinted in *Miscellanies*, 4th ser. (1908), pp. 261–320.

G. P. Gooch, *Life of Lord Courtney* (1920) prints some useful letters from 1899. F. W. Hirst, *In the Golden Days* (1947) publishes the author's diary covering the period of the Manchester meeting; there are some good observations on Hobhouse, and see also Hirst's reviews of *Democracy and Reaction*, *IR*, v (1905), 381–4 and of the *Memoir*, *L*, 22 March 1931, p. 684.

Fry's memoir *Emily Hobhouse* is very important on this period of her life, esp. pp. 86–98, 149–62 for 'methods of barbarism'; see also J. A. Spender, *The Life of Sir Henry Campbell-Bannerman*, 2 vols (1923), i, 335–6. The letters in *Smuts* also contain much on Emily Hobhouse ('the Missis') who took a lifelong maternal interest in the general's welfare, e.g. vol. v, doc. 195, for the lemon cure – on the eleventh day, eleven lemons. See also vol. ii, docs. 385, 388–9, 391, 414, which cover the unavailing representations Hobson made over the native question in late 1908. *William Clarke*, ed. Herbert Burrows and John A. Hobson (1908) prints a fair selection of his writings including his sketches of Courtney and Gladstone, and also 'Bismarck', *CR*, lxxv (1899), 1–17; 'Political defects of the old radicalism', *PSQ*, xiv (1899), 69–86; 'The social future of England', *CR*, lxxviii (1900), 858–69; but not 'The decline in English Liberalism', *PSQ*, xvi (1901), 450–462, which is however noted in the bibliography to Alan J. Lee, 'William Clarke', *DLB*, ii, 94–8. I regard Lee's account, though short, as superior to Peter Weiler, 'William Clarke: the making and unmaking of a Fabian socialist', *Journal of British Studies*, xiv (1974–5), 77–108, whose interpretation is contested by my text.

(II)

There are good articles on Hammond in the *DNB* by Gilbert Murray and in *PBA*, xlvi (1960), 267–94, by R. H. Tawney, which includes a bibliography; see also obituaries listed in bib. notes to epilogue. His papers in the Bodleian Library, Oxford, are full and well preserved; and the letters to the Murrays, spanning more than fifty years, in MP 23a, 23b, are hardly less important. Sidney Ball, 'The moral aspects of socialism', *IJE*, vi (1896), 290–322, was also issued as a Fabian tract. For Hammond's circle at Oxford see Hirst, *In the Golden Days*; also *F. W. Hirst* by his friends (1958), esp. pp. 14ff (but note comment in bib. note to epilogue); Robert Speaight, *The Life of Hilaire Belloc* (1957), esp. pp. 88–9, 147–8; Viscount Simon, *Retrospect* (1952), esp. p. 45; 'Modern Oxford – from a progressive point of view', *PR*, i (1896), 212–24 has a few pertinent comments; see also the review of *Essays in Liberalism*, *PR*, ii (1897), 182–5. Stephen E. Koss, *Sir John Brunner: radical plutocrat* (Cambridge 1970), is good on Hammond's first employer. I have benefited from the exhaustive and often percipient treatment by Douglas Nachod, 'Liberalism and Imperialism; the ideological foundations of anti-imperialist sentiment in Great Britain 1898–1914' (Harvard Ph.D. 1972). There is a glimpse of Barbara Bradby's early life in H. O. Barnett, *Canon Barnett* (1918; cheap edn 1921), pp. 427–9, which Barbara commended in a letter to Lawrence Hammond, 21 March 1919. The composition of both *Charles James Fox* (1903) and *Lord Hobhouse* (1905) can be followed closely through material in HP, which also include much information on the running of the *Speaker*.

(III)

Ada Wallas, *Daguerrotypes* (1929) contains autobiographical sketches on her early years; her letters to Graham Wallas in WP are also helpful in establishing tone and context. For her view of Charlotte Shaw see Beatrice Webb's diary, 27 Sep. 1925; and the diary is, of course, a key document in this section. Beatrice Potter's involvement with Chamberlain in the 1880s is dealt with in the authorities listed in bib. notes to ch. 2, ii; but none of them bring out the significance of this attachment in the period of the Boer War, though Muggeridge and Adam, pp. 163–4, seem on the brink of doing so. Their account suffers from reading the entry for New Year's Day 1901 as referring to a further meeting between Beatrice Webb and Chamberlain rather than back yet again to the highly-charged encounter in July 1900. It is particularly important to consult the MS diary here. Beatrice Webb later inserted a note (ca. 1920) in the entry for 15 June 1899: 'This extract which I have typed myself, rather than give to be copied from my rough typed copy by my secretary, evokes no memory in my mind. But I assume from other entries of this and the following year that it related to my past relations with Joseph Chamberlain. This dramatising of relationships or rather of prospective relationships has always been one of my bad habits.' This protestation will not, I think, be accepted at face value by anyone who has read through the relevant material. Shaw's position is graphically put in his letters to Edward Rose, 14 Dec. 1899, Laurence, ii, 118–19; to George Samuel, 23/24 Dec. 1899, ibid., pp. 121–3; to H. M. Hyndman, 28 April 1900, ibid., pp. 161–3; and to G. F. McCleary, 24 May 1900, ibid., pp. 168–9. His later epistle to Burns, 11 Sep. 1903, ibid., pp. 368–72 is also full of interest. On Olivier and the Boer War E. J. Hobsbawm, 'The lesser Fabians', brings out the essential points, in Lionel M. Munby (ed.), *The Luddites and Other Essays* (1971), pp. 241–4. The diary of Kate Courtney in the Courtney Papers at the L.S.E. is quite useful for the months Oct. 1899 to Jan. 1900.

Sidney Webb, 'Lord Rosebery's escape from Houndsditch', *NC*, l (1901), 366–86, is reprinted in part in *OP*, pp. 220–4. On the Webbs' new policy initiatives see the intelligent and scrupulous study by Geoffrey Searle, *The Quest for National Efficiency* (1971). Bernard Semmel, *Imperialism and Social Reform. English social-imperial thought 1895–1914* (1960) was a seminal study in this field, though it seems to me that some of its seed was broadcast and fell upon stony ground. See S. K. Ratcliffe, *The Story of South Place* (1955), pp. 60–1, for the society's reputation during the Boer War. Wallas's MS notes for 'The decay of Liberalism', given at South Place Oct. 1901, are in WP 16, and though not in connected prose give a full statement of his argument. On the education controversy see Searle, pp. 207–16; McBriar, pp. 198–202, 206–22. Mary Agnes Hamilton, *Sidney and Beatrice Webb* (1933) comments: 'Deep differences of opinion on the Education Act made only the briefest suspension in friendship with Mr and Mrs Graham Wallas' (pp. 152–3); cf. the author's comment on Wallas's 'underlying seriousness of the Nonconformist manse whence he came' (p. 30). The comment on Wallas and the Fabians in Elie Halévy, *Imperialism and the Rise of Labour* (2nd edn 1951), p. 366 can be taken as having Wallas's blessing. For Wells see bib. notes, ch. 5, i.

(IV)

The most important of Hobson's articles on imperialism on which I have drawn are 'Free trade and foreign policy', *CR*, lxxiv (1898), 167–80; 'Capitalism and imperialism in South Africa', *CR*, lxxvii (1900), 1–17; 'The testimony from Johannesburg', ibid., pp. 656–62; 'The proconsulate of Milner', *CR*, lxxviii (1900), 540–54; 'Socialistic imperialism', *IJE*, xii (1901–2), 44–58. The following were substantially incorporated into *Imperialism: a study* (1902): 'The commercial value of imperialism', S, 2 Nov. 1901, pp. 124–6; 'Imperialism as an outlet for population', S, 9 Nov. 1901, pp. 154–5; 'Economic parasites of imperialism', S, 16 Nov. 1901, pp. 179–81; 'Imperialism the policy of investors', S, 23 Nov. 1901, pp. 210–11; 'The financial direction of imperialism', S, 30 Nov. 1901, pp. 245–6; 'Imperialism based on protection', S, 7 Dec. 1901, pp. 275–6 – all in *Imp.*, Pt. 1, chs. 2–5 (main changes here in ch. 2, pp. 30–3, incorporating Hobson's reply to letter from Thomas Cairns, S, 16 Nov. 1901, pp. 186–7). 'The economic taproot of imperialism', *CR*, lxxxii (1902), 219–32, is subject only to minor corrections as Pt. I, ch. 6; likewise 'The scientific basis of imperialism', *PSQ*, xvii (1902), 460–89, as Pt. II, ch. 2 (except section v which is added). Leonard Courtney, 'What is the advantage of foreign trade?', *NC*, liii (1903), 806–12, advanced criticisms which Hobson implicitly took into account in *Imp.* (2nd edn, 1905), pp. 25–6. Hobson's two articles on democracy are virtually contemporary with the 1st edn of *Imp.*, viz 'Ruskin and democracy', *CR*, lxxxi (1902), 103–12; and 'The restatement of democracy', ibid., pp. 262–72, reprinted in *The Crisis of Liberalism* (1909), pp. 71–87.

Richard Price, *An Imperial War and the British Working Class* (1972) goes some way towards suggesting that the pro-Boers exaggerated the strength of popular jingoism. Stephen Koss (ed.), *The Pro-Boers* (1973) is a very useful guide to the polemics of this period and reprints (pp. 25–9) Hobson's despatch from *MG*, 28 Sep. 1899, which is a fair example of his more pointed comments on the Jews. Richard Koebner and Helmut dan Schmidt, *Imperialism. The story and significance of a political word 1840–1960* (Cambridge 1964) is a good general study though rather disappointing on Hobson (chs. 8 & 9) because, despite using all contemporary sources, the viewpoint is retrospective. Their treatment of anti-semitism (pp. 250–6) parallels that of Harvey Mitchell, 'Hobson revisited', *Journal of the History of Ideas*, xxvi (1965), esp. pp. 399–404. I disagree on this point but otherwise find Mitchell's emphasis on the non-economic aspects convincing. D. K. Fieldhouse, 'Imperialism: an historiographical revision', *EcHR*, 2nd ser., xiv (1961–2), 187–209, seems to me a total misunderstanding of Hobson, and though in his exhaustive study, *Economics and Empire 1830–1914* (1973), pp. 39–41, the author's treatment is better, he is still (pp. 46, 53–4, 60) open to the objection that he is applying the wrong criteria. This charge was effectively pressed by Bernard Porter, *Critics of Empire* (1968), p. 216, and still seems to me valid, as indeed does Porter's general treatment which is a model of scholarship and lucidity; see chs. 6 and 7 for *Imperialism*. It is worth noting that the view advanced here of

Hobson's theory is congruent with the work of the two historians who know his writings on imperialism best, viz. Porter and Alan Lee. 'J. A. Hobson, Cobdenism and the radical theory of economic imperialism 1898–1914' by P. J. Cain, *EcHR*, n.s., xxxi (1978), with all its many merits, nonetheless does not persuade me of a variant reading.

Lenin's theory, and the attention given it, have impeded our view of the historical Hobson. The two are neatly disentangled in Eric Stokes, 'Late nineteenth-century colonial expansion and the attack on the theory of economic imperialism: a case of mistaken identity', *Historical Journal*, xii (1969), 285–301. Mary Holdsworth, 'Lenin's *Imperialism* in retrospect', in C. Abramsky (ed.), *Essays in honour of E. H. Carr* (1974), pp. 341–50, is historically unilluminating; but V. G. Kiernan, *Marxism and Imperialism* (1974) contains a full and penetrating essay, pp. 1–68. This led me to Lenin's *Notebooks on Imperialism*, *Works*, xxxix (Moscow 1968), which includes notebook 'Kappa' on Hobson, pp. 405–36. Tom Kemp, *Theories of Imperialism* (1967), ch. 3 on Hobson, esp. pp. 35–8, seems blinkered from Hobson's insights by its own Marxist perspectives. Paul Baran, *The Political Economy of Growth* (Penguin 1973) sees the force of Hobson's argument, though without adopting it. George Lichtheim, *Imperialism* (Penguin 1974), though generally sound, misinterprets underconsumption (pp. 113–14, 172 n.19) as requiring a remedy from the dependent tropical empire (much like Fieldhouse). John Strachey, *The End of Empire* (1959), ch. 6, achieved a notable conflation by making Hobson's an economic theory and Lenin's a colonial theory. This was an interesting misunderstanding in view of the author's comment (pp. 110–11) on Lenin's assertion that Hobsonian reform would be 'not capitalism'; see also ch. 8, iii. It is also historiographically revealing that by 1948 there should be a (misconceived and unnecessary) apology by Brailsford in the sympathetic lecture, *The Life-Work of J. A. Hobson*, pp. 26–7, for Hobson's alleged underestimation of the psychological as against economic reasons for imperialism.

Ch. 4 The State and the Nation

(I)

The letters from Lawrence and Barbara Hammond to Gilbert and Mary Murray have been invaluable for this section. Lawrence's letters (MP 23a) were fairly businesslike, useful on Barbara's health and on the *Tribune* resignation, esp. 30 Jan. 1907. Barbara's letters (MP 23b) were fuller and more imaginative – the series from 14 Feb. 1906 to 15 June 1907 on the *Tribune*, the *Speaker* and the *Daily News* is a wonderful source, esp. 2 Aug. 1906 and 12 Aug. 1906, on which I have drawn heavily. There is a great deal of Hobhouse material here, to be supplemented by his occasional letters to Scott in MGP; these are chiefly in the separate Scott–Hobhouse series but a few letters, e.g. 18 Dec. 1905 quoted in n.1, are in the general series. There are also references to Hobhouse in the letters from Graham to Ada Wallas, WP 43, and in Ada Wallas's diary fragment of 1905, WP 49.

There is an interesting letter on education from Wallas to Hobhouse, 20 Sep. 1906, WP 10 (probably the original, later reclaimed). For Harold Spender see his autobiography *The Fire of Life* (n.d.), esp. ch. xi; and Stephen Spender, *World Within World* (1951), esp. pp. 5–6, 75–83. Wallas's application for a post at Oxford is discussed in his letters with A. E. Zimmern in 1909, WP 4. Hobhouse's arrangements are mentioned in his letters to Scott (MGP) and to Emily Hobhouse, esp. 28 Aug. 1905, Hobhouse Papers. Nos. 3, 5 and 7 Broadlands Road are no longer standing; on their site are twelve expensive modern houses; I assume No. 7 to have been like its neighbours. The story of the *Tribune* has been well told in Alan J. Lee 'Franklin Thomasson and *The Tribune*', *Historical Journal*, xvi (1973), 341–60. For the crisis on the *Manchester Guardian* see David Ayerst, *'Guardian'. Biography of a newspaper* (1971), ch. xxii. Hammond to Hobhouse, draft, n.d. (probably Aug. 1906) is interesting on their relationship and the nature of their understanding. There is one tantalising piece of evidence on why Hammond resigned from the *Tribune*, viz. the TS draft to the Bradbys (HP 34, f.159), which concluded that, even if other reasons were less strong, 'I should still go. And for this reason.' At this point the fragment breaks off.

From the beginning of 1907 the diary of H. W. Nevinson in the Bodleian Library, Oxford, is a source of great value and I have used it a lot especially for the *Nation* lunch. Nevinson drew on it in a general way for *More Changes, More Chances* (1925), esp. pp. 212–19; mostly repeated in *The Fire of Life* (1935) – a favoured title for memoirs by Edwardian journalists. There is a very good study of A. G. Gardiner and the *Daily News, Fleet Street Radical* (1973) by Stephen Koss; see ch. v for this period, and p. 111 for Hammond's resignation. The affidavits on Hammond's health for the Royal Commission in 1912 are in HP 16, and there are letters to Wallas in WP 42. For the *Nation* Alfred F. Havighurst, *Radical Journalist. H. W. Massingham* (Cambridge 1974) chs. vii and viii is a useful survey, with much quotation. *The Heart of the Empire* (1901), ed. C. F. G. Masterman contained essays by nine Cambridge men and has been reprinted (Brighton 1973) with a useful introduction by Bentley B. Gilbert, pp. xi–xxxvii. Lucy Masterman, *C. F. G. Masterman* (1939) contains useful extracts from the author's diary but is disappointing on the *Nation*; it is surprising, e.g., that Hammond 'hardly knew' Mrs Masterman, see Hammond to Ponsonby 2 Jan. 1928, PP, c. 668, ff.124–5. See also 'The New Liberalism of C. F. G. Masterman', by Edward David in Kenneth D. Brown (ed.), *Essays in Anti-Labour History* (1974), pp. 17–41. G. M. Trevelyan, *An Autobiography and other essays* (1949) is pretty unhelpful. G. P. Gooch, *Under Six Reigns* (1958) has some points in ch. vii. Victoria de Bunsen, *Charles Roden Buxton* (1948) is better on the pre-1914 period, and there are also many letters in HP. On Hobson, *Conf.* pp. 82–9 is relevant. There is an interesting comment on Hobson in the *Tribune* period in *Smuts*, ii, doc. 324. Hobson to Mrs E. A. Ross, 13 April 1913, is from the E. A. Ross Papers, State Historical Society of Wisconsin; my copy from Melvyn Stokes. Florence Edgar Hobson, *Ideals. True and False* (1917) contains the two title pieces, from which I quote, which were written before 1914. On Limpsfield see also Margaret Olivier (ed.), *Sydney Olivier*, esp. pp. 92–3, 129, 131. For the *English Review* episode see Hobson to Wallas, 24 June 1909, WP 9, and 2 Oct 1909, WP 4; it briefly became a vehicle for Hobson's group in 1909–10. F. M. L. Thompson, *Hampstead* (1974) is invaluable for the social and economic significance of the topographical points.

(II)

The problem becomes acute in this section of identifying authorship of articles in the *Nation*. For signed or initialled articles I give the author directly; also for articles subsequently republished under the author's name, e.g. in Hobson's *Crisis of Liberalism* (1909) – cited here as *C. of L.* Where there is strong internal evidence, I give the author's name in brackets; and where my attribution is more tentative I add a query. The most important articles used in this section are: Wallas, 'Remember 1880', *S*, 27 Jan. 1906, 408–9; Hobhouse, 'The question of the Lords', *CR*, xci (1907), 1–11, and 'The constitutional issue', ibid., 312–18; (Hobhouse?), 'The master question', N, 9 March 1907, pp. 61–2; (Hammond), 'The crisis in Liberal policy', N, 6 April 1907, pp. 213–14; (Hammond?), 'The party and the land', N, 20 April 1907, pp. 287–8; (Hobson?), 'Mr Asquith's problem', N, 30 March 1907, p. 176; 'The significance of the Budget', N, 20 April 1907, pp. 285–6; (Hobson), '"Earned" and "Unearned"', N, 27 April 1907, pp. 334–5; (Hobhouse), 'The moral of failure', N, 25 May 1907, p. 478; (Hobhouse?), 'Vital aspects of the land question', N, 27 April 1907, pp. 333–4; 'The Government and the party', N, 1 June 1907, pp. 513–14; 'The character of the prime minister', N, 29 June 1907, pp. 653–4; 'Personalities in parliament', N, 31 Aug. 1907, pp. 949–50; (Hobhouse?), 'The Government's problem', N, 12 Oct. 1907, pp. 36–7; 'The moral of Jarrow', N, 6 July 1907, p. 684; 'The fear of socialism', N, 27 July 1907, p. 788; 'Attractiveness in politics', N, 3 Aug. 1907, pp. 820–1; Hobson, 'Socialism in Liberalism', N, 12 Oct. 1907, pp. 37–8 (*C. of L.*, pp. 133–8); Hobson, 'Is socialism plunder?', N, 19 Oct. 1907, pp. 82–3; Hobson, 'Is socialism tyranny?', N, 26 Oct. 1907, pp. 118–19; Hobson, 'Is socialism a spoils system?', N, 2 Nov. 1907, pp. 148–9; Hobson, 'Are riches the wages of efficiency?', N, 9 Nov. 1907, pp. 183–4; Hobson, 'The four-fold path of socialism', N, 30 Nov. 1907, pp. 302–3; Hobson, 'The vision of Liberalism', N, 2 May 1908, pp. 144–5 (*C. of L.*, pp. 91–5); Hobhouse, 'The prospects of Liberalism', *CR*, xciii (1908), 349–58, mainly reprinted as pref. to 2nd edn of *Democracy and Reaction* (1909); 'The limitations of the Pensions Bill', N, 20 June 1908, pp. 405–7; 'A new political development', N, 13 June 1908, pp. 367–8; letter from Ponsonby, N, 15 Aug 1908, pp. 707–8; 'The personality of Mr Burns', N, 24 Oct. 1908, pp. 139–40; (Hobson), 'The finance of social reform', N, 14 Nov. 1908, pp. 243–4, and 'The policy of the supertax', N, 5 Dec. 1908, pp. 367–8, substantially repeated in *MG*, 29 Jan. 1909, 1 Feb. 1909 and 4 Feb. 1909 as 'Taxation and the coming Budget'; cf. (Hobson), 'Land values and the Budget', N, 26 Dec. 1908, pp. 494–5, and 'An equitable Budget', N, 30 Jan. 1909, pp. 662–3; Wallas, letter, *MG*,

1 Dec. 1908; 'Shall the "dominating issue" be dominant?', N, 19 Dec. 1908; 'The effect of "bluff" in politics', N, 30 Jan. 1909, pp. 660–1; 'The remaining work of the Government' and letter from Hobson, N, 27 Feb. 1909, pp. 810–12, 824; 'Trade Boards and sweating', N, 3 April 1909, pp. 8–9; 'A study of the bye-elections', N, 17 April 1909, pp. 80–1; 'The first democratic Budget', N, 1 May 1909, pp. 148–9; 'The attack on the Budget', N, 8 May 1909, pp. 184–5; 'The voice of the Junker', N, 15 May 1909, pp. 232–3; (Hobhouse), 'The overplus of wealth', N, 29 May 1909, pp. 319–20; 'The principles of the Budget', N, 12 June 1909, pp. 374–6; 'The argument for the land taxes', N, 19 June 1909, pp. 408–9; (Hobhouse), 'The coming reality of politics', N, 26 June 1909, pp. 447–8; Hobson, 'The significance of the Budget', *ER*, ii (1909), 794–805; 'The re-heartening of Liberalism', N, 31 July 1909, pp. 628–9; 'The flight of the opposition', N, 7 Aug. 1909, pp. 664–5; 'The Lords and the Land!', N, 11 Sep. 1909, pp. 836–8; (Hobson), 'The social policy of Liberalism', N, 27 Nov. 1909, pp. 354–5; Hobson, 'The extension of Liberalism', *ER*, iii (1909), 673–86 (*C. of L.*, pp. 96–113); Hobhouse, 'The Lords and the constitution', *CR*, xcvi (1909), 641–51; Hobson, 'After the destruction of the veto', *ER*, iv (1909), 111–21 (*C. of L.*, pp. 3–16); Wallas, 'The money-power at war', N, 11 Dec. 1909, pp. 453–5; Hobhouse, 'The contending forces', *ER*, iv (1910), 359–71; (Hobhouse), 'The re-statement of Liberalism', N, 8 Jan. 1910, p. 614.

On the emergence of a Liberal commitment to social policy H. V. Emy, *Liberals, Radicals and Social Politics 1892–1914* (Cambridge 1973) has important points to make though it is a trifle ragged at times. The tactical problem of concentrating the Liberal party's efforts upon one question is the theme of D. A. Hamer, *Liberal Politics in the Age of Gladstone and Rosebery* (Oxford 1972). The excellent study by Neal Blewett, *The Peers, the Parties and the People* (1972) contains in Pt. II an intelligent and thorough appraisal of political developments from the winter of 1908 to the winter of 1910; and for an overall survey Kenneth O. Morgan, *The Age of Lloyd George* (1971) is helpful. The propriety of Churchill's question, 'How did you get it?', was defended by (Hobson), 'The origins of wealth', N, 11 Sep. 1909, pp. 839–40; but it was, of course, no part of the Hobsonian doctrine to make this inquiry of the individual taxpayer, only to make assumptions about certain kinds of wealth; and it is interesting that in *Lib. & Soc. Prob.*, p. 378n. Churchill conceded exactly this point (the preface is dated 26 Oct. 1909). See also C. J. Driver, 'Social and political ideas', in F. J. C. Hearnshaw (ed.), *Edwardian England* (1933), esp. pp. 247–59.

(III)

For the arguments in the press see letter from E. O. Post, N, 19 Oct. 1907, p. 84 and Hobson's adoption of this point in 'The four-fold path of socialism', N, 30 Nov. 1907, pp. 302–3; (Hobhouse), 'The career of Fabianism', N, 30 March 1907, pp. 182–3; (Hobhouse), 'Democracy and the expert', N, 13 June 1908, pp. 375–6; 'Poverty and the state', N, 4 July 1908, pp. 477–8;

'The Poor Law and the family', N, 22 Aug. 1908, pp. 727–8; (Hobhouse), 'The Poor Law Commission' (leader), *MG*, 18 Feb. 1909 and 'The Poor Law Commission's Reports' (leader), *MG*, 20 Feb. 1909; Hobhouse, 'The state in relation to poverty' (six-part series), *MG*, 22 and 24 Feb. 1909, 1, 4, 8 and 15 March 1909; 'Saving and character', N, 2 Jan. 1909, pp. 531–2; 'True conceptions of state help', N, 6 March 1909, pp. 845–6; 'From pensions to insurance', N, 9 Jan. 1909, pp. 566–7; 'The ending or mending of the Poor Law', N, 20 Feb. 1909, pp. 773–4; 'Insurance and unemployment', N, 29 May 1909, pp. 301–2; 'Poor Law reform and the Budget', N, 25 Sep. 1909, pp. 905–6.

Beatrice Webb's diary is, of course, extremely useful and *OP*, ch. vii, prints most of the relevant entries, though on a few minor points the transcription softens Beatrice's attitude in a way that does not do justice to her, e.g. p. 418 adding an exclamation mark – 'no nonsense about democracy!' (15 Nov. 1908) and p. 428 'forming' instead of 'forcing' public opinion (15 May 1909). There are letters from Webb to Scott, 23 Jan. 1909 (MGP) and to Hobhouse, 4 Feb. 1909 (Hobhouse Papers) about the reception of the Minority Report; and cf. Koss, *Fleet Street Radical*, pp. 98–9. The Webbs published their own version of the Minority Report (Cd 4499 (1909) iii) as *The Break up of the Poor Law* and *The Public Organisation of the Labour Market* (1909). For Hobhouse's views on the Report see also *Social Evolution and Political Theory* (1911), pp. 172ff, esp. p. 179 on 'the determined idler' who should get 'discipline and restraint'. J. H. Muirhead, *By What Authority? The principles in common and at issue in the Reports of the Poor Law Commission* (2nd edn 1909) was reprinted from the *Birmingham Daily Post*: I have quoted from the 2nd edition with a postscript written that autumn. A further edn appeared as *The Starting-Point of Poor Law Reform* (1910). The key sections of Churchill's speeches are in *Lib. & Soc. Prob.*, pp. 198–9, 253–73, 297–317. On Churchill's case for the principle of insurance I accept the distinction perceptively drawn in Bentley B. Gilbert, 'Winston Churchill versus the Webbs: the origins of British unemployment insurance', *American Historical Review*, lxxi (1965–6), esp. p. 855; see also Gilbert's *The Evolution of National Insurance in Great Britain* (1966), esp. pp. 271–3 for the meat of Churchill's 'Notes on malingering', 6 June 1909, argued – ironically enough – against Hubert Llewellyn Smith, now his permanent secretary. In her extremely thorough examination of social policy in this period, *Unemployment and Politics 1886–1914* (Oxford 1972), José Harris rightly points to the fact that on the specific point at issue here the Insurance Act retained a moralistic check (p. 314 & n.3). But the principle Churchill was invoking, although it failed to carry this point, was surely the reason for the widespread acceptance of 'insurance' schemes for the next half century. There is now a good biographical study, *John Burns* (1977) by Kenneth D. Brown; see chs. vi and vii for a fair appraisal of his record at the Local Government Board. The socially conservative character of Liberal welfare reform is a theme currently receiving much attention, e.g. Roy Hay, 'Employers and social policy in Britain: the evolution of welfare legislation, 1905–14', *Social History*, i

(1976–7), 435–55. This usually involves stressing the congruence of imperialism with social reform, a case put in a singularly cavalier way in Robert J. Scally, *The Origins of the Lloyd George Coalition. The politics of social-imperialism 1900–1918* (Princeton 1975); for my inability to accept this view see my review, *English Historical Review*, xci (1976), 873–5.

For analysis of unemployment, the study by Harris is very useful, and her excellent biography, *William Beveridge* (1977) is a work of which only time precluded my fuller use. For Beveridge's and Hobson's positions see 'The problem of the unemployed', *SP*, iii (1907), 324–41. Hobson's letter to Samuel, n.d. but ?1903 (Samuel Papers, A 155/III/28) is useful as a child's guide to underconsumption. D. J. Coppock, 'A reconsideration of Hobson's theory of unemployment', *Manchester School*, xxi (1953), esp. pp. 5–7, carefully interprets *The Industrial System* as an anticipation of Keynes, a suggestion made *en passant* by a number of other authors. E. E. Nemmers, *Hobson and Underconsumption* (Amsterdam 1956), though not making this claim, isolates underconsumption rather than the surplus as the core of Hobson's doctrine. The wholly persuasive treatment by Alan J. Lee, 'The social and economic thought of J. A. Hobson' (London Ph.D. 1970) puts the contrary view which I accept here. For Wallas's view on underconsumption see 'The economics of human welfare', N, 27 June 1914, p. 495; for the Hammonds, see *The Village Labourer* (1911), pp. viii, 166; for Hobhouse, 'The overplus of wealth', N, 29 May 1909, p. 319, and *The Labour Movement* (3rd edn 1912), pp. 106–7. Hobson's proposals for taxation were further developed in 'The reconstruction of the income tax', *NC*, lxxv (1914), 644–56. The centrality of a Hobsonian fiscal approach to politics in this period is well argued in H. V. Emy, 'The impact of financial policy on English party politics before 1914', *Historical Journal*, xv (1972). Hobhouse's theory of economic justice is viewed in a different and more unfavourable light in Stefan Collini, 'Liberalism and Sociology', ch. 4, esp. pp. 139–50.

Ch. 5 Human Nature in Politics

(I)

Oliver Hobhouse's notes about his father in *Memoir*, pp. 87ff., pick out many of his personal foibles. His cultural conservatism comes out strongly in *The World in Conflict* (1915), admittedly written under the stress of war; cf. Hobson's *Problems of a New World* (1921), quoted ch. 7, i. The Hammonds' correspondence with the Murrays is a fruitful source of obiter dicta on the marginalia of ethics, esp. cruelty to animals, hunting, vivisection, vegetarianism. See also 'Motor roads and the public', N, 2 Oct. 1909, pp. 7–8. Ada Wallas's diary, though mainly covering the war years, has useful notes on their reading.

John Gross, *The Rise and Fall of the Man of Letters* (1969) provides a sensitive commentary on some of these themes esp. ch. 4 'Some liberal practitioners'. Margaret Drabble, *Arnold Bennett* (1974) is an excellent all-round appreciation; and Newman Flower (ed.), *The Journals of Arnold*

Bennett, i and ii (1932), are full of interest esp. for 1910 when he was writing *Clayhanger* and for the later years of the war when he was prominent in the Writers' Group. H. G. Wells, *Experiment in Autobiography* (1934), e.g. pp. 597–600, on Wallas, has much to offer, and should be supplemented with the very good biography by Norman and Jeanne Mackenzie, *The Time-Traveller* (1973). For Wells and the Fabian Society see his 'The faults of the Fabian', reprinted in the cultural survey by Samuel Hynes, *The Edwardian Turn of Mind* (Princeton 1968), App. C.; and reply to Hobhouse's 'The career of Fabianism', N, 6 April 1907, p. 227. See also Margaret Cole, 'H. G. Wells and the Fabian Society', in A. J. A. Morris (ed.), *Edwardian Radicalism* (1974), pp. 97–113. Beatrice Webb's diary is very full on Wells 1906–10; and see *OP*, pp. 415, 456–7 for the Cambridge Fabians.

Quantity has still not outweighed quality in the extensive published writings about Bloomsbury. Roy Harrod, *The Life of John Maynard Keynes* (1951) remains indispensable despite failings of perspective which more seriously mar its political treatment. Michael Holroyd, *Lytton Strachey: a biography* (1967–8; Penguin 1971) supplies massive documentation and is a useful guide. Quentin Bell, *Virginia Woolf*, 2 vols. (1972) is a biography of great insight and distinction and should be read in conjunction with Leonard Woolf's autobiographical volumes, *Sowing* (1960), *Growing* (1961) and *Beginning Again* (1964), which cover this period. For Keynes's early life, Geoffrey Keynes, 'The early years', in Milo Keynes (ed.), *Essays on John Maynard Keynes* (Cambridge 1975), has unique standing. *JMK*, xv (1971), *Activities 1906–14*, ed. Elizabeth Johnson, prints some material of interest, esp. the letter of 29 Dec. 1909, pp. 39–42; cf. N, 20 Nov. 1909. A much more personal aspect is revealed in the letters of Keynes to Duncan Grant, chiefly 1908–11, but with occasional later ones, in the British Library, Add. MSS 57930–1. Keynes's own autobiographical reflections came in 'My Early Beliefs' (1938), reprinted in *JMK*, x (1972), *Essays in Biography*, pp. 433–50; these receive elucidation in Woolf, *Sowing*, pp. 144–9, 155–6, and in R. B. Braithwaite, 'Keynes as a philosopher', *Essays on John Maynard Keynes*, pp. 243–5. I am quite unable to accept Skidelsky's assertion that before the war Keynes was 'completely uninvolved in the politics of the Left', in 'The revolt against the Victorians', Robert Skidelsky (ed.), *The End of the Keynesian Era* (1977), p. 7; and see also the appraisal of 'Keynes and Cambridge' by John Vaizey, ibid., pp. 10–17. A. C. Pigou, 'John Maynard Keynes', *PBA*, xxxii (1946), 395–414, speaks with the authority of an insider on the Marshallian tradition. On Hobson and Marshall, I am much indebted to the work of A. W. Coats for 'Alfred Marshall and Richard T. Ely: some unpublished letters', *Ec*, n.s., xxviii (1961), 191–4, and more generally his 'Sociological aspects of British economic thought (ca. 1880–1930)', *Journal of Political Economy*, lxxv (1967), esp. 707–14 on Marshall and the Cambridge school.

(II)

Although I draw upon *Human Nature in Politics* in this section, I am not offering a systematic analysis of it, for which Wiener, *Between Two Worlds* should be consulted: but rather trying to pin down Wallas's assumptions about democracy by means of this and other evidence, e.g. 'Credo', notes for Shaw, n.d. (? 1903), WP 10. On the 1910 elections see C. F. G. Masterman, 'How it strikes a contemporary', N, 8 Jan. 1910, pp. 597–9; 'Our "educated" classes', N, 22 Jan. 1910, pp. 669–70; 'The strength of England', N, 22 Jan. 1910, pp. 665–6; Hobson, 'The General Election: a sociological interpretation', *SR*, iii (1910), 105–17 (paper read 22 Feb. 1910); (Hobson), 'The two Englands', N, 26 Feb. 1910, pp. 837–8; cf. (Hobson), 'The mob mind', N, 1 Aug. 1908, pp. 631–2. For attitudes to socialism see the lecture by Wallas, 'Syndicalism', *SR*, v (1912), 247–50, and comment by Hobson, pp. 253–4; cf. 'A new political development', N, 13 June 1908, pp. 367–8. For Labour attitudes see Martin Petter, 'The progressive alliance', *History*, lviii (1973), 45–59; and the very interesting revisionist approach presented with such authority in Kenneth O. Morgan, *Keir Hardie* (1975), esp. ch. 10. Hobhouse's view was argued in 'The prospects of Liberalism', CR, xciii (1908), 349–58, most of which was used as the preface to the 2nd edn of *Democracy and Reaction* (1909; repr. 1972), pp. 247–72. See also *The Labour Movement* (3rd edn 1912), which was a substantial reconstruction, and also *Government by the People* (People's Suffrage Federation, 1910) for the link with woman suffrage. On the role of the intellect (Hobhouse), 'The restatement of Liberalism', N, 8 Jan. 1910, p. 614; 'Oxford and the people', N, 6 Feb. 1909, pp. 710–11; Wallas, 'Let youth but know', S, 20 Jan. 1906, in *Men & Ideas*, pp. 151–5, and 'Oxford and the nation', *Westminster Gazette*, 28 April 1908, ibid., pp. 156–61. The interesting article by Reba Soffer, 'New elitism: social psychology in prewar England', *Journal of British Studies*, viii (1968–9), 111–39, helps set Wallas's views in context. Hobson urged the referendum in 'The conflict with the Lords', *MG*, 14–26 Feb. 1907, reprinted in *Crisis of Liberalism*, pp. 17–49; cf. Hobson, 'The veto for the people', N, 4 May 1907, pp. 378–9. His article, 'The money power in politics', *MG*, 27 Dec. 1909, is attrib. by Alan Lee, and parallels Wallas, 'The money power at war', N, 11 Dec. 1909, pp. 453–5. In view of the ostensibly hopeful tone of *Traffic in Treason* (1914) it is interesting to note Hobson's subsequent view of the Curragh confrontation, in *Democracy after the War* (1917), p. 65: 'Property, in open alliance with organised illegal force, would have fought to recover the constitutional positions it had lost, and would have firmly entrenched itself against future assaults of the people, either in their capacity of an electorate or an industrial proletariat.' For Hammond's retrospective view see 'Liberalism and Labour', *C. P. Scott* (1946), pp. 234–43.

(III)

The progress of *The Great Society* can be traced in considerable detail from the summer of 1910 to the autumn of 1913 through the letters from Graham to Ada Wallas in WP 44–5. What I say here about Hobhouse is chiefly based upon *Democracy and Reaction* (1904), *Liberalism* (1911), *Social Evolution and Political Theory* (New York 1911), *Development and Purpose* (1913), and 'The historical evolution of property, in fact and in idea', in Charles Gore (ed.), *Property: its duties and rights* (1913), pp. 1–31, reprinted in L. T. Hobhouse, *Sociology and Philosophy* (1966), pp. 81–106. C. M. Griffin, 'L. T. Hobhouse and the idea of harmony', *Journal of the History of Ideas*, xxxv (1974), 647–61, is close to my general theme but is seriously marred by some crudities of treatment, e.g. the theoretical contention that Hobhouse only stressed the role of purpose after the First World War (p. 653) and the political point that Ginsberg was wrong to distance Hobhouse from Fabianism (p. 660). John Owen, *L. T. Hobhouse, sociologist* (1974) is a competent synthetic summary but lacks historical sense as to either chronology or context. Peter Weiler, 'The new Liberalism of L. T. Hobhouse', *Victorian Studies*, xvi (1972), 141–61, is better in this respect but I am, in my treatment of the 'fundamental postulate', strongly embattled against Weiler's (pejorative) claim that Hobhouse's 'whole argument rests on this unproved, utopian assumption' (p. 147). John Burrow, *Evolution and Society* (Cambridge 1966), esp. pp. 92–3, 98–9, 101, 219, 267–8, 272–4, is illuminating about the problems of evolutionary social thought, though I think the treatment of Hobhouse has an incisiveness which could easily pass for short shrift. There is an interesting brief account of Hobhouse's thought in relation to Spencer in Geoffrey Hawthorn, *Enlightenment and Despair* (Cambridge 1977), ch. 5. I differ from it in that Hawthorn sees an evolutionary teleology as the crumbling foundation stone of Hobhouse's sociology whereas I see it as an unsafe buttress. In this I believe that I am following Morris Ginsberg; see his essay in Timothy Raison (ed.), *Founding Fathers of Social Science* (Penguin 1969), pp. 154–61, and esp. his introduction to L. T. Hobhouse, *Sociology and Philosophy* (1966), p. xxxvi: 'Many will feel that his attempts to extend the conclusions he reached concerning the evolution of mind in a single planet of our solar system so as to give them a cosmic bearing and to derive from them hopes for the future of the entire universe and of man in it were bound to come up against grave difficulties.' The heaviest guns are undoubtedly those deployed by Stefan Collini, 'Liberalism and Sociology' (Cambridge PhD 1977), esp. ch. 5, and it is with some diffidence that I depart at all from his treatment, and in fact do not do so as regards the political implications. In the justly influential study by Raymond Aron, *Main Currents in Sociological Thought* (1965–8) the two hallmarks of sociology are defined as 'the aim of scientific objectivity and the aim of grasping the social *as such*' (Penguin edn, i, 14). While I think Hobhouse's claims here worth consideration, I cannot go as far as Ronald Fletcher, *The Making of Sociology* (1971), ii, 123–230, in seeking to assimilate Hobhouse to a sort of consensus of the great minds of his age. R. J. Halliday, 'Social Darwinism: a definition', *Victorian Studies*, xiv (1971), 389–405, is a useful account of the evolutionary debate.

For the intellectual climate of this period Noel Annan's Hobhouse Memorial Lecture, *The Curious Strength of Positivism in English Political*

Thought (1959) is one obvious starting point; see also the wide-ranging article by Reba N. Soffer, 'The revolution in English social thought, 1880–1914', *American Historical Review*, lxxv (1970), 1938–64. Michael Freeden, 'J. A. Hobson as a new Liberal theorist', *Journal of the History of Ideas*, xxxiv (1973), 421–43, offers a view of Hobson with considerable stress on the organic paradigm; and his recent book *The New Liberalism* (Oxford 1978) generalises from these insights in a valuable analysis which, however, differs in tone if not substance from my own, e.g. pp. 105–7 preferring Hobson to Hobhouse on the general will. See also David Nicholls, 'Positive liberty, 1880–1914', *American Political Science Review*, lvi (1962), 114–28. The analysis in J. D. Y. Peel, *Herbert Spencer* (1971), chs. 6–8, suggests many parallels esp. with Hobson's organic analogies. Hobson's review of the *Great Society*, *MG*, 10 July 1914, clarifying his position against Wallas, could be seen as a reply to Wallas's review of *Work and Wealth*, N, 27 June 1914, pp. 495–6. For Hobson at his most organic see 'Co-partnership in nature', N, 16 Oct. 1909, pp. 116–17; (Hobson), 'Nature the radical', N, 22 Jan. 1910, pp. 672–3; Hobson, 'Social parasitism', *ER*, iv (1910), pp. 347–58.

On Germany see 'Two schools of socialism', N, 19 Sep. 1908, pp. 856–8; Eduard Bernstein, 'The electoral policy of German Social Democracy', N, 11 Dec. 1909, pp. 456–7; cf. his 'The character of the German workers' insurance', N, 5 Sep. 1908, pp. 798–800; and see Peter Gay, *The Dilemma of Democratic Socialism. Eduard Bernstein's challenge to Marx* (1952; Collier edn 1962), esp. pp. 226–8, 244–7. Bernstein's memoirs, translated as *My Years of Exile* (1921), chs. 7–11, include a lengthy appraisal of the English socialists whom he knew. There are two interesting and neglected essays in Morris Ginsberg (ed.), *Law and Opinion in England in the 20th Century* (1959): by Ginsberg, 'The growth of social responsibility', esp. pp. 14–15, 18–19 on liberal socialism; and by G. D. H. Cole, 'The growth of socialism', esp. pp. 81–3, 92–3 on liberalism and socialism as reform ideologies. The young Cole has attracted much attention: see Anthony W. Wright, 'From Fabianism to Guild Socialism' and Jeffrey Weeks, 'The politics of pluralism', both in *Bulletin of the Society for the Study of Labour History*, 32 (1976), pp. 23–5, 59–66.

(IV)

Wallas, 'From the Second to the Third Reform Bill', *IR*, viii (1906), 228–32, expressed dissatisfaction with traditional historiography. J. L. Hammond and Barbara Hammond, *The Village Labourer 1760–1832* (1911); 2nd imp. 1912; 2nd edn 1913, with new pref. pp. ix–xii; repr. 1919; 3rd edn 1920; 4th edn 1927; Guild Books edn 1948, repr. as paperback edn 1966, with pref. to 4th edn as App. B, pp. 363–7. For general bibliography on the Hammonds as historians see ch. 8, i. I have drawn heavily on the Hammonds' letters in MP 23 for details on the composition of their works. The most significant reviews were by Wallas, N, 11 Nov. 1911, pp. 248–9; and J. H. Clapham, *EcJ*, xxii (1912), 248–55. See J. L. Hammond, 'Making ends meet in the cottage', *L*, 11 Nov. 1936, pp. 893–6, for a later reiteration of the themes of the *Village Labourer*. For modern assessments see E. P. Thompson, *The Making of the English Working Class* (1963; Pelican edn 1968), ch. 7, which extends their line of argument on enclosures; J. D. Chambers and G. E. Mingay, *The Agricultural Revolution 1750–1850* (1966), pp. 85–104, for a sharply critical treatment of their analysis of enclosure, poverty and relation to the labourers' revolt; and E. J. Hobsbawm and George Rudé, *Captain Swing* (1969; Penguin 1973), esp. pp. xix–xxi, which suggests that if the Hammonds came up with several wrong answers about the revolt they were at least asking the right questions.

R. H. *Tawney's Commonplace Book*, ed. J. M. Winter and D. M. Joslin (Cambridge 1972) is a document of high interest; cf. Winter's article drawing upon it, 'R. H. Tawney's early political thought', *Past and Present*, 47 (May 1970), pp. 71–96. Ross Terrill, *R. H. Tawney and his times* (Cambridge, Mass., 1973) is the fullest biographical study. There are good portraits of the Tawneys and the Hammonds in Arnold J. Toynbee, *Acquaintances* (1967), pp. 86–107. Mary Agnes Hamilton, *Remembering My Good Friends* (1944), pp. 83–7, is also good on the Hammonds; cf. p. 136 on the Land Enquiry. The Report of the Land Enquiry Committee, *The Land*, i, *Rural* (1913) includes a long introduction by A. H. D. Acland, citing Tawney (p. lxx) and the Hammonds (p. lxxx). Vol. ii, *Urban* (1914) is half as long again (728/498 pp.). Hobhouse's series, 'The problems of land and labour', also drew heavily on the Hammonds for historical backing: see *MG*, 2, 3, 4, 6, 7, 8, 9 Oct. 1913. For a sensitive treatment of the overtones of historiography see Martin J. Wiener, 'The changing image of William Cobbett', *Journal of British Studies*, xiii (1974), esp. pp. 141–4. H. V. Emy, 'The Land Campaign: Lloyd George as a social reformer', in A. J. P. Taylor (ed.), *Lloyd George: twelve essays* (1971), pp. 35–68, is a good account; also Roy Douglas, 'God gave the land to the people', in A. J. A. Morris (ed.), *Edwardian Radicalism* (1974), pp. 148–61. See also Hobson's paper, 'Rural wages', Rainbow Circle minutes, 12 Nov. 1913. The life of Seebohm Rowntree by Asa Briggs, *Social Thought and Social Action* (1961) is particularly valuable for ch. 3 on Edwardian Liberalism.

Ch. 6 War

(I)

A. J. Anthony Morris, *Radicalism Against War, 1906–1914* (1972) is a full survey, some parts drawing heavily on the work of A. J. Dorey. It does not always resolve matters satisfactorily e.g. pp. 266ff. on Lord Courtney's Committee, on which see also G. P. Gooch, *Life of Lord Courtney* (1920), pp. 568ff.; *Memoir*, p. 48; and Stephen Koss, *Sir John Brunner* (Cambridge 1970), p. 259. The article prepared on behalf of the Foreign Policy Committee, 'Our foreign policy and its reform', *CR*, ci (1912), 466–74, clarifies its structure and intentions; cf. R. C. K. Ensor to Hobhouse, 2 April 1912, in the Hobhouse Papers. Howard Weinroth, 'Norman Angell and *The Great Illusion*: an episode in pre-1914 pacifism', *Historical Journal*, xvii

(1974), 551–74, is a useful survey of the reception of his ideas. See also the autobiography of Norman Angell, *After All* (1951), esp. Pt. II. There are three relevant essays in Morris (ed.), *Edwardian Radicalism*: 'H. N. Brailsford and the search for a new international order', by F. M. Leventhal (pp. 202–17); 'Radicalism and nationalism: an increasingly unstable equation', by Howard Weinroth (pp. 218–33); and 'A study in futility: the British radicals at the outbreak of the First World War', by Marvin Swartz (pp. 246–61).

The Hobhouse Papers in the possession of Mrs J. Balme contain an interesting correspondence between Leonard and Emily Hobhouse during these years; all letters between them (and also to Oliver) are from this source. All letters between Hobhouse and Scott are from the series in MGP unless specified otherwise, in which case they are from the Scott Papers in the British Library; many of these letters have been printed along with the pertinent interview notes (i.e. Scott's 'diary') in Wilson, which is a source of great value in this and the next chapter. I have given the Wilson reference wherever convenient.

The efforts of the British Neutrality Committee are set out in Wallas's memorandum of 6 Oct. 1914, and minutes of the B.N.C., in WP 39, which provide the basic narrative. For Gardiner and the *Daily News* I have relied upon the lucid account in Stephen Koss, *Fleet Street Radical*, pp. 148–50; cf. p. 157 for the urge to enlist. Russell, *Autobiog.*, i, 65, and ii, 16, 45–7, is vivid and generally reliable. There are a number of illuminating letters from the Hammonds to Ponsonby in the early months of the war in the PP in the Bodleian Library; their subsequent correspondence was never again so intimate. Keith Robbins, *The Abolition of War* (Cardiff 1976) is a scrupulously scholarly study based on the author's D.Phil. dissertation (1964); this securely established the story of the 'peace movement' during the First World War, including the role of the U.D.C. This aspect has subsequently been more fully documented and explored in Marvin Swartz, *The Union of Democratic Control in British Politics during the First World War* (Oxford 1971), which I have found very useful. See also John Rae, *Conscience and Politics* (1970) for conscientious objectors.

On Hobhouse's break with the *Nation* see *Memoir*, p. 62; Havighurst, *Radical Journalist*, pp. 235–8; H. W. Nevinson, *The Fire of Life* (1935), pp. 214–15. Nevinson's diary in the Bodleian Library is extremely useful up to the point when the *Nation* group fell apart; see esp. entries for 29 Dec. 1914, 12 Jan. 1915, 16 Feb. 1915, 23 Mar. 1915, 13 April 1915, 18 May 1915, 1 & 8 June 1915. Gilbert Murray, *The Foreign Policy of Sir Edward Grey* (1915) is an important polemical effort; and see Shaw, 'Professor Gilbert Murray's defence of Sir Edward Grey', *NS*, 17 July 1915, pp. 349–51. See also the personal note in G. M. Trevelyan, *Grey of Fallodon* (1937), p. 254n. For attitudes during the early months of the war see Hammond, 'A lesson from the French War', and G. L. Dickinson, 'The Holy War', *N*, 8 Aug. 1914, pp. 698–9 and 699–700; Hammond, 'Workmen and the army', *N*, 5 Sep. 1914, pp. 808–9; Hobhouse, *The World in Conflict* (1915), reprinting eleven short articles from *MG*, March–May

1915; Hobhouse, 'The social effects of the war', AM, cxv (1915), 544–50; Hammond, 'Agricultural labour and the crisis', N, 24 May 1915, pp. 112–113; Hobhouse, 'The soul of civilisation: a dialogue', CR, cviii (1915), 158–65. For Hammond's later view cf. *Faith in France* (Manchester 1946), pp. 226–7 (28 Aug. 1944).

(II)

Lawrence's letters to Barbara Hammond in HP 1–3 are very full during their separation and more use could have been made of them. Wallas, 'Ante-war ideals', N, 2 Oct. 1915, p. 23; and his comment on 'The peacefulness of being at war' (11 Sep. 1915), reprinted in *Men & Ideas*, pp. 95–102, give his views in the autumn of 1915. The main section of Ada Wallas's diary, in WP 49, covers the period 24 Sep. 1915 to 2 Nov. 1918, and has proved of immense value in reconstructing the outlook of Hobhouse, and occasionally Hobson, as well as Wallas himself. Hobson wrote U.D.C. pamphlets No. 15, *A League of Nations* (Oct. 1915) and No. 16, *Labour and the Costs of War* (Jan. 1916); see also his articles, 'Approaches to peace', N, 16 Oct. 1915, pp. 115–16; 'The suppression of free speech', N, 15 April 1916, pp. 68–9; 'Secret trial or no trial', N, 29 April 1916, pp. 123–5; 'The claims of the state upon the individual', N, 10 June 1916, pp. 307–8; 'Liberty as a true war economy', *N*, 29 July 1916, pp. 524–5. Charles Roden Buxton (ed.), *Towards a Lasting Settlement* (1915), includes Dickinson, 'The basis of a permanent peace', pp. 9–36, Hobson, 'The open door', pp. 85–110, and Brailsford, 'The organization of peace', pp. 147–76. Hobson's *The New Protectionism* (1916) has a preface dated 24 June 1916, stating its origin as articles for the *MG*. For his resignation from the Liberal party I am unable to find a better source than *Conf*., p. 126, which must refer to the inter-allied economic conference at Paris in June 1916, as in *Memoir*, pp. 51–2. See V. H. Rothwell, *British War Aims and Peace Diplomacy* 1914–1918 (Oxford 1971), pp. 268–9, which is a thorough and well-organised account with a good grasp of the diplomatic context. On the Bryce Group, there is a set of six drafts of the *Proposals*, Nov. 1914–Aug. 1915, in WP 34, along with Wallas's memorandum of 8 Feb. 1915 and his notes (?Mar. 1915), in WP 34. The lucid article by Martin David Dubin, 'Toward the concept of collective security', *International Organization*, xxiv (1970), 288–318, includes an invaluable appendix collating three of the different drafts with the 1917 published version. Keith Robbins, 'Lord Bryce and the First World War', *Historical Journal*, x (1967), 255–78, is a clear account but does not deal at any length with the Group. There are brief references in Dennis Proctor (ed.), *The Autobiography of G. Lowes Dickinson* (1973), pp. 190–1; E. M. Forster, *Goldsworthy Lowes Dickinson* (1934), p. 164 (and p. 156 for his desire to enlist); Mary Agnes Hamilton, *Remembering My Good Friends* (1944), pp. 136–7, cf. p. 83 for Hammond; Leonard Woolf, *Beginning Again* (1964), pp. 182–3; cf. *Conf*., pp. 103–7. Florence Edgar Hobson, *Ideals. True and False* (1917) includes three war-time papers; see esp. 'Women and internationalism' (Apr. 1915) and 'Must the war go on?' (Nov. 1916). Hobhouse's *Questions of War and Peace*

(1916) reprinted 'The soul of civilisation', with a long, ambivalent, undated dialogue, 'The hope of the world'; and 'The future of internationalism', from an address at the National Liberal Club, 18 Jan. 1916.

For Gardiner's emergence as an Asquithian see Koss, *Fleet Street Radical*, pp. 189–90. On Keynes see Woolf, *Beginning Again*, p. 177; Harrod, pp. 214–15; Holroyd, pp. 620–1; and on Garsington, Hamilton, pp. 73–8. For Massingham's attitude to Asquith see the citations in Havighurst, p. 239, and esp. 'The attack on Free Trade', N, 26 Feb. 1916, pp. 752–3; 'Wayfarer', N, 6 May 1916, pp. 152–3; 'The "letting down" of Liberalism', N, 5 Aug. 1916, pp. 554–6. There is a good political narrative of this period in Trevor Wilson, *The Downfall of the Liberal Party 1914–35* (1966), Pt. 1.

R. H. Tawney, *The Attack, and other papers* (1953) contains 'The attack' (Aug. 1916) and 'Some reflections of a soldier' (from N, 21 Oct. 1916). Ruth Fry, *Emily Hobhouse*, pp. 266ff. deals with her visit to Germany. I quote the Lloyd George interview from *MG*, 29 Sep. 1916. Laurence W. Martin, *Peace Without Victory. Woodrow Wilson and the British Liberals* (New Haven 1958) is a clear survey of the reception of Wilson's policy, making good use of the press. Despite a few errors (e.g. the identification of Hammond as an opponent of the war) it remains of great value. Llewellyn Woodward, *Great Britain and the war of 1914–18* (1967) gives the standard account of all developments; see pp. 235ff. for the American Note. Sterling Kernek, 'The British Government's reaction to President Wilson's "Peace" Note of December 1916', *Historical Journal*, xiii (1970), 721–66, in a highly detailed examination, takes a sceptical view of the tactical manoeuvres here. Ada Wallas's diary, 17 Jan. 1917, on Hobhouse's response may well refer to an encounter a few days previously.

(III)

Paul Barton Johnson, *Land Fit for Heroes. The planning of British reconstruction 1916–1919* (1968) is a very full study with copious citation from departmental papers and it sets Hammond's work properly in context. The Hammonds' work on the *Town Labourer* can be fully reconstructed from their papers, partly as a result of their separation. There is a very interesting series of letters from George Unwin, esp. 14 & 30 July 1914, 6 & 16 Aug. 1914, 1 Sep. 1914, 1 Oct. 1914, in HP 17; and see also below ch. 8, i. For Hammond's indebtedness to Cole at this time compare Cole's *Self-Government in Industry* (1917; ed. J. G. Corina 1972), pp. 40–1, with Jason, p. 108 (quoted in text). See also the interesting article by James Hinton, 'G. D. H. Cole in the stage army of the good', *Bulletin of the Society for the Study of Labour History*, 28 (1974), pp. 76–83. J. M. Winter, *Socialism and the Challenge of War* (1974) focuses on Tawney, Cole and the Webbs; it is a well researched study with many insights to offer; see esp. pp. 136–8 on Whitleyism. On the Romney Street Group see Thomas Jones, *Whitehall Diary*, ed. Keith Middlemas (1969), i, 42; Edna Nixon, *John Hilton* (1946), pp. 53–4, 61–2. For the Idealists and the war see Muirhead, *Reflections*, pp. 172–9; *Bernard Bosanquet and his friends*, pp. 159, 165, in the copy of which in University College London there is a relevant letter from Muirhead to Hilda Oakeley, 7 May 1935, reiterating this point. Stefan Collini, 'Hobhouse, Bosanquet and the state', *Past and Present*, 72 (1976), 86–111, is the authoritative account.

(IV)

A. J. P. Taylor, *The Trouble Makers* (1957; Panther edn 1964) was a pioneering study of radical dissent over foreign policy and it remains unsurpassed; see e.g. its splendid vignette of the 1917 Club, p. 132. On the Club Hamilton, pp. 78–9; H. W. Nevinson, *Last Changes, Last Chances* (1928), p. 128; Woolf, *Beginning Again*, pp. 215–17; and Douglas Goldring, *Odd Man Out* (1935), pp. 267–75, and *The Nineteen Twenties* (1945), pp. 138–52, are all evocative. Anne Olivier Bell, *The Diary of Virginia Woolf*, vol. 1, 1915–1919 (1977), offers contemporary documentation, pp. 57, 94, 99, 102, 115, 209. On the move from Liberalism to Labour, Catherine Ann Cline, *Recruits to Labour* (New York, 1963) is of considerable prosopographical value. For Noel Buxton see also H. N. Fieldhouse's essay in Martin Gilbert (ed.), *A Century of Conflict* (1966), pp. 177–97. In what I write of MacDonald I am strongly influenced by the persuasive interpretation in Rodney Barker, 'Socialism and progressivism in the political thought of Ramsay MacDonald', in Morris (ed.), *Edwardian Radicalism* (1974), pp. 114–30; see also his interesting article 'Political myth: Ramsay MacDonald and the Labour party', *History*, lxi (1976), 46–56. J. M. Winter, 'Arthur Henderson, the Russian Revolution, and the reconstruction of the Labour party', *Historical Journal*, xv (1972), 753–73, is an important and convincing demonstration of the part his Russian visit played in changing his conception of the role of the Labour party. Arthur Henderson, *The Aims of Labour* (1917) shows what he envisaged. See also S. R. Graubard, *British Labour and the Russian Revolution 1917–1924* (1956) for a systematic survey. For the Webbs *BWD*, iii, supplies much background information. L. P. Carpenter, *G. D. H. Cole* (Cambridge 1973) is a painstaking intellectual biography from which I have derived much assistance. It is a pity that it was not able to draw upon Margaret Cole, *The Life of G. D. H. Cole* (1971); and see also Maurice Reckitt's autobiography, *As It Happened* (1941). The Labour Party, *Report of the Executive Committee* (1918), pp. 11–12, *Report of the 19th Annual Conference* (1919), pp. 47–8, and *Report of the 20th Annual Conference* (1920), pp. 39, 41, give some information on the Advisory Committees, but a more exhaustive listing would be helpful. Hobson's 1920. *Dips into the near future* (1918) by 'Lucian' contained satirical articles reprinted from the *Nation* of late 1917; according to H. M. Swanwick's history of the U.D.C., *Builders of Peace* (1924), p. 183, his authorship 'was guessed by one member of the Executive, purely from his style at Executive meetings'.

For the Lansdowne and Labour movement see Robbins, *The Abolition of War*, pp. 150–2. The letters reporting on his mission to Europe which Ray Stannard Baker prepared for Frank L. Polk, Counsellor at the State Department, provide an excellent view of the evolution of British politics in 1918; esp. letters 1–4, 8, 9, and 14. I am indebted to Melvyn Stokes for these copies from the Baker Papers in the Firestone Library at Princeton University. On the Writers' Group see Bennett, *Journals*, ii, 216, 221–3, 235, and Ada Wallas's diary, esp. 16 May 1918. On the Peace, Barbara Hammond's 'Recollections of Peace Conference 1918–19', HP 126, is regrettably only a fragment. There are a few letters of this period in the Keynes–Grant correspondence, BL Add. MSS. 57931. Wilson, pp. 362–78, prints some letters of this period. Keynes's, *The Economic Consequences of the Peace* (1919) is repaginated as *JMK*, ii; and cf. Hammond, 'The catastrophe of Paris', N, 7 June 1919, pp. 286–8. Wilson Harris, *Life So Far* (1954), ch. 6, has some good glimpses of Hammond in Paris. Stephen Koss, *Asquith* (1976) is a scholarly reappaisal, particularly valuable for its insights into his later career.

Ch. 7 Hobson's Choice

(I)

On servants there are some period illustrations in Barbara Hammond's letters to Mary Murray, MP 23b, and in Ada Wallas's diary, June–Sept. 1916, WP 49. For the effect of the war, Arthur Marwick, *Women at War 1914–1918* (1977), p. 163; cf. Pamela Horn, *The Rise and Fall of the Victorian Servant* (1975), ch. 10. For the 1920s, when Lawrence Hammond was working on the *Manchester Guardian* during the summers, his surviving correspondence with Barbara Hammond in HP 4–5 & 12–14 is unusually full and contains many sidelights on Hobhouse, Scott and the running of the paper. *H–L Letters* are an important source in this and the next chapter; Laski's letters were copious, fluent and percipient, but evidently overdrawn at times and not adequate as unsupported testimony. There is a good chapter on Murray in C. M. Bowra, *Memories 1898–1939* (1966), pp. 214–29: and a cameo of the Hammonds ('old-fashioned Fabian Socialists') in Peter Quennell, *The Marble Foot* (1976), pp. 95–6.

(II)

The articles on which I have chiefly drawn are Hammond, 'A tragedy of errors', N, 8 Jan. 1921, 525–32 (1st Irish supp.); (Brailsford), 'Democracy on the defensive', N, 22 Jan. 1921, pp. 573–4; Hammond, 'The character of the Mallow Inquiry', N, 2 April 1921, pp. 10–11; Laski, review of *Our Social Heritage*, N, 9 April 1921, pp. 60–2 (cf. *H–L Letters*, pp. 321, 329); Hammond, 'The terror in action', N, 30 April 1921, pp. 185–92 (2nd Irish supp.); 'Lloyd George for ever and ever?', N, 14 May 1921, pp. 240–1; Wallas, review of *The Acquisitive Society*, N, 11 June 1921, p. 401; 'The passing of Lloyd George', N, 25 June 1921, pp. 458–9; Hammond, 'Ireland under the truce', N, 15 Oct. 1921, pp. 106–7. On attitudes to Lloyd George, the Scott interview notes published in Wilson have much to offer. Michael Bentley, *The Liberal Mind 1914–1929* (Cambridge 1977), esp. pp. 207–19, is a sensitive appraisal of the context in which Liberal attachment to principle became a principle in itself; cf. p. 185 for a hostile verdict on Massingham consistent with my suggestion here. For Massingham's side see H. M. Tomlinson, *H.W.M.*, pp. 125–8, and Massingham's 'Vale' (from *N*, 28 April 1923), pp. 141–2; and the account in Havighurst, pp. 293–307. For Keynes's role, Harrod, pp. 334–8 is fair; Woolf, *Beginning Again*, pp. 92–8, is more ambivalent, and for a sharper reaction, Bell, *Virginia Woolf*, ii, 92. There is a full correspondence on the *Nation* between Scott and Hammond in HP 34. For the L.S.E. in the 1920s see Lord Robbins, *Autobiography of an Economist* (1971), esp. pp. 86–9, 93, 104–5 (on Wallas); Kingsley Martin, *Father Figures* (1966; Penguin 1969), ch. 8; Kingsley Martin, *Harold Laski* (1953), ch. 3; Hugh Dalton, *Call Back Yesterday* (1953), ch. 6.

(III)

Erwin Esser Nemmers, *Hobson and Underconsumption* (Amsterdam 1956) comes into its own on this period, esp. pp. 85–103. T. W. Hutchison, *A Review of Economic Doctrines 1870–1929* (Oxford 1953), pp. 417–23 is a useful introduction. On savings and investment, there is a pertinent letter from Kahn to Keynes in comment on the proofs of the *General Theory*: 'I do not like you saying that saving and investment are "different names for the same thing". They are *different* things (that is the whole point) – they are certainly different acts – but they are equal in magnitude' (*JMK*, xiii, 637). In the *General Theory* (p. 63) the text is adjusted accordingly; but Hobson continually treated them as 'different names for the same activity'. On the consequent difficulty in Hobson's account of investment see Lawrence R. Klein, *The Keynesian Revolution* (1952), esp. p. 137. *A Tract on Monetary Reform* (1923) is reprinted as *JMK*, iv, and *A Treatise on Money* (1930) as *JMK*, v and vi. On 'involuntary abstention' (*JMK*, v, 157) Keynes was departing from D. H. Robertson's term 'automatic lacking' (see p. 154n.). The role of Robertson's *Banking Policy and the Price Level* (1926) is brought out better in Robert Lekachman, *The Age of Keynes* (1967), ch. 3, than in any other general treatment. The excellent article by Lionel Robbins, 'Consumption and the trade cycle', *Ec*, xii (1932), 420n., explicitly based its (perfectly fair) statement of the Hobsonian position upon *The Physiology of Industry* (1889), *The Evolution of Modern Capitalism* (1894), *The Industrial System* (1909) and *The Economics of Unemployment* (1922). It is true that the *Evolution* had gone into a 4th edn (1926), which added a long supplementary chapter. For Keynes's new departure see D. E. Moggridge and Susan Howson, 'Keynes on monetary policy, 1910–1946', *Oxford Economic Papers*, n.s., xxvi (1974), esp. pp. 232–3 for the orthodoxy of the early drafts of the *Treatise*; cf. Keynes, 'Does unemployment need a drastic remedy?', N, 24 May 1924, pp. 235–6, and 'A drastic remedy for unemployment', N, 7 June 1924, pp. 311–12. On Hawtrey's advocacy of the Treasury View see Keith Hancock, 'Unemployment and the economists in the 1920s', *Ec*, n.s., xxvii (1960), p. 311. There is an interesting letter from Keynes to Strachey (5 Jan. 1926): 'I am still too confused in my own mind to know exactly what I want to do. But my sympathies and expectations tend to march in the same direction as yours', *viz.* towards the interventionist remedies urged in *Revolution by Reason*

(1925); see Hugh Thomas, *John Strachey* (1973), p. 52. Keynes's article, N, 24 May 1924, was quoted by Hobson in *Wealth & Life*, p. 242, but misdated. An indication of the subsequent appeal of Hobson's analysis for Keynesians interested in the economics of growth can be seen in the revision of *The Science of Wealth* by R. F. Harrod (4th edn 1950). As will be seen, I have adopted the following formulation from James Meade's brilliant essay 'The Keynesian revolution': 'Keynes's intellectual revolution was to shift economists from thinking normally in terms of a model of reality in which a dog called *savings* wagged his tail labelled *investment* to thinking in terms of a model in which a dog called *investment* wagged his tail labelled savings' (Milo Keynes (ed.), *Essays on John Maynard Keynes* (Cambridge 1975), p. 82). Two useful articles are reprinted in Sidney Pollard (ed.), *The Gold Standard and Employment Policies between the Wars* (1970): L. J. Hume, 'The gold standard and deflation: issues and attitudes in the 1920s', pp. 122–45, and K. J. Hancock, 'The reduction of unemployment as a problem of public policy, 1920–1929', pp. 99–121.

(IV)

On the electoral position of the Liberal party in the 1920s Chris Cook, *The Age of Alignment* (1975) is, despite some inaccuracies, a useful guide. Maurice Cowling, *The Impact of Labour 1920–1924* (Cambridge 1971) traces the process by which a reshaped party system had emerged by 1924, as politicians sought to accommodate themselves to the new role of Labour. The very fine study by Ross McKibbin, *The Evolution of the Labour Party 1910–24* (Oxford 1974) also comes, though by a very different route, to the conclusion that 1924 was the crucial year; see esp. pp. 122–3 for a persuasive explanation of the failure of a progressive strategy. Hammond's subsequent judgment was in his interesting leader, 'The popular front in retrospect', *MG*, 29 April 1938. Wilson, esp. pp. 459–62, prints some pertinent notes and also, p. 468, part of Hobhouse's letter of 7 Nov. 1924; also in *Memoir*, p. 66 (misdated), and see 'The problem', pp. 264–91, his last political reflections. For Massingham, I owed the reference to the letter quoted to Havighurst, pp. 308–9; cf. *H.W.M.*, p. 73: 'All that I'm afraid about the Labour Party is that they'll not be real libertarians (read Whitman's "Libertad").' For Gardiner see his article, 'Wanted: a radical revival', N, 14 May 1921, pp. 243–5, and Koss, *Fleet Street Radical*, pp. 283–4; and Lucy Masterman, *C. F. G. Masterman* (1939), pp. 327–8. Keynes, 'Am I a Liberal' (1925) and 'Liberalism and Labour' (1926) are both in *Essays in Persuasian*, *JMK*, ix, 295–311; the passage on pp. 295–6, on his objections to Labour, did not appear in the original published version. F. M. Leventhal, 'H. N. Brailsford and the *New Leader*', *Journal of Contemporary History*, ix (1974), 91–113, is an extremely useful appraisal; see also Brailsford, *The Life-Work of J. A. Hobson* (1948), p. 13, for Hobson and the I.L.P. There is a good history of the I.L.P. by Robert E. Dowse, *Left in the Centre* (1966); with a soundly-based account of 'Socialism in Our Time', which the *Bradford Pioneer* called 'AN ALTERNATIVE TO GRADUALISM' (p. 122n.). David Marquand, *Ramsay MacDonald* (1977), pp. 452–5, deals very effectively with the controversy, drawing on correspondence between MacDonald and Hobson. For trade-union suspicion of Hobson see Alan Bullock, *The Life and Times of Ernest Bevin*, i (1960), 243–4.

On the Liberal summer school, John Campbell, 'The renewal of Liberalism: Liberalism without Liberals', in Gillian Peele and Chris Cook (eds.), *The Politics of Reappraisal* (1975), pp. 88–113, offers a sympathetic survey, on which he has expanded in *Lloyd George. The goat in the wilderness 1922–31* (1977). Unfortunately this appeared too late for me to benefit fully from it. See also Mary Stocks, *Ernest Simon of Manchester* (Manchester 1963), esp. pp. 69–70, 76–7. William Robson, 'The founding of *The Political Quarterly*', *PQ*, xl (1970), 1–17, is useful, and further correspondence in HP 21 brings out Hammond's role. *We Can Conquer Unemployment* (1929) has a preface by Lloyd George dated 7 March 1929. The Labour Party, *Labour's Reply to Lloyd George. How to conquer unemployment* (1929) has a preface by MacDonald; for Cole's authorship, see Robert Skidelsky, *Politicians and the Slump* (1967), p. 60. Hobson's interesting article, 'Government loans and unemployment', N, 30 March 1929, pp. 903–4, in a sense anticipated Keynes and Henderson, *Can Lloyd George Do It?* (preface dated 1 May 1929), reprinted in *JMK*, ix, 86–125. I do not, however, wish to exaggerate this point since I am unable to accept that 'the concept of the "multiplier" was clearly expounded' in *Can Lloyd George Do it?* (as claimed by Campbell, *loc. cit.*, p. 110). Instead I concur with the view of Ross McKibbin, 'The economic policy of the second Labour government 1929–31', *Past & Present*, 68 (Aug. 1975), pp. 107, 121, that no developed multiplier theory existed at this time. There are obvious dangers of hindsight in interpretation here which are not, I think, altogether avoided in Robert Skidelsky, *Oswald Mosley* (1975), claiming Hobson as a forerunner of Mosley and Keynes (p. 55) and Hobhouse as the exemplar of anti-Keynesian attitudes (p. 154). But if my analysis (esp. ch. 4, iii) holds, such attempts to drive a wedge between them are misconceived.

Ch. 8 The Bleak Age

(I)

The progress of the Hammonds' historical work can be gauged from their papers, esp. Barbara's letters to Lawrence in HP 9–14 and correspondence with Methuens in HP 19–20. There are also a number of fuller letters to the Murrays, esp. Hammond to Murray 17 Aug. 1927, 22 Nov. 1927, 11, 18 & 19 Feb. 1930, MP 23a. For greater clarity this last letter has been punctuated, and abbreviations expanded, as quoted in my text. In the Methuen economic history, J. R. Taylor was to write vol. 4. The Hammonds are criticised for lack of sympathy with Shaftesbury in G. F. A. Best, *Shaftesbury* (1964; Mentor edn 1975), esp. p. 114n.; and, similarly, Ernest Marshall Howse, *Saints in Politics* (1953) writes that the Hammonds 'seem quite incapable of understanding what religion meant to men like Wilberforce and Shaftesbury, and how much it was responsible for the dynamic of their lives' (p. 133n.). R. M. Hartwell contributed an introduction to the new edition of *The Rise of Modern Industry* (1966), reprinted in his *The Industrial Revolution and Economic Growth* (1971), pp. 377–89. This contains useful figures on the numbers printed of the Hammonds' major works; see also pp. 151, 389, for the Hammonds and 'popular consumption'. J. H. Clapham, *An Economic History of Modern Britain*, i, *The Early Railway Age 1820–1850* (Cambridge 1926; 2nd edn 1930; repr, 1939) contains the crucial passages from the first and second prefaces; the treatment of agricultural workers, pp. 127–9, and industrial workers, pp. 548–65 is directly revelant. The terms 'optimists' and 'pessimists' were established by J. L. Hammond in 'The industrial revolution and discontent', *EcHR*, ii (1929–30), 219–20. The famous sentence on 'the standard of comfort' in the *Town Labourer*, p. 36, still stands in the latest edn (1966), p. 47. I call this 'virtually the only categorical statement' having in mind the claim (1st edn, p. 14) quoted below it, which is absent from the later revised version (1966 edn, pp. 26–7). This was one of the passages seized on by A. A. W. Ramsay, 'A socialist fantasy', *QR*, cclii (1929), p. 33; and the Hammonds were able to reply that it had already been excised in the 1928 edition, 'A socialist fantasy: a reply', ibid., p. 290. J. L. Hammond restated the general conclusions of the Labourer trilogy in a number of popular articles and broadcasts, esp. 'The growth of the modern world order' (six parts), *L*, 20 April 1932 (pp. 563–5), 27 April 1932 (pp. 601–3), 4 May 1932 (pp. 639–40), 11 May 1932 (pp. 687–8), 18 May 1932 (pp. 718–19), and 25 May 1932 (pp. 752–3); 'From Tolpuddle to T.U.C.', *L*, 18 April 1934, pp. 639–41, 675; 'The Village' (three parts), *L*, 28 Oct. 1936 (pp. 805–7), 4 Nov. 1936 (pp. 839–42), 11 Nov. 1936 (pp. 893–6); 'Oliver the Spy', *L*, 24 Feb. 1937 (pp. 359–60); 'The life of the worker', *Spec.*, 30 April 1937, pp. 798–9.

The Hammonds' demographic conclusions were challenged by G. T. Griffith, *Population Problems of the Age of Malthus* (1926) and also by M. C. Buer, *Health, Wealth and Population in Eighteenth-Century England* (1926). The authoritative modern survey of these problems, M. W. Flinn, *British Population Growth, 1700–1850* (1970), comments in the bibliography on both these works: 'Now largely of historiographical interest' (pp. 59, 61). Conversely, he calls Barbara Hammond, 'Urban death-rates in the early nineteenth century', *EcH*, i (1926–9), 419–28, an 'invaluable warning' against the reliance Griffith and Buer placed upon their statistical sources. The whirligig of time has been rather busy bringing in his revenges in this field of inquiry; see Flinn's summary, pp. 40–5. The work of Dorothy George, esp. *London Life in the Eighteenth Century* (1925), also suggested that the catastrophic view of the Industrial Revolution should be abandoned. I hope that I have shown that the Hammonds did not resist historical revision; see also here J. L. Hammond's note in the series 'Historical Revisions', *History*, xii (1927–8), 146–8. Their objection was against founding ideological claims upon sweeping inferences that 'welfare' must have improved during the Industrial Revolution – conclusions which have indeed proved historically untenable. Hobhouse, who read Buer et al. at the Hammonds' prompting, commented to Barbara: 'This sudden effort to rehabilitate the Industrial Revolution socially is extremely interesting – part of the general reaction' (25 May 1927, HP 21 f.25).

The standard-of-living controversy, in its classical form, may turn out to have expired in 1974, in which case its tombstone is the admirable volume ed. Arthur J. Taylor, *The Standard of Living in Britain in the Industrial Revolution* (1975), with terminal statements by the editor (pp. xi–lv), E. J. Hobsbawm (pp. 179–88), and R. M. Hartwell and S. Engerman (pp. 189–213); to which might be added M. W. Flinn, 'Trends in real wages, 1750–1850', *EcHR*, 2nd ser., xxvii (1974), 395–413, and Duncan Bythell, 'The history of the poor', *English Historical Review*, lxxxix (1974), 365–77. The general problem has returned very largely to that posed by the Hammonds in *The Age of the Chartists* (1930). The 'qualitative' nature of their case was widely recognised; e.g. the review by T. H. Marshall, *English Historical Review*, xlvi (1931), 657–8. Their concession here to the statisticians (p. 3) is often correctly quoted but incorrectly dated; e.g. Peter Mathias assumes that it first appeared in 1934 with the abridged *Bleak Age* (Taylor, pp. viii–ix), while E. P. Thompson attributes it to 'a late revision of *The Bleak Age* (1947 edition)' in *The Making of the English Working Class* (Pelican edn, 1968), p. 227. This is a small point in itself, but it has served to give a misleading chronology to this historiographical controversy. The important criticism of Silberling's index appeared in T. S. Ashton, 'The standard of life of the workers in England, 1790–1830', *Journal of Economic History*, supp. ix (1949); reprinted in Taylor, at pp. 47–9. In an article first published in 1957, Hobsbawm concluded that 'Clapham has had a surprisingly easy passage, thanks largely to the extreme feebleness of the reply of his chief opponent, J. L. Hammond' (Taylor, p. 63); and pointed out, too, that Ashton's abandonment of Clapham's distinctive argument had not always been realised.

The Hammonds' general perspective on the evidence of possible insurrection has met cogent criticism from Thompson, esp. pp. 629–36, 647–50. They are accused, in effect, of being blinkered by their reformism, or, as Thompson prefers to put it, their 'Fabian persuasion' (p. 647). This is his main criticism of their work. Otherwise, in a remark that echoes Barbara Hammond, he comments: 'The Hammonds, in their lifetime, turned too often towards their critics a genteel cheek of silence; and, after that, they were dead' (p. 934). For a sympathetic general appraisal see R. H. Tawney, 'J. L. Hammond', *PBA*, xlvi (1960), esp. pp. 271–87. There is a solidly-based assessment by Henry R. Winkler, 'J. L. Hammond', in Hans A. Schmitt (ed.), *Historians of Modern Europe* (Baton Rouge, La., 1971), pp. 95–119. The most useful study is Malcolm I. Thomis, *The Town Labourer and the Industrial Revolution* (1974), which offers a full reassessment of the Hammonds' work in the *Labourer* trilogy in the light of subsequent research. An early attack upon them was W. H. Hutt, 'The factory system of the early nineteenth century', *Ec*, vi (1926), 78–93 – in some respects an adumbration of Ramsay's charges. I accept Thomis's judgment that 'the Hammonds stand up very well' in the historical debate over factory conditions (p. 117). There is a much slighter consideration of the Hutt charges in Brian Inglis, *Poverty and the Industrial Revolution* (rev. edn, Panther 1972), pp. 13–35, which is also favourable to the Hammonds here. The articles by Ramsay and the Hammonds, already cited, were concluded by Ramsay's 'A socialist fantasy: the last word', *QR*, ccliii (1929), 113–16. These exchanges account for a large correspondence in HP 22 for Jan.–May 1929. The treatment of the seamen's strike seems a fair test case. The Ramsay charges were pressed in *QR*, cclii, 51–5; the Hammond defence mounted ibid., pp. 273–80. Norman McCord, 'The seamen's strike of 1815 in north-east England', *EcHR*, 2nd ser., xxi (1968), 127–43 is a much fuller treatment than either. He makes clear the distinction between events on the Tyne and the Wear which are muddled in the Ramsay version. He concludes (p. 140) that the strikes appeared to end with most of the men's original demands satisfied, but whereas Ramsay took this at face value, McCord's account goes on to sustain the Hammonds' case that the owners subsequently reneged on the agreed conditions. Indeed the same quotation from General Wynard – 'The conduct of the shipowners, in shifting this distressing business from their own, to the shoulders of the Government, seems to me as disgraceful as it is cowardly' – is used to clinch this point in both accounts (McCord, p. 140; Hammonds, p. 275). Whether the action of the marines should best be described as 'the intervention of the forces of the Crown' (*Town Labourer*, p. 30) or as a 'skilfully planned police action' (McCord, p. 139) will no doubt continue to be a matter of opinion.

(II)

There are several graphic glimpses of the later Wallas in *H–L Letters*, esp. pp. 919–20, 935, 956, 1050, 1064, 1164. Wiener, pp. 197–9, gives an incisive assessment of *Social Judgment*. Kingsley Martin, *Father Figures* (1966; Penguin edn 1969) is generally revealing; see esp. pp. 92–3 on the Wallases and ch. ix on the *Manchester Guardian*. Hammond's papers are a major source for the paper's history at this time and have been put to good use in David Ayerst, *Guardian* (1971). The compilation of C. P. Scott's obituary notices can be reconstructed from the letters between Ted Scott and Hammond 1928–31 in HP 35. See also Rupert Hart-Davis (ed.), *The Autobiography of Arthur Ransome* (1976), chs. 41–2. Malcolm Muggeridge, *Chronicles of Wasted Time*, i, *The Green Stick* (1972) is an autobiography of great insight and literary power, though weak on chronology; ch. iv gives a caustic appraisal of his connexion with the *Guardian*. Kingsley Martin, *Editor* (1968; Penguin edn 1969) deals effectively with the *New Statesman* period. C. H. Rolph, *Kingsley. The life, letters and diaries of Kingsley Martin* (1973), pp. 151–60 gives an account of the choosing of a new editor in 1930; see also C. M. Lloyd to Hammond, 26 June 1930, HP 23.

The best study of the second Labour Government is Robert Skidelsky, *Politicians and the Slump* (1967), but the confidence of some of its judgments is ably questioned by Ross McKibbin, 'The economic policy of the second Labour government 1929–1931', *Past & Present*, 68 (1975), 95–123.

For the reception of the land tax, see letters in N, 9 & 16 May 1931. The 1931 crisis is given close study in David Marquand, *Ramsay MacDonald* (1977), chs. xxv and xxvi, which offer a sympathetic dissection of his difficulties. The accounts of 1931 in Muggeridge, pp. 194–201, and Ayerst, pp. 469–74, interlock to some extent, and usefully supplement the material in HP 35. For Hammond's view of the National Government see 'The teacher in modern life', *Spec.*, 16 April 1932, pp. 549–50. Wallas's final position remains slightly unclear. The entry in Beatrice Webb's diary, which I quote, says as much about her view as his; and H. G. Wells, *Experiment in Autobiography* (1934), p. 600, suggests a more buoyant mood, with its picture of Wallas, only a few months before his death, still full of enthusiasm for Bentham, dilating on 'the "old boy's" abundance and breadth of range'.

(III)

I have found Peter Stansky and William Abrahams, *Journey to the Frontier. Julian Bell and John Cornford: their lives and the* 1930s (1966) extremely helpful. It quotes Bell's letter of 9 Dec. 1933 at length on pp. 108–9. Hugh Thomas, *John Strachey* (1973) is an accomplished biography making good use of Strachey's own papers. Stephen Spender, *World Within World* (1951) is a reflective autobiography, with much to offer on the problems which concern me here, especially when read in conjunction with *Forward From Liberalism* (1937). David Caute, *The Fellow-Travellers* (1973) is a work of which I can hardly speak too highly. It will be seen that Caute's view of the fellow-travellers as heirs to the Enlightenment, projecting their positivistic rationalism on to Russia, has much in common with my approach; I feel that my further distinction of moral and mechanical views helps to explain who was disillusioned – and how. Caute is particularly good on Shaw and the Webbs, and also on Laski. On the Webbs and Soviet communism see Kitty Muggeridge and Ruth Adam, *Beatrice Webb* (1967), ch. 15; Shirley Robin Letwin, *The Pursuit of Certainty* (Cambridge 1965), long note on pp. 374–6; and Gertrude Himmelfarb, 'The intellectual in politics: the case of the Webbs', *Journal of Contemporary History*, vi, 3 (1971), 3–11. E. J. Hobsbawm rightly insists that the Webbs and Shaw 'took socialism seriously, as is shown by their subsequent political evolution. They never doubted that it meant the socialisation of the means of production, distribution and exchange, and they eventually recognised in the Soviet Union the pioneer of a new civilisation', in Lionel M. Munby (ed.), *The Luddites and Other Essays* (1971), p. 232; cf. *Labouring Men* (1964), pp. 254–5. In the passage from *Soviet Communism* (2nd edn, 1937), p. 1214, quoted in my text, the Webbs were essentially using this as their criterion for the new civilisation, adding also planning in support. The further comment is from (Hobhouse), 'Democracy and the expert', N, 13 June 1908, 375–6. There is a useful symposium, 'Reflections on the crisis', *PQ*, ii (1931), 457–84, with contributions from Shaw, Hobson, Laski, Lowes Dickinson, Zimmern, Woolf, Martin and Robson. On Muggeridge, the recent book by Richard Ingrams, *God's Apology* (1977) adds very little to his autobiography, vol. ii, *The Infernal Grove* (1973), esp. ch. 1 on the aftermath of Moscow and the importance of Kingsmill.

For Hobson in the 1930s the works cited in the text can be supplemented by his study of *Veblen* (1936) and, of course, his autobiography which contains many contemporary reflections. 'The state as an organ of rationalisation', *PQ*, ii (1931), 30–45, sought to turn the edge of the vogue term rationalisation towards collectivism. 'Under-consumption and its remedies', *L*, 31 Oct. 1934, pp. 735–6 restated his general views. On the Next Five Years group and similar movements see Arthur Marwick, 'Middle opinion in the thirties', *English Historical Review*, lxxix (1964), 285–98. Hobson's final position is argued in 'A British socialism', *NS*, 25 Jan. 1936 and 1 Feb. 1936; and in 'Thoughts on our present discontents', *PQ*, ix (1938), 47–57. On Keynes's politics, the excellent analysis by Donald Winch, *Economics and Policy* (1969) offers an appendix which is a necessary corrective to the account in Harrod, and has useful comments on Durbin, Cole and the blessed word 'planning'. The otherwise useful intellectual biography by L. P. Carpenter, *G. D. H. Cole* (Cambridge 1973) is weak here e.g. 'Cole felt that young socialists praised Keynes excessively and ignored J. A. Hobson's earlier explanation of the gap between savings and investment' (pp. 178–9). This misses its intended point but accidentally reinforces mine *viz.* that *Cole* is responsible for much misunderstanding here. Keynes's article, 'The dilemma of modern socialism', *PQ*, iii (1933), 155–61, was answered by Rowse, 'Mr Keynes on socialism', ibid., pp. 409–15, following up his earlier 'Socialism and Mr Keynes', *NC*, cxii (1932), 327–42, reprinted in A. L. Rowse, *The End of an Epoch* (1947), pp. 141–59. Many of the political aspects are now ably surveyed in Ben Pimlott, *Labour and the Left in the 1930s* (Cambridge 1977), esp. ch. 4, 'Fabians and Keynesians', which is broadly consistent with my view. On the other hand, Robert Skidelsky, 'The reception of the Keynesian revolution', in Milo Keynes (ed.), *Essays on John Maynard Keynes* (Cambridge 1975), argues that what I call the ideological deficiency of Keynesian economics was less easily remediable (via Labour) and that the problem was 'to *locate* the modernising forces themselves' (pp. 94–5); cf. the reformulation in *The End of the Keynesian Era*, pp. 33–40. I am more in tune with the interesting article by Roger Eatwell and Anthony Wright, 'Labour and the lessons of 1931', *History*, n.s., lxiii (1978), 38–53. Hobson and Durbin thrashed out their differences in 'Underconsumption: an exposition and a reply', *Ec*, xiii (1933), 402–27, and there is a review by Hobson of *Purchasing Power and Trade Depression* in *PQ*, iv (1933), 460–2. E. F. M. Durbin, *The Politics of Democratic Socialism* (4th imp. 1954) has a foreword by Hugh Gaitskell, which neatly summarises the views of this group in the 1930s (p. 9); and see pp. 296 & n. and 305 for Keynesian prosperity measures. See also Michael Postan, 'Political and intellectual progress', in W. T. Rodgers (ed.), *Hugh Gaitskell* (1964), pp. 49–66.

For the evolution of Keynes's thought Donald Moggridge (ed.), *The General Theory and After*, *JMK*, xiii and xiv, is now indispensable. The Hobson–Keynes correspondence of July–Nov. 1931 is printed in *JMK*, xiii.

330–6. The reference to the Banana Parable is to *JMK*, v, 158–60. I have quoted the 1935 correspondence from the clear and convincing account in Alan J. Lee, 'A study of the social and economic thought of J. A. Hobson', (London PhD 1970), pp. 289–97. The most accessible survey of the essential concepts of the *General Theory* is Michael Stewart, *Keynes and After* (Pelican 1967; 2nd edn 1972); but D. E. Moggridge, *Keynes* (1976) has natural advantages as a historical account of the development of Keynes's ideas, one of which was its prior familiarity with the important findings later presented in Susan Howson and Donald Winch, *The Economic Advisory Council 1930–1939* (Cambridge 1977). In a note (p. 183) Moggridge explains that he is contesting two myths, *viz.* (to simplify ruthlessly): 1. Keynesian economics=counter-cyclical employment policies; 2. the *General Theory*=accepted equilibrium theory+rigid wages and a liquidity trap. In general I follow Moggridge here; likewise this account owes much to the brilliant study by G. L. S. Shackle, *The Years of High Theory* (Cambridge 1967), esp. pp. 204, 290–1, on the importance of uncertainty. Thus I am happy to concur in the overall judgment of Ronald L. Meek, 'The place of Keynes in the history of economic thought', in *Economics and Ideology* (1967), that 'Keynes helped to pave the way for a new type of economic thinking which may well transcend all previous economic systems, including his own' (p. 195). I accept Moggridge's argument (see pp. 82, 86–7, 100–1), first put forward in D. E. Moggridge and Susan Howson, 'Keynes on monetary policy, 1910–1946', *Oxford Economic Papers*, n.s., xxvi (1974), 236–7, that public works can be reconciled with the *Treatise* (as a special case), despite the reservation expressed by Lord Kahn, *On Re-reading Keynes*, 4th Keynes Lecture (1974), p. 10 & n. The article by Paul Lambert, 'The evolution of Keynes's thought from the *Treatise on Money* to the *General Theory*', *Annals of Public & Cooperative Economy*, xl (1969), 243–63, is of very considerable importance, esp. on the roles of Kahn and Robinson; though it has in some respects been superseded by D. E. Moggridge, 'From the *Treatise* to the *General Theory*: an exercise in chronology', *History of Political Economy*, v (1973), 72–88, which must be regarded as definitive in its dating of the crucial periods of transition. R. F. Kahn, 'The relation of home investment to employment', *EcJ*, xli (1931), 173–98, pioneered the concept of the multiplier; it was left to Keynes to christen it; Keynes's article, 'The Multiplier', was incorporated into the American edition of 'The Means to Prosperity' (1933), *JMK*, ix, at pp. 341–6. For Keynes's politics in the late 1930s see the important dialogue with Kingsley Martin, 'Democracy and efficiency', *NS*, 28 Jan. 1939, pp. 121–3, which is drawn on to similar effect in D. E. Moggridge (ed.), *Keynes: aspects of the man and his work* (1974), pp. 53–74.

The claim that Hobson anticipated Keynes has been advanced at two levels. The most reputable academic claim is that documented by D. J. Coppock, 'A reconsideration of Hobson's theory of unemployment', *Manchester School*, xxi (1953), 1–21, which I have, on the whole, rejected in ch. 4, ii, and ch. 7, iii. Likewise the argument of David Hamilton, 'Hobson with a Keynesian twist', *American Journal of Economics and*

Sociology, xiii (1953–4), 273–82, seems to me to be historically wrong; but there is a fruitful idea here if it is argued instead in terms of a left Keynesianism which would posit different ideological choices from the (possibly more conservative) actual Keynes, i.e. Keynes with a Hobsonian twist. The other level at which Hobson's supposed claim is pressed is that of the popular mythology of the left, e.g. obiter dicta in Mary Agnes Hamilton, *Remembering My Good Friends* (1944), p. 137, or Martin, *Editor*, p. 172, similar to that quoted from Unwin in my text. See also the introduction by Unwin to the 4th edn of *Imperialism* (1958). In my view the link between these two levels was provided, above all, by Cole. See Margaret Cole, *The Life of G. D. H. Cole* (1971), pp. 208–9, for his general attitude here; also his *Socialist Economics* (1950). His influential popular appraisals of Hobson were chiefly in his reviews of the *General Theory*, *NS*, 15 Feb. 1936, and of *Conf.*, *PQ*, ix (1938), 439–41; 'J. A. Hobson', *EcJ*, l (1940), 351–9; and 'J. A. Hobson', *NS*, 5 July 1958 (under Martin's editorship, of course); cf. the biographical note on Hobson in *OP*, p. 510 (of which Margaret Cole was an editor).

Epilogue Sans Everything

F. W. Hirst, by his friends (1958) contains the short essay by Murray which he was writing at the end of 1955, with its confusion of *Essays in Liberalism by Six Oxford Men*, of whom Murray by then believed himself to have been one, with *Liberalism and the Empire*. The later recollection of Hirst quoted in the text is from the essay by A. F. Thompson. Murray was chairman of the executive council of the League of Nations Union (1923–1938), and joint president (1945–7, 1949–57) and sole president (1947–9) of the United Nations Association. See the *DNB* article by M. I. Henderson. Gilbert Murray, *An Unfinished Autobiography*, ed. Jean Smith and Arnold Toynbee (1960) contains useful contributions from Salvador de Madariaga, Bertrand Russell and Arnold Toynbee. He wrote of his reaction to 1914: 'The prevention of war became, rather suddenly the most important thing in the world' (to Barbara Hammond, 6 Feb. 1952, HP 31 f.57). For Hammond's view of the League see 'Building up world unity', *L*, 25 May 1932, p. 753. He argued the case for ceding a colony in correspondence with Murray; see also his article 'The future of Africa', *Spec.*, 30 Aug. 1935, pp. 316–17. F. M. Leventhal provides a useful analysis in 'Towards revision and reconciliation: H. N. Brailsford and Germany, 1914–1949', in Asa Briggs and John Saville (eds.), *Essays in Labour History 1918–1939* (1977), esp. pp. 175–6, 179–80. Hammond's reflections on Gladstone can be found in 'The romance of nineteenth century politics', *PQ*, ii (1931), 224–40; 'Gladstone's isolation', *Spec.*, 7 April 1933, pp. 492–3; 'Gladstone and the League of Nations mind', in *Essays in Honour of Gilbert Murray* (1936), pp. 95–118 (in which Barbara Hammond, 'The battle for open spaces', pp. 119–40 is also of interest); *Gladstone and the Irish Nation* (1938), to the new edn of which (1964) M. R. D. Foot contributes a knowledgeable Introduction, pp. xix–xxxi; and it was he who took over and finished *Gladstone and Liberalism* (1952). The most stimulating reassessment of

Gladstonian Liberalism in recent years has come from John Vincent, notably in *The Formation of the Liberal Party* (1966) and *Pollbooks: how Victorians voted* (Cambridge 1967) – see esp. p. 47: 'Gladstone created a national theatre for England as Verdi did for nineteenth-century Italy.' A. B. Cooke and John Vincent, *The Governing Passion* (1974) is a detailed study of the Home Rule issue in 1885–6 laying an emphasis upon the 'high politics' of the crisis which may seem disproportionate unless Hammond's account of the Irish implications and of the development of Gladstone's views is also borne in mind. Most recently, Vincent's Raleigh Lecture in History for 1977, 'Gladstone and Ireland', has also suggested that Hammond's perspective led him to overestimate Gladstone's consistency.

The correspondence from the Hammonds in the Murray papers has been of great value, especially on matters like Lawrence's health; see also Hammond to May Wallas, 19 April 1937, WP 48, and Murray to May Wallas, 20 and 24 May 1937, WP 41, for his agreement to write the preface for *Men and Ideas* (1940). The chief contributions to the press are Hammond's leaders, 'England and Europe', *MG*, 10 Dec. 1936, and 'The Popular Front: a retrospect', *MG*, 29 April 1938; Murray's letter to *The Times*, 4 March 1939; Hammond's review 'Between Two Wars', *MG*, 16 May 1939; and the leader, 'The war and democracy', *MG*, 3 Oct. 1940. Many of Hammond's wartime leaders are reprinted in the anonymous volume, *Faith in France* (Manchester 1946), which is usually taken as comprising entirely his own work. I have it on the first-hand authority of A. J. P. Taylor, however, that some leaders (notably 14 July 1944) were not by Hammond at all but by another distinguished historian. On attitudes towards 'appeasement', I have been much influenced by Martin Gilbert, *The Roots of Appeasement* (1966), esp. pp. 179–81; also F. S. Northedge, *The Troubled Giant* (1966), esp. ch. 19. For the *Manchester Guardian's* role, Ayerst, chs. 33–5 is very good; also F. R. Gannon, *The British Press and Germany 1936–1939* (Oxford 1971). For the turn of the tide in favour of Churchill in 1939 see Martin Gilbert, *Winston S. Churchill*, v (1976), pp. 1082–5, 1087, and esp. 1090 for Laski's view that his return would be welcomed 'by most Liberals and by the great bulk of the Labour Party'. Maurice Cowling, *The Impact of Hitler. British politics and British policy 1933–40* (Cambridge 1975) persuasively argues that anti-appeasement helped to legitimate the Labour party and, from 1940, to establish 'the post-war illusion that a régime which had been on the "right side" in relation to Hitler must have embodied an indefeasible centrality for the future' (p. 2). In this respect its thesis is a hostile rendering of the central theme of Paul Addison, *The Road to 1945. British politics and the Second World War* (1975), which is an invaluable account of the triumph of the 'progressive centre', esp. pp. 18, 21, 123, 143, 183–4, 277. I am closely in accord with Addison except where he contends (p. 166) that Keynes, like Beveridge, should be regarded as a technocrat rather than as a Liberal; the party point is well taken, but my argument (esp. chs. 7 and 8) is that his economic approach was crucially affected by his liberal and social democratic outlook in the inter-war period. On the people's war, there is still no better short account than that in

A. J. P. Taylor, *English History 1914–45* (Oxford 1965); see p. 507: 'War socialism was socialism by consent, that is to say, socialism with the difficulties left out.' Alan Sked and Chris Cook (eds.), *Crisis and Controversy. Essays in honour of A. J. P. Taylor* (1976) fittingly contains two useful assessments of the radical effects of the war, by Arthur Marwick and Paul Addison.

For the last phase there are a few relevant articles by Hammond, esp. 'British foreign policy: a summing up', *L*, 13 Feb. 1947 & 6 March 1947, pp. 272–3, 317, 325; 'The Liberal party in perspective', *L*, 30 Sep. 1948. pp. 481–2. The chief obituaries, mainly in HP 149, were: G. P. Gooch, *People and Freedom*, April 1949; Murray and Tawney, *MG*, 9 April 1949; *The Times*, 9 April 1949; Walter Holmes, *Daily Worker*, 11 April 1949; H. N. Brailsford, NS, 16 April 1949; Desmond MacCarthy, *Sunday Times*, 17 April 1949; Hamilton Fyfe, 'Almost the Last', *Tribune*, 6 May 1949; Peter Barry, *Truth*, 6 May 1949. The period between the 1945 General Election and the death of Shaw in 1950 saw the entrenchment of the Fabian interpretation of history; and Shaw continued to attract massive publicity for several years e.g. the newspaper publication of his correspondence with Mrs Patrick Campbell. Barbara Hammond, who had never read 'such disgusting stuff', commented: 'I now understand Leonard Hobhouse's feelings about GBS' (to Murray, 8 Nov. 1952, MP 23b). The letters between her and Murray are inevitably rather scrappy but I have found them of irresistible interest; Murray's take up the volume HP 31; for his position in the 1951 elections see also the statement in *The Times*, 20 Oct. 1951; and for his last article, 'The shadow of barbarism', *Sunday Times*, 16 Dec. 1956. Barbara Hammond's letters were scattered throughout MP 23b when I used them. The final picture of her declining years is based on Arnold J. Toynbee, *Acquaintances* (Oxford 1967), pp. 106–7.

Appendix

Gross effects at death (to the nearest pound)

		died	price index[1] (1867–77=100)
William Clarke	3,272	1901	70
Lord Hobhouse[2]	96,038	1904	70
L. T. Hobhouse	19,423	1929	115
C. P. Scott[3]	18,907	1932	80
Graham Wallas	3,971	1932	80
J. A. Hobson	2,704	1940	128
Beatrice Webb	24,148	1943	155
J. M. Keynes	484,864	1946	186
Sidney Webb	59,420	1947	230
J. L. Hammond	12,797	1949	274
G. B. Shaw	367,234	1950	324
Gilbert Murray[4]	37,525	1957	376
G. D. H. Cole	46,617	1959	356
Barbara Hammond	25,899	1961	354
R. H. Tawney	7,097	1962	360

[1] The *Statist* index of wholesale prices. This has the advantage of a single scale over a long period but is only a rough guide on relative values.

[2] Under a codicil of 1901, the living children of Reginald Hobhouse were to share £15,000; and under a codicil of 1903, Leonard was to receive £2,500 and Emily £1,000 in addition to their shares. These clauses were to become operative on the death of Lady Hobhouse, which happened in 1905.

[3] Other arrangements had already been made for the *Manchester Guardian*.

[4] Murray's children had already been provided for.

Index

Index